THE INTERNATIONAL LAWYER'S DESKBOOK

Edited by

Lucinda A. Low

Patrick M. Norton

Daniel M. Drory

Published by

Section of International Law and Practice

American Bar Association

© American Bar Association 1996

ISBN: 1-57073-166-7

Printed in the United States of America
All Rights Reserved

Published under the direction of the Publications Committee of the Section of International Law and Practice.

Publications Committee Chair: John E. Noyes
Publications Director: Susan Frensilli Williams

PREFACE

This book is designed as a reference tool for lawyers facing international legal problems outside their own areas of expertise. In addition to an overview chapter and a chapter on selecting foreign counsel, there are twenty-four chapters discussing different areas of international law and practice. Each chapter provides an overview of the topic and a compendium of the sources of assistance that the authors consider most useful. The sources of assistance include printed materials (primary and secondary sources), institutional sources such as government agencies, international organizations and non-governmental organizations and, where available, on-line services. Although designed principally for U.S. practitioners, we hope the materials will also be helpful to foreign lawyers.

The book is not intended as a "how to" manual for specific problems or a do-it-yourself guide to international lawyering. All the topics are specialty topics, and they require considerably more knowledge and experience than the reading of a chapter will provide. What we hope this book will do is give the non-specialist reader a basis for dealing intelligently with the problem at hand.

To our knowledge, this is the first time a work of this type and scope has been attempted. It is undoubtedly imperfect; certainly no single volume could aspire to address all of the issues that may arise in the dynamic and complex world of international legal practice. Readers are invited to comment on the selection of topics in this edition, and to suggest topics for future editions. Comments or suggestions should be sent to:

Section of International Law and Practice
American Bar Association
740 15th Street, N.W.
Washington, D.C. 20005
    Attention: Publications Director
    Re: *The International Lawyer's Deskbook* (1996 ed.)

For information on how to become a member of the Section of International Law and Practice, please refer to the insert at the back of the book, or call the Section office at (202) 662-1660.

We would like to thank Susan Frensilli Williams for her able production assistance on the book, John E. Noyes for his suggestions regarding on-line services, Karen Polk and Connie McLean of Miller & Chevalier for library and production assistance, respectively, and K'Ann Richter of Texas Instruments for production assistance. Last but not least, thanks are due to our firms for allowing us to pursue this project, and to our families for their tolerance of the intrusion of the red pen on weekends and holidays.

–The Editors

This book is dedicated to our spouses,

Daniel Magraw, Maureen Norton, and Eve Drory.

–The Editors

ABOUT THE EDITORS

Lucinda A. Low, a member of the California, Colorado, and District of Columbia bars, is a partner in the Washington, D.C. firm of Miller & Chevalier, Chartered. Ms. Low's practice emphasizes complex international business transactions, such as joint ventures and project financings, and U.S. regulation of international business. Ms. Low currently serves as the first woman to be elected to chair the Section of International Practice of the American Bar Association. She has taught International Business Transactions as an adjunct professor at the University of Colorado School of Law, and International Conflicts of Law at American University School of Law. She received her B.A. in Economics and Latin American Studies from Pomona College, and her J.D. from the University of California, Los Angeles School of Law, where she was Editor-in-Chief of the Law Review. Ms. Low speaks Portuguese, French and Spanish and has some knowledge of Italian, Japanese and Russian.

Patrick M. Norton is a partner with the Washington, D.C. office of the law firm of Alston & Bird. Mr. Norton's practice includes both international trans-actions and international dispute resolution. He is currently a member of the Council of the American Bar Association Section of International Law and Practice and was formerly an officer of the Inter-Pacific Bar Association. Mr. Norton previously served at the United States Department of State as Assistant Legal Adviser for East Asian and Pacific Affairs, Assistant Legal Adviser for Near East and South Asian Affairs and Deputy Director of Iranian Claims. He has also served as Counsel to the Senate Select Committee on Intelligence and as an associate with the law firm of Covington & Burling. Mr. Norton is a graduate of the University of Pennsylvania, Oxford University and the Harvard Law School, where he was editor-in-chief of the *Harvard International Law Journal*. He is the author of numerous articles on public and private international law.

Daniel M. Drory is International Trade Counsel to Texas Instruments Incorporated in Dallas, TX. His practice includes international transactions and trade regulatory matters. Before joining Texas Instruments, he was an associate with Wilmer, Cutler & Pickering in Washington, D.C. and London. He graduated from Yale College in 1974 and Stanford Law School in 1978 and also attended Heidelberg University (Germany).

ABOUT THE CONTRIBUTORS

Judith H. Bello is a partner of Sidley & Austin (in the Washington, D.C. office), specializing in international law and trade. In government, she has served as General Counsel and Deputy General Counsel to the U.S. Trade Representative (1985–89), member of the President's Commission on Federal Ethics Law Reform (1989), the number 2 Department of Commerce official administering the antidumping and contervailing duty laws (1982-84), and the Department of State attorney–adviser for trade and transportation (1977–82).

Gary B. Born is the managing partner of Wilmer, Cutler & Pickering's London office, and practices in the field of international dispute resolution. He has published widely in the field, and is the author of *International Civil Litigation in United States Courts* (3rd ed. 1996 Kluwer) and *International Commercial Arbitration in the United States* (1994 Kluwer).

J. Ira Burkemper represents a variety of clients in business immigration matters. Mr. Burkemper has a background in international business that he gained while working in Germany for two multinational automobile manufacturers. He is fluent in German and is conversant in Italian. Mr. Burkemper co–authored an article on business opportunities created by the immigration implications of NAFTA. He is a member of the American Immigration Lawyers Association.

Michael H. Byowitz, a partner with Wachtell, Lipton, Rosen & Katz in New York, has extensive experience in representing companies regarding the U.S. and international antitrust aspects of mergers, acquisitions, joint ventures an corporate takeovers. Mr. Byowitz has represented clients in government and private antitrust litigation, and has advised multinational corporations as to antitrust compliance.

James H. Carter is a litigation partner in the New York office of Sullivan & Cromwell. He is a graduate of Yale College and Yale Law School, a past Chair of the American Bar Association Section of International Law and Practice and a Past Chair of its Committee on International Commercial Arbitration.

Don S. DeAmicis is a partner at Ropes & Gray in Boston, MA, where he specializes in bankruptcy and creditors' rights matters. He has over the past decade represented debtors, creditor committees, financial institutions and other creditors in national default and insolvency cases. Mr. DeAmicis has served as Chair of the International Creditors' Rights and Bankruptcy

Committee of the American Bar Association's Section of International Law and Practice, and has published articles and lectured frequently on international insolvency and creditors' rights matters. He is a graduate of Harvard Law School (1979) and Harvard College (1976).

Gloria F. DeHart is a graduate of Radcliffe (Harvard) College, Cambridge, MA, and Boalt Hall School of Law, University of California, Berkeley, CA. She was admitted to practice in California in January 1966, and before the United Sates Supreme Court in June, 1980. While employed as Deputy Attorney General for the State of California beginning in 1966, she dealt with family support and custody problems, particularly in an international context. Since her retirement from the Attorney General's office in November 1993, she has been employed part-time by the U.S. Department of State as an Attorney Adviser for family law issues in the office of the Assistant Legal Adviser for Private International Law.

Marshall J. Doke, Jr. practices public contract law in Dallas, TX. He is president of the U.S. Court of Federal Claims Bar Association and formerly was Chair of the American Bar Association's Section of Public Contract Law, a member of the ABA Board of Governors, and President of the Boards of Contract Appeals Bar Association.

Donald C. Dowling, Jr., a partner of Graydon, Head & Ritchey in Cincinnati, OH, chairs his firm's International Law Department. He teaches European Union Law at the University of Cincinnati College of Law, and he heads both the American Bar Association's Section of International Law and Practice International Employment Law Committee and the Cincinnati Bar Association's International Law Committee. A graduate of the University of Chicago and the University of Florida College of Law, he has published and spoken around the world on international law topics.

Nathan E. Fagre is Vice President and Deputy General Counsel–International of Occidental Oil & Gas Corporation. Mr. Fagre received an A.B. from Harvard College in 1977, an M.Phil. in International Relations from Oxford University in 1979, and a J.D. from Harvard Law School in 1982.

Edward F. Greene is a partner of Cleary, Gottlieb, Steen & Hamilton, resident in the London office. He specializes in matters relating to U.S. regulation of capital markets and financial institutions. Prior to joining the firm in 1983, he was General Counsel of the Securities and Exchange Commission (1981–82) and Director of the SEC's Division of Corporate Finance (1979–81). Prior to that he was engaged in private practice in New York. Mr. Green received an LL.B. from Harvard Law School in 1966 and an undergraduate degree from Amherst College in 1963.

Barbara R. Hauser, a graduate of Wellesley College and the University of Pennsylvania Law School, has been active in international organizations, particularly in the areas of private client service. Based in Minnesota, Ms. Hauser is the Chair of the Private Client Planning Committee of the ABA Section of International Law and Practice. She is also the President of the Commission on International Laws of Succession for the Union Internationale des Avocats, and an Academician in the International Academy of Estate & Trust Law.

Ambassador Alan F. Holmer is a member of the law firm of Sidley & Austin and is resident in the Washington, D.C. office. The focus of his practice is international trade. In 1990 Ambassador Holmer headed the U.S. delegation to the Bonn Economic Conference. He also previously served as Deputy U.S. Trade Representative (1987–89), General Counsel to the U.S. Trade Representative (1985–87), Deputy Assistant Secretary of Commerce for Import Administration (1983–85), and Deputy Assistant to the President for Intergovernmental Affairs (1981–83). Ambassador Holmer was graduated from Princeton University and Georgetown University Law Center.

O. Thomas Johnson, Jr. is a partner in the Washington, D.C. law firm of Covington & Burling. He received his bachelor's and law degrees from Stanford University. Before joining Covington & Burling, he was with the Office of the Legal Adviser in the Department of State. Mr. Johnson has been involved in questions related to overseas bribery ever since the issue began to receive serious attention in 1975.

Elliot R. Lewis is Associate General Counsel for North American Van Lines, Inc., in Fort Wayne, IN, providing representation in two primary ares: international law and labor and employment law. In 1992, he assisted the company informing the first European van line, UTS Europe, based in Amsterdam. Mr. Lewis graduated from Indiana University School of Law, Bloomington. He currently serves as Co-Chair of the Corporate Counsel Committee and as Vice Chair for Regional Programs, Program Committee, for the ABA Section of International Law and Practice.

Gerold W. Libby is a partner in the Los Angeles office of Whitman Breed Abbott & Morgan, where he specializes in international business and investment transactions, including joint ventures, acquisitions, technology transfers and real estate transactions. He has participated in numerous professional activities and programs, and served a term as Chair of the American Bar Association's Section of International Law and Practice. Mr. Libby received his B.A. from Yale University (1965) and his J.D. from the New York University School of Law (1969).

Rona R. Mears is a partner in the International Section of Haynes and Boone, L.L.P., in Dallas, TX. She also chairs the firm's Americas Practice Group. Her practice is focused on international corporate, joint venture, trade and commercial transactions. She is Texas Co-Chair of the Texas–Mexico Bar Association, and Secretary and Council Member of the American Bar Association's Section of International Law and Practice.

William L. Menard is an associate in the Washington, D.C. office of Gibson, Dunn & Crutcher. Mr. Menard received a B.A. from Williams College in 1983 and a J.D. from Georgetown University Law Center in 1992.

Laurence E. Nemirow is a member of Davis, Graham & Stubbs, L.L.C., in Denver, CO, specializing in corporate and partnership taxation. He graduated from Harvard Law School in 1983.

Angelo A. Paparelli is a partner in the Los Angeles and Irvine, CA offices of the international firm Bryan Cave. Mr. Paparelli is Co-Chair of the Immigration and Nationality Committee of the ABA Section of International Law and Practice, and was a member of the Board of Governors of the American Immigration Lawyers Association from 1988 to 1994. He is certified as a specialist in Immigration and Nationality Law by the State of California, Board of Legal Specialization.

Steven B. Pfeiffer is a partner of Fulbright & Jaworski practicing in the firm's Washington and London offices. He received a B.A. from Wesleyan University in 1969, a B.A. and M.A. in jurisprudence from Oxford in 1971 and 1983, and a J.D. from Yale University in 1976. Mr. Pfeiffer, head of the firm's International Department, practices principally in the field of corporate and commercial law, specializing in international transactions and foreign investment into the U.S., particularly relating to energy matters. He was Chair of the Section on Energy & Natural Resources Law of the International Bar Association from 1992–94.

Peter H. Pfund has been Assistant Legal Adviser for Private International Law in the U.S. Department of State since 1979. His office is responsible for the program of participation by the United States in the private law unification/harmonization work of four international organizations including the Hague Conference on Private International Law. Mr. Pfund attended Amherst College and the University of Pennsylvania Law School. He has served with the Office of the Legal Adviser of the State Department since 1959. He was second to the Legal Division of the International Atomic Energy Agency in Vienna in 1966–68, and served as Legal Adviser of the U.S. Embassy at Bonn in 1973–78.

Robert S. Rich graduated from Yale Law School in 1963, practiced in New York and Paris, and currently is a partner at Davis Graham & Stubbs, Denver, CO. He is Tenth Circuit Regent to the American College of Tax Counsel, and is a regional vice president of the International Fiscal Association.

Edward L. Rubinoff is a partner in the Washington, D.C. office of Akin, Gump, Strauss, Hauer & Feld, L.L.P. who specializes in international trade policy and regulation, including export controls, customs law and trade litigation. He currently serves as Chair of the Export Controls and Economic Sanctions Committee of the American Bar Association's Section of International Law and Practice.

Robert B. Shanks is a partner in the Washington, D.C. office of Morrison & Foerster, where he co-chairs the firm's global Project Development and Finance Group. He specializes in international project finance, privatizations and cross-border investment issues. Mr. Shanks served as Vice-President and General Counsel of the Overseas Private Investment Corporation (OPIC).

James R. Silkenat is partner in Winthrop, Stimson, Putnam and Roberts resident in New York. He is a former Chair of the American Bar Association's Section of International Law and Practice and helps coordinate Winthrop's international practice in New York, where he specializes in the areas of international project finance, M&A, securities and corporate law. He is a former Chair of the ABA's Section Officers Conference and is currently a member of the ABA Board of Governors. He previously served as Legal Counsel of the International Finance Corporation (World Bank Group).

Turner T. Smith, Jr., a Washington, D.C. partner of Hunton & Williams, an international law firm with over 450 attorneys and offices in eight U.S. cities, Brussels, Hong Kong and Warsaw, has practiced environmental law for over 25 years, founded the firm's Brussels office, and heads its international environmental practice.

David K.Y. Tang is the managing partner of Preston Gates & Ellis, based in the Seattle office, where he practices business and real estate law focusing on international commercial transactions and foreign investment matters. He is currently on the Councils of the American Bar Association's Section of International Law and Practice, where he chairs the International Practitioners' Workshop Series Editorial Board, and the Real Property Section. He graduated from Harvard University with an A.B. *magna cum laude*, attended the Hague Academy of International Law and received his J.D. from Columbia University.

Kenneth G. Weigel is partner resident in the Washington, D.C. office of Kirkland Ellis. He has practiced international trade and customs law for over 15 years. His practice includes strategic planning and counseling as well as representation in administrative and judicial proceedings on all issues dealing with the importation of merchandise into the U.S. Mr. Weigel is a past Chair of the Customs Law Committee of the American Bar Association's Section of International Law and Practice, co-author of the treatise, *Antidumping, Countervailing Duty and Other Trade Actions*, and an author of numerous articles on international trade and customs issues. He received his B.A. in Economics with distinction from the University of Michigan and his J.D. with high honors from George Washington University.

Roger D. Wiegley is a partner in the Washington, D.C. office of Winthrop, Stimson, Putnam & Roberts where he practices corporate financing, banking and business law. He represents financial institutions and corporations in a broad range of financial transactions, including securities offerings, asset-backed and other structured financings, securitization programs, credit facilities and trade finance. Mr. Wiegley received a J.D. from the University of Wisconsin in 1977 (*magna cum laude*) and a B.A. from the State University of New York at Buffalo in 1970.

Mary L. Williamson is an attorney at Preston Gates & Ellis, where she practices in the areas of intellectual property and international transactions. She represents a variety of developers, publishers, content producers and distributors of software and other high technology products. Her experience includes work in the general counsel's offices of the Overseas Private Investment Corporation (OPIC) and the Multilateral Investment Guaranty Agency. Ms. Williamson received her J.D. from Stanford Law School, where she was editor of the *Stanford Journal of International Law*, holds an M.A. with distinction from the Johns Hopkins School of Advanced International Studies, and graduated with a B.A. from Stanford University as a member of Phi Beta Kappa.

John R. Wilson is a member of Davis, Graham & Stubbs, L.L.C., in Denver, CO, where his practice principally involves corporate and international transactions. He is a 1986 graduate of Stanford Law School and an Adjunct Professor in the Graduate Tax Program of the University of Denver, teaching international taxation.

TABLE OF CONTENTS

CHAPTER 1

THE INTERNATIONAL PRACTICE OF LAW

The Editors

This chapter provides an overview of international legal practice and the general resources that are available to lawyers confronted by international legal issues. The following chapters will discuss specific areas of international legal practice and sources of assistance in each area.

I.   INTRODUCTION

Practicing lawyers are increasingly confronted by commercial transactions and disputes with an international dimension. Goods, services, and capital cross international boundaries more frequently and in greater quantities than was imaginable only a few years ago. Significant commercial negotiations typically involve performance in more than one jurisdiction and parties of different, sometimes several, nationalities. If a dispute arises, the courts of more than one country and, in many cases, arbitral or other private tribunals as well, may have jurisdiction. Special rules will determine the proper forum, the procedures followed by that forum, and the enforcement of any resulting decision.

The common thread running through these diverse situations is the potential applicability to a transaction or dispute of one or more sets of laws that do not apply to transactions or disputes between nationals of the same country. From the standpoint of a U.S. practitioner, there are four such bodies of law: (1) U.S. laws, generally federal statutes, that specifically regulate international transactions or disputes and may apply not only to conduct within the United States but also extraterritorially; (2) the laws of foreign countries; (3) public international law; and (4) conflict of laws rules (or "private international law"), which determine which of several potentially applicable laws courts or arbitral tribunals will apply to a transaction or dispute, and which vary from jurisdiction to jurisdiction. Special rules developed by non–governmental international organizations (such as the International Chamber of Commerce) may also be incorporated into commercial agreements and can, in some instances, be of great assistance in clarifying the parties' intentions or conforming an agreement to international practice.

International legal practice now involves virtually every area of human endeavor. In some areas, important aspects of an international transaction or dispute may still be determined by local laws. (*See, e.g.,* Chapter 6, *Secured Transactions,* Chapter 9, *Securities Law,* Chapter 20, *Creditors' Rights and Bankruptcy.*) At least four areas, however, involve distinctly international legal issues and commonly confront private practitioners. These are trade, investment, technology transfer, and disputes.

A.　International Trade

The sale of goods or services across national boundaries gives rise to a number of issues not present in domestic sales.

First, the movement of the goods or services will itself be subject to regulation. The exporting and importing countries (and countries of transshipment as well) will regulate the entry or exit of goods or services from their territories – prohibiting some, imposing restrictions or requirements on others, levying customs duties or other charges on still others. (*See* Chapter 13, *Export Controls, Sanctions and Antiboycott Laws,* and Chapter 12, *Customs Law.*) These national laws, sufficiently complex in themselves, are further complicated by a web of international agreements that restrict the rights of states to regulate international commerce. Multilateral conventions (GATT, the WTO agreements), regional arrangements (NAFTA, the European Union) and bilateral trade agreements often limit an importing country's right to restrict trade in goods and services. Similarly, international sanctions may prohibit exports to or transactions with particular countries (*e.g.,* current United Nations sanctions against Libya and Iraq) or in particular products (*e.g.,* the Missile Technology Control Regime). The consistency of national laws with international obligations of this kind is the source of negotiation and dispute on many levels, public and private. (*See* Chapter 16, *Trade Remedies and Benefits Programs.*) As new areas of national regulation are drawn into international trade agreements or applied extraterritorially, the complexities increase. (*See, e.g.,* Chapter 11, *Environmental Law,* and Chapter 23, *International Labor and Employment Law.*) If the goods and services are being procured by a foreign government, or financed by the U.S. government, special rules will apply. (*See* Chapter 15, *Government Procurement.*)

Second, the contract of purchase and sale may be subject to one or more national laws. The buyer and seller of the goods or services will typically stipulate to an applicable national law in their contract, and that choice will be respected in most jurisdictions. The state in whose territory the contract is performed may, however, have mandatory laws that will preempt the parties' choice, in whole or in part. Antitrust laws, securities laws, implied warranties designed to protect consumers, and rules concerning the enforcement of security interests are typical examples. The country of origin of the goods or services may also have laws that apply to activities outside its borders, if those activities have an effect in the state of origin. (*See* Chapter 8,

International Antitrust, Chapter 9, *Securities*, Chapter 11, *Environmental Law*, and Chapter 23, *International Labor and Employment Law*.)

The purchase and sale agreement may also be subject to international rules. The parties may stipulate to the application of the United Nations Convention on Contracts for the International Sale of Goods,[1] or, in the absence of a stipulation of an applicable law, the Convention may apply if the parties' respective countries adhere to the Convention. Many contracts will also incorporate trade terms, such as the INCOTERMS promulgated by the International Chamber of Commerce ("ICC"), to specify by convenient abbreviations (FOB, CIF, etc.) the parties' payment and delivery obligations. (*See* Chapter 2, *International Commercial Transactions*.)

Third, international sales of goods or services are frequently accompanied by a number of ancillary agreements – contracts for the carriage of the goods, insurance agreements, letters of credit, other financing or security arrangements, etc. Each is also potentially subject to more than one set of laws. International maritime conventions and customary rules of admiralty, for example, may apply to the carriage of goods or to insurance contracts. International letters of credit almost invariably incorporate by reference the ICC's Uniform Customs and Practices for Documentary Credits. (*See* Chapter 5, *International Payment Methods*.) Export financing and insurance may be procured from specialized institutions such as the Export–Import Bank of the United States, with their own statutory restrictions, policies, and procedures. (See Chapter 3, *International Financing* and Chapter 4, *Political Risk Insurance*.)

Fourth, if the seller uses an agent or distributor in a foreign country, the agency or distributorship agreement will generally be governed, in whole or in part, by that country's laws. Many countries have enacted laws to protect local agents and distributors by, for example, permitting termination only upon the occurrence of specified events or the payment of termination fees or by requiring that all disputes be resolved in local courts. Local labor laws may, in some instances, also apply to agents. (*See* Chapter 2, *International Commercial Transactions*.) Payments to agents and distributors represent one of the many contexts in which issues under the U.S. Foreign Corrupt Practices Act may arise. (*See* Chapter 14, *The Foreign Corrupt Practices Act*.)

Fifth and finally, trade transactions (and the auxiliary agreements they generate), raise distinct tax issues under U.S. law, under foreign law, and under international agreements. (*See* Chapter 10, *U.S. Taxation of International Transactions*.)

B. *International Investments*

Investments by nationals of one country in the territory of another raise a different set of issues. Many countries prohibit foreign ownership in certain sectors of the economy or specify limitations on the percentage ownership that a foreign investor may hold in those sectors. Others require prior approval of foreign investments or regular reports by foreign investors providing details of their holdings. (For United States laws of this nature, see Chapter 21, *Foreign Investment in the United States*.)

International investments may take a great many forms – a stock or asset purchase, a joint venture, establishment of a new, wholly foreign-owned entity, portfolio investments, etc. Where the investment involves a contractual agreement, the parties may generally choose the law to apply to that agreement. Again, however, some local laws may be mandatory, *e.g.*, those applying to corporate governance, ownership of real property, labor, or employment. In some instances, too, local securities and anti-competition laws will apply. (*See* Chapter 8, *International Antitrust* and Chapter 9, *Securities Law*.) U.S. laws with extraterritorial application may also affect the foreign investment, depending on its ownership structure and activities.

In a trade contract, a company may be able to structure its activities so as to avoid local taxation. This will not, however, be possible in an investment context unless the investment is in a tax haven jurisdiction or the host country grants a tax holiday. International investments therefore typically require detailed tax planning to address the intersection of local and U.S. tax laws. (*See* Chapter 10, *U.S. Taxation of International Transactions*.)

The financing of international investments, especially project financing, where lenders look principally to the project and not to the general credit of the project sponsors, is a rapidly evolving area, attracting specialized sources and issues. Private sector projects may be financed by a combination of public and private sources. On the public side, the World Bank and some of the regional development banks have private sector affiliates that provide debt and sometimes equity financing. The Overseas Private Investment Corporation ("OPIC"), a U.S. government-owned entity, is another source for loans and loan guarantees for U.S. investment abroad. (*See* Chapter 3, *International Financing*.)

Insurance issues, especially against political risks, also frequently arise with respect to international investments. The need to provide protection against these risks has spawned specialized government agencies to provide coverage not available, or not available at economical rates, in the private sector. (*See* Chapter 4, *Political Risk Insurance*.)

International investments may also be subject to various issues of public international law. Hundreds of bilateral investment treaties and the recently signed European Energy Charter Treaty[2] now impose obligatory standards, often quite detailed, for the treatment of foreign investors. The WTO agreement on investment is limited in scope, but the OECD has recently undertaken efforts to negotiate a general multilateral investment treaty. Customary public international law also imposes restrictions on the treatment of foreign nationals and, more specifically, on the terms on which a host country may expropriate the assets of foreign nationals.

C.   Technology Transfers

Technology transfers constitute one of the fastest-growing areas of international commercial activity. These can be stand-alone transactions (*i.e.,* technology sales, licenses, or franchises) or transactions that occur in connection with a trade or investment transaction. The commercialization of computer software occurs largely through licensing, and the explosive growth in software activity has generated its own sub-body of law in this area.

Technology transfers may be subject to specific regulation by both the exporting country and the recipient country. The United States subjects technology transfers to export controls that in some areas are more far-reaching than its controls on the export of goods. (*See* Chapter 13, *Export Controls, Sanctions and Antiboycott Laws.*) The importing country may regulate royalty payments or other aspects of the transaction under laws governing licenses as technology transfers, or customs or tax laws.

The licensing or franchising of technology also implies that the grantor has rights in the technology that are legally cognizable in the recipient country. Intellectual property rights such as patents, trademarks, and copyrights are territorial in nature. A network of treaties has therefore been created to facilitate the obtaining of rights in other jurisdictions. (*See* Chapter 7, *Intellectual Property Rights.*) Companies contemplating an international technology transfer and their counsel need to be familiar with this network and develop a strategy for technology protection well in advance of any actual transfer.

Technology transfers also raise distinct issues under U.S. and local tax laws, and activity in this area requires tax planning. (*See* Chapter 10, *U.S. Taxation of International Transactions.*)

D.   International Dispute Resolution

Disputes arising out of the international sale of goods or international investments constitute yet another distinct area of international legal practice, which may be divided into three general issues: (1) determination of the forum in which the dispute can or must be resolved; (2) procedural rules applicable to adjudication of the dispute in that forum; and (3) enforcement of the resulting decision in other jurisdictions. (*See* Chapter 18, *International Litigation,* and Chapter 19, *International Commercial Arbitration.*)

Courts, with limited exceptions, will enforce a choice-of-forum clause in an international contract. Because parties to international contracts are generally unwilling to submit their disputes to adjudication by one another's national courts, and because it is easier to enforce an arbitral award than a foreign judgment, most international contracts provide for arbitration. Arbitration clauses, too, are typically enforceable in most jurisdictions. When the contract does not include a choice-of-forum or arbitration clause, all of the issues associated with the establishment of personal and subject matter jurisdiction will be presented, generally with special features recognizing limitations on the host state's rights to prescribe conduct outside of the state or to adjudicate disputes involving individuals or corporations not legally present within the state.

Any international dispute brought before a forum, arbitral or judicial, will involve a host of procedural issues. Service of process, rights to pre-hearing discovery, interlocutory relief, evidentiary standards, authentication procedures, and similar issues will necessarily arise. Local conflict of laws rules ("private international law") will also determine which substantive laws will apply to various aspects of the transaction or dispute. All judicial systems and all of the major international arbitral institutions provide more or less developed rules as to how to deal with these issues in an international context.

Some of these rules are also now established by international treaty. The Hague Conventions on Service of Process[3] and the Taking of Evidence Abroad,[4] for example, provide agreed rules and procedures for dealing with service of process and discovery issues. Many of the world's leading trading countries are parties to these Conventions, albeit often with reservations. The Hague Convention Abolishing the Requirement of Legalisation for Foreign Public Documents[5] establishes an authentication mechanism and is even more widely accepted. (*See* Chapter 17, *Legalization of Documents for Use Abroad*.)

Enforcement of a court judgment or arbitral award presents different issues. Generally, enforcement of court judgments is a matter of comity rather than a matter of legal obligation. Practice in this regard varies widely, depending on such factors as reciprocity and similarity of the legal systems involved. Some regional organizations also facilitate the enforcement of decisions of one another's courts by convention. *See, e.g.*, European Communities Convention on Jurisdiction and Enforcement of Judgments in Civil and Commercial Matters ("EEC Judgments Convention" or "Brussels Convention"),[6] and the Inter-American Convention on the Taking of Evidence Abroad and Additional Protocol.[7] The United States is not currently party to any bilateral or multilateral convention of this nature.

The enforcement of arbitral awards is, in comparison, relatively straightforward. Most of the world's major trading nations, including the United States, are now parties to the United Nations Convention on the Recognition and Enforcement of Foreign Arbitral Awards (the "New York Convention"),[8] which provides for the enforcement of arbitral awards rendered in the territory of one contracting state in the territories of the other contracting states. The exceptions are limited and generally construed narrowly. Many of the countries in the Western Hemisphere are also parties to the Inter-American Convention on International Commercial Arbitration (the "Panama Convention"),[9] which applies enforcement rules within the region similar to those of the New York Convention. (*See* Chapter 19, *International Commercial Arbitration*.)

E.   Other

The preceding sections discuss commercial transactions and disputes. International legal issues arise in non–commercial contexts as well. Because people move across borders, national immigration laws have had to address personal as well as business immigration. (*See* Chapter 22, *Immigration and Nationality.*) Other family law issues – marriage, divorce, adoption, child custody – can have an international dimension. Certain of these situations have given rise to international agreements, while others remain largely governed by national law. (*See* Chapter 25, *Family Law.*) Family wealth transfer – wills, trusts and estates – also increasingly defy national boundaries. (*See* Chapter 24, *Wills, Trusts, Estates and Related Taxes.*) Bankruptcy, individual or corporate, is still largely governed by national law, but international issues are increasing. (*See* Chapter 20, *Creditors' Rights and Bankruptcy.*)

II.   SOURCES OF ASSISTANCE

The various bodies of law potentially applicable to these diverse situations are not conveniently collected in one place. A lawyer confronted with an international transaction or dispute must therefore be prepared to find assistance in several places.

A.   General

There are three basic sources of law with which every international lawyer in the United States should be familiar.

First, as in other areas of the law, the American Law Institute has attempted to summarize U.S. international legal practice in a "Restatement" – in this case, *The Restatement of the Foreign Relations Law of the United States, Third.* As its title suggests, the principal focus of the "*Restatement Third*" is public international law – "foreign relations law." Many provisions will be too theoretical or too political to be of more than academic interest to most practitioners. Nevertheless, the *Restatement Third* is significant because it establishes an overall architecture for international legal issues, making it possible to fit a particular problem into that architecture and to identify related issues. Further, the *Restatement Third* does address many specific issues that arise in commercial legal practice, including the jurisdiction of national legislatures to prescribe rules (*e.g.*, antitrust, securities) for conduct outside their borders, the jurisdiction of national courts to adjudicate such conduct, immunities of foreign states, and certain areas of international trade and monetary law. For each, it provides a succinct statement of the authors' view of the current state of the law, together with numerous comments and illustrations, including citations.

The *Restatement Third* is not authoritative. It purports to state only U.S. practice. Many of its provisions were contentious when adopted, and even U.S. courts have sometimes interpreted the law quite differently. Nevertheless, for many issues the *Restatement Third* is an excellent place to start.

Second, the American Society of International Law has published a comprehensive two-volume collection of *Basic Documents of International Economic Law*, which includes the most important inter-governmental agreements governing international trade and finance, international investments, international litigation, and similar issues. Each is prefaced by a brief explanatory introduction, and each includes a useful bibliography. *Basic Documents* includes most of the original texts to which an international practitioner would wish to refer and is currently on-line on LEXIS–NEXIS (ITRADE/BDIEL) and WESTLAW.

Third, every international lawyer should be familiar with *International Legal Materials* ("*ILM*"), a bimonthly publication of the American Society of International Law. *ILM* provides international lawyers with recent official developments – treaties, statutes, important judicial and arbitral decisions, etc. It generally provides full original texts and brief summaries. English translations are provided for documents in other languages. *ILM* is in its 34th year of publication, and most of the significant public law developments of recent years are to be found in its pages. *ILM* is also now available on WEST-LAW.

A number of other periodicals cover recent developments in the field. Finding information in these periodicals on a specific issue is a serendipitous process, but an article or a note by an expert on, for example, recent changes in the foreign investment laws of a particular country, can be well worth a quick search. Three periodicals are worthy of special note: (1) *The International Lawyer*, published quarterly by the American Bar Association's Section on International Law and Practice; (2) *The International Business Lawyer*, published monthly (one issue for July–August) by the Section on Business Law of the International Bar Association; and (3) *Corporate Counsel's International Adviser*, published monthly by Business Laws, Inc.

B.   *International Legal Issues Online*

Every international lawyer should also be familiar with the extensive collections of materials available from LEXIS–NEXIS and WESTLAW. It is not practicable to list here all of the collections now accessible online from these two services. Suffice it to note that each includes original source materials encompassing: U.S. statutes, regulations, treaties, and case law; similar materials for an expanding list of foreign jurisdictions; and an array of periodicals reporting on and analyzing international legal developments around the world. *See* III., Sources of Assistance. Many recent developments appear online before they are available in hard copy. Access to these materials is, accordingly, a significant enhancement to any lawyer's international legal practice.

Additional sources of assistance are also increasingly available on the Internet. Developments in this area are so rapid that one hesitates to summarize them. A general description of legal sources on the Internet and how they may be accessed may be found in *The Lawyer's Guide to the INTERNET*, recently published by the ABA Section of Law Practice Management. There are also several very useful and readily accessible sources for legal materials at Stanford, Cornell, and Indiana Universities. A collection particularly useful to international lawyers is the International Trade Law Library, maintained by the University of Tromsø, Norway. Another important source of assistance for international legal materials or advice is INT-LAW, an electronic discussion group of international and foreign law librarians on the Bitnet. (*See* III., Sources of Assistance.) Note that all Internet materials are subject to questions of authority, accuracy, and currency, and that a number of difficult, and generally unresolved, issues of copyright and privacy laws may affect use of these materials.

C.   *United States Laws*

There is no single source for the numerous U.S. laws that apply to international transactions or disputes. Again, however, LEXIS–NEXIS and WESTLAW both maintain extensive on-line libraries devoted solely to U.S. international materials, and the various Internet sources cited in the Bibliography would also provide access to most of the materials likely to be of interest to an international practitioner. Sources for U.S. laws applicable to specific areas of international practice are identified in the other chapters of this book.

D.   *Foreign Laws*

Obtaining reliable information on foreign laws requires consultation with local counsel. (*See* Chapter 26, *Selecting and Working with Foreign Counsel.*) Indeed, providing advice on foreign law that is not based on such consultation can give rise to malpractice issues. Nevertheless, it is frequently both necessary and helpful to have at hand the text of foreign laws or explanations as to how they apply.

With more than 200 countries in the world today, however, finding reliable texts of foreign laws, much less reliable English translations, is an uncertain process at best. CCH publishes the full texts of the principal laws of a number of countries in loose-leaf with periodic updates. These are perhaps the most reliable collections. CCH and Matthew Bender also publish guides to doing business in various countries. These are generally of high quality and can be very useful. LEXIS–NEXIS and WESTLAW also are adding foreign statutes to their libraries, generally in the original language, and it may be possible to access other foreign laws on the Internet. (*See* III., Sources of Assistance.)

Several publications also attempt to collect in one place the texts of the commercial laws of foreign jurisdictions likely to be of interest to private U.S. practitioners. (*See* III., Sources of Assistance.) These collections suffer from inherent problems. It is often difficult to place a commercial statute in its broader legal framework, and keeping the texts up to date is a Herculean task at which the publishers only partially succeed.

Similarly, *The Economist* and some of the major accounting firms periodically publish summaries of the laws of countries likely to be of commercial interest. (*See* III., Sources of Assistance.) These summaries, too, can be very useful. Lawyers need to be cautious, however, about using such secondary sources, and the summaries also tend to go out of date.

Finally, the United States Commerce and State Departments provide assistance in specific areas. Commerce provides a broad array of information in various publications and through various services. Many of these publications and services are identified in Commerce's *A Basic Guide to Exporting*. Of particular note are the National Trade Data Bank, which assembles a broad range of trade data and is updated monthly, and summaries of investment laws in foreign countries, which are available through a "Flash Fax" system (202–482–1064). The responsible desk officers at the Commerce Department, or the commercial officers of the Foreign and Commercial Service at major U.S. Embassies, can often supplement these materials with additional information or advice as to where additional information may be obtained. (Call Commerce at 202–482–5777 and ask for specific country desk.)

The State Department publishes guidelines on service of process, discovery, and other litigation issues for many countries. These materials can also be supplemented by the State Department's Office of American Citizens Services. (*See* III., Sources of Assistance, for telephone numbers.)

E.   *Public International Law*

Public international law can be divided into inter-governmental treaties[10] and the customary "law of nations." Treaties are more likely to be of interest to private practitioners since they often set out rules of law directly applicable in the jurisdictions of the parties. Bilateral tax and investment treaties, for example, may have important consequences for private transactions. Similarly, multilateral conventions often establish rules for international judicial assistance, limitations on import regulations, etc.

For treaties and international conventions to which the United States is a party, the Treaty Affairs Staff of the Office of the Legal Adviser at the Department of State publishes an annual *Treaties in Force*, which lists, as of January 1 of each year, the treaties to which the United States is a party, the other parties to the treaty, dates of signing and coming into force, etc. Subsequent developments are reported in *ILM*, and current information can be obtained directly from the Treaty Affairs Staff (202–647–2044). Each U.S. treaty is sequentially numbered in the Treaties and Other International Agreements Series ("T.I.A.S.") and subsequently in the United States Treaties ("U.S.T.") series. Lack of funds in recent years has delayed many of these publications. All agreements in force for the United States are available on line through LEXIS–NEXIS or WESTLAW almost immediately.

Treaties to which the United States is not a party are more difficult to locate. Agreements of significance can often be found in *ILM*. The United

Nations Treaties Series ("U.N.T.S.") attempts to publish all international treaties but is generally years behind. The Treaty Affairs Office at the Department of State can sometimes be of assistance in locating or identifying a treaty between third parties. For more definitive information, however, it is best to refer to local counsel in one of the countries in question or to the appropriate embassies.

The best sources for customary international law are collections of state practice and treatises by scholars. Most of the collections of state practice have involved U.S. diplomatic practice, which are particularly relevant for U.S. lawyers but not necessarily accepted by foreign governments and lawyers. These collections began in the nineteenth century. The best known modern collections are *Hyde, Hackworth,* and *Whiteman.* (*See* III., Sources of Assistance.) The Department of State has attempted to update *Whiteman* with annual *Digests of International Law*. A lack of funds has, again, placed the publication of this series behind schedule, and the Department is currently in the process of issuing a cumulative collection for 1981–88. The Department also makes the more important recent developments available to the public by publishing a section on U.S. practice in the quarterly issues of the *American Journal of International Law*.

There are numerous treatises on public international law. The continued validity of some of the older and more traditional texts is subject to a great deal of doctrinal controversy. The more frequently cited texts in English, including those most often cited by U.S. courts, include *Oppenheim, O'Connell, Brierly,* and *Brownlie.* (*See* III., Sources of Assistance.) There are also well-known treatises on public international law published in, among other languages, French, German, Spanish, and Italian.

F.   *Private International Institutions*

A number of private or quasi–private institutions promulgate rules that may be used to govern particular issues or kinds of transactions. Perhaps the best general example is the various arbitration institutions that publish and administer international arbitrations. (*See* Chapter 19, *International Commercial Arbitration*.)

By far the most significant, however, is the International Chamber of Commerce. The ICC supervises the International Court of Arbitration (an administrative rather than a judicial body), which promulgates and maintains rules for arbitration and conciliation and has administered international arbitrations for many decades. The ICC also maintains panels of experts in other fields, which promulgate, *inter alia*, INCOTERMS, the Uniform Customs and Practices for Documentary Credits (the "UCP"), Uniform Rules for Contract Guarantees, and Uniform Rules for Collections. These systems of technical rules are frequently incorporated by reference in private international contracts. The ICC publishes numerous guides explaining these rules and summarizing related technical areas. The ICC's Banking Commission also

provides advisory opinions interpreting the UCP, which it periodically publishes. These materials are commendable for their clarity and succinctness.
Most recently, the ICC has published model agency and distributorship
agreements, together with floppy disks that permit private practitioners to
load the model agreements directly onto their computer systems.

G.   *Private International Law*

Private international law is international law that is intended to govern
the relationships of private parties. It includes – but is not limited to – international rules governing applicable law to a transaction or matter. It also
includes international commercial law, family law, procedural law in international disputes, and others.

There are several public institutions actively involved in the development of private international law. These include UNCITRAL, UNIDROIT, the
Hague Conference, and the Organization of American States ("OAS"). Their
products include treaties (conventions), uniform laws, guidelines, and principles. It is up to individual countries whether to adopt the treaties and uniform laws these bodies develop. Some have been widely-accepted; others
have not. Each of the major bodies is discussed briefly below; additional contact information is set forth in the Sources of Assistance. In addition, several
chapters of the book discuss particular rules in more detail.[11]

1.   UNCITRAL

The United Nations Commission on International Trade Law ("UNCITRAL")
is a subsidiary organ of the United Nations, created in 1966. The United States is
one of sixteen members of the Commission. UNCITRAL's best-known product is the United Nations Convention on Contracts for the International Sale
of Goods, referred to earlier in this Chapter. A related convention, the United
Nations Convention on the Limitation Period in the International Sale of
Goods, was ratified by the United States in 1994 and entered into force for
the United States on December 1, 1995. Both of these are discussed in more
detail in Chapter 2, *International Commercial Transactions*. At this writing,
UNCITRAL's pending projects include: a model law on electronic data interchange; uniform rules for assignment in receivables financing; cross-border
insolvency; and a convention on independent guarantees and standby letters
of credit. It has also developed three other instruments to which the United
States is not a party: a 1988 Convention on International Bills of Exchange
and International Promissory Notes (*reprinted in* 28 I.L.M. 177 (1989)); a
Convention on Liability of Operators of Transport Terminals in International
Trade (*reprinted in* 30 I.L.M. 1506 (1991)); and a Model Law on International
Credit Transfers (*reprinted in* 32 I.L.M. 588 (1993)).

2. UNIDROIT

The International Institute for the Unification of Private Law ("UNIDROIT") is an independent intergovernmental body of 56 members, including the United States. UNIDROIT has developed several conventions in the area of private international law, and has also recently published a set of principles for international commercial contracts.[12] The UNIDROIT-developed conventions are: Convention on International Factoring (*reprinted in* 27 I.L.M. 943 (1988)) (*entered into force*, May 1, 1995; signed but not ratified by the United States); Convention on International Financial Leasing (*reprinted in* 27 I.L.M. 931 (1988)) (*entered into force* May 1, 1995; signed but not ratified by the United States); and a Convention on the International Return of Stolen or Illegally Exported Cultural Objects (*see* draft, *reprinted in* 34 I.L.M. 1330 (1995) *and* Introductory Note by Harold S. Burman, 34 I.L.M. 1322 (1995)). Other pending projects include rules for the recognition and enforcement of security interests in mobile equipment, and guidelines for international franchising.

3. The Hague Conference

The Hague Conference on Private International Law is an inter–governmental body with 41 members, including the United States. The Hague Conference has developed a number of conventions in the areas of conflicts of laws, procedural issues in transnational disputes, and personal status and family law. The procedural conventions are discussed in more detail in Chapter 18, *International Litigation*; the family law conventions are considered in Chapter 25, *Family Law*. The Hague Conference also adopted a Convention on the Law Applicable to Contracts for the International Sale of Goods (*reprinted in* 26 I.L.M. 1573 (1987)), which is not yet in force, and which is designed to replace a 1955 Hague Convention on the same subject, which is in force but to which the United States is not a party.

4. The OAS

The OAS has convened five specialized conferences on private international law (CIDIP–I through CIDIP–V). These conferences have dealt with choice of law, procedural issues in transnational litigation, and commercial law topics. One of the Conventions, the Inter–American Convention on Letters Rogatory, and an Additional Protocol, have been ratified by the United States (*reprinted in* 14 I.L.M. 399 (1975) *and* 18 I.L.M. 1238 (1979), respectively). (*See* Chapter 18, *International Litigation*.)

III.   SOURCES OF ASSISTANCE

A.   *U.S. Statutes, Regulations, and Case Law*

Lexis–Nexis maintains an International Trade Library (Itrade), which includes federal international case law, statutes, regulations, and agency decisions.

Westlaw maintains libraries for federal international law cases, statutes, rules, regulations, and administrative law decisions (primarily Customs). The library prefix is Fint–.

See also the Internet sources cited below.

B.   *Foreign Statutes and Laws*

Foreign Law: Current Sources of Codes and Basic Legislation in Jurisdictions of the World (3 vols., loose-leaf) (Thomas H. Reynolds & Arturo A. Flores eds., 1989).

Claire M. Germain, Germain's International Law Research: A Guide For Attorneys (1991–).

International Encyclopedia of Comparative Law (11 vols.) (R. David, *et al.* eds. 1973).

International Encyclopedia of Laws (R. Blanpain ed., 1991).

Martindale–Hubbell Law Digest, Canadian and International Law Digest (annual).

CCH and Mathew Bender & Company each publish extensive collections of foreign laws and guides to those laws.

Lexis–Nexis: Statutes of Australia, China (in English), England, and France (in French); state and federal Mexican legislation (in Spanish); selected texts of Russia and Eastern Europe (in English); European Community law. Case law of Australia, Canada, England, France (in French), Ireland, Mexico (in Spanish), New Zealand, and Scotland.

Westlaw: Statutes of China (Chinalaw), Russia and the C.I.S. (Rusline), commercial laws of Eastern European countries (Int-Eeurope), and the official European Community data base (Celex).

The China Law Reporter (published quarterly by the ABA Section of International Law and Practice)

Inter-American Legal Materials (copies of recent laws and regulations in the original language and, when available, in English translation; published twice a year by the ABA Section of International Law and Practice).

The Official Journal of the European Communities and other European documents are available on CD-ROM, with periodic updates, from Vista InterMedia Corporation (Stamford, CT).

COMMERCIAL LAWS OF THE WORLD (Foreign Tax Law Publishers, Inc.).

THE ECONOMIST INTELLIGENCE UNIT, INVESTING, LICENSING & TRADING CONDITIONS ABROAD (for individual countries; various publication dates).

PRICE WATERHOUSE, INFORMATION GUIDE SERIES ("DOING BUSINESS IN _____"; various publication dates).

U.S. DEPARTMENT OF COMMERCE, A BASIC GUIDE TO EXPORTING (1992) (in addition to basic rules and procedures for exporting, summarizes a broad range of official publications and information sources of the United States Government and various international organizations).

U.S. DEPARTMENT OF COMMERCE, The National Trade Data Bank (export promotion and international trade data collected by 15 U.S. Government agencies; updated monthly; available on CD-ROM).

U.S. DEPARTMENT OF COMMERCE, "Flash Fax" information on investment laws in specific countries: (202) 482-1064.

U.S. DEPARTMENT OF STATE, guidelines on service of process and discovery procedures in specific countries. Call appropriate regional desk at Office of American Citizens Services: Africa (202-647-4994); Americas (202-647-3712); East Asia (202-647-3675); Europe (202-647-3444); Near East and South Asia (202-647-3926).

Szladits, *Foreign Law in English*, 34 AM. J. COMP. L. 180 (1986) (bibliography).

C. *Treaties*

For treaties to which United States is a party:

U.S. DEPARTMENT OF STATE, UNITED STATES TREATIES AND OTHER INTERNATIONAL AGREEMENTS (multi-volume, 1950-) (on-line on WESTLAW as USTREATIES).

U.S. DEPARTMENT OF STATE, TREATIES IN FORCE (annual).

I. KAVASS & A. SPRUDZS, UST CUMULATIVE INDEX *1950-70* (1973; Supp. 1, 1977; Supp. 2, 1985; loose-leaf).

CHARLES BEVAN, TREATIES AND OTHER INTERNATIONAL AGREEMENTS OF THE UNITED STATES OF AMERICA, 1776–1949 (12 vols., 1968–74).

W. MALLOY, TREATIES, CONVENTIONS, INTERNATIONAL ACTS, PROTOCOLS AND AGREEMENTS BETWEEN THE UNITED STATES OF AMERICA AND OTHER POWERS, 1776–1909 (4 vols. 1910; *reprinted* 1968).

LEXIS–NEXIS: U.S. treaties from 1789 (INTLAW/USTRTY).

NAFTA is available, with supporting commentary, on CD–ROM from the ABA Section of International Law and Practice.

For non–U.S. treaties:

M. J. BOWAN & D. J. HARRIS, MULTILATERAL TREATIES: INDEX AND CURRENT STATUTES (1984, periodic supplements). The Multilaterals Project of the Fletcher School of Law and Diplomacy is attempting to make these materials available on the Internet:
http://www/tufts.edu/departments/fletcher/multilaterals.html.

WESTLAW maintains copies of European Community treaties (CELEX–TRTY).

D.   *Official Documents*

BASIC DOCUMENTS OF INTERNATIONAL ECONOMIC LAW (2 vols.) (S. Zamora & R. Brand eds. 1990) (on–line on LEXIS–NEXIS (ITRADE/BDIEL) and WESTLAW).

E.   *Secondary Sources*

1.   Books

Editorial Staff of the George Washington Journal of International Law and Economics, GUIDE TO INTERNATIONAL LEGAL RESEARCH (2d ed. 1993).

The following are leading sources primarily for public international law:

AMERICAN LAW INSTITUTE, RESTATEMENT OF THE LAW (THIRD) OF THE FOREIGN RELATIONS LAW OF THE UNITED STATES (1986) (on–line on WESTLAW as REST–FOREL).

J. L. BRIERLY, THE LAW OF NATIONS (6th ed. 1963).

IAN BROWNLIE, PRINCIPLES OF PUBLIC INTERNATIONAL LAW (4th ed. 1990).

CHARLES CHENEY HYDE, INTERNATIONAL LAW (3 vols., 2d. ed. 1947).

ANTOINE-CHARLES KISS, RÉPERTOIRE DE LA PRATIQUE FRANÇAISE EN MATERIÈRE DE DROIT INTERNATIONAL PUBLIC (1962).

D. P. O'CONNELL, INTERNATIONAL LAW (2 vols., 2d. ed. 1970).

OPPENHEIM'S INTERNATIONAL LAW (Vol. I, PEACE, R. Jennings & A. Watts ed., 9th ed. 1992; Vol. II, WAR AND NEUTRALITY, H. Lauterpacht ed., 7th ed. 1958).

CHARLES ROUSSEAU, DROIT INTERNATIONAL PUBLIC (5 vols. 1970–1983).

U.S. DEPARTMENT OF STATE, DIGEST OF UNITED STATES PRACTICE IN INTERNATIONAL LAW (annual 1973–80; cumulative, 1981–88).

ALFRED VERDROSS & BRUNO SIMMA, UNIVERSELLES VÖLKERRECHT (3d ed. 1984).

MARJORIE WHITEMAN, DIGEST OF INTERNATIONAL LAW (14 vols. 1963–71).

2.   Periodicals

International Legal Materials (American Society of International Law, bimonthly) (on–line on LEXIS-NEXIS from January 1980: ITRADE/ILM).

The International Business Lawyer (Business Law Section, International Bar Association, monthly, one issue for July–August) (on–line on LEXIS-NEXIS from Winter 1981: ITRADE/INTLAW).

The International Lawyer (Section of International Law and Practice, American Bar Association, quarterly).

Corporate Counsel's International Adviser, (Business Laws, Inc., monthly).

F.   On-Line Services

LEXIS-NEXIS maintains extensive International Law (INTLAW) and International Trade (ITRADE) Libraries.

WESTLAW maintains an extensive International Law library and database.

G. BURGESS ALLISON, THE LAWYER'S GUIDE TO THE INTERNET (ABA Section of Law Practice Management, 1995).

Erik J. Heels, *The Legal List, Law-Related Resources on the Internet and Elsewhere* (1094) is available in hardcopy from:

> Erik J. Heels
> The Legal List
> 39 Main Street
> Eliot, ME 03903–2234

– also available on e–mail via anonymous FTP: ftp://ftp.midnight.com/pub/Legal List/legallist.txt.

The U.S. Department of State offers a "Private International Law Databse" with current developments in private international law at UNCITRAL, UNIDROIT, and the OAS. It is accessible at: http://www.his.com/~pildb/.

ABA sources are available at: Section of International Law and Practice home page: http://www.abanet.org.

The Section's Internet Listserve Discussion Group is at: ABAINTINV@cali.kentlaw.edu.

The American Society of International Law list for members of its International Economic Law Group is at: ASILIELG@cali.kentlaw.edu.

The International Trade Law Library at the University of Tromsø, Norway is available at:
http://www.ananse.irv.uit.no/trade_law/nav/trade.html.

The University of Helsinki is also a good source of information on inter-national trade and economics: http://www.helsinki.si/~Isaarine/internat.html.

Some of the better World Wide Web sites for legal research generally are:

Legal Information Institute of Cornell University Law School: http://www.law.cornell.edu/lii.table.html.

Virtual Law Library at Indiana University School of Law: http://www.law.indiana.edu/law/lawindex.html.

Chicago–Kent College of Law's Guide to Legal Resources: http://www.kentlaw.edu/lawnet/lawlinks.html.

Int–Law for foreign and international law librarians is served out of the University of Minnesota (INT–LAW@UMINN1.BITNET).

G.   *Other*

ICC publications may be obtained from:
ICC Publishing, Inc.
156 Fifth Avenue, Suite 308
New York, New York 10010
(212) 206-1150

United Nations Commission on International Trade Law (UNCITRAL):
Vienna International Center
P.O. Box 500
A-1400 Vienna, Austria
Tel.: (011) 43-1-71131-4060
Fax: (011) 43-1-237485

International Institute for the Unification of Private Law (UNIDROIT):
Via Panisperna 28
00184 Rome, Italy
Tel.: (011) 39-6-6994-1372
Fax: (011) 39-6-6994-1394

Hague Conference on Private International Law
6, Scheveningseweg
2517 KT The Hague
The Netherlands
Tel.: (011) 31-70-363-3003
Fax: (011) 31-70-360-4867

Organization of American States (OAS)
17th Street and Constitution Avenue, N.W.
Washington, D.C.
Tel.: (202) 458-3407
Fax: (202) 458-6029

ENDNOTES

[1]   *Done* at Vienna, April 11, 1980; *entered into force* January 1, 1988. Annex I, Final Act of the U.N. Conference for the International Sale of Goods, 1980, U.N. Doc. A/CONF. 97/19, U.N. Sales No. E.82.V.5. English text *reprinted in* 52 Fed. Reg. 6264 (1987).

[2]   *Done* in Lisbon, Dec. 17, 1994, *reprinted in* 34 I.L.M. 382 (1995). The Energy Charter Treaty was signed by more than 40 OECD, Eastern European, and Commonwealth of Independent States countries. Ratification by 30 countries is necessary to bring it into force.

[3]   *Done* at The Hague November 15, 1965; *entered into force* February 10, 1969; 20 U.S.T. 361; 658 U.N.T.S. 163.

4 *Done* at The Hague March 18, 1970; *entered into force* October 7, 1972; 23 U.S.T. 2555; 847 U.N.T.S. 231.

5 *Done at* The Hague October 5, 1961, *entered into force* October 15, 1981; T.I.A.S. 10072, 527 U.N.T.S. 189.

6 Comprised of several declarations and protocols, which are published in consolidated and edited form in 26 O.J. EUR. COMM. No. C 97/1, April 11, 1983. Originals are *reprinted in* 18 I.L.M. 20 (1979).

7 January 30, 1975, OAS Treaty Series No. 44, *reprinted in* 14 I.L.M. 328 (1975). Additional Protocol, May 24, 1984, OAS Treaty Series No. 65, *reprinted in* 24 I.L.M 472 (1985).

8 *Done* at New York June 10, 1958; *entered into force* June 7, 1959; for the United States December 29, 1970; 21 U.S.T. 2517, 330 U.N.T.S. 38 (1958).

9 *Done* at Panama January 30, 1975; *entered into force* June 16, 1976; for the United States October 27, 1990; OAS Treaty Series No. 42, *reprinted in* 14 I.L.M. 336 (1975).

10 For purposes of international law, a "treaty" is any binding written agreement between countries. It therefore subsumes both those agreements constituting "treaties" for U.S. constitutional purposes and other international agreements referred to in U.S. practice as "executive agreements."

11 The authors wish to acknowledge the contributions of Professor Peter Winship and Harold Burman to Section II.G. of the chapter.

12 UNIDROIT PRINCIPLES OF INTERNATIONAL COMMERCIAL CONTRACTS (1994).

CHAPTER 2

INTERNATIONAL COMMERCIAL TRANSACTIONS

Rona R. Mears

I.   INTRODUCTION

A.   *Defining International Commercial Transactions*

Resources vary in their definitions of the term "international commercial transactions." It is generally understood, however, to include a wide range of cross-border business dealings. In particular, the term refers to the activities of merchants and to transactions involving the sales and distribution of goods and services among parties in different countries. But it may also include a variety of related cross-border commercial dealings that cover nearly all of the means by which businesses market their products and services and make investments across national borders.

There are certain principal legal issues that most international commercial transactions have in common. These are discussed below in section I.C. Other legal issues that arise primarily in specific transactions are set out in section II. Distinct legal issues do not, however, arise solely in connection with formulating international commercial transactions; they also are presented in adversarial and regulatory contexts. Section III (Sources of Assistance) identifies resources that provide more detail on the legal issues and transactions discussed in this chapter.

B.   *The Law Applicable to International Commercial Transactions*

The legal issues that arise in international commercial transactions must be viewed within a broad framework of applicable law, including U.S., foreign and international law. (*See* Chapter 1, *The International Practice of Law*.) Any one or a combination of these laws may apply, and the international practitioner must be inclusive in examining and determining applicable law. The extent to which party autonomy, *i.e.*, the designation by the parties of applicable law, will be recognized for the range of issues raised by the transaction is a threshold issue.

U.S. law, for instance, applies to the exit of goods from the U.S.; the primary example of such U.S. regulation is export controls. U.S. law also applies to certain aspects of taxation (including tax-based export inducements) and to areas in which U.S. law has an extraterritorial reach, such as export controls and antitrust regulation. In addition to U.S. federal law, provisions of U.S. state law or local regulations also may apply to such areas as taxation, environmental regulation, health standards, transportation and other issues.

Foreign law—that is, the law of the non-U.S. trading or investment jurisdiction (often called the "host" jurisdiction)—is applicable to customs and entry of goods, cross-border exit of capital or entry of people, establishment of joint ventures or direct investments in the host jurisdiction, and the day-to-day operation of businesses in the foreign country, including tax, labor, environmental, corporate accounting and reporting, and myriad other local regulations.

International law may also apply to international commercial transactions. Among the most common examples are treaties such as the U.N. Convention on Contracts for the International Sale of Goods ("CISG") and the multilateral trade agreements to which the U.S. is a party, such as the North American Free Trade Agreement ("NAFTA") or the General Agreement on Tariffs and Trade ("GATT"). In addition, bodies of customary international law such as the International Chamber of Commerce's INCOTERMS may also apply.

The discussions below identify the law or laws that may be applicable to the primary legal issues common to most international commercial transactions and the particular legal issues raised in certain transactions.

C. *Principal Legal Issues Presented by International Commercial Transactions*

Certain legal issues dealt with in international transactions have domestic parallels, but many do not. As a result, it is not appropriate to assume that domestic commercial contracts will work for an international transaction. Differing jurisdictions and special cross-border issues make it necessary to view international commercial transactions somewhat differently from their domestic counterparts, and to revise domestic contracts or to draft new international contracts accordingly.

Even though international commercial transactions are diverse, some legal issues are common to nearly all of them. First, most of these transactions are based on an international commercial contract. That contract is the foundation of the transaction, defines its principal legal issues, and is its primary legal document. Also common to these dealings is cross-border movement of one or more of the following: goods, services, capital, information, technology, people, or profits. In addition, most transactions involve international financing arrangements, and all of them face the challenges of cross-border dispute resolution. Long-term transactions such as foreign direct investments present additional legal issues related to establishing and maintaining an on-going business operation in a foreign country.

In providing legal advice on international commercial transactions, the transnational lawyer may encounter any–or even all–of the principal legal issues summarized below. These issues are grouped under four major headings: international contracting; cross–border movement; financing and currency issues; and other general issues.

1.   International Contracting Issues

   a.   Power of Private Parties to Contract Cross–Border;
         Applicable Law

Virtually all jurisdictions recognize the rights of private parties to establish their own contractual arrangements and to bind one another to the law of the contract. Such principles are implicit under common law and are explicitly set forth in civil law codes.

The legal framework for contracting may differ, however, from one jurisdiction to another, and may set forth varying standards for when the contract is formed, whether it is valid and enforceable, and what local requirements must be met. The first issue to address is applicable law: what law will control this contract; how is it likely to be enforced; will the jurisdictions involved recognize a choice of governing law by the parties? There may, for instance, be significant advantages to designating the law of the foreign country (of a venture partner or sales customer), and to planning on enforcement in the foreign jurisdiction. Such a choice depends on the particular advantages the foreign law may offer or the ease of enforcement. In large transactions involving financings, for instance, New York law is often mutually agreed upon because it is a well-developed body of commercial law with extensive precedents. For similar reasons, English law is a frequent choice for maritime contracts. Or there may be customs of trading that indicate a commonly adopted pattern of governing law, such as the frequent use of the law of the vendor's country for sales of goods contracts.

For certain types of contracts there may be an international convention which provides a body of law that is designated to govern. The best example is contracts for sales of goods that are between parties whose home countries are signatories to CISG.[1] The convention is a well-formulated sales code (somewhat like the U.S. Uniform Commercial Code) that sets out explicit answers to such questions as when the contract is formed, and what the respective rights of the parties are. (*See* a discussion of CISG at section II.A.5.)

Another recent development in the international law of contracting is the promulgation of the UNIDROIT (International Institute for the Unification of Private Law) Principles of International Commercial Contracts,[2] a set of recommended rules (analogous to our domestic *Restatements*) relating to formation, interpretation, validity and other issues pertaining to international contracts. Although not a treaty, the Principles may emerge as an accepted formulation of customary international law and assist international lawyers of differing jurisdictions to reach a common ground for drafting all types of international commercial contracts.

Most jurisdictions recognize the power of the parties to choose the governing law of a commercial transaction contract. There are, however, provisions in some legal systems that mandate the applicable rule of law in certain situations and do not permit that rule to be altered by the parties' choice of law or forum. Such situations generally relate to public policy or to specific types of transactions, such as technology transfer agreements that may be required to use host country law, especially in developing countries. In general, the trend is toward allowing parties to choose governing law. International conventions such as the European Communities Convention on the Law Applicable to Contractual Obligations (1980) and the CISG are examples of such agreements that support party choice. This choice should be made and negotiated at the earliest possible time so that the contract may be drafted with the governing law in mind. All of the following issues must be considered in relation to the critical determination of what law is to govern the contract.

b.   Contract Formation; Letters of Intent and Term Sheets

Jurisdictions vary in their rules regarding formation; the CISG, for instance, does not require a writing, while at the other extreme some centralized economies may impose many formal requirements to reach contract formation. Letters of intent, heads of agreement, memoranda of understanding, term sheets and other comparable preliminary contract documents should be treated with special care. One needs to be very explicit about what the parties are legally binding themselves to do: Simply negotiate further? Reimburse expenses in the case of failure to go forward? Compensate the non-breaching party?

c.   Elements, Validity and Form of Contract

Over many decades of increasing international commercial activity, cross-border contracts have developed many common elements and look remarkably similar in form to domestic U.S. contracts and to each other. However, the precise elements required and the contract form that is valid varies depending on applicable law. An initial draft done in one jurisdiction should be reviewed by local counsel for validity, enforcement and proper form in any foreign jurisdiction involved and in relation to governing law. If the contract must be registered, a certain form and translation into local law may be required.

d.   Procedural Formalities

Notarization, registration with a government agency, or even preliminary approvals may be required for certain contracts in some jurisdictions. It is necessary to determine what these requirements are early in the drafting process and to allocate responsibility for meeting them. Notarization in particular is a more complex and highly formal process in civil law jurisdictions, which involves the services of a type of professional (*notaire*) not found in the United States. (*See* Chapter 26, *Selecting and Working with Local Foreign Counsel*.)

Notarization in the U.S. may also require legalization for the notarized document to be acceptable as authentic. (*See* Chapter 17, *Legalization of Documents for Use Abroad.*)

> e. Responsibility for Foreign Laws; Pending Government Approvals

Provisions should be included delegating responsibility for compliance with foreign law. Often, although not always, this responsibility is delegated to the foreign party, with the U.S. party retaining oversight or control over critical issues. This arrangement is based on an assumption that the foreign party and its legal counsel have the knowledge and access to accomplish compliance more efficiently. The contract may have to be contingent on receiving certain government approvals, and documentary proof of approvals and compliance with all foreign jurisdiction requirements should be provided to each party and will likely be a condition to any closing.

> f. Allocation of Risk

Risks may be allocated between the parties by agreement in the contract to a considerable extent. Governing law, including U.S. or foreign law, conventions such as CISG, or even customary rules such as trade terms for sales of goods (*see* discussion in section II.A.2.) play a role in risk allocation. It is essential, however, to verify with foreign legal counsel that risks allocated in the contract are enforceable under foreign law to the extent intended by the parties. In some cases, risks cannot be allocated: For instance, in many countries certain risks of termination of agents and distributors may not be allocated to them because of protective legislative regimes.

> g. Currency Issues

Many international commercial transactions involve payments in currency. The exchange control regime (both current and historical) of the foreign country should be understood to identify risks to be managed through contractual provisions, insurance or other mechanisms. Contracts should address key currency issues: What is the currency of denomination (i.e., what type of currency is used to specify the amount to be paid)? What is the currency of payment (this may differ from the currency of denomination, raising exchange risk considerations)? Who will bear the risk of foreign exchange variations? How will restrictions on availability and use of foreign exchange be handled? What currency reporting requirements must be met, and by which party? (*See* Chapter 3, *International Financing,* and Chapter 4, *International Payment Methods.*)

> h. *Force Majeure;* Supravening Government Action

In many parts of the world, the likelihood of dramatically changing circumstances makes the *force majeure* clause an essential element in international commercial contracts. Clauses dealing with the consequences of supravening government action may be handled separately or incorporated in a *force majeure* clause. It is necessary to distinguish among hardship, *force majeure*, special risk clauses, and civil law concepts such as changed circumstances and frustration. Counsel must be certain that the clause is drafted with precision and that terms are fully defined to ensure effectiveness and enforceability.

i.   Term and Termination

Like other contract elements, the term of a contract and termination rights must be drafted in light of applicable law. Termination in particular often deserves special attention if foreign law governs the contract, because of traditions of protective legislation in some countries for technology transfer contracts or foreign representative arrangements.

j.   Choice of Forum; Dispute Resolution; Stipulated Remedies

Choice of the type of dispute resolution to be used and the forum in which it will occur are as important as the choice of governing law. International commercial contracts in all parts of the world increasingly specify arbitration as the means to resolve disputes; other forms of alternative dispute resolution are used less frequently because of the differences among them in various countries. Whether litigation or arbitration is stipulated, the choice of forum must be carefully analyzed in relation to local procedural rules. (*See* Chapter 18, *International Litigation* and Chapter 19, *International Commercial Arbitration.*) It is very common for cross–border contracts to stipulate remedies on the occurrence of certain events, thus altering–and making more predictable–the results of dispute resolution in foreign jurisdictions.

k.   Governing Language

Contracts for cross–border transactions usually involve parties of differing native languages. An early agreement between the parties should be reached as to what language will be used for the contract. It is most efficient and least likely to lead to confusion if one language is used for drafting, negotiations, and the final version of the contract. For many reasons, however, it may be helpful or necessary to translate the contract into a second language, or multiple languages, either during negotiations or in the final version. Differences in language often result in differing interpretations of contract terms. It is essential, therefore, that the contract specify a governing language; when issues arise that require interpretation, the governing language will prevail. The decision as to governing language should take into account issues of enforceability, requirements for registration in foreign jurisdictions and any mandatory specifications for contract language that may exist for certain sector, government or other types of contracts in some countries.

l.   Enforceability

All international contracts should be reviewed for enforceability by foreign counsel if foreign law governs or if performance or enforcement occurs in a foreign jurisdiction.

2.   Cross-Border Movement Issues

When goods or people or capital cross national borders, the laws of both the country from which they exit and the country they enter will apply. In addition international agreements such as trade agreements (*e.g.*, NAFTA) or trade terms (such as INCOTERMS) may govern certain aspects of the border crossing. The international lawyer should always think in terms of three questions: What will it take to leave the country of origin? What will it take to enter the country of destination? What international agreements may complicate or facilitate the border crossing? These questions raise customs, export controls and sanctions, immigration, foreign exchange, currency movement disclosure and other legal issues discussed elsewhere in this book.

3.   International Financing Issues

Nearly all international commercial transactions raise issues related to international financing: assuring payment, using special financing instruments created for cross-border dealings, obtaining insurance or other government assistance to support the transaction. (*See* Chapter 3, *International Financing*, Chapter 4, *Political Risk Insurance*, and Chapter 5, *International Payment Methods*.)

4.   Other General Issues

Additional issues common to international commercial transactions are discussed in the other chapters of this book. Virtually every transaction will present potential tax issues. (*See* Chapter 10, *U.S. Taxation of International Transactions*.) Many will also involve important questions of intellectual property rights (*see* Chapter 7, *Intellectual Property Rights*) and compliance with environmental regulations (*see* Chapter 11, *Environmental Law*). If a transaction involves the host country government, issues of sovereign immunity and act of state (*see* Chapter 18, *International Litigation*) and payments to government officials (*see* Chapter 14, *The Foreign Corrupt Practices Act*) may also have to be considered.

II.   SPECIFIC TYPES OF INTERNATIONAL COMMERCIAL TRANSACTIONS

Legal issues associated with international commercial transactions arise primarily in the context of negotiating and documenting the transaction. This section discusses specific types of international commercial transactions.

A.   *Contracts for International Sales of Goods*

These agreements may be as simple as a one-time purchase order, or as complex as a long-term sales/supply agreement with provisions for quotas, price adjustments and a term of several years. What all of these agreements have in common is that they provide for cross–border sales of goods. The law applicable to contracts for sales of goods is most often designated explicitly by the parties in the agreement. If none is designated, a court or arbitral tribunal may apply the law of its home jurisdiction or may look to business customs and apply the law of the vendor's country. If both parties are from countries that are signatories of CISG, that Convention will apply if the contract is silent concerning governing law. Local courts may conclude that CISG governs even when U.S. state law is stipulated (assuming the other party is from a CISG contracting state), because the federal Constitution requires state courts to enforce CISG as a treaty and the supreme law of the land.[3] To analyze successfully the legal issues raised by these contracts, applicable law should first be determined.

General legal issues discussed in section I.C. that are applicable to these agreements include international contracting issues, cross–border movement issues such as customs, export controls and antiboycott compliance, and cross–border financing issues. Most important, contracts for the international sale/purchase of goods also raise numerous special issues.

1.   Battle of the Forms

In routine sales of goods, it is frequently the business custom to exchange forms as a means of forming the contract. The buyer often submits a pre–printed purchase order form to the seller, and the seller responds by sending back an order and shipping confirmation on the seller's own preprinted form. This practice leads to the so–called battle of the forms, which refers to ambiguities or even failure legally to form a contract resulting from inconsistencies of terms in the forms exchanged. In the United States, the Uniform Commercial Code ("UCC") includes provisions that recognize the intent of the parties and that soften the general common law rule that any change in the terms of an acceptance of an offer constitutes rejection.

Particular caution must be taken to avoid an international battle of the forms, since pre–drafted purchase orders and confirmation forms are likely to have been drafted under conflicting legal regimes. Domestic forms for sales of goods should only be used if they have been reviewed carefully and adapted to the international context, with applicable law specified. Further, the legal result of a battle of the forms may be different depending on whether the UCC or CISG applies, the latter being somewhat less flexible in recognizing the intent of the parties.

2.   Terms of Trade

Trade terms are short conventions used to define the rights and obligations of a buyer and seller with respect to the transfer of goods. More specifically, trade terms clarify the allocation of costs and risks associated with the delivery and payment of goods. For example, an *f.o.b.* term requires that a seller deliver the merchandise to a common carrier at the port of shipment. In contrast, a *c.i.f.* term requires that a seller arrange for and pay all charges for insurance and transportation. Consequently, in the event of an increase in freight charges, the increase falls upon the buyer in an *f.o.b.* contract, but upon the seller in a *c.i.f.* contract.

On a broad scale, trade terms fall into two major categories: terms relating to delivery contracts and terms relating to shipment contracts. Delivery contracts extend the seller's delivery obligation to the country of destination, while shipment contracts end the seller's delivery obligation in the seller's own country. Thus, a buyer and seller can allocate the various costs, risks, and obligations related to the delivery of goods by specifying the appropriate trade term in the sales contract.

The International Chamber of Commerce has developed an internationally recognized set of trade terms known as INCOTERMS (INternational COmmercial TERMS). INCOTERMS provides buyers and sellers a uniform standard for communicating and using trade terms in international commercial transactions. INCOTERMS apply to transactions when the parties expressly incorporate them into the contract, and may also be used by courts or arbitral tribunals as the standard of international customary law to settle trade terms disputes, even when INCOTERMS have not been expressly incorporated in the contract. It is highly desirable for trading parties to use a frame of reference such as INCOTERMS for the trade terms used in their contracts to avoid the ambiguity that may result from using such terms without an established referent.

3.   Documentary Character of International Sales of Goods

To meet the needs of international traders and sources of trade financing, numerous documents are required to effect an international contract for the sale of goods. These documents are usually required to be absolutely accurate and timely, and serve a variety of purposes. The transnational lawyer should be familiar with the form and effect of the commercial invoice, the packing list, the bill of lading, the certificate of insurance, the draft or bill of exchange, the letter of credit, and the certificate of inspection or quality, as well as customs documents such as certificates of origin, export or import licenses, health or safety certifications and export declarations. (*See* Chapter 3, *International Financing* for more discussion of documentation related to financing, and Chapter 12, *Customs Law*, on customs documents.) Although most transactions still rely on paper–based documentation, there is increasing use of electronic data interchange ("EDI"). (*See* Section II.G. below.)

4.   Warranties/Inspection/Product Liability

Warranties for the products being sold, as well as rights of inspection and specific standards for acceptance, should be set forth definitively in the sales contract. Both business customs and specific laws related to these issues differ throughout the world, so precision and inclusiveness in drafting these clauses are especially important. Consideration should also be given to the substantive law governing the contract, whether the UCC, CISG or foreign law, because each may produce differing results on these matters. In certain jurisdictions, statutory warranties are mandatory and may not be disclaimed or limited in the contract; they simply must be recognized as a cost of the transaction. If limitation or disclaimer of a statutory warranty is possible, it is necessary to determine the precise language required to make an express disclaimer or limitation effective.

Clauses should include names of products warranted (or any that are not), length of the warranty, the remedies that are available, how to make a claim, and, if applicable, merchantability and fitness for purpose representations. Likewise, the specific rights of buyer to inspect and the standards for acceptance of the goods, should be included. It is necessary to give special consideration to the risk of product liability claims under the law of the jurisdiction where the product will be sold and obtain advice from local legal counsel regarding whether there are ways to manage those liabilities. In most countries these liabilities will not be as likely, or the potential amount of damages as threatening, as they are in the U.S. for foreign sellers marketing products here.

5.   U.N. Convention on Contracts for the International Sale of Goods ("CISG")

CISG is the product of a concerted effort to develop a uniform law on the international sale of goods, and has been adopted by countries representing virtually every major type of legal system in the world. The United States became a party to CISG in 1986. CISG applies automatically to international sales of goods transactions in which the buyer and seller have their respective places of business in different countries, and CISG has entered into force in both countries. CISG does not govern consumer sales or sales of services. The contracting parties, however, may choose to exclude the application of CISG or to vary the effect of any of its provisions. Also, the application of CISG is subject to any reservations or declarations a country may have made when ratifying the Convention.

CISG serves the same gap–filling function as the UCC, albeit in the international sale of goods context, and many of CISG's provisions are comparable to those found in the UCC. Specific similarities may be found in the provisions on warranties, course of dealing and usage of trade, excuse, remedies, and adequate assurances of performance, among others. Major differences between CISG and the UCC, however, do exist in certain areas. Under contract formation, for example, CISG requires that an acceptance essentially "mirror" the terms of an offer, whereas the UCC allows for greater discrepancy in the terms. Other key differences include concepts quite foreign to the UCC, such as fundamental breach (Art. 49(1)), avoidance (Art. 49(1)), and *Nachfrist* (notice requirement if the seller does not deliver on time) (Art. 47(1)). Ambiguities in CISG provisions regarding the statute of limitations have been clarified by the adoption of a companion convention on limitations.[4]

Extensive commentaries have been published on CISG, including article-by-article comparisons with the UCC, which are particularly helpful for practitioners familiar with UCC provisions. *See* Sources of Assistance at III.A.2.f.

6. Industry–Specific Issues and Forms

Some legal issues arise in a specific industry context. Numerous trade groups have published forms of contracts that are industry–specific providing sample clauses and annotations that address these issues; for example, the construction contract of the International Federation of Consulting Engineers (Revised Fédération Internationale des Ingénieurs–Conseils ("FIDIC") Conditions for Works of Civil Engineering Construction and for Electrical and Mechanical Works).

B. *Sales Agency or Distribution Agreements*

One of the most common ways to market a product in a foreign jurisdiction is by means of a foreign sales agent or distributor located in the country where the goods will be sold. In general, the sales agent is a person or company that finds buyers and assists with marketing, typically works on a commission basis, and does not take title to or possession of the products. A distributor is an independent person or company that buys and resells for its own account, obtains a profit by marking up the price on the product for resale, and takes on the risks of buying and holding inventory in the foreign market. Any such arrangements should be documented by a written agreement that clearly states the status of the foreign representative and sets out the parties' mutual obligations.

Foreign law in the jurisdiction where the agent or distributor (together sometimes referred to as *"representative"*) is operating plays a significant role, and such arrangements should not be undertaken without the advice of local legal counsel. For instance, under the local laws of some countries there exist different types of foreign representatives with varying legal characteristics. In certain jurisdictions the *del credere* agent acts as a surety, guaranteeing payments by the customer to the principal, often for additional compensation. In Germany, a veritable array of options for representation exists, including several types of agents as well as other forms of intermediaries.

Some countries have highly developed regimes of law designed to provide protection for local parties serving as sales representatives for foreign companies. It is essential to know these local laws and the potential liabilities they create before embarking on a binding relationship. In addition to the particular issues discussed below, the general issues of international contracting, cross–border movement and financing may apply to these agreements.

1. Local Restrictions

Some jurisdictions have restrictions as to who may serve as the representative of a foreign company selling goods in the local marketplace. In the

Middle East, for instance, it is not unusual for local law to mandate that the representative be a "local" person or company. This may require that an individual representative be a citizen of the jurisdiction or that a company serving as a representative must be organized under the laws of, or owned by citizens of, the foreign country. In some countries, such restrictions may only apply to representatives marketing to government entities. Before a representative is selected, local restrictions should be reviewed thoroughly.

In addition, there may be requirements for registration, reporting or other types of disclosure when agreements are entered into by foreign countries with local representatives. These requirements may add further burdens, such as translation, notarization and legalization of the agreements before they can be registered.

2.   Distribution Agreements as Sale of Goods Contracts

Distribution agreements call for the sale of goods by the manufacturer to the foreign distributor, with all of the related issues that arise in any contract for the international sale of goods. This factor is frequently overlooked, and key elements of the sale of goods aspect of the agreement are omitted. In addition to general contracting issues, the distribution agreement should deal with terms of trade, sales documentation, warranties, inspection, cross–border movement of goods, financing, sales quotas, price adjustments and any other sale–of–goods contract terms applicable to the arrangement.

3.   Exclusivity

It is not unusual for a representative to be given some type of exclusivity. The agreement should be precise in specifying the kind of exclusivity granted (for instance, whether it simply grants a territory in which no other representatives will be named, also limits the manufacturer's right to sell, or limits the representative from selling competing products) because local customs and regulations often differ in their understanding of the term "exclusive."

Further, the local jurisdiction's competition laws should be reviewed to see whether exclusive arrangements are permitted with representatives. (*See* Chapter 8, *International Antitrust*.) Although U.S. law generally permits exclusive representation, the European Union ("EU"), for instance, has detailed competition regulations affecting both distribution agreements and sales agency agreements that may restrict the exclusivity that the parties want. Even if exemptions from the EU regulations are available, a careful review of representative agreements in relation to the regulations is essential.

4.   Termination

Protective legislation in many countries provides statutory compensation to representatives in the event of termination. In the European Union, a directive requires each member state to provide certain minimum standards for the benefit of representatives. The payment amounts may be considerable and must be taken into consideration as a cost of entering into such an arrangement. It is necessary to determine what provisions of local law may affect termination, and to draft the term and termination provisions of the representative agreement carefully with the specific legal requirements in mind.

C.   Countertrade Agreements

Normally a sale of goods is structured as an exchange of goods for money. However, an increasingly common arrangement involves barter–or some variation–perhaps involving complex parallel agreements to buy products, to take goods as compensation for sales of technology or to balance quotas of reciprocal sales of goods contracts. Although many names are used for these arrangements–offset, counterpurchase, and others–the term *"countertrade"* is used most frequently to refer to them collectively.

The countertrade contract raises general issues of international contracting, cross–border movement of goods, and perhaps international financing if parallel agreements are used. In addition, countertrade presents special issues: definition of the trade obligation, pricing, time periods and reciprocal calculation of compensation, all of which must be very specific. These issues are typically governed by national laws; there are no international agreements on countertrade. More than one contract is often advisable to establish parallel arrangements for buyer and seller to purchase goods reciprocally. (*See* Chapter 5, *International Payment Methods.*)

D.   Contracts of Carriage and Air/Marine Insurance

In connection with a sale of goods, distribution agreement or countertrade contract, there will be associated contracts that provide for transportation and insurance of the goods. Whether it is the seller or buyer who is required to provide transportation and insurance is controlled by the agreement between the parties and, in particular, the trade terms as discussed above.

Often the buyer or seller will work with a freight forwarder who arranges the necessary transportation both domestically (to the port of disembarkation) and internationally. Often, too, goods are transported with a single contract of carriage by use of a *"through bill of lading"* or *"combined transport document."* Intermodal transportation – the combined use of truck, ship and perhaps air – has become popular and is simplified by containerization in which goods are packed in one container that moves from one mode of transportation to another. Insurance is critical to whichever party bears the risk of loss during transportation and deserves special attention in relation to the type of goods and the perils or liabilities that they may face en route.

Transportation contracts may be governed by complex statutory or treaty regimes such as the U.S. Carriage of Goods by Sea Act ("COGSA," 46

USC §§ 1300–1315) or by international conventions such as the Convention for the Unification of Certain Rules Relating to International Transportation by Air (the "Warsaw Convention," 49 Stat. 3000; T.S. No. 876, signed at Warsaw October 12, 1929).

Contracts of carriage and insurance are highly specialized. The services of an experienced and reputable freight forwarder are critical in making the arrangements, and the advice of legal counsel with expertise in this area should be sought if particular legal issues arise.

E.   *Service Contracts*

International trade now often involves the contracting for sales of services. Management consulting, advertising and promotion, architectural design, environmental and civil engineering, business advisory, and technological consulting, are just a few of the types of services that companies may contract to provide cross–border. General legal issues of contracting as discussed in section I.C. are important for service contracts, as are issues of immigration if technicians or managers will cross borders to perform services (*see* Chapter 22, *Immigration and Nationality*) and employment law (*see* Chapter 23, *International Labor and Employment Law*). Issues of taxation (*see* Chapter 10, *U.S. Taxation of International Transactions*) may also affect how service agreements are structured and how compensation is earned.

The laws of the foreign jurisdiction will control many aspects of the transaction. Some services by foreigners (*e.g.*, engineering) may require special licensing or registration under local law, or may be prohibited unless performed in partnership with a local licensed professional. In addition, it is necessary to consider whether the pattern of activity in the foreign country created by a service agreement constitutes a presence that requires registration, subjects the service provider to local taxation or makes it advisable to set up a local business entity to provide limited liability in the host country.

Increasingly, international trade agreements are playing a role in establishing the legal framework for cross–border services. NAFTA, for instance, includes a chapter on Cross–Border Trade in Services (Chapter 12) that sets out fundamental principles on rights of establishment, standards of treatment and other matters such as licensing and certification, and an entire chapter on financial services (Chapter 14). GATT, although less comprehensive in its impact than NAFTA, also incorporates an agreement on services.

In the service sector, differences in culture and business customs as well as language make it critical that arrangements take into account the traditions of the particular service sector and that all contract provisions are set out precisely.

F.   *Technology Licensing and Technology Transfer Agreements*

The international technology licensing agreement grants to another person the right to use all or some portion of an intellectual property right–a patent, trademark, trade name, business know–how or other. Every license necessarily involves the transfer of technology to another, but there are also so–called technology transfer agreements that over time or immediately fully transfer both the substance of the technology and the intellectual property rights for agreed compensation. Further, parties may enter into international research and development agreements that provide for on–going shared activity that produces new technology which will be owned and used by the parties.

All of these agreements involve general international contracting issues (section I.C. above) and in particular intellectual property issues (*see* Chapter 7, *Intellectual Property Rights*). Thus, for instance, the licensor or grantor must have its intellectual property rights protected in the foreign jurisdiction in order to be able to transfer them–license their use–to another party in that jurisdiction. Applicable law may be difficult to determine. Many jurisdictions allow freedom of the parties to contract for licensing or technology transfer, just as for other agreements. However, some countries–especially those that are developing economically–have special restrictions on these contracts. There may be a requirement that local (host or receiving jurisdiction) law govern the contract, that the agreements be pre–approved by the government, or that they be registered with a local agency. Some jurisdictions have enacted special technology transfer legislation that incorporates such provisions, or even requires that licensed technology rights become the full property of the local licensee after a specified period. Determining the local law requirements for licensing or technology transfer should be the first step taken by the international lawyer.

Computer hardware, software and related technologies are of special importance to many countries that need to obtain this technology. Some jurisdictions are adopting specialized legal regimes for the sector–*e.g.*, the "informatics" statute in Brazil[5]–that must be reviewed if the contract includes licensing or transfer of computer–related technology. Local rules concerning the ability to reverse–engineer, the enforceability of "shrink–wrap" licenses, encryption, and other aspects important to licensors do not necessarily mirror their U.S. counterparts.

In addition to general contracting issues, cross–border movement (of information, people, equipment) and financing issues as discussed above at section I.C., other particular issues for licensing and technology transfer are:

> 1. Granting Language. Viewed as the most important clause in the license, the granting provision must clearly set out what is permitted, and provide the licensor with adequate control over the grantee's scope of activity.

2. Grant–Back. Often a licensor wants to ensure that advances to the technology that result from the licensee's activity will revert to the licensor. Such clauses may not be enforceable in some jurisdictions or even may be expressly prohibited.

3. Warranties. Customarily there are numerous warranties required from the licensor (*e.g.*, proper and valid title to the rights), but there may also be implied warranties in certain countries under local law and these should be carefully reviewed.

4. Payment. Often payment for a license is made as a royalty and is limited to productivity. Amounts may be controlled by local law or even prohibited when a patent is pending.

G.   *Electronic Data Interchange Agreements*

Trading partners enter into agreements to exchange data electronically to exchange trade documentation or in any other situation in which the regular, fast and cost–efficient exchange of information is essential to a business relationship. Technologically–rich companies that have international licensing, technology transfer, research and development or management consulting agreements increasingly use EDI arrangements. Existing legal regimes do not yet address legal issues of EDI; most rules on EDI are industry guidelines or come from groups such as the International Chamber of Commerce, which has published rules for interchange of trade data by teletransmission, (Uniform Rules of Conduct for Interchange of Trade Data by Teletransmission (UNCID), ICC Publication No. 452, 1987). EDI agreements must be drafted with unusual care and with reference to such industry guidelines or uniform rules because there is virtually no law to rely on in case of controversy or dispute. Other issues to address in such agreements include standards for creation and transmission of data, arrangements with outside providers (of the EDI system), if applicable, security measures and responsibilities in the event of system failures.

H.   *Franchising Agreements*

Franchising is an elaborated method of licensing and distribution. It has become one of the most widely–used methods for international expansion of restaurants, hospitality businesses, and retail outlets. The franchisor licenses the right to sell products and/or services, using the franchisor's intellectual property–typically trade names, trademarks, business know–how or even an entire business system–in return for an initial payment plus on–going royalties based on sales. The franchise agreement forms the essential nexus of the arrangement and often provides for standards of quality control and reporting to which the franchisee must adhere, as well as providing inspection rights for the franchisor. Agreements may be made with individual foreign franchisees or may take a variety of forms such as master franchising or area development agreements that give expansion or sublicensing rights to a key foreign collaborator.

In the U.S., the legal regime governing franchising is well-developed, but this is not the case throughout much of the rest of the world. In determining applicable law in the host country of the franchisee, it is necessary to review not only any existing "franchising law," but also to consider whether provisions of licensing, distribution, technology transfer, competition or even joint venture laws, may be applicable. If franchising is not recognized as a distinct method of doing business and there are no franchising laws *per se*, considerable ambiguity may exist regarding the franchise's legal status, and this should be discussed with foreign legal counsel. Under whatever regime applies there may be local registration requirements and disclosure regulations. Even if no local disclosure requirements exist, U.S. franchisors often supply information substantially similar to that required in the United States, since there is the possibility that allegations of inadequate disclosure could be pursued under U.S. law in U.S. courts.

The terms of the franchise agreement include many that are found in licensing and distribution agreements. For example, just as a distribution agreement provides for sale of goods and should incorporate the applicable contract terms for a sale of goods contract, likewise most franchises include an agreement that the franchisee will buy goods (perhaps food ingredients or retail store inventory) from the franchisor. Sale of goods contract terms should therefore be included. Other special issues are training and operational support by the franchisor, royalties, fees, reimbursements, and other forms of compensation, and their tax implications, and standards for quality and quantity of performance.

Although many of these issues are similar to those encountered in a domestic franchising arrangement, each incorporates special considerations that arise from the cross-border context of the franchise and the foreign jurisdiction involved. For this reason, domestic franchise agreements must be carefully adapted for the international transaction.

Franchisors may also resort to providing capital to help initiate franchising expansion, resulting in complex arrangements such as hybrid franchising/joint venture agreements or franchise/direct foreign investment strategies that raise additional legal issues, as described below regarding joint ventures and outbound direct investment.

I.   *Equity and Contractual Joint Ventures*

The joint venture is a type of partnership arrangement between two or more existing and on-going business entities from different countries, which come together to undertake a business activity of a limited term or to start a new business enterprise for an extended life. The venturers share in profits, losses, liabilities and management of the undertaking. The joint venture agreement forms the foundation of the arrangement, but it is often accompanied by numerous corollary documents. The joint venture may be of the *"contractual"* type, in which the agreement alone sets out all details of the venture, and no new business entity is formed. Or it may be an *"equity"*-type joint venture in which the joint venture agreement provides that a new business entity will be formed in the host jurisdiction—often a corporation or a similar limited liability entity, in which venturers own set percentages of shares to reflect their relative venture interests—and the legal regime of the new business entity becomes the controlling framework for the venturers' relationship. Contractual joint ventures may be very short-term by comparison and entered into for discrete projects or for other very specialized purposes. The international sales consortium agreement or *"teaming"* arrangement, in which companies bid together on a single project or government procurement may be structured, for instance, as a short-term contractual joint venture arrangement. The term *"strategic alliance"* is often used to refer to an arrangement that is structured as a contractual or equity joint venture, and that usually involves two or more businesses of significant size that are undertaking together a new business venture that is limited in scope.

Local law of the host jurisdiction is applicable to the new business operation. Some countries will have a special law just for joint ventures that prescribes certain legal requirements for mixed foreign-local joint ventures. Alternatively, such requirements may be part of the jurisdiction's foreign investment law. In some countries, the joint venture (either equity or contractual or both) will not be recognized and the applicable law may be difficult to locate, so local legal advice becomes critical.

Particular attention should be given to the tax status of a contractual joint venture because it may vary widely from one jurisdiction to another; for instance, under U.S. law the contractual joint venture will generally be treated as a partnership for tax purposes. For larger strategic alliances of significant market players, competition laws of the applicable jurisdictions may impose special requirements for disclosure, reporting or approvals. The contractual joint venture must also contend with properly using the local venturer as the entity of record in the host jurisdiction, since no new joint business entity exists.

The general issues of international contracting as well as cross-border movement issues, financing and the investment establishment and maintenance issues discussed in section I.C. above apply to the joint venture agreement. Of special importance are legal issues related to the letter of intent (or the preliminary joint venture agreement, as it is often called) and to issues of management control, minority shareholder rights, dispute resolution mechanisms, and applicable law. Numerous ancillary agreements between the venturers also frequently are involved for matters such as licensing, supply arrangements, management consulting, or distribution services.

J.   Broker Agreements

Brokers are used extensively in international commercial transactions throughout the world. They may serve a wide variety of functions, but generally they act as independent parties who are not empowered to bind the principals but who, for agreed compensation, bring together the transaction parties. Such arrangements are recognized under the national law of most jurisdictions, but care should be given to drafting the broker agreement so that it will not be deemed an agency relationship, thereby triggering local agency laws and protective legislation.

K.   Turnkey and BOT Agreements

Projects in foreign countries that require the building of a facility often go forward under turnkey project agreements, which set out the responsibilities of the contractor or vendor to finish the facility and "turn the key" over to the purchaser for immediate use. Numerous variations on the turnkey arrangement also are used. For instance, the "BOT" (build–operate–transfer) agreement provides that the builder operates the facility for a specified time period to obtain a guaranteed return and then transfers ownership to the government. The BOT also has produced additional variants, such as the "BOO" (build–operate–own) and others. These agreements raise general issues of contracting and often are similar to construction agreements with provisions for sub-contracting. They also may incorporate innovative international financing arrangements. Parties usually may specify applicable law in the contract, but the ability to do so may be restricted by the nature of the project (for instance, public works), the origin of the financing, or the fact that the contract is with a government entity. FIDIC and UNCITRAL have prepared standard contracts, model clauses and general resources addressing legal issues specific to construction and turnkey projects. (*See* Chapter 15, *Government Procurement*, for additional issues that arise if the turnkey project agreement is with a government and is granted pursuant to a bidding process.) Background information on these types of project agreements is available from the Overseas Private Investment Corporation.

L.   Energy/Mining; Concessions/Development Agreements for the Exploitation of Natural Resources

Another extensive category of international commercial transactions involves those related to foreign participation in the exploitation of natural resources. Mining and energy are usually the sectors that come to mind, but transactions may also relate to forestry, fishing, seabed exploitation and even corporate agricultural ventures. Concessions and agreements for development in these areas are highly specialized, and the local law of the foreign jurisdiction where the resources are located is particularly critical and generally mandatory. Natural resources usually are specially protected under either distinct legal regimes or the constitution of the host country. Further, many of the best opportunities in this sector are in developing countries where there often exist sensitivities and proprietary attitudes about natural resources as well as tough regulation of foreign investment.

A clear understanding of the relevant property rights under local law for the specific resource involved (as well as generally) is the starting point for analyzing these transactions, but it must also include such matters as what type of dispute resolution and applicable law will be allowed and how the investor can be protected in case of intervening government action that either changes the business aspects of the operation or results in expropriation or nationalization of the investor's operations. Bilateral treaties with the host country may provide some reassurance in these latter cases, and these should be closely reviewed. Political risk insurance offered by entities such as the Overseas Private Investment Corporation ("OPIC"), the Multilateral Investment Guaranty Agency ("MIGA") or private sector insurers may also be available to provide protection for investments. (*See* Chapter 4, *Political Risk Insurance*.) Particularly troublesome in many areas of the world are the potential effects of a change in government leadership on the attitudes and resulting regulation of foreign investment in natural resource exploitation.

M. *Outbound Direct Investment*

The establishment and management of a business in a foreign jurisdiction (usually in the form of foreign direct investment) presents a cluster of legal issues that are shared whether the investment is made by establishment of a joint venture, by starting a foreign wholly-owned subsidiary, or by other means. As distinct from other international commercial transactions, the foreign direct investment involves the cross-border transfer of capital and usually the establishment of an ongoing business operation in the foreign country. Other cross-border business ventures that do not fully meet the definition of foreign direct investment may also raise these legal issues: for instance, a hybrid franchise/joint venture; a representative office; turnkey project operations; or distribution arrangements, including foreign investor ownership or other participation.

1. **Foreign Investment Regulation**

Foreign investment rules are determined by local law. There are limited restrictions on investment barriers under the recent WTO Agreement on Trade Related Investment Measures ("TRIMS"), but no broad multilateral agreement on investment exists (although the negotiation of such an agreement is under discussion at the OECD).[6] Virtually all jurisdictions have some kind of regime that regulates foreign investment. Often such a regime surprises U.S. businesspersons and lawyers, because foreign investment regulation in the U.S. has traditionally been so limited relative to the regimes in foreign countries.

In the U.S., nevertheless, we do limit foreign investment in certain sectors, require reporting by foreign investors, in some states restrict foreign ownership of land, and otherwise control inbound investment by foreigners. (*See* Chapter 21, *Foreign Investment in the United States.*)

Outside the U.S., much more comprehensive–and often onerous–foreign investment regulations may be encountered, particularly in jurisdictions that are less economically developed. Such countries often have complementary regimes that provide for control of foreign investment but also make available attractive incentives such as tax holidays to attract such investment. More highly industrialized nations are usually the opposite, having few restrictions on foreign investment but also offering few incentives.

Foreign investment laws frequently determine: whether and to what extent certain sectors are open to foreign investment (utilities, communications, transportation and defense sectors often are not); whether the foreigner must have a local partner, and in what percent interest; whether the investment must be pre–approved, registered, or simply notice provided; and whether incentives are available. These are threshold issues that must be considered by the international lawyer before all others to ensure that the project is legally feasible. Sources in this chapter's bibliography provide secondary guidance on this issue, but foreign counsel should also be consulted for recent developments or to interpret the regulatory environment.

2.   Choice of Business Entity

Foreign direct investments that involve the establishment or continuation of an on–going business require a careful examination of the alternatives for the business entity under which it will operate. Most countries have legal entities that are relatively comparable to such U.S. entities as the corporation, limited liability company, partnership, sole proprietorship and branch. In addition, most jurisdictions provide for the *"representative office,"* a very limited type of establishment for purposes of doing market research or publicizing a product line, but not for sales or other profit–making activities.

In general, limited liability entities–in whatever specific form–are preferable to shield the investor from liability in the local jurisdiction. Often a U.S. special–purpose subsidiary is established to own the foreign limited liability company, in an effort further to shield the non–U.S. activities from home jurisdiction assets. The final choice of a foreign business entity should be made in consultation with foreign counsel and tax counsel based on a close examination of alternative entities and their attributes and requirements (which may differ significantly from the United States), local marketplace acceptance, business customs and taxation issues. Sources are available that provide surveys of corporate or other business entities in various jurisdictions. (*See* Sources of Assistance at III.A.2.c.)

3. Contracting for Control

Any foreign investment involving a local partner raises the issue of control: Who is to make day-to-day operational decisions, and how are key business decisions such as acquisitions, large borrowings, declaration of bankruptcy, to be made? Often the venturer or partner who puts in the most capital is least qualified to make business decisions–especially about day-to-day operations in the foreign country. Therefore, special control arrangements that do not directly reflect percentages of ownership interest or capitalization may be desirable. Key issues are: whether the host country foreign law allows such special control arrangements; how they should be documented and how enforceable they are; and, under the foreign investment law, whether such arrangement is legally permitted. In jurisdictions requiring a set percentage of local (host country) ownership, the usual assumption is that effective control will directly reflect the local ownership interest. In such countries, special control arrangements that differ from ownership interests may be difficult to accomplish.

4. Local Regulations and Reporting Requirements

All foreign jurisdictions have local regulations and reporting requirements for business entities. These may also include special accounting procedures and periodic public or confidential statistical filings. Once a foreign investor has entered the host country, all of these local requirements apply to the new or acquired business. Note that these reporting and regulatory demands are in addition to those created by the host country's investment law. Local accountants and foreign counsel are the best source of information on these regulations and the practicalities of compliance.

5. Risks of Nationalization or Expropriation

Foreign investors must face issues related to the threat that a host country may expropriate or nationalize the investment. The law of the host country should be reviewed, as well as government agreements such as Bilateral Investment Treaties, Friendship, Commerce and Navigation Treaties, and trade agreements such as NAFTA, if applicable. There may be laws or contractual provisions that reduce the threat of nationalization or expropriation, or provide for appropriate compensation. Another alternative is to consider political risk insurance, which may cover nationalization of investments. (*See* Chapter 4, *Political Risk Insurance*.)

6. Antitrust

U.S. or foreign competition law may be applicable to joint ventures, mergers and acquisitions, licensing agreements, distribution arrangements or franchising. (*See* Chapter 8, *International Antitrust*.)

7. Other

In certain foreign jurisdictions, additional issues such as availability of investment incentives, limitations on repatriation of capital or profits through exchange controls, and government intervention in a foreign investor's dealings may also be present. International lawyers should consult local legal counsel and one or more of the country-specific resources available regarding these issues.

N. *Mergers and Acquisitions*

Often a foreign investment occurs by means of a merger with or acquisition of a company in the target foreign jurisdiction. Foreign investment regulations of the host country may restrict mergers or acquisitions in certain sectors, or may dictate the degree of ownership interest that may be acquired, effectively blocking the proposed transaction. In certain legal regimes there may be more resistance to foreigners' acquiring a business owned by locals than there is to a new start-up enterprise. Certain companies (often those that have been privatized) may have barriers to foreign ownership written into their corporate charter, which should be reviewed at the earliest possible time. Local attitudes toward acquisition by foreigners directly affect the regulatory regime and must be considered.

Due diligence should be performed, just as for domestic acquisitions, but this may be difficult if the local business environment is unfamiliar with the exhaustive examinations to which U.S. acquirors are accustomed. Compromises may need to be made and the advice of local legal counsel sought to determine what elements of due diligence are critical. Public sources of financial information about companies are often unavailable, and getting public or even private recommendations may be difficult. In such situation, the network of professionals–accountants, bankers, chamber officials and lawyers–known to local legal counsel will be the best resource.

Researching title to property, debt obligations, free and clear company ownership, tax status and other matters require detailed knowledge of the local laws. Further, the extraterritorial reach of U.S. securities laws, particularly the anti-fraud provisions, as well as U.S. antitrust laws, may result in their covering the transaction. Competition or securities regulations under the law of the foreign jurisdiction also must be considered. Because these rules will not necessarily parallel U.S. rules, compliance may be quite complex. (*See* Chapter 8, *International Antitrust* and Chapter 10, *Securities Laws.*)

Hostile takeovers of foreign companies provide special challenges if preapprovals, registrations or notices are required of the foreign investor during a period in which the intentions are preferably kept confidential. Some domestic acquisitions raise these legal issues because there are foreign subsidiary companies in the target company family.

Statutory mergers may face particular hurdles because of differences in corporate laws of the target jurisdiction and a lack of parallel management and ownership framework to make merger feasible. Finally, the tax consequences of these mechanisms for foreign investment on both sides of the border have to be analyzed to determine the best structure for the transaction. (*See* Chapter 10, *U.S. Taxation of International Transactions.*)

O.   Real Property Contracts

The acquisition or leasing of real property may occur independently or may be an integral part of an outbound foreign investment, joint venture or other commercial transaction. Title to real property and the forms of contracts for sale or leasing are uniquely the product of the local law of the jurisdiction where the property is located. With the help of local legal counsel, numerous special issues must be reviewed: Are foreigners allowed to own property? Are there special restrictions that limit foreign ownership rights? What verification of clear and free title is available? How does real property financing work (if applicable and available)? What zoning, environmental or other regulations apply?

Contracts should be reviewed by foreign counsel for proper form and opinions or certified documentation obtained regarding enforceability, clear title and proper transfer. In civil law countries, the *notaire* and not a lawyer may be the principal local service provider. Additional assistance will be necessary if a trust arrangement is required under local law that grants beneficial ownership to the foreign investor.

P.   Privatizations

In recent years, many developing countries have offered government-owned entities and service enterprises for sale to foreign investors as well as local private parties. Contracts for privatization acquisition often include many of the legal issues discussed above under mergers and acquisitions of private companies. The contracts are with governments, however, and often are the result of complex government-run bidding processes. Documentation is very detailed and issues of sovereign immunity arise in the contracting process. There may also be restrictions on governing law, method of dispute resolution, means of payment or other matters under the national law of the host jurisdiction either because the transaction is a privatization or because the sectors involved (frequently utilities, transportation, banking and the like) are specially protected.

Q.   Cross-Border Portfolio Investments

The term *"portfolio investment,"* viewed in the context of international commercial transactions, refers to cross-border purchases of instruments such as securities, bonds, futures, or certificates of deposit. Such investments often are called *"indirect"* investments to distinguish them from direct foreign investments such as building a manufacturing plant or establishing a business. Unique cross-border or foreign instruments, such as American Depositary Receipts ("ADRs") which represent foreign securities on deposit in a foreign country, also are traded on U.S. stock exchanges. Although purchases and sales occur in the U.S., ADRs may be viewed as cross-border portfolio (or indirect) investments. Another example of an instrument that is unfamiliar to many investors is the foreign-issued corporate bearer share, for which title passes to whoever physically holds the share certificate.

If instruments purchased are issued abroad and traded on foreign exchanges, investors will not have the degree of protection offered by U.S. securities laws. Further, the rights of a holder of such instrument–a matter controlled under foreign law–may be very different from the rights that the investor is familiar with in the U.S. Other legal issues that may arise include those related to provisions of the purchase contract, the currency of payment (for purchase or dividends), whether ownership of the particular instrument is allowed to a foreigner under applicable law, liquidity restrictions and tax consequences.

III. SOURCES OF ASSISTANCE

A. Books

1. General

INTERNATIONAL BUSINESS PLANNING: LAW AND TAXATION (UNITED STATES) (6 vols., William P. Streng and Jeswald W. Salacuse eds. 1988; current to 1995). (Of special interest are Volumes 2 and 3 on export transactions and technology transfer and Volume 4 on foreign investments; useful appendices of forms, statutes and regulations; regularly updated.)

INTERNATIONAL CONTRACT MANUAL (5 vols., Albert H. Kritzer ed. 1994). (Quintessential guide especially for export contracts, but checklists good for all types of international contracts. Extensive CISG analysis and country handbooks on exporting to various areas.)

GREGORY LETTERMAN, LETTERMAN'S LAW OF PRIVATE INTERNATIONAL BUSINESS (3 vols., 1990, Supp. 1991). (The "hornbook" of private international transactions; broad-ranging content and well-organized with detailed paragraph numbering system.)

NEGOTIATING AND STRUCTURING INTERNATIONAL COMMERCIAL TRANSACTIONS: LEGAL ANALYSIS WITH SAMPLE AGREEMENTS (Shelly P. Battram and David N. Goldsweig eds. 1991). (Published by the ABA Section of International Law and Practice; covers most basics with a focus on practicalities and drafting tips.)

PAUL H. VISHNY, GUIDE TO INTERNATIONAL COMMERCE LAW (2 vols., 1981, updated through 1993). (Two volumes of greater detail on transactions discussed in this chapter; especially strong on export–import, technology transfer and foreign representatives.)

2.   Particular Topics

a.   Contracting

UNIDROIT PRINCIPLES OF INTERNATIONAL COMMERCIAL CONTRACTS (American Society of International Law ed. 1994). (May be ordered directly (ISBN 88-86449-003, US$75) from UNIDROIT, 28 Via Panisperna, I-00184 Rome, Italy.)

b.   Agency and Distribution

THOMAS F. CLASEN, INTERNATIONAL AGENCY AND DISTRIBUTION AGREEMENTS (3 vols., 1991, updated through 1994). (Individual country chapters written by local counsel cover the basics of agency and distribution law.)

c.   Establishment; Business Entities

INTERNATIONAL CORPORATE PROCEDURES (3 vols., Leonard S. Sealy ed. 1992, updated through 1994). (For each country, well-organized review of limited liability companies, partnerships, branches, joint ventures, with basic requirements plus local taxation and accounting summary.)

DIGEST OF COMMERCIAL LAWS OF THE WORLD (8 vols., updated in part to 1995). (Country-by-country digest of basic laws for many jurisdictions of the world; each includes a section on partnership and business associations including types of entities and basic requirements. Includes many remote jurisdictions not found in other compilations.)

d.   Joint Ventures

JAMES A. DOBKIN, et al., JOINT VENTURES WITH INTERNATIONAL PARTNERS (3 vols., 1989, updated through 1994). (Country-by-country summaries of applicable local law; volume on "Structure and Negotiation with Forms" has comprehensive survey of legal issues and drafting tips; numerous forms.)

DAVID N. GOLDSWEIG & ROGER H. CUMMINGS, INTERNATIONAL JOINT VENTURES: A PRACTICAL APPROACH TO WORKING WITH FOREIGN INVESTORS IN THE U.S. AND ABROAD (1990). (Concise analysis of key issues in context of hypothetical; special emphasis on joint venturing in developing countries.)

e.   Licensing and Technology Transfer

L. ECKSTROM & S. SZCZEPANSKI, ECKSTROM'S LICENSING IN FOREIGN AND DOMESTIC OPERATIONS (4 vols., 1972, updated through 1994). (Comprehensive survey of licensing and technology transfer issues plus country-by-country reviews. For exhaustive selection of forms, see associated publication: ROBERT

GOLDSCHEIDER, ECKSTROM'S LICENSING IN FOREIGN AND DOMESTIC OPERATIONS: THE FORMS AND SUBSTANCE OF LICENSING (2 vols. 1978; looseleaf, periodically supplemented).)

f. Trade in Goods

GUIDE TO THE INTERNATIONAL SALE OF GOODS CONVENTION (2 vols., updated to 1995). (Basic materials, commentaries, comparison table of CISG and UCC provisions; includes U.N. Convention on the Limitation Period in the International Sale of Goods.)

INTERNATIONAL TRADE REPORTER–EXPORT SHIPPING MANUAL (3 vols., updated to 1995). (Covers export regulation and documents required for most countries of the world; updated regularly so very current information.)

g. Turnkey Projects and Construction Sector

UNCITRAL LEGAL GUIDE TO DRAWING UP INTERNATIONAL CONTRACTS FOR CONSTRUCTION OF INDUSTRIAL WORKS (New York: United Nations Document A/CN/9/SER.B/2 (1988).) (Comprehensive guide with forms and model clauses. May be ordered from United Nations by referencing U.N. Publication Sales No. E.87.V.10 (ISBN 92–1133300–8 04200 P).)

h. Countertrade

Chapter 25, *Countertrade*, in INTERNATIONAL CONTRACT MANUAL, cited above at I.A. (This chapter serves as a handbook on countertrade, including its history, rationale and various structures with numerous examples of countertrade deals and a discussion of documentation.)

B. Periodicals

1. General

Corporate Counsel's International Adviser. Monthly. Chesterland, Ohio: Business Laws, Inc. (Broadly ranging topics but strong in trade, commercial transactions and foreign business laws.)

2. Trade; Export–Import

International Trade Reporter. Weekly. Washington, D.C.: The Bureau of National Affairs, Inc. (Valuable updates on trade policy, U.S. and foreign regulation and enforcement; articles and document reprints on topics related to international commerce.)

C.   On-Line Services

1.   LEXIS–NEXIS

Examples of periodical materials with particular transactional emphasis are:

- *The International Lawyer* from Winter 1981
- *International Trade Reporter* from July 1984
- *BNA International Trade Daily*

2.   WESTLAW

Examples of periodical materials are:

- D&B–International Dun's Market Identifiers (company information)
- *International Trade Reporter* from 1986
- *BNA International Trade Daily* from September 1987

ENDNOTES

1   U.N. Doc. A/CONF. 97/19 (1981), Annex I, English version, *reprinted in* 52 Fed. Reg. 6264 (1987) *and in* 19 I.L.M. 668 (1980).

2   The American Society of International Law (ed.), May 1994.

3   *See* Winship, *Changing Contract Practices in the Light of the United Nations Sales Convention: A Guide for Practitioners,* 29 Int'l Law., 525, 538 (1995).

4   1974 U.N. Convention on the Limitation Period in the International Sale of Goods, *reprinted in* 13 I.L.M. 952 (1974); 1980 Protocol, *reprinted in* 19 I.L.M. 696 (1980).

5   The Informatics Law (Brazil), Law No. 7232, enacted October 29, 1984.

6   One notable exception is the 1994 European Energy Charter Treaty, *reprinted in* 34 I.L.M. 360 (1995), which arose out of the European Energy Charter Conference and creates a multilateral regime for foreign investment.

CHAPTER 3

INTERNATIONAL FINANCING

James R. Silkenat and Roger D. Wiegley

I.   INTRODUCTION

The term "international financing" encompasses an extremely broad spectrum of transactions. In a general sense, an international financing is any loan or investment in which two or more participants are located in different national jurisdictions or in which relevant property, either the object of the transaction or collateral, is in a national jurisdiction other than that of the participants. When the term is used in a more specific sense, the context usually suggests a transaction involving two or more national jurisdictions, such as trade finance, cross-border lending or investment by U.S. companies in non-U.S. affiliates.

Although the term may have many applications, international financings do share some general characteristics or, more precisely, some potential risks. Many of these risks are not encountered in domestic financing transactions. Indeed, the "art" of international financing from the lawyer's perspective is to understand all the risks in a particular transaction, to learn the various ways of mitigating these risks and the costs associated with (and efficacy of) each of these mitigating techniques, and then to explain all of this to a client in a way that will enable him or her to make an informed business decision. This task, which is never easy, is made more difficult by the fact that much of the risk assessment is a matter of guesswork and many of the "solutions" devised by lawyers over the years have not been tested in courts.

In one respect, this entire book is about the types of risks that can arise in international financing. Each chapter deals with one element of risk or the response to a particular risk created by legal institutions or legal regimes. It may sound obvious, but it is nonetheless true that the more one learns about the subjects covered in the other chapters of this volume, the better able one will be to identify issues, judge their importance and formulate responses. There will always be a certain amount of uncertainty – sometimes an uncomfortable amount – but this, after all, is the situation in which a creative lawyer can make the greatest contribution.

After providing a brief overview of financing sources, this chapter will focus on the risks encountered in international financing. These risks can generally be placed in four categories: credit or investment risk; transfer risk; currency risk; and political risk. There are also some special issues to consider when dealing with a public sector entity in another country.

II.   CREDIT OR INVESTMENT RISK

It is taken for granted that the creditworthiness of a U.S. borrower or the financial strength of an investment candidate in the United States, public or private, can be determined with a high degree of accuracy, assuming a reasonably diligent investigation. The same cannot always be said when the borrower or the investment candidate is not located in the United States or in another country with a highly developed economy. For example, if a lender wants to run a credit check on a prospective borrower in a developing economy, can the lender obtain reliable data? Can the lender rely on the borrower's financial statements? Do the accounting principles in the borrower's country produce results that are materially different from U.S. GAAP? Are asset values over-stated? Some foreign governments require annual upward revaluation of assets to compensate for inflation, even though this may overstate the productive value of the assets. Are all liabilities shown, including contingent liabilities? What level of scrutiny is brought to bear by auditors in the borrower's country? Are historic trends in operating results adjusted for inflation? Is fraud commonplace due to lack of public and private enforcement mechanisms? These same questions are relevant when the transaction is an equity investment rather than a loan.

Of course, many of these questions are not the responsibility of the international lawyer. On the other hand, lawyers can and do find ways to minimize business risks. When this talent is applied to problems of cross-border credit risk, the lawyer can contribute by finding well-qualified lawyers, accountants, bankers and other professionals in the jurisdiction where the borrower or investment candidate is located.

The next step is formulating the right questions. Here, too, the lawyer can play an important role because he or she is, by virtue of a lawyer's professional training, likely to phrase questions in a way that produces unambiguous answers. Needless to say, it is critical that the right questions be asked when different cultures are involved. Frequently, important basic information is not conveyed because one party making a loan or an investment assumes that a particular business practice is common to both cultures, while the other party, such as a professional adviser in a foreign country, does not volunteer information about local practices on the assumption that the lender or investor will ask about anything that he or she does not know. There are no easy steps to finding the right questions, but it helps to think through not only the issues that can arise in a domestic transaction, but also the assumptions one makes about the reliability and meaning of various kinds of information provided by a borrower or an investment candidate.

III.   TRANSFER RISK

"Transfer risk" refers to the difficulties that foreign borrowers or foreign affiliates encounter in converting domestic earnings into a foreign currency such as U.S. dollars. Transfer risk arises because of exchange controls that are imposed by a government.

A.   Exchange Controls

The demand for convertible foreign currencies in developing economies far exceeds the supply. One way to resolve this shortfall is to have a free market wherein demand and supply factors determine the price of the currency. The other method, which is more common in developing economies, is for the government to establish a fixed exchange rate for its currency but at the same time establish procedures for the rationing of the scarce foreign currency according to priorities.

The highest priorities are loans from the multilateral development banks, payments for essential imports and bank interest charges on public sector loans. Only if the available foreign currency exceeds these requirements will the authorities, by means of a licensing system, allocate the excess to private companies needing to service debt, repatriate profits or import consumer goods. Governments have their own reasons for rationing by means of exchange controls rather than allowing the allocation to be made through a free market. Some governments try to use exchange rates as a means of keeping the prices of food and essential imports relatively low. Other governments use the exchange controls for more overtly political reasons.

In the most extreme form of exchange control, the government assumes complete control of the currency. Local residents must surrender all foreign exchange earnings to the authorities and in turn must formally apply to the authorities for the foreign currency they need to meet their requirements. Some countries employ a multiple exchange rate system wherein different rates are used for different types of transactions. In general, entities that the country's authorities want to encourage are allowed to buy foreign currency at a relatively low exchange rate, or to sell the foreign currency they earn at a relatively high exchange rate, whereas the opposite is true for entities the country wants to discourage. Still another form of exchange arrangement calls for a free market wherein demand and supply factors determine the price of the currency, but only for certain categories of products and services, while for other categories the supply of foreign currency is rationed according to the objectives of the country's authorities.

A practical and easily accessible source of information regarding the exchange control practices of a country is the U.S. Department of Commerce country desk officer. The desk officer maintains current information on the exchange application and allocation procedures within the assigned country. To make an inquiry, call (202) 482-2000 and ask for the country desk officer.

In August of each year the International Monetary Fund (IMF) publishes the "Annual Report on Exchange Arrangements and Exchange Restrictions." The report includes country-by-country comprehensive descriptions of the exchange systems of most countries of the world. Equally important, the publication reports the existing exchange controls and regulations of each country. The information is updated in "International Financial Statistics," the monthly publication of the IMF. Both publications are available for purchase from the Publications Office of the International Monetary Fund, Washington, D.C.

A commercial source for exchange control information is the FCIB–NACM Corporation. It is an association of credit and finance executives in exporting and banking that holds a roundtable discussion in various cities each month. The members report their worldwide payment practices and credit experiences. The address is: FCIB–NACM Corp., Metro Center One, 100 Wood Avenue South, Iselin, New Jersey 08830–2716; telephone (908) 548–2820; fax (908) 548–2582.

B.   *Minimizing Transfer Risk*

It is difficult to predict the likelihood of currency inconvertibility in a developing economy because governments change, economic priorities change and exchange ratios, which affect the availability of foreign currency, change. There are, however, a few ways to deal with transfer risk. One way is to obtain political risk insurance (discussed below, section V, "Political Risk"). Another is to identify a use for local currency. This second technique is easier for multinational corporations than it is for commercial lenders, but even for lenders there may be users for local currency that offer a creative solution to an unexpected problem. For example, if the borrower's country has a major export commodity, the party holding local currency may be able to use the currency to purchase the commodity in the country and then sell it through a broker outside the country for an amount payable in the desired currency. Alternatively, if the borrower has foreign earnings from exports, it may be possible to take a pledge of the borrower's foreign receivables outside the national jurisdiction of the borrower, although this would be a solution only in the extreme case where the exchange controls in the borrower's country prevent the borrower from using the foreign currency that it earns.

IV.   CURRENCY RISK

When future payments or distributions are payable in a foreign currency, there is the risk that the foreign currency will depreciate in value before the foreign currency payment is received and is exchanged into U.S. dollars. Of course, there would be a profit from the currency exchange should the price of the foreign currency increase, but most lenders and investors would gladly give up the possibility of currency exchange profit if they could eliminate the risk of currency exchange loss.

Currency risk is not covered under insurance policies that cover political risk. One solution to the problem of currency risk is to require the borrower to make payments in the desired currency. In the case of, say, a joint venture, the foreign partner could be required to make all of its contributions in the same currency as the other partner. This solution raises other issues. In the case of a loan, if the borrower is located in a developing economy and the borrower has no source of foreign currency, such as export sales, it may simply be unable to generate enough local currency to meet its payment obligation at the prevailing exchange rate. Thus, the currency risk is replaced with a credit risk. In the case of a joint venture, the foreign partner that bears the currency risk may soon come to feel that it is making a contribution to the venture that is disproportionate to its rewards.

Where two major currencies are involved, unless the transaction is a loan (where the lender typically insists upon repayment in the currency of the national jurisdiction in which the lending branch is located), neither party may be willing to assume the other party's currency risk. In that situation, a party expecting to receive foreign currency may want to eliminate exchange risk through a hedging transaction.

A.   *Exchange Rates and Foreign Exchange Market*

An exchange rate is the amount of currency that can be bought or sold for a certain amount of another currency. Currencies of the major economies are traded among banks for their customers and for themselves and by foreign exchange dealers.

The foreign exchange market consists of two markets: the spot market and the forward or future market. The spot market is for foreign exchange delivered within two business days; the forward market is for foreign exchange to be delivered three or more days in the future, typically one, two, three or six months after the transaction date. Transactions in the spot market are executed at the rate of exchange prevailing at the time the transaction is made. In quoting a spot rate, the bank will quote a bid and offer rate for the particular currency. In quoting the forward rate of a given currency, a bank will give a rate at which it is willing to buy the currency (the bid rate) and a rate at which it is willing to sell a currency (an offer rate) for delivery at a specified future date.

In a completely free exchange market, the relationship between the spot and forward rates of a currency will be determined by the relationship between the interest rates in the given country and the rest of the world. In a free market, the currency with the higher interest rate will sell at a discount in the forward market; the currency with the lower interest rate will sell at a premium in the forward market.

The foreign exchange market provides three methods for protection against the decline in the value of a foreign currency to be received in the future: covering in the forward market; covering through the money market;

and currency options. Each of these methods is described below, using as an example an invoice for payment in French francs in six months.

B.   *Forward Market Hedging Technique*

Under this method a party would enter into a forward exchange contract with its bank that provides for the delivery to the bank of the French franc payment to be received in six months. The bank would agree to pay a designated amount for the French francs which would be the six months' rate for francs.

This hedging action assures a sum certain at the end of 180 days regardless of any changes in the exchange rate. There are limitations, however. Banks are reluctant to enter into a futures contract with small customers or for small amounts. Also, the ability to deliver the currency six months in the future is only as good as the creditworthiness of the obligor. If the obligor does not pay the French francs six months in the future, the other party is still obligated to deliver francs to the bank. The party with the obligation to deliver francs to the bank may have to purchase the currency in the spot market or compensate the bank for any loss. Finally, the forward market is thin, *i.e.*, few banks are willing to hedge for any period beyond six months to one year.

C.   *Money Market Hedging Technique*

A party could borrow French francs in the Eurocurrency market, convert the francs into U.S. dollars in the spot market, invest the proceeds in the U.S. money market to earn interest (or use the funds for working capital), and then repay the franc loan when payment is received from the buyer. The net cost is the interest differential between the cost of the loan in francs and return on the U.S. dollar investment.

This hedging method may be the preferred form of hedging if the borrowed funds are used to replace a higher cost borrowing. This method assumes that a party has access to the Eurocurrency market. In reality, small companies and/or small transactions may be shut out of the market because of the banks' reluctance to deal with small accounts. Also, the margins a bank charges for loans are higher than the margins it charges for a foreign transaction. Finally, there is the risk that the obligor may not pay on the due date, which means that the contracting party will not have the francs to pay the amount due the bank.

D.   *Currency Options*

This method gives one party the right (but not the obligation) to buy or sell a specific amount of currency at a specified exchange rate on or before an agreed–upon date. The option has the advantage that, if the exchange rate moves in favor of the option holder, the option can be exercised, thus protecting the holder against loss. If the rate moves against the option holder, he or she can let the option lapse but take a profit by selling the foreign currency in the spot market. Thus, there is no downside risk but there is potential for gain.

The two basic types of options are the call option, which provides the contract holder with the right to purchase an agreed amount of foreign currency at a specified price, and the put option, which provides the contract holder with the right to sell an agreed amount of foreign currency at a specified price. The specified price at which the option can be bought or sold is called the exercise or striking price. The buyer of the put option contract pays to the seller of the contract a fee, called the premium. The buyer makes the decision of whether or not to exercise the option. No matter how much the exchange rate moves, the holder of a put option cannot lose more than the premium because there is no binding requirement that he or she exercise the option. However, there is no limit on the amount of possible gain.

Foreign currency options are a good technique to protect against contingent risk exposure when a bid for a foreign project has been submitted but there is doubt as to whether the bid will be accepted. The potential foreign receivable can be hedged with a put option. If the bid is not accepted, the option need not be exercised and the cost of hedging is limited to the premium; if the bid is accepted, the put option ensures that the hedging party can sell the foreign currency received, at the striking price, and thus be protected against the risk of an adverse movement in the exchange rate. Furthermore, the premium is known at the time of the bidding which allows the hedging party to incorporate the hedging costs into the bid price. If the hedging party is not the successful bidder, it can sell the option to recapture the value of the option between the date of the sale and the expiration of the option contract. It can thus recover some of the premium that was paid. If, instead, the hedging party had entered into a forward contract to sell the potential foreign currency receipts, and the bid were not accepted, it would have remained obligated to engage in a foreign exchange transaction which could have been risky.

Foreign currency options can be bought over–the–counter from a bank or from a broker who has access to the Philadelphia Stock Exchange and other markets that trade options. If the currency option is purchased over–the–counter, i.e., from a bank, the amount, premium, strike price and maturity date are decided between the buyer and seller. If the option is purchased through a transaction on one of the exchanges, the amount, fees, strike price and maturity date are standardized.

V. POLITICAL RISK

Political risks include war, hostilities, civil strife, rebellion, revolution, insurrection, acts of terrorism, confiscation, expropriation and government intervention in the operations of a company's business. Such political events occur unexpectedly and are therefore impossible to predict. When making a loan to or an investment in a developing economy, it might be prudent to obtain political risk insurance. Political risk insurance can be obtained from the Overseas Private Investment Corporation ("OPIC"), the Multilateral Investment Guaranty Agency ("MIGA"), Export–Import Bank of the United States (Eximbank) and a few private insurers, such as Lloyds of London and American International Group. (*See* Chapter 4, *Political Risk Insurance.*)

A.   OPIC

OPIC is a self–sustaining U.S. government agency that was created to encourage U.S. investment in developing countries. Most developing countries are eligible for OPIC programs, with a few exceptions based on U.S. foreign policy considerations.

OPIC provides U.S.–government–backed loan guarantees and direct loans for overseas investments by U.S.–owned companies. In addition, OPIC provides political risk insurance for new investments and significant expansions of existing investments in eligible countries.

OPIC's terms generally limit the maximum insurable amount to 90 percent of an investment's value for equity, up to a maximum of $200 million per risk, per project. This per–project limit may be exceeded on a case–by–case basis. OPIC insurance coverage is long–term, up to 20 years. OPIC's insurance is backed by an excellent history of paying claims, by OPIC's substantial reserves and, ultimately, by the full faith and credit of the United States Government.

OPIC's policies insure against all three major categories of political risk: (1) confiscation, expropriation, or nationalization; (2) transfer risk (currency inconvertibility); and (3) damage to physical assets or lost income due to political violence, including war, revolution, insurrection and civil strife. The agency does not, however, insure against commercial risks.

OPIC insures against *de facto* or "creeping" expropriations, as well as outright nationalizations. However, OPIC expropriation insurance is "all or nothing" coverage. No compensation is available for a partial expropriation of the investor's business that merely diminishes its value.

OPIC's inconvertibility coverage is only available to the extent that a legal right to convert local currency into hard currency exists at the time of the policy's issuance. Thus, the agency insures the continuance of a foreign exchange right; inconvertibility insurance is not available to parties who invest in countries that do not maintain any right of conversion and repatriation. The risk that a currency may be devalued is not insurable through OPIC, as it is regarded as a commercial risk.

Generally, OPIC's political violence coverage can extend to damage or destruction of physical assets. For institutional lenders, the agency has extended its policies to cover liability for principal and interest payments on loans or payments under technical assistance agreements where a form of political violence has caused a default. This coverage, like coverage for "creeping" expropriation, is subject to careful scrutiny as a result of the potential blurring of commercial and political factors. OPIC looks carefully to ensure that a failure to make payment is in fact attributable to a political event and not to commercial difficulties of the borrower or a contracting party.

B. MIGA

MIGA, which was established by a convention sponsored by the International Bank for Reconstruction and Development (the "World Bank"), was created to provide guarantees against non-commercial risk in order to encourage the flow of capital into and among developing countries.

MIGA's support is available to individual and corporate investors in countries that contribute to MIGA's capital. The MIGA Convention lists four broad categories of non-commercial risk:

(1) the risk of transfer resulting from host government restrictions on currency conversion and transfer;

(2) the risk of loss resulting from actions of the host government that eliminate or diminish the foreign investor's investment;

(3) the repudiation or breach of government contracts in the cases where the investor has no access or limited access to a competent judicial or arbitral forum; and

(4) the risk of armed conflict and civil disturbance.

Eligible investments for MIGA guarantee contracts would be new investments, made for medium or long term, that are expected to contribute positively to development in the host country.

Although the concept of MIGA has been around for several decades, it was only established officially in April 1988 and only signed its first insurance contract at the beginning of 1990.

MIGA's coverage can be provided for up to 20 years. It is designed to supplement both private insurers and the investment insurance agencies of national governments (such as OPIC). At present, MIGA's coverage is limited to $50 million per project.

As of the end of 1994, 147 countries had signed the MIGA Convention (including the U.S.).

C.   Eximbank

Eximbank is a U.S. government agency that facilitates export financing of U.S. goods and services. Eximbank promotes exports by providing a wide range of financing support, including loans and loan guarantees, export credit insurance, and project financing.

Eximbank's loan guarantees provide repayment protection for loans from private lenders to creditworthy buyers made for the purpose of financing the cost of exported U.S. goods and services. Eximbank guarantees are backed by the full faith and credit of the United States. Most guarantees provide coverage against non-payment for any reason, whether commercial or political. A guarantee covering only political risks is also available for certain transactions, and it is the only type of guarantee available where there is common ownership between the U.S. exporter and the foreign buyer, as in the case of exports by a U.S. company to its foreign subsidiary. Covered political risks include war, cancellation of an existing export or import license, expropriation, confiscation of (or intervention in) the buyer's business, and transfer risk (new government policies preventing the conversion of a foreign deposit into dollars). Losses due to currency devaluation are not considered a political risk. Commercial risks cover non-payment for reasons other than specified political risks, including deterioration of the buyer's market, fluctuations in demand, unanticipated competition, shifts in tariffs, technological change, buyer insolvency and natural disasters.

D.   Private Insurance

Political risk insurance from private sector insurers tends to focus on shorter term risks, such as trade credits. Such insurance is usually limited to one, two or, at most, three years, renewable at the option of the insurer. Insurance against political violence is generally not available from private sector insurers, and private inconvertibility insurance is not available in many countries that are served by OPIC and MIGA.

E.   Monitoring Political Risk

The following publications are recommended sources of information on economic and political conditions within a country or countries of interest:

- *Political Risk Letter.* Monthly newsletter that summarizes the service's latest political risk forecasts. Address: Political Risk Services, 6320 Fly Road, Suite 102, P.O. Box 248, East Syracuse, NY 13057-0248; telephone: (315) 431-0200.

- *International Country Risk Guide.* Monthly report by Political Risk Services that includes financial, economic and political risk forecasts and ratings for 130 countries. (See above for address.)

- *Country Reports.* Quarterly publication, with annual supplements, that reviews current economic, political and business conditions and prospects for 180 countries. Address: Economist Intelligence Unit Ltd., 15 Regent Street, London SW1Y 4LR England; telephone: 011–44–171–830–1000.

- *Rundts Weekly Intelligence.* Reviews important current world business, economic and political developments on a weekly basis. Address: S.J. Rundt & Associates, Inc., 130 East 63rd Street, New York, NY 10021; telephone: (212) 838–0141.

VI. DEALING WITH PUBLIC SECTOR ENTITIES

Conducting business with public sector entities in developing economies – airlines, transit companies, public utilities, municipalities, state governments and government ministries – can be frustrating and expensive. There are few public officials who can act without bureaucratic constraints. Moreover, it is difficult to assess the public sector entity's ability to pay.

The assumption throughout this discussion is that the transaction involving the public sector entity is structured so that the central government is either the obligor or guarantor, which means that the creditor is looking to the full faith and credit of the central government for repayment. This concept is referred to as "sovereign risk."

A. Risks

Appraisal of a government's ability to meet its obligations requires an analysis of government finances, external public debt and other economic data. Not many credit managers have this expertise.

While a private sector obligor will make its decision on the basis of business considerations, the public sector decision may be political and/or require "facilitating payments." A private sector obligor can make a decision relatively quickly whereas the public sector obligor may take weeks and even months to reach a decision because of bureaucratic procedures.

Moreover, there is continuity of management in the private sector. In developing economies, however, frequent changes in government are not uncommon. The new head of state invariably appoints new ministry officials who understandably become preoccupied with macro–economic problems rather than transactions with or payments due to foreigners.

B. Central Government Guarantee

It is difficult, if not impossible, to determine whether the public sector entity can contract foreign debt or have the resources to service the debt for its own account. For this reason experienced commercial lenders usually require the guarantee of the Ministry of Finance or Central Bank or a satisfactory financial institution whenever a public sector entity is the proposed obligor.

It is important to be aware of the difference in the quality of credit whenever the public sector transaction is structured with the Ministry of Finance or Central Bank as guarantor instead of as obligor. When the central government is the obligor, funds for repayment are provided in the overall budget. The funds are there when needed for repayment. When the central government is the guarantor, there may be no funds budgeted. Special legislative action may be required for authorization of the payment, which can mean considerable delays in securing payment by the guarantor.

C.   *Facilitating Payments*

It is not uncommon for public officials to request "facilitating payments." U.S. companies and lenders should bear in mind that the Foreign Corrupt Practices Act of 1977 makes certain payments, offers of payment, and gifts to foreign officials, foreign political parties, or foreign political candidates illegal if made for the purpose of obtaining, retaining, or directing business to any person. (*See* Chapter 14, *The Foreign Corrupt Practices Act.*)

A payment by a U.S. company in violation of the Foreign Corrupt Practices Act exposes that company to criminal prosecution. Moreover, U.S. entities making the illegal payments may find later on, with a change in government, that the new government will use the illegal payment as an excuse not to pay. Or, once begun, the illegal payments may have to continue in order to obtain repayment of the amounts owed.

D.   *Sovereign Risk Appraisal*

The following sources of information can be useful in an assessment of a foreign sovereign.

- *Institutional Investor,* a monthly periodical, surveys banks around the world. The banks are asked to grade the creditworthiness of the governments on a scale of from 1 (least creditworthy) to 100 (most creditworthy). The findings, published twice a year in the periodical (March and September), have the advantage of reporting the combined perceptions of the various banks. Address: 488 Madison Avenue, 12th Floor, New York, NY 10022; telephone (212) 224-3300.

- *Euromoney,* a monthly publication of Euromoney Publications Ltd., London, also ranks governments. The Euromoney rankings of countries is based upon the announced terms of credits extended to the governments rather than on anyone's opinion. This system provides the analyst with a basis for knowing what the trends have been for credits to an individual country and allows a comparison with the patterns for other countries. Address: Euromoney Publications Ltd., Nestor House, Playhouse Yard, London EC4 5EX England; telephone 011-44-171-779-8935.

- Eximbank's economists analyze individual countries using quantitative and qualitative information obtained from a variety of sources. On a semiannual basis they prepare brief written reports on more than 150 countries where Eximbank is allowed to do business. These reports, which are updated as warranted between semiannual country policy reviews, describe the positive and negative economic aspects of a country, with emphasis on the external economic and financial situation, and the country's ability to service its international debt. Eximbank's country reports are for staff use only. However, U.S. companies and banks can call or visit the Eximbank economist to obtain an informal briefing.

VII.   SOURCES OF FINANCING

In today's international economic climate, it is common to use different types and sources of financing to fund different types of ventures. Further, in complex financings, it is often common to use different financing sources for different stages and components of the venture (equity funds, for example, to finance feasibility studies, preliminary design and engineering; short-term revolving bank credits during the construction period; export credits for major equipment purchases; and development or commercial bank loans for longer term financing).

The principal source of private financing for most international projects today is commercial loans. The source of these loan funds can be local or multinational, syndicated or not. Deciding whether (and how) to use commercial loans will depend in most cases on the specifics of the country and business sector involved and the overall creditworthiness of the borrower.

In addition to the private, commercial sources of capital that are available for financing of international projects and ventures, multilateral financial institutions have also become an important source of such funding, both in terms of equity and debt capital. Although they are by no means the only sources of such financing, the World Bank and its affiliated institutions alone provided more than $20 billion in loans and credits for international project financing in the past year. The financial institutions which provide this type of financing can generally be divided into four categories: First, there is the World Bank group, *i.e.*, the International Bank for Reconstruction and Development (usually referred to as the World Bank), the International Development Association (the Bank's soft-loan window) and the International Finance Corporation (which makes loans and equity investments in the private sector). A second category is composed of the regional development banks, such as the Asian Development Bank in Manila, the Inter-American Development Bank in Washington and the African Development Bank in the Ivory Coast. Third, there are a variety of country-oriented development institutions, similar to the Agency for International Development ("AID") and Eximbank, which provide project financing with regard to goods supplied from a particular country. Finally, there are the privately-owned development institutions such as PICA, in Asia, and the ADELA Group, in Latin America. All of these institutions of course work with private commercial and investment banks in providing or arranging for loan funding for international joint ventures and other development projects. Each of these financial institutions will have its own rules and procedures for financing.

VIII.   CONCLUSION

For any particular type of international financing, be it trade finance, project finance, secured lending, a joint venture investment, or other type of transaction, there are customary forms of documents and typical contractual issues that require negotiation. It is impossible to cover all of the documents and all of the issues in a chapter such as this. Suffice it to say that there are books and professional conferences devoted to each type of international financing, and frequently these books and conferences will focus on a particular country or region. It is always a worthwhile investment of time and money to consult these sources before embarking on a new international transaction. It is also important to consider the forest before examining the trees. What is the objective of the transaction? What are the risks? What kind of information is needed to fully assess the risks?

When these questions have been considered, the structural issues can be addressed: creating enforceable security interests, obtaining credit support or insurance coverage, minimizing taxes, early termination or "exit strategies," leasing vs. sale considerations, off-shore depositories, etc. The resolution of these structural issues will depend upon the facts of a particular situation. It is impossible to generalize about the "best" structure, except to state the obvious: the best structure is one that minimizes the risk to your client and does so in a practical, efficient and cost-effective manner, while avoiding risks for the other party that jeopardize the success of the transaction. It is hard to overemphasize the importance of risk assessment for the lawyers in international financing. Indeed, an important role of the lawyer in any transaction is to understand and allocate risk. International financings are no different. They just make the task more complex and more challenging.

IX.   SOURCES OF ASSISTANCE

A.   *Published Sources*

1.   Books and Specific Articles

THE ABA GUIDE TO INTERNATIONAL BUSINESS NEGOTIATIONS (J. Silkenat & J. Aresty eds. 1994).

J. BARBEAU AND M. AINSLIE, A GUIDE TO FOREIGN INVESTMENT IN THE UNITED STATES (1989).

Blassberg & Gooding, *Facilitating and Financing International Acquisitions, in* ACQUISITIONS, MERGERS, SPIN-OFFS AND OTHER RESTRUCTURINGS 1993 (PLI Com. Law and Practice Course Handbook Series).

Bohn, *Eximbank's Role in International Banking and Finance,* 20 INT'L LAW. 829 (1986).

Fitzgerald, *Overview of Risks in International Financing, in* PROJECT FINANCING FROM DOMESTIC TO INTERNATIONAL 1995 (PLI Com. Law and Practice Course Handbook Series).

Hudes, *Protecting Against Inconvertibility and Transfer Risk: An Outline of Trade Financing Programs of the Export-Import Bank of the United States,* 9 HASTINGS INT'L AND COMP. L. REV. 461 (1986).

INTERNATIONAL BORROWING (D. Bradlow & W. Jourdin eds. 1984).

McQuiston, *Drafting an Enforceable Guaranty in an International Financing Transaction: A Lender's Perspective,* 10 INT'L TAX & BUS. LAW. 138 (1993).

Silkenat, *The Role of Multilateral Financial Institutions in Financing International Investments, in* COUNSELING EMERGING COMPANIES IN GOING INTERNATIONAL (A. Gutterman ed. 1994).

SOVEREIGN LENDING: MANAGING LEGAL RISK (M. Gruson & R. Reisner eds. 1984). Publisher: Euromoney Publications Ltd., Nestor House, Playhouse Yard, London EC4 5EX England; telephone: 011-44-171-779-8935.

10-10E SECURITIES LAW SERIES, INTERNATIONAL CAPITAL MARKETS AND SECURITIES REGULATION (H. Bloomenthal & S. Wolff eds. 1995).

2. Periodicals and Newsletters

Country Reports. Publisher: Economist Intelligence Unit Ltd., 15 Regent Street, London SW1Y 4LR England; telephone: 011–44–171–830–1000.

Country Risk Service. Publisher: Economist Intelligence Unit Ltd. (see above).

Euromoney. Publisher: Euromoney Publications Ltd. (see above).

Eximbank Letter. Publisher: International Business Affairs Corp., 4938 Hampden Lane, #346, Bethesda, MD 20814; telephone: (301) 907–8647; fax: (301) 907–8650.

International Financial Law Review. Publisher: Euromoney Publications Ltd. (see above).

Institutional Investor (March and September issues). Publisher: Institutional Investor, 488 Madison Avenue, 12th Floor, New York, NY 10022; telephone: (212) 224–3300.

International Country Risk Guide. Publisher: Political Risk Services, 6320 Fly Road, Suite 102 – P.O. Box 248, East Syracuse, NY 13057; telephone: (315) 431–0511.

International Monetary Fund, *Annual Report on Exchange Arrangements and Exchange Restrictions.* Publisher: IMF Publications Services, 700 19th Street, N.W., Washington, D.C. 20431; telephone: (202) 623–7430; fax: (202) 623–7201.

IMF Statistics Dep't, *International Financial Statistics.* Publisher: IMF Publications Service (see above).

International Trade Finance Report. Publisher: The Morgan Williams Group, Inc., P.O. Box 22, Rutherford, NJ 07070; telephone: (201) 933–9626; fax: (201) 939–2137.

Political Risk Letter. Publisher: Political Risk Services (see above).

Rundts Weekly Intelligence. Publisher: S.J. Rundt & Associates, Inc., 130 East 63rd Street, New York, NY 10021; telephone: (212) 838–0141.

B. *Institutional Assistance*

> U.S. Department of Commerce
> 14th and Constitution, N.W.,
> Washington, D.C. 20230
> Telephone: (202) 482–2000

For a listing of country desk officers, their telephone and fax numbers, call 1–800–USA–TRADE.

> Export–Import Bank of the United States
> 811 Vermont Avenue, N.W.,
> Washington, D.C. 20571
> Telephone: (202) 565–3200 or (800) 565–EXIM
> Fax: (202) 565–3210

> International Monetary Fund
> 700 19th Street, N.W.,
> Washington, D.C. 20431
> Telephone: (202) 623–7000
> Fax: (202) 623–4661

> Overseas Private Investment Corporation
> 1100 New York Avenue, N.W.,
> Washington, D.C. 20527
> Telephone: (202) 336–8400
> Fax: (202) 408–9859

> The World Bank
> 1818 H Street, N.W.,
> Washington, D.C. 20433
> Telephone: (202) 477–1234
> Fax: (202) 477–6391

CHAPTER 4

POLITICAL RISK INSURANCE

Robert B. Shanks

I. INTRODUCTION

The political risks of investing in developing countries and emerging market economies are perceived to be significantly greater than the conceptually similar regulatory and governmental risks affecting investments in developed counties. This perception arises in part from the fact that many developing countries, particularly those in the process of converting from socialist to market-based economies, lack a system of well-tested commercial laws, so long taken for granted in the developed western democracies, to enforce contractual rights and obligations and to protect private property rights from arbitrary government interference. The perception also arises from recognition that the development process itself is fraught with uncertainty as rapid political, economic and social changes often give rise to forces that are difficult to predict and may be impossible even for governments to control. In an era when political risk forecasting remains more art than science,[1] companies investing in or trading with developing countries and their lenders often seek additional protection by obtaining guarantees and political risk insurance.[2]

II. TYPES OF POLITICAL RISK

A. *Political Risks Facing Overseas Investments*

The basic political risks against which investors and lenders seek protection through political risk insurance include: (1) expropriation or nationalization; (2) inconvertibility of local currency earnings into hard currency, or government refusal to allow hard currency to be remitted out of the country (transfer risk); (3) political violence, including war, revolution, civil strife and terrorism; and (4) government repudiation of, or interference with, contractual obligations entered into by government-controlled entities.

Political risk insurance is generally available to cover these categories of political risk. Insurance is generally not available, however, to cover the heightened commercial risks of investing in, or trading with, developing countries and emerging markets. The distinction between political and commercial risks is therefore of some importance, even though in the real world it is often difficult, and sometimes impossible, to categorize an event as either purely political or purely commercial. For example, if a government-owned utility enters into an agreement to purchase all of the power produced by a privately-financed generating facility, and the utility subsequently defaults on that obligation, the resulting loss could be characterized as either commercial or political, depending upon the reasons for the default. If the failure resulted from the utility's lack of funds necessary to meet its payment obligation, the loss could be described as "commercial," even though the commercial failure might have political roots in the government's monetary policy or the government's adoption of an energy regulatory policy that prevented the utility from charging and collecting market-based rates for power, thereby ensuring that tariffs would not be sufficient to cover the cost of building new generating facilities. If, however, the government acted to frustrate an investor's efforts to enforce its contractual rights against the utility, or to enforce performance guarantees issued by the government to the foreign investor or its lenders in support of the utility's purchase obligation, the government's action might well constitute an expropriatory act qualifying for compensation under a political risk insurance policy. Similarly, a failure of a government entity to perform under a fuel supply agreement with a private generator could result from either a commercial failure or a political act.

1.   Specific Insurable Political Risks

a.   Expropriation

This risk includes both outright nationalization and "creeping" or *de facto* expropriation. The U.S. and other industrialized countries take the view that nationalization is lawful only if it is undertaken for a public purpose, is not arbitrary or discriminatory, and is accompanied by prompt, adequate and effective compensation. *See Restatement (Third) of the Foreign Relations Law of the United States* § 712 (1987).

Outright nationalization is straightforward, but increasingly rare. When it occurs, the principal issue is usually the adequacy of compensation offered by the government.

"Creeping" or *de facto* expropriation refers to host government actions that fall short of outright nationalization, but nevertheless effectively deprive investors of fundamental rights in, or control over, their property. Short of nationalization, a host country can act politically to affect an investment in a variety of ways. Taxation and regulation, for example, are political acts, but they are presumptively lawful exercises of a government's political powers even though they may adversely affect an investor's rights in, or control over, its investment. A host government can also breach, or cause a government controlled entity to breach, an agreement with an investor. Such breaches can be categorized either as political or commercial acts, again depending upon the circumstances.

The Overseas Private Investment Corporation ("OPIC"), the U.S. government agency that insures U.S. investments in friendly developing countries (22 U.S.C. §§ 2191 *et seq.*), defines expropriation as an act or series of acts that satisfy all of the following requirements:

> The acts are attributable to a foreign governing authority which is in *de facto* control of the part of the country in which the project is located;

> The acts are violations of international law (without regard to the availability of local remedies) or material breaches of local law;

> The acts indirectly deprive the investor of fundamental rights in the insured investment (rights are "fundamental" if without them the investor is substantially deprived of the benefits of the investment); and

> The violations of law are not remedied and the expropriatory effect continues for one year.

b.   Currency Inconvertibility and Transfer Risk

This risk encompasses an investor's inability to convert local currency earnings into U.S. dollars or other hard currency or to remit hard currency out of the country to pay dividends or loans denominated in hard currency or to repatriate capital. Inconvertibility and transfer risk are distinguishable from the risk of currency devaluation. Whenever an investor receives payment in currency that is not freely convertible, it runs the risk that the currency of payment will depreciate against foreign exchange. Thus, when the investor converts the payment, it may be worth less than expected. Although there is clearly a political element to the setting of currency exchange rates, currency devaluation is regarded as a commercial risk. Devaluation is not an insurable risk, although it may be mitigated through hedging arrangements and other commercial devices. (*See* Chapter 3, *International Financing.*)

Insurance is available from various public sources to protect investors against adverse changes in laws or regulations providing for convertibility of local currency into hard currency and transfer of hard currency revenues out of the country. For example, OPIC deems currency inconvertible if the investor is unable legally to convert earnings from or returns of the foreign investment into U.S. dollars through any channel for a period of 90 days.

c.   Political Violence

This risk includes the occurrence of war, revolution, insurrection, terrorism, and civil strife. Insurance against this risk may cover the loss of business income and/or damage to physical assets. OPIC defines "political violence" as a violent act undertaken with the primary intent of achieving a political objective, such as declared or undeclared war, hostile action by national or international armed forces, civil war, revolution, insurrection, civil strife, terrorism, or sabotage.[3]

d. Contract Repudiation

Insurance may also be obtained to cover a government's failure to honor a contractual obligation. In project financings for power and other major infrastructure projects, for example, the foreign investor typically enters into a concession or tolling agreement and other contracts with state-owned enterprises. In project financings for power generation facilities, the generator typically enters into an energy conversion or power sales agreement with a state utility, which agrees to purchase all electricity generated and to make capacity payments based on the installed capacity of the generating facility. These payments are calculated to cover, at a minimum, all debt service for the project and, thereby, to make it financeable. Payments typically are denominated in hard currency, or are indexed to hard currency, to mitigate foreign exchange risk in meeting hard currency debt obligations. The utility also agrees to pay additional fees upon the actual delivery of power to the grid.

If for any reason the utility fails for an extended period to meet its obligation to make capacity payments, the project will default on its obligations to its creditors. In the typical situation, where the sponsor and lenders lack confidence in the creditworthiness of the state utility, they will seek credit enhancements in the form of performance undertakings or guarantees from the government backing the utility's obligation. Both the utility's payment obligation and the government's enhancement of that obligation may be subject to enforcement through international arbitration. Political risk insurance is available to cover investors and lenders against the risk that the government will refuse to arbitrate, obtain an award in its favor by fraud or duress, or fail or refuse to pay an award rendered in favor of the insured investors or lenders.

B. *Political Risks Affecting Export Transactions*

The same types of political events that threaten investments can also disrupt export transactions. Insurance is generally available to cover the following risks associated with selling or contracting abroad:

1) Losses associated with the "wrongful calling" of bid, performance, advance payment and similar guaranties or other "on demand" instruments posted by sellers in favor of buyers;

2) Certain acts by governments in contravention of contracts, including contract repudiation, embargoes or revocation of import or export licenses;

3) Nonpayment or default due to currency inconvertibility or political violence; and

4) Losses due to confiscation of equipment or inventory or damage or nonpayment due to political violence.

III.   SOURCES OF POLITICAL RISK INSURANCE

Political risk insurance is available to cover investments from OPIC and its counterpart bilateral agencies in the other OECD countries, from the World Bank Group's Multilateral Investment Guarantee Agency (MIGA) and from a select group of private sector insurers. Political risk insurance covering risks associated with export sales transactions is available from the Export-Import Bank of the United States (Ex-Im Bank), from the export credit agencies of the other OECD countries, and from certain private insurers.[4]

A.   *Political Risk Insurance for Investments*

1.   **Overseas Private Investment Corporation**

a.   Structure and Organization

OPIC is a self-sustaining independent U.S. government agency. Its mandate is to encourage U.S. private investment in developing countries. OPIC provides political risk insurance for new investments and expansions of existing investments in eligible countries.[5] OPIC will cover up to 90 percent of equity investments and up to 100 percent of loans to eligible investments. OPIC recently increased its coverage limit to a maximum of $200 million per risk, per project. Coverage is long-term, up to 20 years. OPIC's political risk insurance is backed by the full faith and credit of the United States; and OPIC has an excellent history of paying claims.

It is important to emphasize several features of OPIC's coverage. First, OPIC can cover only political risks, not commercial ones. Second, OPIC can insure only new investments, including expansions or modernizations. Third, OPIC insurance is based on the underlying contractual relationship that the investor has negotiated. In other words, OPIC insures against the risk that the host government will unlawfully interfere with the terms of the underlying contract; it does not insure that the underlying agreement is a good one or that the investment will result in a profit.

b.   Eligibility Criteria

Because OPIC is a U.S. government agency, statutory and policy restrictions affect eligibility of investors and investments under OPIC's programs. The most significant of these limitations are set forth below.

Eligible investors include U.S. citizens, entities incorporated in the U.S. (if more than 50 percent beneficially owned by U.S. citizens), and entities incorporated outside the U.S. if more than 95 percent beneficially owned by U.S. persons or nationals.

As a development institution, OPIC attempts to assist investments that would not go forward without OPIC insurance. Investors are therefore required to register their projects with OPIC prior to entering into an irrevocable commitment to invest. Investors who have not registered their projects nevertheless may be eligible for coverage if, for example, they provide in their contract that the investment is contingent upon obtaining political risk insurance from OPIC or another other appropriate source. The investment must be a "new" investment, including modernization or expansion of an existing facility.

OPIC will cover up to 90 percent of an equity investment and up to 100 percent of loans by an eligible lender, up to a maximum of $200 million per risk, per project.

OPIC will not assist any investment in a "runaway" plant or an investment that would result in a significant net loss of jobs in the U.S. OPIC is also required to be sensitive to the U.S. balance of payments (i.e., U.S. exports) in deciding whether to assist an investment.

OPIC screens projects for environmental risks and will not finance or insure any project that poses unreasonable risks to the host country's environment.

2. The Multilateral Investment Guarantee Agency

a. Structure and Organization

MIGA was organized as an agency associated with the International Bank of Reconstruction and Development (the "World Bank") in 1988. MIGA's purpose is to encourage the flow of investments to developing countries by providing:

> guarantees (insurance) to foreign investors against currency transfer, expropriation, war, revolution or civil disturbance, and breach of contract risks; and

> advisory services to developing member countries on their attractiveness to foreign investment.

b. Eligibility

Coverage under MIGA is subject to eligibility requirements similar to, but distinct from, those for OPIC insurance. Some of the most significant requirements are set forth below:

Eligible investors include nationals of a member country, entities incorporated and having their principal place of business in a member country, and entities having a majority of their shares owned by nationals of member countries. Eligible investors also include nationals of the host country, if the assets to be invested are obtained from abroad.

MIGA can insure new investments between member countries where the investment project is located in a developing country. Investments must comply with the laws of the host country and must be consistent with the host government's developmental objectives and priorities.

MIGA can insure equity or debt up to 90 percent of the investment amount, subject to a per project, per coverage limit currently set at $50 million.[6] No minimum amount of investment is required.

MIGA will insure only political, not commercial, risks.

MIGA will insure equity interests and other forms of direct investment such as loans and loan guarantees made by equity holders. Coverage may be extended to other forms of investment, including management and service contracts and licensing agreements.

Certain types of investments, such as those related to military purposes, are not eligible.

The host government must approve an investment before coverage is extended. MIGA can deem that approval to have been obtained, however, if the host government has not objected to the investment within a reasonable period.

MIGA has the option to seek to enter into an agreement with the host country concerning treatment of investments guaranteed by MIGA. Unlike OPIC, however, MIGA is required to enter into such an agreement only if it is not satisfied that the host country can provide fair and equitable treatment and adequate legal protection for the investment.

3. Private Political Risk Insurance

A select group of private insurers also cover investments against certain political risks. It is generally more difficult to describe the coverages available from the private market in part because this information may be confidential, and in part because the market has been in a state of flux during the past several years.

The largest private political risk insurer in the U.S. is American International Group ("AIG"). In recent years, AIG has written political risk insurance, sometimes in combination with specialized commercial coverages, for oil and gas drilling rigs, the transportation industry, kidnapping, ransom and extortion, and special coverages for the entertainment industry.

Other major private political risk insurers include Lloyds of London, the Chubb Group, and Citicorp through its subsidiary Citicorp International Trade Indemnity, Inc. ("CITI"). A significant recent new entrant into the field is Exports Insurance Company, headquartered in New York.

In general, private political risk insurance offers some important benefits but also lacks some important advantages, compared with insurance offered by national agencies. Private insurers are not encumbered by the policy constraints affecting public agencies, such as restrictions on investor, project or country eligibility. Insurance for expropriation, usually referred to as "confiscation, expropriation and nationalization," is generally available in the private market. Private coverage is also generally available to cover the risk of arbitrary draw-downs of standby letters of credit posted as advance payment guarantees or performance bonds. Limited private coverage is also available against the risk of currency inconvertibility. Private coverage is generally not available, however, to cover war risks affecting land-based assets.

Although the private market for political risk insurance can trace its roots back centuries to Lloyds' early coverage of marine risks, the market for land-based political risks is still developing. The huge increase in world trade and investment flows of recent years could well lead to significant new developments in the form of new entrants, new types of coverage and new partnerships between public and private political risk insurance providers.

B.   *Export Credit Insurance*

Export credit insurance is available to cover the risk that the buyer of exported goods or services will default based on certain political events, as well as certain other risks discussed above in section II.B of this chapter. The primary sources of this form of coverage are the Eximbank and its counterpart export credit agencies in the other OECD countries, as well as certain private sector insurance providers, including AIG, Lloyds, CITI, and Exporters Insurance Company.

Eximbank is an independent U.S. government agency that supports U.S. exports through various financing mechanisms, including export credit insurance, loan guarantees and direct loans. Eximbank's programs differentiate on the basis of short-, medium- and long-term transactions. The repayment term for short-term sales is 180 days for consumables and 360 days for capital goods and equipment. Medium-term transactions typically range from 181 days to five years and may qualify for insurance, guarantee and debt loan programs. Long-term transactions are those of longer than five years' duration and qualify for guarantees and loans. Eximbank supports only goods and services being exported from the U.S. containing at least 50 percent U.S. content. Short-, medium- and long-term financing is generally available.

Eximbank offers both short- and medium-term export credit insurance policies, including the following:

• **Multi-buyer policies** provide coverage for an exporter's short-term credit sales (generally up to 180 days). Under multibuyer export credit insurance, a range of coverage options and credit limits is available. Premiums are based on a number of factors, including length of terms offered, buyer type, spread of country risk, transaction type, and previous export experience.

• **Single-buyer policies** insure short- or medium-term single or repetitive sales to the same buyer. The single-buyer policy covers losses caused by political events, including war, revolution, changes in certain export or import laws, foreign exchange convertibility, or commercial events, such as insolvency and protracted default. Premiums are set according to a risk-based pricing system.

• **Bank letter of credit insurance** protects banks against losses on irrevocable letters of credit issued by foreign banks in connection with financing U.S. exports. This policy can reduce the risks concerning confirmations and negotiations of irrevocable letters of credit issued by overseas financial institutions. It covers both commercial and political risks in connection with the failure of an overseas financial institution (issuing bank), whether sovereign or private, to make payment or reimbursement to the insured bank on an irrevocable letter of credit of the issuing bank.

• **Financial institution buyer credit export insurance** can reduce the risks on a direct buyer credit loan or a reimbursement loan made to a foreign buyer through an Eximbank Financial Institution Buyer Credit Insurance Policy (the Buyer Credit Policy). A direct buyer credit loan is a loan extended to a foreign entity by a financial institution for the importation of U.S. manufactured or produced goods. A reimbursement loan is the financial institution's reimbursement of a buyer's payments to the U.S. supplier. In either case, repayment is based upon a buyer's obligation to the financial institution. This policy affords coverage against commercial defaults and political events that could result in nonpayment under the buyer's obligation.

• **Small business credit insurance** provides enhanced protection for short-term credit sales by small companies. The policy provides coverage on the insured percentage of a loss resulting from a buyer default arising from the political risks defined in the policy, including war, revolution, cancellation of an import or export license, currency inconvertibility, or for commercial reasons. Rates are determined by the length of the credit terms and type of buyer with respect to each shipment.

IV.   CONCLUSION

Political risk insurance is an important tool for managing the heightened risks of cross-border investments and export transactions. The availability of this type of insurance is increasing in step with growing demand from the increased cross-border investment and trade flows of recent years. It is reasonable to expect that this growing demand will lead to new entrants into the field and new types of coverage in the coming years as trade flows increase and developing countries rely increasingly on the private sector to finance their infrastructure needs.

V. SOURCES OF ASSISTANCE

A.   Statutes; Treaties

12 U.S.C. §§ 635–635t (Eximbank).

22 U.S.C. §§ 2191–2206b (OPIC).

Convention Establishing The Multilateral Investment Guarantee Agency, *done* October 11, 1985, *entered into force* April 12, 1988, *reprinted in* 24 I.L.M. 1598 (1985); *codified in* Multilateral Investment Guarantee Agency Act, Pub. L. No. 100–202, Section 10(e) (1987), 101 Stat. 1329–34, 22 U.S.C. § 2901c *et seq.*

B.   Books

Thomas L. Brewer, Kenneth David & Linda Y.C. Lim, Investing in Developing Countries: A Guide for Executives, Ch. 10 (1986).

Financing Third World Development: A Survey of Official Project Finance Programs in OECD Countries (Fariborz Ghadar ed. 1987).

International Political Risk Management: New Dimensions (Fariborz Ghadar & Theodore H. Moran eds. 1984).

Managing International Political Risk: Strategies and Techniques (Fariborz Ghadar, Stephen J. Korbrin & Theodore H. Moran eds. 1983).

Navigating New Markets Abroad: Charting A Course for the International Business Person (David M. Raddock ed. 1993).

Robert B. Shanks, *Federal Government International Financing and Insurance Programs, in* Counseling Emerging Companies in Going International (Alan S. Gutterman ed. 1994).

Robert B. Shanks, *Investment Protection For Projects In Eastern Europe and the Soviet Union: OPIC, MIGA And Bilateral Investment Treaties, in* Legal Aspects of Trade and Investment in the Soviet Union and Eastern Europe 1990 (Eugene Theroux ed. 1990).

C.   Periodicals

Robert B. Shanks, *Traders Eye Policy Shift on China,* The National Law Journal, June 13, 1994, at C1.

D.   *Institutional Contacts*

World Bank

World Bank–MIGA	Chief Guarantee Officer
1868 H St., N.W.	World Bank–MIGA
Washington, D.C. 20006	1868 H St., N.W.
202/473-5245	Washington, D.C. 20006
Policy and Legal Issues	202/473-6163
	Guarantee Issues

OPIC

Information Officer	Auto Info Line
OPIC	202/336-8799
1100 New York Ave., N.W.	Auto Fax line
Washington, D.C. 20527	202/336-8700
	Request a fax of a specific document

Eximbank
Export–Import Bank of the U.S.
811 Vermont Ave., N.W.
Washington, D.C. 20571
202/565-3946
Fax: 202/565-3380

Principal Official Agencies
Insuring Export and Investment Exposures[7]

Country	Agency	Export coverage?	Investment coverage?
Argentina	Compania Argentina de Seguros de Crédito a la Exportacion S.A. (CASC)	Yes	No
Australia	Export Finance and Insurance Corproation (EFIC)	Yes	Yes
Austria	Oesterreichische Kontroll-bank Aktiengesellschaft (OEKB)	Yes	Yes
Belgium	Office National du Ducroire (OND)	Yes	Yes
Canada	Export Development Corporation (EDC)	Yes	Yes
Cyprus Republic	Export Credit Insurance Service, Ministry of Commerce and Industry (ECIS)	Yes	No
Denmark	Eksportkreditadet (EKR)	Yes	No
Finland	Valtiontakuukeskus (FGB)	Yes	Yes
France	Compagnie Française d' Assurance pour le Commerce Extérieur (COFACE)	Yes	Yes
France	Société Française d'Assurance Crédit (SFAC)	Yes	No
Germany	Hermes Kreditversicherungs-Aktiengesellschaft (HERMES)	Yes	No
Germany	Treuarbeit Aktiengesellschaft (TREUARBEIT)	No	Yes
Hong Kong	Hong Kong Export Credit Insurance Corporation (HKEC)	Yes	No
India	Export Credit Guarantee Corporation of India Limited (ECGC)	Yes	Yes
Indonesia	PT. Asuransi Ekspor Indonesia (PT. ASEI)	Yes	No

Country	Agency	Export coverage?	Investment coverage?
Israel	The Israel Foreign Trade Risks Insurance Corporation Ltd. (IFTRIC)	Yes	Yes
Italy	Sezione Speciale per l'Assicurazione del Credito all 'Esportazione (SACE)	Yes	Yes
Italy	Societá Italiana Assicurazione Crediti S.p.A. (SIAC)	Yes	No
Jamaica	National Export–Import Bank of Jamaica Limited (EXIMJ)	Yes	No
Japan	Export–Import Insurance Division International Trade Administration Bureau, Ministry of International Trade & Industry (IED/MITI)	Yes	Yes
Korea	The Export–Import Bank of Korea (EIBK)	Yes	Yes
Malaysia	Malaysian Export Credit Insurance Berhad (MECIB)	Yes	No
Mexico	Banco Nacional de Comercio Exterior S.N.C. (BANCOMEXT)	Yes	No
Netherlands	Nederlandsche Credietverzekering Maatschappij N.V. (NCM)	Yes	Yes
New Zealand	Export Guarantee Office (EXGO)	Yes	Yes
Norway	Garanti–Instituttet for Eksportkreditt (GIEK)	Yes	Yes
Portugal	Companhia de Seguro de Créditos, S.A. (COSEC)	Yes	Yes
Singapore	ECICS Ltd. (ECICS)	Yes	No
South Africa	Credit Guarantee Insurance Corporation of Africa Limited (CGIC)	Yes	Yes
Spain	Compañia Española de Seguros de Crédito a la Exportación S.A. (CESCE)	Yes	No
Spain	Compañia Española de Seguros de Crédito y Caución S.A. (CESCE)	Yes	No

Country	Agency	Export coverage?	Investment coverage?
Sri Lanka	Sri Lanka Export Credit Insurance Corporation (SLECIC)	Yes	No
Sweden	Exportkreditnämnden (EKN)	Yes	Yes
Switzerland	Geschäftsstelle für die Exportrisikogarantie (ERG)	Yes	Yes
Switzerland	The Federal Insurance Company Limited (FEDERAL)	Yes	No
Turkey	Export Credit Bank of Turkey (TURK EXIMBANK)	Yes	No
UK	Export Credits Guarantee Department (ECGD)	Yes	Yes
UK	Trade Indemnity plc (TI)	Yes	No
USA	Export–Import Bank of the United States (EXIMBANK)	Yes	No
USA	Overseas Private Investment Corporation (OPIC)	No	Yes
Zimbabwe	Zimbabwe Credit Insurance Corporation Limited (ZCIC)	Yes	No
Multilateral	Multilateral Investment Guarantee Agency (MIGA)	No	Yes

ENDNOTES

[1]   For example, few experts predicted the fall of the Shah in Iran, the Gulf War in response to Iraq's invasion of Kuwait, or the rapid disintegration of the former Eastern Bloc. Similarly, there was little warning presaging Mexico's 1995 financial crisis.

[2]   The subject of loans and loan guarantees available from international financial institutions, such as the World Bank, the International Finance Corporation, the various regional development banks, the U.S. Overseas Private Investment Corporation ("OPIC") and export credit agencies, like the Export–Import Bank of the United States is closely related to the subject of political risk insurance and is discussed in Chapter 3, *International Financing.*

[3]   OPIC does not insure against damage caused by acts undertaken primarily to achieve labor or student objectives. In contrast, the World Bank's Multilateral

Investment Guarantee Agency (MIGA) does not exclude labor or student–motivated violence from its standard definition of political violence coverage.

4   The table preceding these endnotes lists the principal official agencies insuring against export and import exposures, as well as political risk insurance for invest-ments.

5   OPIC's finance program is described elsewhere in this treatise.

6   As this chapter was being written, MIGA was planning a capital increase that could have the effect of raising its per project and per country limits.

7   This table is reprinted with the permission of the author from Felton McLellan Johnston, *Political Risk Insurance: Conservative if Costly, a Back-up Option After Identifying Serious Vulnerabilities*, in NAVIGATING NEW MARKETS ABROAD: CHARTING A COURSE FOR THE INTERNATIONAL BUSINESS PERSON (David M. Raddock ed. 1993).

CHAPTER 5

INTERNATIONAL PAYMENT METHODS

Nathan E. Fagre and William L. Menard

I.   INTRODUCTION

International transactions, from the simple sale of goods and services across national borders to the construction of large industrial projects, present the parties with special or heightened risks of non–payment or non–performance compared to those arising in domestic transactions. In international sales contracts, goods are often transported over great distances. When the seller has delivered the goods but the buyer fails to pay, the seller may be forced to resell his goods at the foreign location at a loss rather than reship them. Because the governing law is often uncertain, and because national legal systems and jurisdictions overlap and are often inconsistent, redress for breach of contract may be difficult to obtain. Further, in international transactions buyers and sellers frequently are strangers, with no established course of dealing with one another and with little established custom upon which to rely. The primary purpose of the payment systems and the performance guarantees described in this chapter is to reduce these uncertainties and risks.

The risks of non–payment in international transactions have spawned a host of mechanisms for securing payment, often through the use of third–party credits or guarantees. The scope and complexity of many international transactions has similarly given rise to the creation of a variety of devices to secure performance by the parties of their contractual obligations. Payment and performance guarantees can be given by private institutions, such as banks, or by government or quasi–governmental organizations, such as the Overseas Private Investment Corporation ("OPIC"). (*See* Chapter 4, *Political Risk Insurance*.) The payment and guarantee mechanisms described in this chapter are often used in domestic transactions but are particularly important in the international context.

II.   CONTRACTUAL PAYMENT ISSUES

Most international contracts must address at least three payment issues: the price terms themselves; the time of payment; and the currency of payment. The price terms and timing issues are similar to those in domestic transactions but have unique aspects. Currency issues generally arise only in international contracts.

A. Price Terms

The price terms for international sales of goods typically include specifications for where the goods are to be delivered, whether shipping and insurance charges are included in the price, and which party is responsible for obtaining export and import clearances. A series of abbreviations known as "INCOTERMS" (INternational COmmercial TERMS), developed by the International Chamber of Commerce ("ICC"), permit these issues to be addressed succinctly and efficiently. Many of the terms closely resemble their UCC counterparts (FOB, CIF, and so forth), but the potential complexities of dealing with export and import procedures add important nuances to these common terms and have led to the introduction of additional terms not contemplated by the UCC. The ICC publishes a very useful guide to INCOTERMS that sets out, both in text and graphically, the precise connotations of each term.[1]

B. Time of Payment

Any delay in payment for goods involves some element of credit and accompanying liquidity problems for the parties. These issues are significantly magnified in international transactions where the goods may be in transit for relatively long periods of time. The seller may not be willing or able to defer payment until the buyer has received the goods. Likewise, the buyer may not wish to pay for the goods long before he will obtain them and be able to sell them himself. Time of payment is, therefore, even more important in international sales contracts than in domestic transactions.

The parties can adjust these issues through the sales prices themselves or by providing for advance or installment payments. In many instances, however, neither party is able or willing to undertake the liquidity risk. Government instrumentalities therefore often step in to provide the necessary liquidity. In the United States, for example, the Export–Import Bank, generally by guaranteeing credits through private banks, will finance many export transactions.

C. Currency Risk

In an international transaction, either or both of the parties will be paying or receiving payment in a foreign currency. Exchange rate fluctuation or inconvertibility may present significant risks.

Rate fluctuation is generally protected against either by some form of contractual indexing or by hedging. In an indexing arrangement, the parties will peg the price to one or more currencies (or to Special Drawing Rights, a basket of currencies) or perhaps require payment in different currencies (*e.g.*, half in the seller's national currency and half in the buyer's currency). More typical in a simple sale of goods transaction, the buyer will hedge by taking a forward transaction in the futures currencies market in the currency in which the payment is to be made. For more complicated or recurring transactions, the seller may take out a loan in the currency in which he expects to be paid. (*See* Chapter 3, *International Financing.*)

Inconvertibility or exchange rate controls present different problems. The risk of future inconvertibility can be allocated in the contract or insured against. (*See id.;* and Chapter 4, *Political Risk Insurance.*) Current exchange controls may preclude a sale altogether. For certain countries, however, the United States Agency for International Development ("USAID") requires, in order to administer governmental development assistance programs, substantial quantities of local currencies that are not generally convertible. USAID will assist U.S. exporters in making sales in these countries by accepting payment from the local buyer in his currency and paying the U.S. exporter in dollars from funds appropriated for the assistance program. USAID's Commodity Import Programs are reported in the *Commerce Business Daily* and the *A.I.D. Procurement Information Bulletin.*

III. PAYMENT METHODS

A. *Direct Payments*

In domestic transactions the parties generally use direct payment methods. These include cash, checks, wire transfers, promissory notes, and negotiable bills of lading. These payment methods often prove to be too risky or inconvenient in the international context. Cash is risky to transport, and checks may be dishonored upon presentment, leaving the seller with little recourse after the goods have been delivered. Payment in advance by the buyer gives security to the seller but subjects the buyer to the risk that the goods will not be shipped.

B. *Negotiable Instruments*

The two principal forms of negotiable instruments used in international trade are the bill of exchange and the promissory note. In the former, the seller presents the bill of exchange (or "draft") to the buyer, together with the shipping documents. The bill directs payment to the seller or a third party at whatever time payment is due under the contract. The buyer accepts the bill by signing it and returning it to the seller. The seller may then be able to take the bill to his bank and negotiate it to the bank for a discounted payment that takes into account the period of time before the buyer becomes obligated to pay and the risk of non–payment. The promissory note is generally a simple written promise to pay on a specified date. It, too, is negotiable at a discount.

When the seller is confident of the buyer's creditworthiness, these instruments are widely used in international trade. Because that confidence is often lacking in international transactions, however, it is common to require some form of bank guarantee as well. In some legal systems, for example, the buyer's bank may guarantee payment by placing an "aval" directly on the instrument. This still leaves a negotiating bank with the risk that the foreign bank will not pay. The seller, moreover, will be an endorser of the instrument and hence liable if this occurs.

C.   *Documentary Collections*

In order to give greater security to the seller in international transactions, the parties frequently turn to a device known as *payment on collection* or *documentary collection*. Under this approach, the seller presents to his bank all the documents required for the buyer to take possession of the goods, including all transport documents (*e.g.*, bills of lading), insurance documents, and commercial invoices, and instructs the bank not to deliver the documents to the buyer until the buyer pays the draft (a *sight draft*) or accepts it for payment at a specified later date (a *time draft*). In the latter case, the banks have no independent payment obligation to the seller, who remains at risk for the non–payment of the draft.

D.   *Letters of Credit*

The *documentary letter of credit* is the most important and perhaps the most widely used payment instrument in international trade transactions. By interposing an independent payment obligation by a bank between the buyer and the seller, the letter of credit significantly reduces the risk to each.

1.   **Parties to the Letter of Credit**

Letters of credit have at least three parties, and in many cases there are additional parties. The *account party* is typically the buyer in the transaction and applies to a bank to issue the letter of credit on its behalf. The *issuer* or *issuing bank* is the bank that issues the letter of credit on the buyer's behalf. The *beneficiary*, usually the seller in the transaction, is the party entitled to receive payment under the letter of credit.

In addition to these parties, a letter of credit transaction may include an *advising bank*, usually located in the same country as the beneficiary. The advising bank would typically have a correspondent banking relationship with the issuing bank and would notify the credit to the beneficiary. A *nominated* or *paying bank* is a bank, also typically located in the beneficiary's country, authorized in the letter of credit to make payments under the credit against presentation of documents by the beneficiary. The paying bank may be, but is not always, the advising bank. Where the paying bank undertakes an independent payment obligation, it is deemed to be a *confirming bank*. The beneficiary has a right of action to enforce payment against a confirming bank but not against an advising or nominated bank.

Key to the functioning of these relationships is the "independence principle." Each of the several contractual relationships among these parties is independent of the others. There is an underlying contract for the sale of goods between the buyer (the account party to the credit) and the seller (the beneficiary of the credit); the account party has a contractual relationship with the issuing bank; and the issuing bank has a contractual relationship with the beneficiary – and each of these contractual relationships is legally independent of the others. If a confirming bank is involved, the beneficiary also has an independent contractual relationship with that bank (it has rights against the issuing bank as well if the confirming bank fails to pay); and a fourth independent contractual relationship is created between the issuing and confirming banks.

2. How the Letter of Credit Works

A letter of credit is initiated upon an application by the account party to the issuing bank. The application typically will ask for the name and address of the beneficiary, the amount and method of payment, a description of the goods and the method of shipment, and, most important, the documents to be presented by the beneficiary in order for the credit to be paid. For the transnational shipment of goods, the presentment documents typically include the seller's draft or demand for payment, a bill of lading, insurance documents, a certificate of origin, and the like, often in multiple copies. Typically, the issuing bank requires the account party to collateralize the payment amount of the credit.

Upon acceptance of the application, the issuing bank sends the letter of credit to the advising or confirming bank, and the latter delivers the letter of credit to the beneficiary. If a confirming bank is involved, there will typically be a separate document restating the terms of credit and indicating the confirming bank's direct obligation to pay the beneficiary.

Upon shipment of the goods, the beneficiary, *i.e.*, the seller of the goods, presents to the designated paying bank all documents called for in the letter of credit. Because the letter of credit is an obligation of the issuing (or confirming) bank totally separate from and independent of the underlying contract for the sale of goods, the obligation of the issuing (or confirming) bank to pay the credit is based upon the proper presentation of specified documents. The documents must conform strictly to the terms of the credit. Even minor discrepancies may permit, or require, dishonor of the request for payment, although courts differ as to how strict the conformity must be. In practice, banks when confronted by non-conforming documents, especially when the non-conformities are minor, will often ask the account party if it is prepared to accept the discrepancies.

If a confirming bank is involved, it will pay the beneficiary against presentation of conforming documents, and then present the documents to the issuing bank for reimbursement. The confirming bank assumes the risk that it will not be reimbursed if it has honored non-conforming documents or if, for some reason, the issuing bank is unable to pay.

The issuing bank then presents the documents to the account party for reimbursement. Again, if the documents are non-conforming, the account party will not be obligated to reimburse the bank. In many, but not all, instances the documents will include original documents of title, *e.g.*, a bill of lading, which the account party must then present to the shipper to obtain the goods and complete the transaction. The account party's right to refuse reimbursement for non-conforming documents arises from the difficulties it may have in obtaining the goods if the documentation is not proper.

The "independence principle" prohibits the banks involved in these transactions from looking to whether the underlying sales contract has been satisfactorily performed when they are reviewing the documents. As a result, there may be instances where the seller has delivered non-conforming goods but receives payment under the letter of credit because the documents presented to the paying bank conform to the requirements of the letter of credit. In such a case, the buyer's only recourse is ordinarily to sue the seller for breach of contract.[2] Buyers are, therefore, generally careful in stipulating what documents will permit payment and, where circumstances permit, they often require that the documents include pre-shipment certification of quality and quantity of the goods by an independent party.

There are variations of these procedures. In some instances, the issuing or confirming bank only accepts the documents for payment at a later date. The acceptance itself, however, may permit the beneficiary to be paid by discounting the bank's acceptance.

Timing is often very important. Because the documents typically include title to goods in transit, they must pass through the system quickly if the buyer is to obtain the goods promptly. The paying bank has only a few days in which to honor or dishonor the documents.[3] Failure to act will constitute dishonor, and failure to specify grounds for dishonor within the required period will constitute waiver of those grounds.

3. Fees and Costs

Separate fees are generally charged for issuing, advising, confirming, amending, and paying the credit, as well as negotiating and accepting drafts. Parties to a letter of credit should be aware of the fees associated with each activity as well as which party is responsible for each of these fees.

4. Sources of Law

Although letters of credit are often used in international transactions, they are largely governed by national laws. In the United States, letters of credit are governed by provisions of Article 5 of the Uniform Commercial Code ("UCC"), which has been adopted in substance by all fifty states.

The Uniform Customs and Practice for Documentary Credits ("UCP"), developed by the International Chamber of Commerce, provides a set of rules for banks issuing international letters of credit. First promulgated in 1933 by the ICC, the current 1993 revision of the UCP is referred to as the "UCP 500." The UCP is a voluntary code of international practice widely applied by banks around the world through agreement of the parties to different national instruments. Virtually every international letter of credit will stipulate that the UCP applies. The Banking Committee of the ICC periodically renders advisory opinions interpreting the UCP and collects and publishes these opinions. Although not binding, the Banking Committee's opinions are generally regarded as authoritative.

The provisions of the UCC and the UCP are generally consistent with one another, and the courts try hard to find such consistency. When that is not possible, they generally treat the incorporation of the UCP in a letter of credit as a contractual term, subject to such requirements of the UCC as they deem mandatory.

5.   Variations on the Letter of Credit

There are a number of variations on the standard documentary credit. These include:

a.   Standby Letter of Credit

A *standby letter of credit* is similar in form to a documentary credit, but payment is made only in the event that one of the parties fails to perform its obligations under the contract. Instead of producing the typical shipping documents called for in a documentary letter of credit, under a standby letter of credit the beneficiary provides documents evidencing the occurrence or non-occurrence of an event specified in the instrument. Standby credits, in effect, function as performance guarantees and are used by U.S. banks because they are prohibited by law from issuing the bank guarantees that are used elsewhere in the world. Standby credits are frequently required for large construction contracts in the Middle East. Standby credits are now subject to the UCP 500.

b.   Transferable Letter of Credit

A *transferable letter of credit* is a form of documentary credit that the beneficiary may transfer, in whole or in part, to one or more third parties. This form of letter of credit is often used by traders with multiple suppliers or creditors because it allows the trader to utilize the credit to secure his payment obligations to his suppliers or creditors.

c.   Back-to-Back Letter of Credit

A *back-to-back letter of credit* is a letter of credit issued upon the security of an existing letter of credit. The back-to-back letter of credit is typically used by a middleman buyer who intends to resell the goods immediately. On the security of his own customer's letter of credit, the middleman buyer can have a letter of credit issued for the benefit of the seller. Upon receipt of the shipping documents under the primary credit, the middleman buyer's bank will pay the seller and turn around and present the documents for payment to the ultimate buyer's bank under the second credit. The middleman will not generally take possession of the documents. His bank will pay him the difference between what it receives from the ultimate buyer and what it has to pay to the seller. By using two instruments, the middleman can also effectively prevent his suppliers and customers from learning the prices at which he is buying and selling the goods.

d.   Revocable Letter of Credit

Most letters of credit are irrevocable, meaning that they cannot be altered or amended without the consent of all parties. A *revocable letter of credit* may be altered, amended, or canceled unilaterally by the issuing bank, and as a result is not commonly used.

E.   *Countertrade*

A lack of convertible currency has caused a number of countries in recent years to eschew cash payments altogether and revert to variations on barter – the exchange of goods for goods. These *"countertrade"* arrangements have assumed several, often very sophisticated, forms. Pure barter is the direct exchange of goods. *"Counterpurchase"* involves separate, parallel contracts, each paid for in currency, whereby the seller under one contract engages in the second contract to buy goods from the buyer's country. In some instances, the "buyback" is of other goods produced by the buyer itself; in others, the counterdeliveries are unrelated to the initial purchase. Anticipatory purchases by a seller from his buyer's country to build up countertrade "credits" are sometimes referred to as *"junktims."* (*See* Chapter 2, *International Commercial Transactions.*)

Related forms of non–cash payments may be involved in construction or capital investment agreements. A foreign supplier of, for example, a factory may agree to be paid in the output of the factory. Or, the supplier may agree to use a certain percentage of local supplies or labor in either the initial construction or in subsequent manufacturing.

All of these agreements tend to involve complex legal relationships. Generally, there are at least two and sometimes several inter–related contracts, and the implications of failure to perform one contract on continued performance of the other(s) must be carefully thought through. Often, too, important governmental interests will be present, and the parties must deal with some degree of governmental regulation.[4]

F.   *Factoring and Forfaiting*

To solve their liquidity problems, and sometimes to shift the risk as well, exporters often discount their receivables from foreign buyers to an intermediary bank or other financing institution. In a *"forfaiting"* arrangement, the *"forfaiteur"* – *i.e.*, the bank – agrees to have no recourse against the exporter so long as the exporter performs under the contract by delivering conforming goods. The *forfaiteur* ordinarily will not simply accept the risk of the buyer's payment, but will require a bank aval or guarantee from the buyer's country.

In a factoring arrangement, the bank typically buys the exporter's receivables, again at a discount, as they arise. There are numerous variations on this basic arrangement, including both recourse and non–recourse terms.[5]

IV.   SOURCES OF ASSISTANCE

A.   *U.S. Statutes*

Article 2 of the UCC sets forth the general principles of sales law applicable in the United States and has been adopted by every state except Louisiana. Article 3 of the UCC sets forth the principles of law applicable to negotiable instruments in the United States and has been adopted by all fifty states. Article 5 of the UCC sets forth the principles of all applicable to U.S. letters of credit and has been adopted by all fifty states.

B.   *Foreign Statutes and Laws*

Bills of Exchange Act, 1882, ch. 61 (United Kingdom).

C.   *Treaties*

Uniform Laws on Bills of Exchange and Promissory Notes, June 7, 1930, 143 L.N.T.S. 257. The Uniform Laws have been adopted by more than twenty countries, primarily in Europe, and provide uniform rules for bills of exchange. Many common law countries, including the United Kingdom, have not accepted the convention and use their own rules for bills of exchange.

United Nations Convention on Contracts for the International Sale of Goods, April 11, 1980, S. Treaty Doc. No. 9, 98th Cong., 2d Sess., *reprinted in* 15 U.S.C.A. app. at 53 (West Supp. 1995).

D.   *Other Official Documentation*

INTERNATIONAL CHAMBER OF COMMERCE, UNIFORM CUSTOMS AND PRACTICE FOR DOCUMENTARY CREDITS (ICC Pub. No. 500, 1993).

E.   *Secondary Sources*

1.   **Books**

AMERICAN BAR ASSOCIATION, LETTERS OF CREDIT AND FINANCIAL INSTITUTIONS (1989).

NEGOTIATING AND STRUCTURING INTERNATIONAL COMMERCIAL TRANSACTIONS (S. Battram & D. Goldsweig eds. 1991).

DEL BUSTO, ICC GUIDE TO DOCUMENTARY CREDIT OPERATIONS FOR THE UCP 500 (ICC Pub. No. 416A, 1986).

JOHN F. DOLAN, THE LAW OF LETTERS OF CREDIT (2d ed. 1991; Cumulative Supp. 1995).

W. FOX, INTERNATIONAL COMMERCIAL AGREEMENTS (1988).

M. GRUSON, INTERNATIONAL COMMERCIAL AGREEMENTS (PLI Com. L. & Practice Course Handbook Series No. 592, 1991).

H. HARFIELD, BANK CREDITS AND ACCEPTANCES (5th ed. 1974).

HORN & WYMEERSCH, BANK–GUARANTEES, STANDBY LETTERS OF CREDIT AND PERFORMANCE BONDS IN INTERNATIONAL TRADE (1990).

INTERNATIONAL CHAMBER OF COMMERCE, STANDARD DOCUMENTARY CREDIT FORMS FOR THE UCP 500 (ICC Pub. No. 516, 1993).

KURKELA, LETTERS OF CREDIT UNDER INTERNATIONAL TRADE LAW (1985).

A. LOWENFIELD, INTERNATIONAL PRIVATE TRADE (1981).

MCCULLOUGH, LETTERS OF CREDIT (1993).

ROWE, LETTERS OF CREDIT (1985).

C. SCHMITTHOF, EXPORT TRADE; THE LAW AND PRACTICE OF INTERNATIONAL TRADE (5th ed. 1986).

WOOD, LAW AND PRACTICE OF INTERNATIONAL FINANCE (1980).

2. Periodicals

Butterworth's Journal of International Banking and Finance.

International Contract Advisor.

International Trade Finance.

Journal of International Banking Law.

Letter of Credit Update.

Letters of Credit Report.

3. Specific Articles

Bergsten, *A New Regime for International Independent Guarantees and Standby Letters of Credit: The UNCITRAL Draft Convention on Guaranty Letters*, 27 INT'L LAW. 589 (1993).

Brill & Bjorkman, *Federal Court Jurisdiction over International Banking Transactions*, 110 BANKING L.J. 125 (1993).

Chaterjee, *Persisting Controversy as to "Reasonable Time" Under the Documentary Credit Mechanism: An Overview of the 1993 UCP for Documentary Credits*, 6 J. INT'L BANKING L. 235 (1994).

Davenport & Smith, *The Governing Law of Letters of Credit Transactions*, BUTTERWORTH'S J. INT'L BANKING & FIN. L. 3 (Jan. 1994).

Dolan & van Huizen, *International Rules for Letters of Credit: A Final Report*, BANKING & FIN. L. REV. 173 (1994).

Dolan, *Weakening the Letter of Credit Product: The New Uniform Customs and Practice for Documentary Credits*, 14 J. INT'L L. BUS. 184 (1994).

Gavigan, Note, *Wysko Investment Company v. Great American Bank: A New Attack on the Usefulness of Letters of Credit*, 14 J. INT'L L. BUS. 184 (1993).

Leacock, *Fraud in the International Transaction: Enjoining Payments of Letters of Credit in International Transactions*, 17 VAND. J. TRANS. L. (1984).

Lipton, *Uniform Regulation of Standby Letters of Credit and Other Private Demand Security Instruments*, 10 J. INT'L BANKING L. 402 (1993).

Mattout, *Letters of Indemnity in Shipping Transactions: Legal Aspects*, 8 J. INT'L BANKING L. 320 (1991).

McGivern, *International Letters of Credit and Their Use in Agricultural Export Situations*, 37 ARK. L. REV. (1983).

Nasburg, *Loan Documentation: Basic But Crucial*, 36 BUS. LAW. 884 (1981).

Rowe, *Automating International Trade Payments —Legal and Regulatory Issues*, 4 J. INT'L BUS. L. 234 (1987).

Sandler, *The Future of Small Business Export Financing: Improving the Small Business Administration's Export Revolving Line of Credit*, 27 G.W.J. INT'L L. & ECON. 107 (1993).

Stack, *The Conflicts of Law in International Letters of Credit*, 24 VA. J. INT'L L. 171 (1983).

F.   *On-Line Services*

LEXIS, ITRADE Library.

G.   *Institutional Assistance*

The Export–Import Bank of the United States, 811 Vermont Avenue, N.W., Washington, D.C. 20751, (202) 556–3946.

International Chamber of Commerce, 156 Fifth Avenue, New York, NY 10010, (212) 206–1150.

Overseas Private Investment Corporation, 1100 New York Avenue, N.W., Twelfth Floor, Washington, D.C. 20527, (202) 336–8799.

United Nations, Office of Legal Affairs, Treaty Section, New York, NY 10017, (212) 963–3918.

United States Agency for International Development. Commodity Import Programs reported in *Commerce Business Daily* and *A.I.D. Procurement Information Bulletin*. Further information may be obtained at (703) 875–1058.

The World Bank Group, 1818 H Street, N.W., Washington, D.C. 20433, (202) 623–7000.

ENDNOTES

1   *See* INTERNATIONAL CHAMBER OF COMMERCE, INCOTERMS 1990 (Pub. No. 460, 1990).

2   If the documents are fraudulent, however, a court may enjoin payment. This

fraud exception was first adopted by New York courts. *Sztejn v. J. Henry Schroeder Banking Corp.*, 177 Misc. 719, 31 N.Y.S.2d 631 (Sup. Ct. 1941). Its scope remains controversial, but it has been adopted in the UCC (§ 5-114(2)(b)).

3   Under the UCC, the paying bank usually has three banking days in which to honor the documents. UCC § 5-112(1)(a). The exact number of days may, however, vary from state to state. Under the ICC's Uniform Customs and Practices ("UCP"), discussed in Section III.D., the bank has a "reasonable time," not to exceed seven business days, to honor the documents. UCP 13(b).

4   *See*, International Law Institute, DOING COUNTERTRADE: A PRACTICAL GUIDE (2d ed. 1994); Andres B. Santamaria, "Countertrade," in N. HORN (ed.), THE LAW OF INTERNATIONAL TRADE FINANCE 39 (1989).

5   *See*, Horst-Ulrich Jaeger, "Export Factoring and Forfaiting," in N. HORN (ed), THE LAW OF INTERNATIONAL TRADE FINANCE 277 (1989).

CHAPTER 6

SECURED TRANSACTIONS

Gerold W. Libby

Obtaining a security interest in collateral of a borrower, customer or other debtor will often be an important part of an international transaction in which financing is extended, whether a loan, a sales transaction where a seller is financing the transaction, or another financing transaction. This chapter introduces some general legal issues relevant to security interests and discusses obtaining security interests in real and personal property under foreign law. Along the way it addresses governing law and conflict of law issues.

I.   INTRODUCTION

Security interests constitute only one type of security that a lender, manufacturer/seller or other party extending financing in an international transaction will wish to consider. In undertaking such a transaction, consideration must be given also to the availability of government or private guarantees, including parent company guarantees, and the availability, structuring and proper drafting of letters of credit, to name two of the most common forms of security used in international financing transactions. (*See* Chapter 3, *International Financing*, Chapter 4, *Political Risk Insurance*, and Chapter 5, *International Payment Methods.*)

In addition, other important bodies of law must be considered to understand fully the implications of a particular security interest. Issues of title to collateral must be considered if the extent of the benefits of the security interest are to be understood. And the interplay between the legal framework for security interests and applicable bankruptcy and other creditors' rights law may be essential to a full understanding of the legal effect of a security interest. (*See* Chapter 20, *Creditors' Rights and Bankruptcy.*)

With the exception of certain specific categories of collateral, notably aircraft and ships, creating a security interest in the context of an international financing transaction will almost always require compliance with the local law of one or more jurisdictions. Other than in those limited, exceptional cases, there is no body of international law governing the creation of security interests or applicable to a determination of the rights associated with them.

Many jurisdictions provide for the creation of mortgages or other liens against real property which will generally be familiar to United States lawyers. However, very few jurisdictions have systems for the creation of security interests in other property, *i.e.*, tangible and intangible personal property, which offer the detail and sophistication provided by Article 9 of the Uniform Commercial Code ("UCC"),[1] the primary legal framework in all 50 states applicable to creation of security interests in personal property. Moreover, numerous pitfalls can be found in the security interest laws of jurisdictions around the world. Thus, a lawyer involved in this area will often encounter the twin devils of legal principles that are unfamiliar and perhaps not well developed, but which may require precise technical compliance if a valid security interest is to be created.

Although the personal property security interest law in most foreign jurisdictions differs markedly from Article 9 of the UCC, a lawyer who becomes involved in foreign security interest law will benefit greatly from having at least a general grounding in Article 9. Such Article 9 issues as the proper description of collateral subject to a security interest, the distinction between creation and perfection of a security interest, the distinction between the security interest and the underlying debt obligation, and the application of a security interest to after-acquired property, usually have relevance in a security interest obtained under foreign law, and review of Article 9 law would be a useful first step in the analysis. Competent local counsel will also be key. (*See* Chapter 26, *Selecting and Working with Foreign Counsel.*)

II.   SECURITY INTERESTS IN REAL PROPERTY

Most foreign jurisdictions, and all Western European countries, provide a legal mechanism for creation of a security interest in real property owned by a debtor which grants the secured party the right to priority repayment of indebtedness from the auction sale of the property. Just as is the case in the United States, it is usually necessary to exercise care in complying precisely with the technical requirements of that law.

In those jurisdictions where foreign ownership of real property either is not permitted or is subject to special restrictions, a foreign financing party will encounter limitations on its ability to acquire a security interest in that property. In Switzerland, for example, foreign ownership of real property is not permitted, and mortgages on such property are as a practical matter unavailable. Communist countries historically did not permit private owner-ship of real property, and in the formerly communist jurisdictions of central and eastern Europe and the Newly Independent States, the law concerning real property mortgages is comparatively new and not well-developed.

The term "mortgage" is used in many countries to refer to a security interest in real property. However, in England and some other common law countries the more common term is the "charge," which refers to a security interest over real and personal property. In those countries the document creating the security interest, in both real and personal property, is the "debenture." The term "deed of trust", familiar in much of the United States, is generally not found abroad.

In some cases real property mortgage law is national, but in others it is local. In the latter situation, there can be gaps within the country. China is an example: Some major cities have a mortgage law, others do not, and a national or uniform provincial mortgage framework does not exist. But whether applicable law is local, provincial or national, it is virtually always the case that as a matter of conflict of laws, the law of the place where the real property is located will govern as to all issues regarding an interest in that property, including, among others, the effect of a mortgage, priority rules, whether a mortgage itself or only the underlying debt may be assigned, and rights of enforcement and redemption.

At the risk of overstating a vital point, care must be exercised in drafting mortgage instruments. For example, in many common law jurisdictions, the power to sell the mortgaged property must be expressly set forth, and various other rights, such as the appointment of a receiver to receive income from mortgaged property, will be lost if not expressly provided for. Careful attention must also be paid to local formalities as to witnesses, seals and the like.

The mortgage law in some countries entails significant notarial fees and related charges. In France, for example, fees and taxes may amount to almost one percent of the secured debt. In Germany, a statutory table imposes significant charges. It is appropriate to note in this regard that in numerous foreign jurisdictions notarial procedures and charges are more important, and much more costly, than is the case in the United States. (For a further discussion of the notary, or *notaire*, in civil-law systems, see Chapter 26, *Selecting and Working with Foreign Counsel*. In some jurisdictions significant delays can be encountered in obtaining requisite notarial review of mortgage documentation.

In most Western jurisdictions it is possible to receive and record or otherwise register a mortgage denominated in U.S. dollars or some other well-recognized currency. However, in other parts of the world only mortgages in local currencies will be recognized, thereby creating a foreign exchange risk in the context of an underlying transaction not denominated in the local currency.

A common technique to be considered in addressing such a problem is a so-called "maintenance of value" provision in the underlying transaction document, which would require the debtor to provide additional collateral in the event of a loss of value of collateral as a result of exchange rate fluctuations. Some jurisdictions, even though they require registered or recorded mortgages to be denominated in local currency, will permit the mortgage to index the local currency value of the collateral to the rate of exchange relative to the currency of the underlying debt obligation.

An array of due diligence issues, beyond the scope of this chapter, should also be considered in determining whether to seek a mortgage on foreign real property in the first place. Most of these issues would fall under the heading of considering the scope of the rights of the creditor if foreclosure becomes necessary. These issues would include: determination of the priority under local law of a mortgage in relation to other preferential creditors, *e.g.*, tax authorities; determination of the extent to which a mortgage on real property will attach to buildings and/or other fixtures, as well as crops, located on the real property; consideration of the procedures to be invoked in the event of foreclosure and of the practical ease of realizing on the mortgaged real property; and the legal effect on a senior mortgage of a junior mortgage on the same real property.

Some jurisdictions offer security interest devices that create security interests in real as well as personal property, although in most cases the registration or other public recordation of security interests will require separate filings in appropriate real property and personal property security interest registries. The most prominent security interest of this type is the "floating charge" under English law[2] and found as well in other common law countries; this is discussed in more detail below. Mexico offers a purchase money security interest, either a *credito refaccionario* or a *credito de habilifaccion o avio*, which can cover both real and personal property, although as a purchase money security interest the loan proceeds must be used to purchase the property that is the subject of the security interest. Finland has a system somewhat akin to the English law floating charge regime, entailing execution by a debtor of debenture notes which may identify specific real and/or personal property as collateral.

III.   SECURITY INTERESTS IN PERSONAL PROPERTY

Security interests in personal property, both tangible and intangible, may be obtained in most countries with a developed legal system and are widely used in both the loan and the acquisition/sale contexts. However, there are numerous important differences in applicable law from one jurisdiction to another. Familiarity with Article 9 of the UCC will afford a beneficial orientation to the subject, but most legal regimes in this area in other countries are quite different from the UCC.

Unlike mortgages and other secured transactions involving real property, international secured transactions involving personal property are more likely to involve multiple jurisdictions, and therefore to raise conflict of law issues. The UCC permits parties broad choice–of–law latitude in general, but contains relatively restrictive rules concerning the law applicable to security interest perfection. Intricate fact situations can give rise to numerous jurisdictions whose law should be considered for security interest purposes, *e.g.*, the place where the debtor is incorporated, the place where the debtor has a place of business, the place where the prospective collateral is located, and, in the case of goods in transit, the destination of the goods. Generally speaking, in the absence of an effective choice of law, courts give greatest weight in determining governing law to the location of personal property. The

Restatement of Conflicts provides that as between the immediate parties, the validity and effect of a security interest in personal property are determined by the law of the state that, with respect to the particular issue, has the most significant relationship to the parties, the property, and the security interest. *Restatement (Second) of Conflict of Laws, §251 (1988).*

Most jurisdictions have separate systems for creation and recordation of security interests in particular types of collateral, notably ships and aircraft. Thus, the usual first step in analyzing security interests in personal property is to determine whether the proposed collateral is covered by such a specialized system. If it is not, recourse must be made to the jurisdiction's general legal framework concerning security interests.

Two somewhat conflicting and noteworthy themes in foreign law have developed over the years in connection with security interests in personal property. One is the "floating charge," mentioned above, which initially developed under English law and is available in a number of other common law jurisdictions. The other is the law of civil law jurisdictions, which have generally moved in hesitating fashion toward the kind of comprehensive, integrated personal property security interest system so familiar under Article 9 of the UCC. This hesitancy may be due to the general rule in civil law jurisdictions giving all creditors equal rights to satisfaction of claims against a debtor's collateral, so that legislative provisions creating and defining special rights for secured creditors are exceptions that usually are strictly construed.

A. *The Floating Charge*

The floating charge is a comprehensive lien under English law which can be used to create a security interest in *all* of the assets of a debtor, including both real and personal property. In addition to England, it is accepted in such common law jurisdictions as New Zealand and Australia.[3]

The floating charge requires execution by a debtor of an instrument identified as a debenture, the contents of which must be prepared with care. The floating charge is actually created by filing, which is analogous to perfection under the UCC. In England, filing is undertaken at Companies House, in London, and must be made within 21 days after execution. Additional registrations must be made for unregistered land, registered land, and patents and trademarks. The floating charge is said to become a "fixed" charge when it "crystallizes," which occurs when the debtor goes into liquidation, or when an event of default occurs and the secured party takes steps to enforce his security, *e.g.*, by the appointment of a receiver. Hence, it is important in drafting the debenture to link crystallization to events of default. Until crystallization, the debtor may deal with the collateral in the ordinary course of business, and it is not necessary for a specific release of inventory to be obtained on each occasion.

Floating charge principles entail some drawbacks from the standpoint of a secured creditor, particularly with respect to the priorities of secured interests. A party holding a floating charge, a "chargee," will be subordinate to claims for liquidation expenses, certain taxes, and certain wages and salaries. Further, the floating charge will rank after executions that are completed before crystallization, which usually leads to providing in transaction documentation that a relevant event, *e.g.*, issuance of a judgment against the debtor, will itself be an act of crystallization. Prior to crystallization, a debtor can deal in or with the collateral and a third party purchaser may acquire title to the collateral from the debtor free and clear of the floating charge even if the purchaser has actual notice of the charge. Hence, the floating charge will apply only to assets to which the debtor has title at the time of crystallization.

Two other important points regarding floating charges should be mentioned. First, they may be used only in connection with debtors that are companies, not individuals or partnerships. And the floating charge is not always enthusiastically recognized by jurisdictions that have not adopted it. This has resulted in a body of case law over conflict issues, and strongly suggests that a party seeking a security interest in assets of an English (or Australian or New Zealand) company that are located in both floating charge and non-floating charge jurisdictions should take steps to obtain and perfect security interests in both those categories of jurisdictions.

B.   *Civil Law Security Interests*

The law has developed quite differently in most civil law jurisdictions. Most major civil law jurisdictions provide for security interests in personal property, but there are significant variations from one jurisdiction to another, particularly as to types of collateral eligible for coverage and as to perfection. It is therefore difficult and dangerous for the practitioner to make assumptions based on experience with some other jurisdiction.

The legal frameworks of most civil law countries in the area of personal property security interests are derived from the pledge, and consist of various eclectic and often incomplete additions to basic pledge law which have been made over the years. For example, the French Civil Code and the French Commercial Code contain elaborate provisions regarding the possessory pledge, where the secured party takes possession of the pledged collateral. The French pledge, or *nantissement*, has been expanded so as to permit a lender effectively to obtain a security interest over a debtor company's business, including goodwill, as well as machinery and equipment.[4] The *nantissement* is created by contract and becomes effective against third parties on filing with the Commercial Registry of the district in which the collateral is located. However, a *nantissement* does not cover inventory, which, in general, may be the subject of a security interest only by means of a possessory pledge. Similarly, in Belgium the *nantissement* is available, but only to a

European Union bank or other financial institution, as to inventory only to the extent of 50 percent of value, and only to the extent funds are actually loaned by the secured party. In Japan, security interests in most types of personal property may be acquired, but except for certain specialized categories of personal property, there is no filing mechanism whereby third parties have constructive notice of such security interests, so that a secured party has recourse only against the proceeds from sale to third parties. Security interests in personal property are available in Spain and will be characterized as mortgages or pledges depending upon the nature of the collateral.

Another theme in some civil law jurisdictions is the frequent use of conditional sales in seller financing transactions. In Germany, for example, security interests of the type provided for by Article 9 of the UCC are unknown. Instead, where a seller extends credit, the seller will retain title to the goods until full payment has been made, in a transaction known as an *Eigentumsvorbehalt*. Because there is no mechanism for public registration of a conditional sale, retention of title without more will afford little protection where goods are resold to a bona fide third-party purchaser. In order to remain secured, a seller will often require the buyer simultaneously to assign proceeds and any other rights resulting from resale. Such "extended retention of title" agreements (*verlängerter Eigentumsvorbehalt*) are generally recognized and enforced by German courts. In the typical case, where the buyer defaults the seller is entitled to retrieve any goods sold under the conditional sales agreement and remaining in the buyer's inventory, to recover any proceeds from the resale, and to recover from the buyer any deficiency. So-called title retention contracts, or *venta con reserva de dominio*, are also widely used in Mexico.

Some civil law jurisdictions use a trust device in connection with credit in a sale transaction. For example, under Mexican law, a trust device known as the *fideicomiso* will permit a vendor to lend funds to a bank, which can in turn lend to a debtor/customer, who in turn provides collateral to the bank. In the event of default, the bank can sell the collateral without invoking a judicial procedure. The trust arrangement operates as a transfer of title to the goods in question, so that the vendor secured by the trust would prevail over creditors of the debtor who would otherwise have a preference. Note that under Mexican law only a bank or credit institution may act as a trustee, so that a vendor could not itself take collateral from the debtor and foreclose without a judicial proceeding. In Germany and the Netherlands as well, security interests in tangible personal property may be granted by a fiduciary transfer of title to a security trustee or collateral agent. In these trust arrangements there may or may not be a public registration or recordation system. Although the trust documents do not automatically create floating liens, after-acquired property can usually be made subject to the trust arrangement by having debtors/customers submit periodic lists of newly-acquired assets. Where public recordation of a trust arrangement does not exist, for purposes of due diligence in the context of an acquisition, new loan or otherwise, its existence must be ascertained directly from the debtor/customer.

C. *Intangible Personal Property*

The personal property security interest laws of many jurisdictions entail different rules for intangible (as opposed to tangible) personal property, with intangible personal property including accounts receivable and other contract rights, trademarks, patents and other intellectual property rights, and stock certificates and other negotiable instruments. The law in some countries, particularly civil law jurisdictions, is derived from the possessory requirements associated with pledges, and requires specific identification of the intangibles in question and notice to a third-party debtor (in the case of receivables and other contract rights). Other jurisdictions provide for registration of security interests in intangibles. The English law floating charge can apply to intangibles and does not require specific identification at the time the charge is given, although notice must be given to third parties of assignment of specific contract rights. Under French law, receivables and other contract rights may generally be pledged only after registration with a local tax office, by notification to debtors. An exception, the *bordereau Dailly*, eliminates those requirements, but it is unclear whether it is available to lenders other than French banks.

Security interests in intellectual property rights may require registration or other filing with a national registry of the rights in question. Security interests in stock certificates and other negotiable instruments will almost always require a possessory pledge, which in some jurisdictions can be accompanied by actual registration with the issuer corporation of the name of the secured party.

The irregularities in the legal frameworks applicable to personal property security interests in many civil law jurisdictions should not be overstated. In most cases the law is clear, and well-developed practices are in place. The point is that in many cases these frameworks are not highly integrated, but instead result from numerous statutory amendments over time. This results in inconsistency from one jurisdiction to another. The point cannot be made too strongly that the practitioner confronting this subject must take each jurisdiction on its own terms and become comfortable with its particular law as well as practice.

IV.   SECURITY INTERESTS IN SHIPS AND AIRCRAFT

Security interests in ships and aircraft are the subject of unique and specialized bodies of law, and are noted here only for purposes of completeness. No lawyer should undertake responsibility in this area without a firm grounding in the applicable law. Unlike the jurisdiction-specific legal frameworks concerning security interests in real and personal property, security interests in ships and aircraft are affected by well-established international law in the form of multilateral conventions directed specifically to that subject.

A. Security Interests in Ships

The 1958 Geneva Convention on the High Seas establishes a general duty of each signatory state to establish a legal framework for the registration of ships of its nationality, and ships are thus registered on a national, as opposed to multinational, basis. Some jurisdictions require a degree of national ownership of a ship that is registered under its flag, whereas other "open register" states, *e.g.*, Panama, Liberia and Honduras, do not.

Proper ship registration is necessary for effective registration of a ship mortgage, which is likewise undertaken on a national basis. Ship mortgage law varies with the jurisdiction and entails a high degree of procedural and formal requirements. The British Merchant Shipping Act of 1894, as amended, remains English law and is the model in numerous – but not all – present and former United Kingdom jurisdictions. Liberian law concerning registration of ship mortgages is derived almost entirely from the United States Ship Mortgage Act of 1920.

Maritime liens, which enable a claimant to assert a lien on a vessel in order to satisfy claims for damages or injury resulting from collision, for example, tend now to be less substantial in amounts than the large sums utilized in the purchase or construction of ships. In addition, insurance is often available against major lien claims. Nonetheless, maritime liens remain significant.

The international law concerning ship mortgages and maritime liens, including relative priorities, includes the 1926 Brussels Convention on Maritime Liens and Mortgages, as well as the subsequent 1967 Brussels Convention. The United States is not a party to either Convention, but amendments to the United States Ship Mortgage Act of 1920 have brought United States law into conformity with the Conventions, which provide for the recognition of a ship mortgage if it complies with the law of the so-called flag state of the vessel in question. Numerous details concerning priorities and other procedural aspects of ship mortgages are left to national law. A host of conflict-of-law issues can arise in connection with ship mortgages and maritime liens. The conflicts analysis usually requires a determination of the proper forum for enforcement of a ship mortgage, a determination of the law to be applied by that forum in analysis of the validity of a ship mortgage and priorities, among others, followed by a determination of the substantive rules of that law.

B. Security Interests in Aircraft

Aircraft mortgage law is derived to a considerable extent from the law concerning ship mortgages, with national frameworks for the creation and registration of aircraft mortgages. Aircraft owned by national airlines can usually be financed on the credit of the borrower. In the case of private ownership, so-called title financing, including equipment trusts, is common.

Aircraft engines and other aircraft parts will often constitute an important part of aircraft collateral, but national legal systems vary in their efficacy in bringing those items within the coverage of aircraft mortgages.

The 1948 Geneva Convention on the International Recognition of Rights in Aircraft establishes a framework for recognition among signatory parties of registered aircraft mortgages. Under the Convention, the validity of an aircraft mortgage is determined by reference to the law of the flag, *i.e.*, the jurisdiction of registration. The Convention applies to contractually created mortgages, as opposed to common law and judicial liens, and establishes the priority of properly registered mortgages over competing claims in countries which are parties to the Convention.

V.   SOURCES OF ASSISTANCE

A.   *Books*

1.   General

DIGEST OF COMMERCIAL LAWS OF THE WORLD series (various dates, Oceana Publications, Inc.) (series of individual country legal reports which include summary coverage of local security interest law).

PHILIP WOOD, LAW AND PRACTICE OF INTERNATIONAL FINANCE (1980) (includes comprehensive treatment of security interests in international financial transactions with emphasis on English law and ship mortgages).

2.   United States Law

SECURED TRANSACTION GUIDE, Commerce Clearing House (1969 –) (five loose-leaf volumes).

JAMES J. WHITE & ROBERT S. SUMMERS, UNIFORM COMMERCIAL CODE (1988).

3.   English Law

J. R. LINGARD, BANK SECURITY DOCUMENTS (1985).

B.   *Articles*

1.   General

A. M. Garro, *The Reform and Harmonization of Personal Property Security Law in Latin America*, 59 REVISTA JURIDICA DE LA UNIVERSIDAD DE PUERTO RICO 1 (1990).

Gerald Shea and Peter Shabecoff, *Guarantees and Security in European M&A*, 14 INT'L FIN. L. REV. 13 (July 1995).

2. Specific Countries

Australia – I. Cameron, *Company Charges and the Australian Law Reform Commission: Scrutinizing the Department of Utter Confusion*, 12 COMPANY & SEC. L. J. 357 (1994).

Australia – C. Sexton, *Security over Intellectual Property in Australia,* 13 EUR. INTELL. PROP. REV. 65 (1991).

Canada – B. MacDougall, *The Debtor's Interest in Personal Property Under the Personal Property Security Act*, 33 ALBERTA L. REV. 80 (1994).

Canada – B. J. Roth, *Article 9 North of the 49th: Its Development in Canada's Personal Property Security Acts*, 27 UCC L. J. 251 (1995).

Canada – J. S. Ziegel, *Secured Transactions in Personal Property and the Federal-Provincial Conflict in Canadian Bankruptcy Law*, 46 S.C.L. REV. 877 (1992).

China – T. P. Chen, L. Qian and M. S. Scromela, *Security Devices for Credit Transactions in China,*24 INT'L LAW. 85 (1990).

China – R. Oechshi, *The Developing Law of Mortgages and Secured Transactions in the People's Republic of China*, 5 CHINA L. REP. 1 (1988).

China – Deborah S. Prutzman and Howard H. Jiang, *Lending to Projects and Enterprises in China,*13 INT'L FIN. L. REV. 35 (1994).

China – M. A. Sobel and D. Zhang, *Foreign Secured Lending in China: Socialism and Property*, 52 LAW & CONTEMP. PROBS. 185 (1989).

Czech Republic – Pavel Holec, James Kiernan and Joseph Jacob, *Secured Lenders Face Uncertainty Under New Czechoslovak Rules*, 11 INT'L FIN. L. REV. 34 (1992).

Finland – Lauri Peltola, *Secured Lending under Finnish Law*, 11 INT'L FIN. L. REV. 36 (1992).

France – Stephen H. Haimo, *A Practical Guide to Secured Transactions in France*, 58 TUL. L. REV. 1163 (1994).

Great Britain – H. N. Bennett and C. J. Davis, *Fixtures, Purchase Money Security Interests and Dispositions of Interests in Land*, 110 LAW Q. R. 448 (1994).

Great Britain – B. Collier, *Conversion of a Fixed Charge to a Floating Charge by Operation of Contract: Is It Possible?* 4 AUSTRALIA J. CORP. L. 488 (1995).

<u>Great Britain</u> – J. Hudson, *The Case Against Secured Lending*, 15 INT'L REV. L. & ECO. 47 (1995).

<u>Israel</u> – J. Weisman, *Floating Charges: Recent Developments Under Israel Law*, 41 CURRENT LEGAL PROBS. 197 (1988).

<u>Japan</u> – M. T. Kawachi, *The New Law of Asset Securitization in Japan*, 17 U. PUGET SOUND L. REV. 587 (1994).

<u>Mexico</u> – David W. Barowsky and Carlos A. Babuard, *Secured Transactions in Mexico*," 28 INT'L LAW. 263 (1994).

<u>Mexico</u> – Robert G. Gilbert & Carlos A. Parra, *The Financing of Commercial International Transactions and the Rights of Secured Parties in Mexico*," 6 INT'L L. PRACT. 9 (1993).

<u>New Zealand</u> – D. Webb, *Secured Transactions in New Zealand: Time For an Overhaul*" 1994 NEW ZEALAND L. J. 233 (1994).

<u>Russia</u> – E. Osakwe, *Law of Banking and Security Transactions: A Biopsy of Post-Soviet Russian Commercial Law*, 14 WHITTIER L. REV. 301 (1993).

<u>Russia</u> – P. G. Woods, student author, *From Feudal to Modern: The Evolution of Real Estate Finance in Russia*, 8 EMORY INT'L L. REV. 749 (1994).

<u>Taiwan</u> – J. K. Winn, *Security Interests Under the Laws of the Republic of China on Taiwan: An Introductory Guide*, 23 TEX. INT'L L. J. 395 (1988).

ENDNOTES

1   UNIFORM COMMERCIAL CODE OFFICIAL TEXT AND COMMENTS (1972).

2   Not to be confused with a "floating lien" under the UCC, which, although applicable to virtually all personal property, does not apply to real property.

3   It was formerly recognized as well under federal Canadian law. However, Canada has abolished its federal legislation in this area, leaving the Canadian provinces and territories free to establish their own personal property security interest frameworks. Most have enacted Personal Property Security Acts derived substantially from Article 9 of the UCC. Quebec is the notable exception, where a civil law regime is employed.

4   As is the case in most civil law jurisdictions, the basic statutory framework concerning personal property security interests under French law is found in the French Civil Code with respect to non-commercial transactions and in the French Commercial Code with respect to commercial transactions.

CHAPTER 7

INTELLECTUAL PROPERTY RIGHTS

David K.Y. Tang and Mary L. Williamson

I.   INTRODUCTION

Issues involving intellectual property rights should be considered during the planning process for every international transaction. Intellectual property is at the heart of some transactions, such as international software development contracts and joint ventures in biotechnology research. In other cases, such as distribution agreements involving trademarked products, confidential customer information, or copyrighted manuals and other end user documentation, intellectual property rights are an important but less obvious factor in a proposed relationship.

A client involved in an international transaction may need to accomplish one or more of the following goals: acquire a foreign party's intellectual property; license its own intellectual property rights to a foreign entity; or jointly develop intellectual property with a foreign concern. A lawyer who is counseling a party to an international transaction should consider the need for intellectual property ownership and license provisions, royalty and other payment terms, termination clauses, and other intellectual property–related clauses in the contracts.

Clients should also be apprised of the need to consider foreign intellectual property laws. A U.S. company that infringes intellectual property rights that are recognized by a foreign jurisdiction – regardless of whether the United States recognizes the same rights – could find itself sued for infringement in that country's courts or have its exports seized by the local customs authorities. U.S. companies should also investigate applicable foreign rules for registering license agreements and gaining approval of royalty arrangements, and should be alert to antitrust and technology transfer policies in foreign jurisdictions that may affect their intended transactions. (*See* Chapter 8, *International Antitrust*; Chapter 13, *Export Controls, Sanctions and Antiboycott Laws.*)

International legal norms for protecting intellectual property rights are likely to become more consistent and stronger as a result of the recent "Agreement on Trade–Related Aspects of Intellectual Property Rights," commonly referred to as the "TRIPs Agreement," which is part of the Uruguay Round agreements that led to formation of the World Trade Organization (the "WTO"). All countries that choose to participate in the WTO (and thereby get the benefits of the Uruguay Round of trade liberalization) must accede to the TRIPs Agreement, although less developed countries may implement the intellectual property protections required by the Agreement over a number of years (generally four years, but less developed countries may take up to a maximum of 11 years to implement certain patent–related measures). The TRIPs Agreement both incorporates and builds on existing multilateral agreements concerning intellectual property, including most prominently the Berne Convention and the Paris Convention, both of which are discussed below.

II.   INTERNATIONAL RECOGNITION OF INTELLECTUAL PROPERTY RIGHTS

Intellectual property rights include patents, trademarks, trade secrets, copyrights, mask work rights (for semiconductor chip designs), and a variety of related or "neighboring" rights such as moral rights and the rights conferred in some jurisdictions by inventor's certificates. These rights are territorial in nature, meaning that an owner or licensee must file or otherwise qualify for and obtain intellectual property protection on a country–by–country basis. For example, a U.S. patent or trademark registration does not confer rights outside the United States (although its owner may benefit from certain procedural protections in obtaining protection overseas). Similarly, while a copyrighted work created in the United States may be recognized and receive national treatment in foreign jurisdictions that are parties to the Berne Convention or certain other conventions, a U.S. copyright itself will not have extraterritorial effect. The principle of territoriality makes it vital to plan ahead in order to protect the value of products that embody U.S. intellectual property rights and that will be involved in international transactions.

III.   SPECIFIC INTELLECTUAL PROPERTY RIGHTS

A.   *Patents*

Under U.S. law, new, useful, and nonobvious inventions embodied in a tangible thing or process may be eligible for patent protection. The owner of a patent has the right to exclude others from making, using, or selling the invention for a limited period of time. Similar criteria define what is patentable subject matter in other jurisdictions, but important differences exist among countries or jurisdictions with respect to the scope of patentable inventions (*e.g.*, whether genetically–altered plants and animals or diagnostic and therapeutic methods are subject to patent protection). Some nations impose compulsory licensing requirements or other technology transfer requirements on patent owners.

The TRIPs Agreement requires that countries accede to the most recent draft of the Paris Convention, which is the primary multilateral convention governing patent protection. WTO members will also be required to implement a patent protection term of 20 years, issue both product and process patents, and limit compulsory licensing laws and policies.

B.   Trademarks

A trademark is any word, name, symbol, design or device, or any combination of these, that identifies the source of goods or services and distinguishes them from the goods or services of others. In general, a mark may not be confusingly similar to the marks of others who provide similar products or services, and it should not be merely descriptive of the goods or services in question. In the United States, trademark rights (and rights in service marks) are established and maintained through the adoption and actual use of a mark in conjunction with the associated good or service. Registration, although beneficial, is not required. In contrast, many foreign jurisdictions have minimal or nonexistent use requirements, so that the first entity to register a mark can own that mark even if it has been used and registered by other parties in other countries. A trademark registration is generally valid for a specified period and is then renewable.

The U.S. has acceded to several trademark treaties under which U.S. trademark owners receive national treatment in member states, but no centralized process exists whereby U.S. trademark registrations can be registered and protected in foreign jurisdictions. Under the Paris Convention (discussed above in connection with patents), an applicant for U.S. trademark registration has six months after filing in the U.S. to file a trademark application in member countries, within which period the filing will be deemed to have occurred as of the date of the U.S. filing. Filings must be done country-by-country. Another treaty, the Madrid Protocol, entered into force on December 1, 1995, and allows residents of member countries to file a single trademark registration application in all member countries. Membership in the Madrid Protocol is limited, however, and prospects for U.S. accession are low.

The TRIPs Agreement requires signatory countries to establish procedural safeguards for obtaining and maintaining rights in both trademarks and service marks. Such safeguards include implementing trademark registration systems that allow examination of applications, publication of marks, and an opportunity for others to oppose the registration of such marks by bringing timely challenges. WTO members must recognize a trademark licensee's use of a mark as qualifying for protection, so that the activities of a U.S. company's foreign manufacturers or distributors may be sufficient to retain protection in jurisdictions that require continuing use of trademarks in order to obtain such protection.

C.   Trade Secrets

Under U.S. laws, a trade secret is valuable and confidential business or technical information that gives its possessor an advantage over competitors. Information that is generally known to the public will not usually qualify for trade secret protection. The key to maintaining a trade secret is keeping it confidential, including by retaining strict control over physical materials (*e.g.,* documents or computer files) that contain or embody the trade secret. A trade secret is theoretically limitless in duration, as long as its secrecy is maintained, but it may be lost through independent creation or derivation by another.

Trade secret law varies among U.S. jurisdictions, and even more so internationally. Generally, in foreign jurisdictions that recognize trade secrets, the law protects against trade secret misappropriation, which refers to obtaining the trade secret by improper means such as theft, industrial espionage, bribery, or breach of a confidential relationship or other legal obligation. In some countries, a trade secret must be used or disclosed to the owner's detriment before the owner can bring any protective legal action. Some countries protect only tangible information as trade secrets, so that oral disclosures and intangible know-how that is exchanged as part of a transaction or joint venture do not qualify for trade secret protection.

Apart from limited provisions in the North American Free Trade Agreement ("NAFTA"), the TRIPs Agreement is the first international convention to address trade secret protection. It defines a trade secret as being (i) not generally known among or readily accessible to persons who would normally deal with such information, (ii) having commercial value as a consequence of such secrecy, and (iii) being preserved by reasonable steps taken by its owner to protect the secrecy of the relevant information. However, the scope of protection provided by the TRIPs Agreement is limited. A plaintiff seeking relief in a national court for trade secret misappropriation may be required to prove that the defendant knew or was grossly negligent in not knowing that it was acquiring trade secrets through behavior that is "contrary to honest commercial practices."

D.   Copyrights

Under U.S. law, copyrights arise in original works of authorship that are fixed in a tangible medium of expression. Examples of works protected by U.S. copyright law include literary works, musical recordings, photographs, movies, and software programs (in both object code and source code form). A copyright owner has an exclusive right to reproduce, distribute, and display and perform publicly the copyrighted work (for applicable categories of works), and to prepare derivative works (*e.g.,* translations, screenplays, and photographs) based on such work.

The United States is a party to the Berne Convention for the Protection of Literary and Artistic Works, which provides that a copyright arises automatically in a work at the time of its creation. Berne Convention countries accord national treatment to copyright holders from other member countries. The agreement has been revised five times since its inception in 1886; the most recent substantive modifications, joined by the United States, were made in 1971. Different countries adhere to the texts from different years, and thus have made varying commitments concerning copyrights within the Berne Convention framework. Furthermore, some member countries have entered official reservations to the convention exempting themselves from certain provisions.

Signatories of the WTO accords will be required to implement the core provisions of the most recent text of the Berne Convention and will be subject to additional substantive and procedural copyright protection provisions set forth in the TRIPs Agreement. The intended result is greater consistency and stricter standards for international copyright protection, although less-developed WTO member countries will be entitled to phase in necessary reforms gradually.

IV.   TRANSACTIONS INVOLVING INTELLECTUAL PROPERTY RIGHTS

Intellectual property rights are transferred through assignment agreements and licenses. In an intellectual property assignment, all right, title, and interest in an intellectual property right (*e.g.*, a patent or copyright) is conveyed to the assignee. In a license agreement, the intellectual property owner grants either exclusive or nonexclusive rights for specified uses of its intellectual property in exchange for royalties or other consideration. For example, an author may assign all right, title, and interest in an article to the journal that has commissioned it, or he may license the journal to publish the article and portions thereof in the print format, while reserving digital electronic publishing and other distribution rights for himself.

A license agreement should specify its term, the geographic territory and fields of use that it covers, the circumstances under which the license can be terminated or revised, whether it is exclusive or nonexclusive, whether the licensee can assign or sublicense any of its license rights, and what quality control requirements may apply. The agreement should also define which party will own any modifications or improvements made by the licensee to the licensed property, and what uses may be made of such modifications or improvements by each party. Noncompetition arrangements, exclusive or nonexclusive licenses to such improvements, and assignments back to the original licensor are among the options for disposing of such rights.

The tax implications of a technology transfer arrangement also merit close attention. Payments under license agreements, which are typically denominated as one-time license fees and/or royalties, are frequently subject to withholding taxes in the licensee's country, but certain license and fee structures may result in more favorable treatment than others.

Both licensors and licensees should research whether any U.S. export or foreign import restrictions apply to the intellectual property being licensed (*e.g.*, transfers of encryption software could run afoul of both). Although the U.S. export licensing regime is more liberal now than during the height of the Cold War, significant regulatory hurdles for certain technologies and destinations remain in place. (*See* Chapter 13, *Export Controls, Sanctions and Antiboycott Laws.*)

Some foreign jurisdictions require that technology license agreements be approved by, or at least registered, with the government in order to take effect or for royalty payments to be made using foreign exchange. Licensors should be especially alert to possible impediments to their receiving royalty payments in hard currency, either because of failures to comply with local policies on obtaining advance approvals for technology licenses or because of changing foreign monetary policies.

Intellectual property owners must tread a fine line between protecting their intangible rights and seeking to extract too much leverage from such rights. Licenses that tie grants of intellectual property rights to purchasing requirements or that require royalties beyond the term of the underlying right (*e.g.*, a patent term) may constitute misuse of intellectual property and violate U.S. or foreign antitrust laws. Requirements that a licensee assign or license back to the licensor any intellectual property that the licensee develops in the course of using licensed intellectual property may also be subject to challenge. (*See* Chapter 8, *International Antitrust.*)

U.S. licensors of intellectual property should also be wary of mandatory technology transfer laws and policies which may override the contractual terms governing license arrangements in some jurisdictions (usually in developing countries). For example, know-how developed by the foreign licensee may be deemed to be the property of the licensee at the end of the license term regardless of the ownership provisions of the original agreement. Over time, implementation of the TRIPs Agreement should lessen such risks to technology licensors, but national laws and policies that are intended to promote technology transfer and protect domestic inventions will likely persist and remain relevant to structuring international transactions in the years to come.

V.   ENFORCEMENT ISSUES

A U.S. owner of intellectual property will generally want to enforce its rights within the United States if at all possible. This may lead to including a U.S. choice of law in a licensing or assignment agreement. The enforceability of such clauses depends in part on where the agreement may be deemed to be performed, and also on whether enforcement of the agreement under U.S. law would conflict with the public order or essential public policies of the foreign party's jurisdiction. Notwithstanding any use of such a clause, an intellectual property–related contract should authorize the owner of any intellectual property rights to seek injunctive relief in any jurisdiction and forum in order to protect its property promptly and effectively.

U.S. laws provide a variety of remedies against intellectual property infringement that do not depend on a contractual choice-of-law provision. Under the Lanham Act, U.S. courts may assert jurisdiction over extraterritorial actions that have a sufficient effect on U.S. interstate or international commerce (including, in some cases, diversions of foreign sales away from U.S. exporters or reentry of counterfeit goods into the United States). The Customs Service is authorized to seize various categories of infringing goods at the border upon application by the intellectual property owner. (*See also* Chapter 16, *Trade Remedies and Benefits Programs*, which discusses a similar remedy ordered by the U.S. International Trade Commission under "Section 337.")

Intellectual property owners may also choose to pursue remedies in foreign jurisdictions, both through private lawsuits and, often more effectively, by exerting political pressure on local civil and criminal prosecutors. Software, video game, and other industries that suffer from high levels of foreign counterfeiting have achieved some success in enhancing enforcement of intellectual property laws overseas by lobbying both the U.S. government and relevant foreign governments. Sanctions used to enforce intellectual property rights in foreign jurisdictions include both civil and criminal penalties, as well as more immediate actions such as seizure and impoundment of counterfeit or pirated goods.

Finally, various multilateral, regional, and bilateral trade agreements protect U.S. companies' intellectual property rights in foreign jurisdictions, and provide an additional layer of enforcement mechanisms. The newly-formed WTO has jurisdiction over disputes involving the multilateral obligations of its members concerning copyrights, patents, trademarks, trade secrets, and other forms of intellectual property. Member countries can take complaints to the WTO for adjudication under its dispute resolution provisions, a process that creates an avenue for elaborating on worldwide standards and practices concerning intellectual property. Regional and bilateral options include raising complaints in connection with the NAFTA or the 1995 anti-piracy agreement between the United States and the People's Republic of China. Private parties can call on the U.S. government to enforce the terms of such agreements, and the NAFTA in particular contains detailed procedures for invoking dispute resolution mechanisms if a member country violates the intellectual property protection or other terms of such agreement. (For further discussion of related trade remedies, specifically "Section 301," *see* Chapter 16, *Trade Remedies and Benefits Programs*.)

VI.   SOURCES OF ASSISTANCE

A.   U.S. Law

1.   Statutes

The Patent Act, 35 U.S.C.A. §§ 1–376 (1984 & Supp. 1995).

The Lanham Act, 15 U.S.C.A. §§ 1051 – 1127 (1976 & Supp. 1995) (governing trademarks).

Uniform Trade Secrets Act, 14 U.L.A. 433 (1990 & Supp. 1995).

The Copyright Act of 1976, 17 U.S.C.A. §§ 101–1101 (1977 & Supp. 1995).

2. Regulations

Patent & Trademark Office, Department of Commerce, 37 C.F.R. §§ 1–150 (1994).

Copyright Office, Library of Congress, 37 C.F.R. §§ 201–259 (1994).

B. International Agreements

Berne Convention for the Protection of Literary and Artistic Works, Sept. 9, 1886, 331 U.N.T.S. 217.

Convention Revising the Paris Convention of March 20, 1883 for the Protection of Industrial Property, July 14, 1967, 21 U.S.T. 1583, 24 U.S.T. 2140, T.I.A.S. 6923, 7727.

Final Act Embodying the Results of the Uruguay Round of Multilateral Trade Negotiations, GATT Doc. MTN/FA (Dec. 15, 1993).

Patent Cooperation Treaty, June 19, 1970, 28 U.S.T. 7645, T.I.A.S. 8733.

Universal Copyright Convention, Sept. 6, 1952, 6 U.S.T. 2732, 216 U.N.T.S. 133. (The U.S. is also a party to this Convention, but it is less widely–accepted than the Berne Convention.)

C. Secondary Sources

1. Books

L. ECKSTROM & S. SZCZEPANSKI, ECKSTROM'S LICENSING IN FOREIGN AND DOMESTIC OPERATIONS (1972, with updates).

A. JACOBS & A. GREENE, TRADEMARKS THROUGHOUT THE WORLD (1989, with updates).

M. NIMMER, NIMMER ON COPYRIGHT (1978, with updates).

M. NIMMER & P. GELLER, INTERNATIONAL COPYRIGHT LAW AND PRACTICE (1994, with updates).

J. SINNOTT & J. BAXTER, WORLD PATENT LAW AND PRACTICE (1968, with updates).

S. STEWART, THE LAW OF INTERNATIONAL COPYRIGHT AND NEIGHBORING RIGHTS (1983, with updates).

2. Law Review Articles

Davis, *Combatting Piracy of Intellectual Property in International Markets: A Proposed Modification of the Special 301 Action*, 24 VAND. J. TRANSNAT'L L. 505 (1991).

Mensik, *Selected Topics Regarding Software Licensing in Europe*, 6 J. PROPRIETARY RTS. 21 (1994).

Oman, *Intellectual Property After the Uruguay Round*, 42 J. COPYRIGHT SOC'Y OF THE U.S.A. 18 (1994).

Smith, *Obtaining Trademark and Copyright Enforcement in the United States for Infringement Abroad*, 6 J. PROPRIETARY RTS. 8 (1994).

Note, *Preventing Software Piracy Through Regional Trade Agreements: The Mexican Example*, 20 N.C.J. INT'L L. & COM. REG. 175 (1994).

CHAPTER 8

INTERNATIONAL ANTITRUST

Michael H. Byowitz

I.   INTRODUCTION

The United States, the European Union and most of its member states, Canada, Mexico and several other jurisdictions have enacted and enforce antitrust laws to maintain free and open competition in their markets. Violation of applicable antitrust laws may have serious consequences for firms and individuals who are involved. The possible impact of antitrust laws needs to be considered in many commercial transactions.

Antitrust laws generally prohibit agreements, understandings and other concerted activities that unreasonably restrain commerce. In that regard, antitrust statutes draw a significant distinction between arrangements among competitors (referred to as horizontal restraints) and arrangements with distributors, customers or suppliers (referred to as vertical restraints). In the United States, many restrictive arrangements among competitors are deemed illegal *per se.* By contrast, many arrangements with customers and suppliers are evaluated under a rule–of–reason approach which focuses on market factors, business justifications and actual injury to competition.

Apart from concerted action, antitrust laws generally prohibit abusive practices by dominant firms. Unlawful monopolization is generally defined as the possession of monopoly power plus an element of improper conduct, although what is deemed improper varies considerably among jurisdictions.

A number of competition laws prohibit anticompetitive mergers and acquisitions. The laws of the United States and some countries abroad also create comprehensive merger control regimes with mandatory premerger notification and waiting period requirements for all transactions exceeding, or involving parties that exceed, specified thresholds as to transaction value, annual revenues or market shares.

The need for sensitivity to antitrust concerns does not stop at the border. The United States antitrust laws apply not just to conduct within the United States, but also to actions wholly abroad that affect import commerce or that have direct, substantial and reasonably foreseeable effects on domestic or export commerce. For example, the United States antitrust authorities routinely assert jurisdiction over foreign mergers that affect the U.S. market.

Similarly, U.S. enforcement action may be taken against foreign cartels that affect U.S. prices or U.S. exports. Moreover, the European Union and a few of its member states have enforced their merger controls against foreign mergers affecting their markets. The competition laws of a number of foreign jurisdictions contain prohibitions similar to the basic provisions of U.S. antitrust laws.

Antitrust laws are complex. Their application depends on the particular facts at issue, and their terms vary from jurisdiction to jurisdiction. This summary is intended as an overview of antitrust principles of the United States and other countries to help the reader recognize potential antitrust concerns. Like other chapters of this deskbook, it is not intended as a comprehensive discussion of the laws of any country, or as a substitute for seeking legal advice in appropriate situations.

Many states of the United States have enacted their own antitrust laws. In addition, U.S. federal law, the law of many individual states, and the laws of jurisdictions outside the United States prohibit unfair methods of competition and unfair or deceptive acts and practices such as deceptive labeling. A discussion of these laws is outside the scope of this chapter, but anyone proposing to transact business in the United States or abroad needs to consider their possible applicability.

II.   SUBSTANTIVE PROHIBITIONS[1]

A.   *Horizontal Restraints: Relations with Competitors*

In the United States, certain trade restraints have been identified by the courts as so restrictive of competition and so lacking in justification that they are treated as illegal *per se* and condemned regardless of their business purpose and irrespective of whether any injury to competition has in fact taken place. Such offenses are most likely to result from understandings between competitors and to be prosecuted as felonies. The competition laws of a number of jurisdictions outside the United States also prohibit such cartel activities.

The classic example of unlawful concerted activity among competitors is a formal or informal agreement to "fix" or "stabilize" prices. The prohibition against naked price-fixing covers much more than simply setting a specific dollar price or price range. Many agreements among competitors that directly or indirectly affect prices, whether higher or lower, are prohibited. A violation may occur when two competitors agree on terms or conditions of sale such as discounts, credit or payment terms. In addition to naked price-fixing agreements, the antitrust laws also prohibit formal or informal agreements or understandings with competitors to (i) coordinate bidding, (ii) divide markets, customers, suppliers or lines of business, (iii) restrict output or production capacity, or (iv) boycott or refuse to do business with certain suppliers or customers.

It is not only formal or express agreements that are forbidden. Any kind of informal or "gentlemen's agreement" – or other tacit or implied understanding concerning price or other matters of competitive significance – is equally forbidden.

There need not be evidence of an explicit unlawful agreement in order to establish the existence of an antitrust violation. Unlawful arrangements may be inferred from circumstantial evidence. Casual conversations among competitors about fixing prices or dividing business, together with evidence that competitors subsequently offered the same prices or split up business, can be interpreted on an after–the–fact basis as a violation of the antitrust laws.

There are instances in which horizontal agreements may be permissible as serving legitimate business purposes. For example, under United States antitrust law, competitor cooperation with respect to exchange of credit information, labor union relations or industry–wide advertising promotions is lawful under certain circumstances.

Trade associations frequently serve legitimate business purposes. However, participation in trade association activities requires vigilance from an antitrust perspective, because they involve meetings of competitors. Employees participating in trade association activities – or, indeed, in any outside professional or social gathering involving competitors–need to be sensitive to avoiding improper communications concerning matters of competitive significance. Product standardization may also raise antitrust issues, particularly where it serves as a basis for stabilizing prices or reducing competition in an industry.

Joint ventures among competitors also can raise serious issues under antitrust laws. Antitrust authorities may challenge so–called joint ventures that do not involve any integration of resources and are in fact no more than attempts by horizontal competitors to restrict competition. On the other hand, *bona fide* joint ventures – those that produce a combined entity that is more efficient than either partner alone – may be evaluated under a more lenient standard than price–fixing activities. Examples of integrative efficiencies that may result in more favorable treatment of joint ventures include economies of scale, synergies resulting from pooling complementary resources, facilitating entry into new markets, and the sharing of risks. Certain joint ventures limited to production and/or research and development may be subject to more lenient antitrust treatment than joint ventures which also include sales and marketing activities.

B.   *Vertical Restraints: Relationships with Customers and Suppliers*

Firms that do not enjoy market power are free, as a general matter, to do business or not to do business with whomever they choose. Antitrust laws prohibit certain vertical restraints when they are the product of "agreements" with distributors or customers. As a result, firms should decide to select customers and suppliers on an independent basis, and such decisions should not be the result of an agreement with a competitor, or with a competing customer or supplier, not to do business with certain customers or suppliers.

In the area of vertical restraints, antitrust laws may allow a non–dominant firm to achieve through independent action what would be unlawful if achieved through agreement with another company. Whether a particular policy is the product of unilateral or concerted action may be difficult to determine as a legal matter. As a result, any plan to restrict a dealer or distributor in the various ways described below should be reviewed in advance with antitrust counsel for the appropriate jurisdiction(s).

1.   Resale Price Maintenance

Resale price maintenance or vertical price fixing occurs when a customer and supplier agree on the price the customer will charge for the supplier's product. Resale price maintenance is illegal *per se* under the antitrust laws of the United States and certain jurisdictions abroad. In other foreign jurisdictions, resale price maintenance is illegal only when engaged in by a dominant firm.

In the United States, the *per se* prohibition of resale price maintenance applies only if the practice is found to be the product of concerted action, as opposed to the action of a single firm. It is axiomatic that under U.S. law, a supplier may lawfully announce its suggested resale price and then refuse to sell to customers that do not observe its policy. Liability may arise, however, if the supplier goes beyond immediate termination by seeking to convince or coerce an offending dealer to change its ways, or by enlisting other dealers to assist in carrying out the policy. Under these circumstances, the conduct may be deemed to be the product of an agreement between manufacturer and distributor, rather than unilateral conduct by the manufacturer. For this reason, close consultation with experienced counsel is necessary to avoid serious legal pitfalls in the United States. Although suggesting resale prices is also permissible in certain other jurisdictions which treat vertical price fixing as *per se* illegal, even unilateral terminations of non–compliers may be prohibited.

2.   Territorial and Customer Restrictions

Many manufacturers wish to confine their third–party distributors in reselling their products to a particular territory or to specified customers or classes of customers. In the United States and some jurisdictions abroad, such vertical restrictions and customer restraints will be judged under a rule–of–reason approach, and frequently will be found lawful when the firm using them does not have market power and/or they promote increased inter–brand competition. More stringent rules may apply in other jurisdictions, including the European Union, where a fundamental purpose of competition law is to promote a single integrated market.

3.   Exclusive Dealing and Requirements Contracts

Exclusive dealing arrangements in favor of a manufacturer or supplier restrict or eliminate a dealer's ability to source and sell competitive products. A manufacturer's unilateral policy of refusing to sell to dealers that carry competitive products will normally not raise antitrust concerns, absent a sufficiently large position to confer market power on the manufacturer. Seeking a commitment from the customer not to deal in competing lines may be defensible in a number of circumstances in certain jurisdictions, but the same set of facts may give rise to a violation in other jurisdictions.

Requirement contracts obligate buyers to purchase all or most of their requirements from particular sellers. Such contracts present antitrust issues like exclusive dealing arrangements and may violate the laws of some jurisdictions under certain circumstances.

4.   Tying Arrangements

Tying arrangements – the practice of forcing a customer to purchase one item in order to obtain another item that the customer really wants – are frequently condemned under antitrust laws. Accordingly, sellers should leave their customers free to purchase only those items that they want, and not require customers to purchase unwanted items as a condition to their being permitted to purchase what they do want.

Prohibitions against tying arrangements generally do not apply to legitimate efforts to sell several products or multiple services in a package, as long as the seller is prepared to sell each of the products or services separately at realistic prices where offering separate products or services is economically feasible. Thus it is often permissible to agree with a customer to provide multiple products provided that the customer is not required to accept one product in order to procure the other. In addition, tying arrangements may be permissible if, under the circumstances, the impact on competition or trade is insignificant, or the products must be sold together for technological reasons.

5.   Reciprocal Dealing

Situations in which a business utilizes its purchasing power to gain customers for its own products may raise antitrust issues similar to tying arrangements. If a supplier is compelled to make purchases in order to acquire or keep a sales account, such reciprocal dealing arrangements may be condemned.

6.   Price Discrimination

In the United States, the Robinson–Patman Act makes it unlawful for a seller to discriminate in price between competing customers who purchase commodities of like grade and quality. A price difference alone will not violate the Act. It is also necessary to establish that the difference in price caused injury to competition among manufacturers or competing customers.

Even where the plaintiff can show that a price differential that injured competition, a seller can nonetheless prevail in a Robinson–Patman Act lawsuit by demonstrating that the price concession falls within one of a number of statutory defenses. These include the so–called "meeting competition" and "cost justification" defenses.

Some jurisdictions abroad prohibit price discrimination. Others do not.

C.   *Business Arrangements and Agreements Among Affiliated Corporations*

In the United States, there are circumstances under which a parent company can be found to have conspired for antitrust purposes with a subsidiary or other corporate affiliate. As a result, there may be antitrust limitations on a firm's ability to coordinate business activities with subsidiaries and affiliates. In the United States, those limits do not apply to unincorporated divisions.

D.   *Intellectual Property Licensing*

Patent, trademark and copyright license agreements may cause antitrust concerns if they are among competitors. Such agreements may also raise antitrust issues when the owner of an intellectual property right seeks to place vertical restrictions on a licensee's use of the intellectual property.

E.   *Monopolization: Abuses by Dominant Firms*

In addition to prohibiting collective action among competitors, antitrust laws proscribe certain actions of a single firm that constitute monopolization or attempted monopolization. Unlawful monopolization is often defined as the possession of monopoly power plus an element of improper conduct.

Monopoly power consists of the power of a single firm unilaterally to control prices or exclude actual or potential competitors with respect to the market for a particular product or service. A market for antitrust purposes might be limited to a single product line or a relatively small geographic area.

Possessing a dominant position with a very high market share generally is not by itself illegal under antitrust laws. For example, a firm may achieve substantial market share through historical accident or superior business acumen and competitive success. Antitrust laws do prohibit certain actions of a predatory, discriminatory or unreasonably exclusionary nature in order to maintain a monopoly position. Such prohibitions include predatory pricing (i.e., pricing below an appropriate measure of cost for the purpose of eliminating competitors in the short run and raising prices in the long run) and misuse of judicial or regulatory process for the purpose of eliminating actual or potential competition. Antitrust laws also prohibit seeking to leverage a dominant position in one market into another market.

There are important differences among antitrust prohibitions applicable to dominant firms. For example, U.S. law prohibits acquiring a monopoly position by improper methods, as well as certain attempts to monopolize. By contrast, the dominance provisions of some jurisdictions abroad apply only to firms that already enjoy a dominant position. In addition, the U.S. antitrust laws do not address excessive prices charged by monopolists who obtained that position lawfully; that issue is left to be addressed, if at all, by a specific regulatory regime. The antitrust laws of some other jurisdictions may prohibit a monopolist from charging excessive prices, even if its monopoly position was obtained lawfully.

F.   *Merger Control*

The United States, the European Union ("EU") and several of its member states, Canada, Mexico and a number of other countries have enacted extensive merger control statutes that prohibit anticompetitive stock or asset acquisitions and other forms of merger or partial merger. These laws require notification to the antitrust enforcement authorities of all transactions meeting specified thresholds.

Most antitrust merger control statutes prohibit mergers and acquisitions that create a dominant firm, *i.e.*, a firm with the ability unilaterally to raise prices above competitive levels. The laws of the United States and some jurisdictions abroad also prohibit transactions that make more likely the prospect of successful oligopolistic practices by post–merger market participants, for example, by reducing uncertainty about rivals' intentions, thereby facilitating parallel pricing.

In determining whether to oppose a merger or acquisition, most antitrust authorities take into account an appropriately defined relevant market, the market participants, market concentration, entry conditions, and an analysis of whether the exercise of market power is rendered more likely by the merger. The specific market shares and/or concentration levels that will cause a challenge on antitrust grounds tend to be somewhat lower in the United States than in a number of other jurisdictions.

Guidelines issued by the enforcement authorities of the United States and Canada set forth in detail the analytic frameworks employed by their respective competition authorities to evaluate transactions. Enforcement authorities in other countries generally have not issued such guidelines.

Some antitrust laws create mandatory prior notification regimes for mergers and acquisitions (*e.g.*, the U.S., the EU, Canada, and Mexico), while others impose mandatory or voluntary postmerger reporting requirements (*e.g.*, the United Kingdom and Australia). Under mandatory prior notification regimes, reportability is determined by whether the proposed transaction (and/or the parties thereto) exceed specified thresholds. These thresholds vary considerably among jurisdictions.

For example, the notification requirements in the United States imposed under the Hart–Scott–Rodino Act use thresholds based both on the size of the parties and the size of the transaction, with the result that filings are required for most transactions at or above $15 million in value and for some transactions below that level. The EU's thresholds are based entirely on the size of the parties, and are set at very high levels. The combined firm must have worldwide turnover of 5 billion European Currency Units ("ECU") and each party must have EU turnover of 250 million ECU. Some countries abroad have notification thresholds based on the combined firm's market share in the country or a substantial portion thereof.

Statutes with mandatory premerger notification requirements impose waiting periods (of varying lengths) before proposed transactions may be completed. Notification and waiting period requirements are designed to preserve the ability of antitrust enforcers to investigate the competitive effects of proposed transactions, and to attempt to block those that are deemed anticompetitive. The level of information required in initial filings under notification regimes varies considerably, as does the quantity of documents and information that the parties may be required to submit in the course of a full premerger investigation.

III.   ENFORCEMENT

In the United States and Canada, certain violations of antitrust laws may result in criminal liability. Individuals found guilty of a criminal violation of antitrust laws in these jurisdictions may be subject to imprisonment and significant fines. Most antitrust laws abroad do not impose criminal liability, although several contain provisions establishing very substantial administrative sanctions.

In countries abroad that effectively enforce their antitrust laws, conduct by officers or employees deemed improper may subject their firms to substantial fines as well as broad–ranging injunctions governing future conduct that could have a significant adverse impact on a firm's day–to–day operations. In addition, U.S. antitrust violations may expose a firm to civil suits for treble damages by private parties who suffer loss by reason of the violations, and prevailing plaintiffs (but not defendants) may recover attorney's fees. Such lawsuits can be extremely costly to defend, both in terms of monetary costs and lost time of officers and employees. Although certain foreign jurisdictions allow for private actions in theory, substantial impediments to successful recovery exist as a practical matter. Jurisdictions outside the United States have embraced neither treble damages nor one–sided attorney's fee provisions. Indeed, a few countries have enacted so–called "blocking statutes," which seek to deny enforcement of the trebled feature of the award.

IV.   SOURCES OF ASSISTANCE

A.   *U.S. Statutes and Regulations*

The U.S. antitrust laws include the Sherman Antitrust Act, 15 U.S.C. §§ 1–7 (1988), the Clayton Antitrust Act, 15 U.S.C. §§ 12–27 (1988 and Supp. V 1993), and the Federal Trade Commission Act, 15 U.S.C. §§ 41–58 (1988). Noteworthy provisions include Section 1 of the Sherman Act, 15 U.S.C. § 1 (contracts, combinations and conspiracies in restraint of trade), Section 2 of the Sherman Act, 15 U.S.C. § 2 (monopolization and attempts to monopolize), Section 6a of the Sherman Act, 15 U.S.C. § 6a (application of Sherman Act to conduct occurring outside United States), Section 7 of the Clayton Act, 15 U.S.C. § 18 (anticompetitive stock or asset acquisitions), Section 2 of the Clayton Act, 15 U.S.C. § 13, commonly referred to as the Robinson–Patman Act (1988) (price discrimination), Section 5 of the Federal Trade Commission Act, 15 U.S.C. § 45 (catch–all provision), and the National Cooperative Research & Production Act, 15 U.S.C. §§4301–4306 (1993) (enhanced statutory protection for research and certain production joint ventures).

Mandatory premerger notification and waiting period requirements are imposed by Section 7A of the Clayton Act, 15 U.S.C. § 18a, commonly referred to as the Hart–Scott–Rodino ("HSR") Act (enacted in 1976), and the HSR regulations, 16 C.F.R Parts 801–803 (initially promulgated in 1978).

B.   *Foreign Statutes and Laws*

Canada – The Competition Act of 1986 prohibits, among other things, horizontal and vertical restraints (§§ 45, 61, 77), predatory pricing (§§ 50(1)(c), 79), price discrimination (§ 50(1)(a)), abuse of dominance (§§ 78, 79), and anticompetitive mergers (§§ 91–100). The Competition Act also establishes a mandatory premerger notification regime with size of party and size of transaction thresholds which focus on Canadian operations, assets and sales (§§ 108–110).

The European Union – The principal antitrust provisions are set forth in two articles of the Treaty Establishing the European Economic Community, at Rome, Mar. 5, 1957, 298 U.N.T.S. 47 (commonly referred to as the Treaty of Rome). Article 85 deals with agreements in restraint of trade and Article 86 prohibits abuse of dominance. Mandatory premerger notification and waiting requirements apply to certain transactions which are prohibited if deemed "incompatible with the Common Market." *See Council Regulation (EEC) No. 4064/89 of 21 December 1989 on the control of concentration between undertakings* (the "Merger Regulation"). Transactions falling above the thresholds are subject to the exclusive competence of the European Commission, while those falling below are subject to the laws of the appropriate member states. *See* regulations and notices implementing the Merger Regulation, including:

Commission Regulation (EC) No. 3384/94 of 21 December 1994 on notifications, time limits and hearings; Commission Notice 94/C 385/01 on the distinction between concentrative joint ventures (subject to the Merger Regulation) and cooperative joint ventures (subject to Article 85 and national law); Commission Notice 94/C 385/04 on calculation of turnover; Commission Notice 94/C 385/02 on the notion of a concentration; Commission Notice 94/C 385/03 on the notion of undertakings concerned; and *Commission Regulation (EC) No. 3385/94 of 21 December 1994 on the form, content and other details of applications and notifications* (for cooperative joint ventures).

The United Kingdom – The United Kingdom prohibits cartels and other restrictive trade practices (Restrictive Trade Practices Act 1976) and collective and individual resale price maintenance (Resale Prices Act 1976). A mechanism exists under the Fair Trading Act 1973 for the investigation of monopoly situations and under the Competition Act 1980 for the investigation of anti-competitive practices. These Acts mean that matters such as excessive pricing, discrimination and tie-ins can be investigated and controlled. The Fair Trading Act also provides a mechanism for the investigation of certain mergers that could be detrimental to competition or to the public interest generally. Specific legislation has been passed to regulate competition in relation to sectors such as telecommunications, gas, electricity and water.

France – Competition law in France is based on the Ordinance of December 1986 regarding free market pricing and competition. There are prohibitions on anticompetitive agreements (Article 7), abuse of dominance (Article 8), refusals to deal (Article 30), resale price maintenance (Article 34), and discriminatory practices (Article 36(1)). The statute provides for the control of certain mergers involving parties exceeding specified combined turnover or market share thresholds (Article 38 *et seq.*). There is no mandatory premerger notification regime.

Germany – The principal antitrust law is the Gesetz gegen Wettbewerbsbeschränkungen, enacted in 1958 and last amended in 1990. It includes prohibitions on agreements and concerted practices that restrain competition (§§ 1, 25, 38), price fixing (§ 15), mergers that create or strengthen a dominant market position (§ 24), and abuse of dominance (§ 22). There is a mandatory prior notification requirement for acquisitions involving parties whose combined worldwide turnover exceeds specified thresholds. (§§ 23(2), 24a(i).)

Italy – Act 287 on The Protection of Competition (October 10, 1990) contains provisions based on Articles 85 and 86 of the Treaty of Rome and the EU Merger Regulation.

Mexico – The Federal Law of Economic Competition of 1992 became effective in June 1993. The statute prohibits monopolies (Article 8), most horizontal restraints (Article 9), as well as certain vertical restraints and exclusionary conduct engaged in by a dominant firm (Articles 10-13). There is also a merger control regime prohibiting anticompetitive transactions (Articles 16-19) and imposing mandatory premerger notification and waiting period requirements for all transactions exceeding specified thresholds (Articles 20-22).

Australia – The principal antitrust statute is the Trade Practices Act of 1974. The statute prohibits agreements that substantially lessen competition, agreements that fix prices and boycotts (§ 45), vertical restraints including resale price maintenance, tying and exclusive dealing arrangements which substantially lessen competition (§§ 47-48), stock or asset acquisitions that substantially lessen competition (§ 50), and misuse of a substantial degree of market power (§ 46). There are voluntary authorization and notification procedures for mergers, acquisitions and some other conduct which requires the Trade Practices Commission to make a determination within a specified time period based on a competitive detriment/public benefit test and which bars subsequent challenges of notified matters.

Many other countries have enacted competition laws with widely varying provisions. These countries include but are not limited to Spain, Denmark, Norway, Sweden, various Central and Eastern European countries, various South American countries, Japan, Korea, and New Zealand. The competition laws of many countries are reviewed in detail in J. Garrett, cited *infra*. Some of these competition laws have not been actively enforced in a manner designed to enhanced consumer welfare, while others were enacted relatively recently.

C.   *Treaties*

Article 1501 of the North American Free Trade Agreement ("NAFTA") imposes obligations on the three NAFTA signatories (the U.S., Canada and Mexico) to enact and effectively enforce competition laws aimed at enhancing consumer welfare. Article 1504 establishes a working group on trade and competition law consisting of representatives of the antitrust enforcement authorities of the signatories.

D.   *Other Official Documents*

United States – The analytic framework used by the federal enforcement agencies in a number of areas are set forth in several sets of guidelines. *See U.S. Department of Justice and Federal Trade Commission Horizontal Merger Guidelines* (1992), *reprinted in* 4 TRADE REG. REP. (CCH) ¶ 13,104; *U.S. Department of Justice and Federal Trade Commission Antitrust Guidelines for the Licensing of Intellectual Property* (1995), *reprinted in* 4 TRADE REG. REP. (CCH) ¶ 13,132; *U.S. Department of Justice and Federal Trade Commission Antitrust Enforcement Guidelines for International Operations*

(1995), *reprinted in* 4 TRADE REG. REP. (CCH) ¶ 13,107; and *Statements of Antitrust Enforcement Policy and Analytical Principles Relating to Health Care and Antitrust,* Jointly Issued by the U.S. Department of Justice and Federal Trade Commission (1994), *reprinted in* 4 TRADE REG. REP. (CCH) ¶ 13,152.

HSR Act – The Statement of Basis and Purpose as to the original HSR regulations is reported at 43 Fed. Reg. 33450 *et seq.* (1978). The Statement of Basis and Purpose as to various changes to those rules are reported at 44 Fed. Reg. 66781 (1979), 48 Fed. Reg. 34427 (1983), 52 Fed. Reg. 7066 (1987), 52 Fed. Reg. 20058 (1987), and 54 Fed. Reg. 21425 (1989).

Canada – The Canadian Bureau of Competition Policy has published enforcement guidelines in a number of areas, including merger enforcement, price discrimination and predatory pricing. These guidelines are reprinted in Davies, Ward & Beck, cited *infra.*

E.   Secondary Sources

Important secondary sources concerning the U.S. antitrust laws include AMERICAN BAR ASSOCIATION ("ABA") SECTION OF ANTITRUST LAW, ANTITRUST LAW DEVELOPMENTS (3d ed. 1992); TRADE REGULATION REPORTER; P. AREEDA & D. TURNER, ANTITRUST LAW: AN ANALYSIS OF ANTITRUST PRINCIPLES AND THEIR APPLICATION (1978); and J. VON KALINOWSKI, ANTITRUST LAWS AND TRADE REGULATION (1995). *See also* PRACTICING LAW INSTITUTE, BASIC ANTITRUST LAW (1994).

For guidance on constructing an antitrust compliance policy under U.S. law, see W. HANCOCK, MATERIALS ON ANTITRUST COMPLIANCE PROGRAMS (2d ed. 1995), ABA SECTION OF ANTITRUST LAW, COMPLIANCE MANUALS FOR THE NEW ANTITRUST ERA (1990), and W. COMEGYS, ANTITRUST COMPLIANCE MANUAL (2d ed. 1992). *See also* M. MACARTHUR, ASSOCIATIONS AND THE ANTITRUST LAWS (U.S. Chamber of Commerce 1994).

On the issue of reportability under the Hart–Scott–Rodino Act, important sources include: FEDERAL TRADE COMMISSION, PREMERGER NOTIFICATION SOURCE BOOK (1990); two introductory guides published by the FTC, entitled WHAT IS THE PREMERGER NOTIFICATION PROGRAM? AN OVERVIEW (January 1991) and TO FILE OR NOT TO FILE: WHEN YOU MUST FILE A PREMERGER NOTIFICATION REPORT FORM (January 1991); ABA SECTION OF ANTITRUST LAW, PREMERGER NOTIFICATION PRACTICE MANUAL (1991) (collection and discussion of FTC staff informal interpretations of HSR reporting requirements); S. AXINN, B. FOGG, N. STOLL & B. PRAGER, ACQUISITIONS UNDER THE HART–SCOTT–RODINO ANTITRUST IMPROVEMENTS ACT (1995); and 1A M. LIPTON & E. STEINBERGER, TAKEOVERS & FREEZEOUTS CH. 7 (1995).

Reference materials on competition laws outside the United States include DAVIES, WARD & BECK, COMPETITION LAW OF CANADA (1994); F. FINE, MERGERS AND JOINT VENTURES IN EUROPE: THE LAW AND POLICY OF THE EEC (2d ed. 1994); L. RITTER, *et al.*, EEC COMPETITION LAW, A PRACTITIONER'S GUIDE (1991); M. HEIDENHAIN & H. SCHNEIDER, GERMAN ANTITRUST LAW (4th ed. 1991); and J. GARRET, WORLD ANTITRUST LAW & PRACTICE (1995).

ENDNOTES

1   See Section IV for relevant citations.

CHAPTER 9

SECURITIES LAW

Edward F. Greene

I. INTRODUCTION

Most jurisdictions regulate capital raising activities, as well as trading in the secondary market. In general, the former are more heavily regulated than the latter. In any jurisdiction, the following questions should be asked with respect to a securities offering to assess the level of applicable regulation:

•   What is the nature of the capital raising activity? An initial public offering typically is regulated more extensively than an offering by a more seasoned company.

•   What business is the company in? Collective investment vehicles are usually subject to more stringent rules than industrial companies.

•   How will the issue be sold? In the U.K., for example, if only professional investors are approached, there is no requirement to deliver a prospectus and publicity surrounding the offering is permitted. In the United States the test is not whether the investor is professional but sophisticated. If only sophisticated investors participate, there is also no requirement to deliver a prospectus, but there are limits on press and other publicity during the course of an offering.

•   What kind of security is being offered? In some jurisdictions, certain instruments such as commercial paper are exempt from the requirements that otherwise might apply to a debt or equity issue.

•   If the offering is to be sold to the public generally, is there a requirement to deliver a prospectus and, if so, what rules determine its content? In some jurisdictions (Sweden, for example), the content is established by the stock exchange on which the securities are listed. In others, such as the United States, there are prescribed forms, established by an administrative agency.

•   Will there be a press campaign in connection with an offering? In some jurisdictions, the only information about the offering must be in the prospectus. Others permit newspaper and other media stories and ads designed to generate interest in the offering. Others also permit underwriters to distribute research reports about the company before or during the offering.

•   Is the offering being conducted outside the domestic market? If so, what rules apply? Those of the market in which the offering is made? Those of the domestic market? Both? Most jurisdictions apply the same standards to offerings to local investors, regardless of where the issuer is located. However, some jurisdictions such as the U.K. will defer in some instances to the accounting standards of another market rather than apply local rules.

•   Who can participate in selling securities in the offering? Must they be licensed? Most jurisdictions require distribution participants to be licensed as a broker–dealer.

•   What liability attaches if the offering goes wrong and to whom? The company? The directors? The underwriters? The accountants? What is the standard of liability? Absolute? Negligence? Fraud? The liability provisions vary greatly throughout the developed markets, and should be understood before conducting an offering, especially in a cross–border context.

•   What are the consequences of a public offering? Some jurisdictions require ongoing reporting to the markets on a periodic basis. Other subject companies to certain books and records provisions.

It is beyond the scope of this chapter to discuss in detail how each market differs in regulating securities transactions. Suffice it to say that they are regulated in most markets. What follows for illustrative purposes is a description of the regime in the United States, with comparisons where appropriate. Although the United States regulates to a greater extent than most other markets, regulatory convergence is occurring, and the model in the United States exerts a great deal of influence by reason of the size of its market.

II.   THE U.S. MODEL

Regulation of securities transactions and market participants in the United States occurs at both the federal and the state level. Federal regulation proceeds primarily through the operation of statutes enacted by Congress, together with rules promulgated thereunder by the Securities and Exchange Commission ("SEC"), the administrative agency with oversight responsibility in this area. Each state in addition has its own laws, though generally they conform to each other. The discussion that follows focuses on the scope and orientation of the most important of these: the Securities Act of 1933 (the "Securities Act"), which governs the initial distribution of securities; the Securities Exchange Act of 1934 (the "Exchange Act"), which governs the resale of securities in secondary market transactions; and the Investment Company Act of 1940 (the "Investment Company Act"), which regulates collective investment vehicles such as mutual funds.[1]

By and large, the goal of U.S. federal securities regulation is to provide potential investors access to the information they require to make an informed decision regarding whether to invest in a given security. Federal regulatory authorities, in contrast to those in certain states and non-U.S. jurisdictions, do not evaluate or pass upon the merits of particular securities, nor is there a queue governing who may have access to the market and at what times. Accordingly, the primary method of U.S. federal securities regulation is mandatory disclosure. Extensive disclosure obligations permeate the U.S. securities laws, most fundamentally in the Securities Act requirement that a prospectus be prepared and delivered in connection with public offerings of securities, and in the Exchange Act requirement that companies whose securities are widely held or exchange-listed file periodic reports about their business and financial condition. To buttress these disclosure provisions, each statute sets out express remedies for investors who purchase securities on the basis of incorrect or incomplete information. Other jurisdictions, such as Japan, have comparable disclosure provisions but limit the types of companies that can raise money publicly and impose a queue.

III.   INITIAL OFFERINGS OF SECURITIES

Like most jurisdictions, the United States regulates to a much greater extent distributions of new securities than secondary market trading in outstanding securities. The Securities Act regulates at the federal level initial offerings of securities to the public. Essentially, the Securities Act provides that every offer and sale of a security involving the use of U.S. jurisdictional means must be registered with the SEC, unless a specific exemption is available. Each of the various elements of this principle requires some elaboration.

A.   Definition of a "Security"

The definition of a "security" for purposes of the Securities Act – and thus, the scope of the transactions covered by the Act – is extremely broad. (Essentially the same definition applies for purposes of the Exchange Act.) The definition has evolved slowly and with difficulty over the years. It is subject to a fair amount of uncertainty at the margins, and so cannot really be reduced to any concise formula, but it expressly extends to "any interest or instrument commonly known as a 'security'" and includes all garden-variety forms of equity and debt securities, as well as investment contracts. The point to be emphasized here, then, is simply that the international lawyer must be

alert to the possibility that any proposed transaction in any market in which
an investment opportunity is to be bought or sold may involve the offer and
sale of a "security" within the meaning of the local law, thus triggering the
application of laws that, if not anticipated, may have unwelcome consequences for the transaction.

B. Registration Under the Securities Act

In the United States an issuer of the securities (the "registrant") must
prepare a registration statement to offer securities to the public. The registration statement consists primarily of a prospectus containing information that
meets specific disclosure requirements established by regulation. The registration statement is filed with the SEC and is subject to a process of administrative review and comment that aims to ensure compliance with the SEC's
disclosure requirements. Only the registrant can file a registration, even
though the sellers of securities are existing shareholders. By contrast, in other
jurisdictions, the document is the responsibility of the seller of securities.

The content of the registration statement is prescribed in forms promulgated by the SEC. The forms incorporate detailed rules concerning the type
and level of disclosure about the registrant's business that must be provided
in the prospectus. These rules require the inclusion of financial statements
that are audited in accordance with U.S. generally accepted auditing standards, that comply with (or, in the case of non–U.S. registrants, are reconciled
to) U.S. generally accepted accounting principles, and that meet additional
requirements as to format and presentation.

The depth and breadth of disclosure in the prospectus does not depend
on the nature of its intended audience – in a registered public offering, the
same information is required whether securities are to be marketed only to
sophisticated institutions and investment professionals or to a wider audience including retail investors. The SEC has in certain contexts streamlined
the registration process to alleviate some of its burden and expense. For
example, in recognition of the continuous disclosure to the trading markets
that many companies are required to make through the filing of periodic
reports pursuant to the Exchange Act, prospectuses filed by such companies
are now allowed to incorporate information by reference to other SEC filings,
and "shelf registration" procedures are available which permit securities to be
registered in advance and distributed at any time without additional action
by the SEC staff. These techniques are being implemented in other jurisdictions, such as Canada. At the other end of the scale, there are special registration forms for small businesses, which eliminate certain requirements as to
the form and content of disclosure. There are also separate forms for U.S. and
non–U.S. issuers, although the applicable accounting and disclosure rules are
generally the same for domestic and foreign companies.

The registration obligation is supported by certain prospectus delivery
requirements, which provide that the prospectus must be sent to each pur-

chaser during the offering and, in certain cases, for a period thereafter. In addition, every sale of a security underwritten or allotted to an underwriter or dealer must be accompanied by a prospectus, whenever the sale occurs.

Most jurisdictions regulate the content of prospectuses in a manner similar to the United States. The major differences are: (i) the rules governing content and their source (*i.e.*, the Listing Directive of the European Union and the Companies Act of 1984 in the U.K., as contrasted to the rules of an administration agency such as the SEC, which can be changed without legislative action); (ii) who reviews the document, if at all (in some jurisdictions only the stock exchange on which the securities are listed reviews the document); (iii) whether the prospectus must be pre-cleared before distribution to the public; and (iv) the period of time during which it must be delivered.

C.   *Exemptions from Registration*

Many jurisdictions exempt certain transactions from the requirement to prepare and deliver a prospectus. In the United States, for example, there are two types of exemptions. First, the Securities Act enumerates certain "exempted securities" as to which registration is not required under any circumstances. Among these are short-term debt obligations, specifically, any note that matures by its terms within nine months of issuance, the proceeds of which are used by the issuer for current transactions. Commercial paper is generally issued in the United States under this exemption. Also exempted are securities issued by U.S. banks and U.S. branches of foreign banks, and by the government of the United States, the several states or their political subdivisions (but not, significantly, securities issued by foreign governments).

The second type of exemption applies to "exempted transactions." Of these, the most important is the exemption for "transactions by an issuer not involving any public offering" – so-called "private placements." The term *"public offering"* is not defined in the Securities Act, but during more than half a century, a substantial body of case law and SEC regulatory practice has developed concerning private placements by U.S. issuers. Standardized procedures and documentation have also evolved to allow transactions to proceed with assurance that the private placement exemption from registration may safely be relied upon.

In addition, to permit greater certainty in planning transactions intended to qualify as private placements, SEC rules provide certain private placement "safe harbors." Generally speaking, under U.S. law, a safe harbor is a set of detailed procedures for ensuring compliance with a general principle. If the procedures are properly followed, any doubts about how the general principle will be applied can be eliminated. On the other hand, if compliance is imperfect in one or more respects, the argument may still be made that the general principle itself commands the result that compliance with the safe harbor would have achieved. Rule 506 of Regulation D under the Securities Act provides issuers of securities with a safe harbor for "limited" offerings.

Broadly, under Rule 506 an offering will be deemed a good private placement so long as the securities are purchased only by (a) an unlimited number of "accredited investors" and (b) no more than 35 other buyers. The definition of *accredited investor* includes banks, insurance companies, pension plans, officers and directors of the issuer, and natural persons meeting certain individual income or net worth thresholds. With respect to the buyers who are not accredited investors, the issuer must reasonably believe that each such buyer, individually or together with an investment advisor meeting certain criteria, has the knowledge and experience required to evaluate the merits and risks of the investment. The rule also contains certain information delivery requirements and forbids the use of any general solicitation or general advertising in connection with the offering.

Many foreign jurisdictions also exempt private placements. The availability of the exemption typically depends upon: (i) the number of investors (*e.g.,* in Japan, no more than 50 can participate); (ii) the nature of the investor (*e.g.,* in the U.K. the test is whether the person's ordinary activities involve him or her in acquiring, managing or disposing of investments (as principal or agent)); (iii) whether there is general publicity about the offering; and (iv) how soon the securities are resold to public.

If a security is issued in a private placement, the practitioner must ascertain whether there are any restrictions on subsequent resales. In the United States, for example, securities acquired in a private placement are deemed "*restricted.*" Restricted securities may be resold in ordinary brokerage transactions subject to restrictions as to the availability of information and the manner and overall volume of sales only after the expiration of a two-year holding period and may be resold free of such restrictions only after the expiration of a three-year holding period. In the interim sales are permitted on a private placement basis to similar institutions, but the shares remain "restricted" until the two- and three-year periods from the time of the sale elapse. The restrictions are imposed to prevent indirect distributions to the public in violation of the registration provisions. Other jurisdictions, such as France, do not restrict subsequent sales as long as the initial purchasers were eligible and investors.

D.   *Transactions Outside the Home Market*

With the increasing globalization of the securities market, securities are frequently sold outside the domestic market. The securities placed abroad, however, will frequently be resold into the domestic market, especially if most of the trading in the issuer's securities occurs in that domestic market. Practitioners must consider whether any reflow may violate the domestic rules applicable to public offerings. For example, in the United States, there is no express exemption in the Securities Act covering offers and sales that are made outside the United States; if there is any use of U.S. jurisdictional means in connection with the initial issuance or subsequent resale of securities into the United States, the registration requirement may apply. The U.S. authorities are concerned if securities distributed abroad are expected or intended to be resold in the United States shortly after sales abroad.

Given the expansive interpretation of U.S. jurisdictional means by the U.S. courts, offerings by foreign and (especially) U.S. issuers, even if carefully structured, are obviously vulnerable in this regard. The growing internationalization of the securities markets, in particular the desire of U.S. institutional investors to acquire foreign securities as part of their diversified worldwide portfolios, focused attention on the question whether the registration requirements of the Securities Act should not be subject to more rigorous territorial limitation. The same trend, meanwhile, fueled interest, both at the SEC and in the investment community, in a clear set of rules for determining the circumstances under which resales into the United States of unregistered securities originally placed abroad ("flowback") could be made without violating the registration requirement. The SEC adopted Regulation S in response to these concerns.

Basically, Regulation S states that the registration requirements of the Securities Act apply only to offers and sales of securities made inside the United States. Equally important, it sets forth two relevant safe harbors. The first safe harbor applies to offers and sales by issuers or other distributors of securities (e.g., underwriters). To qualify for this safe harbor, the securities must be sold in an "offshore transaction" (one in which the buyer is outside the United States when the buy order originates or that is effected on the physical floor of a foreign securities exchange) without the use of any "directed selling efforts" in the United States (activities undertaken for the purpose, or that reasonably could be expected to have the effect, of conditioning the U.S. market for the securities being offered resulting in flowback). Depending on the status of the issuer and the nature of the offering, certain additional requirements must be met as well. These additional requirements relate to a "restricted period" following the initial placement abroad during which securities may not be sold into the United States, to "offering restrictions" on the manner in which securities may be marketed, and to the delivery of "notice" describing to the purchaser the applicable restrictions on resale. In general, these additional requirements are least restrictive when it is least likely that securities offered abroad will flow back into the U.S. market ("Category 1") and most restrictive when adequate information about the issuer is not publicly available in the United States and U.S. market interest is sufficient to suggest that offerings of the issuer's securities outside the United States may not come to rest abroad ("Category 3"). When adequate information about the issuer is publicly available in the United States ("Category 2"), the concerns about securities flowing into the United States are reduced, and the restrictions fall between these two extremes.

The second safe harbor permits securities that are initially offered abroad, or sold in the United States in a private placement, to be resold immediately abroad by persons other than an issuer or distributor so long as the offshore transaction requirement (defined slightly more broadly in this context) is met and there are no directed selling efforts in the United States in connection with the resale. This aspect of Regulation S has been important primarily in increasing the attractiveness of privately placed securities of non–U.S. issuers – the liquidity of such securities has been enhanced by allowing resales to be made immediately outside the United States into their principal trading market, encouraging foreign issuers to seek access to the U.S. capital market through private placements.

E.   *Civil Liability*

The liability a defendant may face for improper conduct in buying or selling securities will vary from jurisdiction to jurisdiction and may result in multiple exposure. Remedies and sanctions for improper securities activities typically can be sought in three basic ways: through civil litigation, administrative proceedings by a governmental agency or self–regulatory organization and/or criminal prosecutions. In many countries, particularly the United States, the same conduct can give rise to liability based on more than one statutory provision, and this liability can be enforced in legal actions brought by both governmental entities and private parties. Thus, the international lawyer must be sure to understand the potential liabilities for a securities transaction in each particular jurisdiction at issue.

In civil litigation, private parties seek to recover losses suffered as a result of the defendant's conduct, or request injunctive relief to compel or enjoin action. These private rights of action either arise from express statutory provisions or are implied, *i.e.*, created by judges to provide remedies for violations of statutes that are silent as to possible remedies. Administrative agencies such as the SEC may also bring civil actions to seek forfeiture of illegally obtained profits, civil monetary penalties, which may be greater or less than damages awarded in a private civil suit, and/or injunctive relief.

The United States has draconian express statutory remedies with respect to public offerings. First, if a security has been sold without being registered, and the seller fails to sustain the burden of establishing an available exemption, the buyer is entitled, within the prescribed limitations period, to rescind the transaction and get back its purchase price. The same is true in the case of non–compliance with the Act's prospectus–delivery requirements. Second, there are express remedies if a registration statement is, by virtue of a misstatement or omission, materially misleading. Liability attaches regardless of the purchaser's ability to prove reliance or causation; liability is absolute with respect to the issuer, and extends to the officers and directors of the issuer, the underwriters, and the accountants and other experts who have taken responsibility for some part of the registration statement, in each case unless such person can show it exercised "due diligence" in connection with the preparation of the registration statement. In contrast, the remedies for insider trading have been implied by the courts and can be substantial.

The SEC may also bring an administrative proceeding for certain violations in connection with the public offering and has the power to impose civil penalties or to obtain cease and desist orders mandating an immediate halt to the improper conduct. The SEC may not bring criminal proceedings even though it is an agency of the federal government. Those proceedings may only be brought by the Department of Justice. Defendants who are convicted face substantial fines and, in the case of individuals, terms of imprisonment.

If liability is imposed on officers or directors, the international practitioner should consider whether indemnities from the company are permissible or enforceable. The SEC has take the position that indemnities of officers, directors and underwriters against the consequences of their negligence are not enforceable as a matter of public policy, and the courts have generally sustained that position. Insurance is permissible, however. Indemnification is more generally available in the U.K.

IV.   THE SECONDARY MARKET FOR SECURITIES

Most jurisdictions also regulate financial intermediaries participating in the domestic capital market as well as trading activities in the secondary market. Although the U.S. again has the most developed regime, in general countries regulate the same types of activities. Under the Exchange Act, the U.S. has: rules requiring registration and periodic reporting by companies with exchange–listed or widely held securities; rules governing the conduct of market intermediaries (other than investment advisors); rules mandating adequate recordkeeping and internal accounting controls, and the Foreign Corrupt Practices Act ("FCPA") which proscribes bribery of foreign officials and other corrupt practices on the part of issuers of registered securities;[2] rules regulating the solicitation of proxies in connection with shareholder voting; rules governing the conduct of tender and exchange offers; rules requiring major shareholders to report the existence of and changes in their holdings of a company's shares; and rules prescribing penalties for manipulative or deceptive practices in connection with sales of securities, and for trading on inside information. By and large, foreign companies are subject to these rules to the same extent as domestic U.S. companies, including the FCPA (although the SEC's proxy rules, for obvious reasons, do not apply to the internal corporate affairs of non–U.S. companies).

A.   *Exchange Act Registration*

Most jurisdictions require ongoing disclosure to the secondary market following a public offering. Often these conditions are imposed by the stock exchange on which the securities are listed. The U.S. rules, however, impose requirements irrespective of any listing. The Exchange Act requires any U.S. company (i) that has a class of securities listed on a U.S. securities exchange or a class of equity securities quoted in the NASDAQ system of the National Association of Securities Dealers, Inc. (described below) or (ii) that has a class of equity securities held of record by more than 500 persons and $5 million or more in assets[3] to register such class with the SEC, and thereafter to file periodic reports. Foreign companies are also subject to registration under the Exchange Act and periodic reporting obligations if (i) they have a class of exchange-listed securities or "NASDAQ"-quoted equity securities or (ii) subject to a limited exception,[4] they exceed the asset and shareholder thresholds described above and 300 or more of the holders of the relevant class of securities are in the United States. By contrast, foreign companies whose securities are traded in the U.S. over-the-counter market (with prices quoted in the "pink sheets" and on an electronic bulletin board operated by the NASD), even if they exceed the asset and shareholder thresholds, may avoid Exchange Act registration, with its attendant periodic reporting obligations, if they undertake to furnish to the SEC reports and other information they make available in their home markets. In addition, every company, U.S. or foreign, making a public offering of debt or equity in the United States must file periodic reports under the Exchange Act so long as the securities offered are held by at least 300 persons.

Ongoing disclosure requirements under the Exchange Act differ for U.S. and foreign issuers. U.S. issuers file annual, quarterly, and interim reports. Foreign issuers, however, are required to file only an annual report, with interim reports required only to the extent they are made available by the issuer for legal reasons or as a matter of practice.

B.   Regulation of Market Participants

The Exchange Act, like legislation in many other countries, regulates a wide variety of market activities and participants. It requires disclosure of ownership in excess of five percent of any class of equity registered under the Exchange Act and requires filings and disclosure in connection with tender and exchange offers for five percent or more of any such class. Many jurisdictions have similar obligations to disclose interests in equity securities in excess of a specified percentage–three percent, for example, in the U.K. In addition, the Exchange Act regulates all persons acting in the United States as broker-dealers, clearing agents, information processors or securities depositaries. The only exception, an important one, is for banks acting as broker-dealers, which are generally exempt from registration under the Exchange Act and therefore subject to oversight only by their bank regulators. While only the entity performing the service, not its holding company, if any, is regulated, the SEC was recently empowered to require a registered broker-dealer to obtain certain financial information about its unregulated affiliates and to restrict upstream distributions in certain instances. Because the failure to obtain a license can be a criminal offense, practitioners should carefully review whether any intermediary acting in the market must be licensed.

In addition, the Exchange Act is similar to the laws of other countries in that it regulates securities exchanges and contains broad rules barring manipulative market conduct on or off the floor of an exchange. These market manipulation rules are also applied in certain circumstances to activities on markets outside the United States. The principal markets in the United States are the New York Stock Exchange, Inc., the American Stock Exchange, Inc. and the National Association of Securities Dealers Automated Quotation system, "NASDAQ," an over-the-counter formal quotation system for dealers. The exchanges and the NASD, which oversees the over-the-counter market in the United States and is the operator of NASDAQ and NASDAQ/NMS, are self-regulatory organizations ("SROs"). The SROs are required to regulate their member broker-dealers in the public interest, and their rules are subject to review and approval by the SEC. Virtually every broker-dealer must be a member of the NASD. While other jurisdictions have SROs, they are not as extensively regulated as are SROs in the United States.

The Exchange Act also requires each issuer that has registered a class of equity securities under the Exchange Act or otherwise has a periodic reporting obligation and its subsidiaries (domestic or foreign) to maintain accurate books and records and an adequate system of internal controls. It bars certain foreign corrupt payments by any company, U.S. or foreign, and it prohibits any officer or director from lying to the firm's auditors. These provisions are not common outside the United States.

C.   Insider Trading

For a long time, the United States was the only market that prohibited trading on the basis of material non-public information. Other countries, such as the U.K., Japan and Germany, have now followed suit, and such trading is now regulated in most markets, although what constitutes the offense differs from market to market. Unfortunately, the SEC and Congress have never defined the offense, in contrast to member states of the European Union, where the offense is statutory. As a result, while the penalties are severe in the United States, the conduct prohibited is uncertain. Its contours have been established through application by the courts – sometimes at the behest of the SEC (in its enforcement capacity) and sometimes in suits brought by private parties – of a broad general prohibition against fraud to particular fact patterns involving trading while in possession of undisclosed material information. In essence, the offense consists of trading in breach of a fiduciary obligation or misappropriating information. Regulation of insider trading reflects an important characteristic of the regulation of U.S. financial markets in contrast to other markets, for example in Europe. Often the U.S. rules are general in scope and must be fleshed out through interpretation by the staff of the SEC and litigation by both the government and the private bar. For this reason, many of the rules about market conduct have their origin in decisional law construing the statutory and regulatory framework. In any event, practitioners in any jurisdiction must be extremely careful when advising market participants on the law of insider trading.

Both civil and criminal penalties can arise from violations of the U.S. insider trading law. The SEC can bring a civil action for injunction and "disgorgement" of profit gained (or loss avoided) against a person who trades in violation of the law. A civil fine of up to three times the disgorgement amount can be imposed by a court at the SEC's behest. Under certain circumstances, the SEC may also seek civil penalties against "controlling persons" (e.g., the employer and supervisors) of an insider trader where such persons have disregarded the likelihood that the subordinate would improperly trade on information gleaned through employment. Criminal proceedings can be brought by the U.S. Department of Justice against persons who willfully violate insider trading laws. A conviction can result in fines of up to $1 million and/or imprisonment of up to 10 years for natural persons or fines of up to $2.5 million for violations by a company or other entity. Each trade can be prosecuted as a separate count of misconduct.

V.   COLLECTIVE INVESTMENT VEHICLES

Collective Investment Vehicles ("CIVs") are usually regulated because of abuses in the past. Moreover, the regime is usually quite strict, and often prevents a CIV from raising funds outside its domestic market. The rules, including those relating to its taxation, are often complex. Thus, it will come as no surprise that the U.S. Investment Company Act is one of the most complex of the U.S. securities laws.

The Investment Company Act covers a wide range of companies, and provides a good checklist of the types of entities that might be regulated in other jurisdictions as CIVs. Every "investment company" is subject to regulation, unless expressly exempt or excluded. An "investment company" is defined not only in terms of its purpose but also in terms of the assets it holds, to minimize the possibility that an entity could inappropriately escape regulation. Thus, not only is every entity that holds itself out as being engaged primarily in "investing, reinvesting or trading in securities" covered but any entity that is engaged in the business of investing, reinvesting, owning, holding or trading in securities and holds as little as 40 percent of the value of its assets in securities (other than U.S. government and agency securities and securities of majority owned subsidiaries that are not themselves investment companies).

Moreover, the Investment Company Act's remedial purposes have provided the basis for the SEC's broad view of the definition of "security" in the Act. Although that definition is virtually identical to the definitions found in the other U.S. securities laws, the staff of the SEC has consistently taken the position that a variety of instruments and items that are not securities under those other statutes – such as commercial bank loans, affiliate loans, certain insurance instruments, commercial and other ordinary-course credit arrangements, and the like – are securities for the purposes of the Act.

Any investment company that is not excluded or exempted not only must register with the SEC but also must be structured so that it fits within the definition of one of three categories of investment company. The requirements applicable to a registered investment company depend in part on its classification. If a company does not fit within one of these categories, it cannot register and therefore cannot do business unless an exemption is available under the statute or granted by the SEC.

There is no doubt that conventional mutual funds and investment companies are intended to be the primary subjects of Investment Company Act regulation. The combination of the asset–based definition of investment company and the broad interpretation of the definition of security, however, has also brought within the regulatory range of the Investment Company Act other sorts of entities, sometimes referred to as "inadvertent investment companies," for which the appropriateness of Investment Company Act regulation is far less obvious. These companies include certain holding companies that own controlling, but less than majority, interests in other companies, foreign banks and insurance companies and their holding companies, and finance subsidiaries whose assets consist of loans to their parents and affiliates.

The Investment Company Act contains a number of provisions excluding particular types of entities either from the definition of investment company or from the operation of the Act. In addition, the Act grants authority to the SEC to exempt entities either from any of its specific provisions or from its provisions generally, where such exemption is "necessary or appropriate in the public interest and consistent with the protection of investors and the purposes fairly intended by the policy and provisions" of the Act. Although this exemptive authority provides necessary flexibility to a rigid statute, in recent practice such exemptions have been both expensive and time–consuming to obtain: other than in cases of routine relief identical to previously granted exemptions, this process now typically requires several months and often longer where novel issues are presented.

A registered investment company is subject to very significant ongoing disclosure requirements. However, in contrast to the other U.S. federal securities laws, the primary focus is on substantive regulation. Such regulation extends to: the make–up and conduct of the board of directors; transactions between an investment company and its promoters, underwriters, advisers and other affiliated persons; issuance of debt or other "senior" securities and other borrowings to create leverage; investment in other companies; and securities custody arrangements.

The Investment Company Act regulates foreign investment companies by restricting their offerings of securities in the United States. A foreign investment company is prohibited under the Act from making a public offering in the United States unless it has received an order from the SEC registering it as an investment company, which order generally would impose conditions that parallel the provisions of the Act. The requirements that must be met to obtain such an order are such that, with the exception of a few Canadian investment companies, U.S. public offerings by foreign investment companies are effectively prohibited. Although the Investment Company Act does not explicitly address private offerings by foreign investment companies, the SEC staff has attempted to place stringent limitations on such offerings that are derived from the rules applicable to U.S. private investment companies.

VI.   CONCLUSION

Most jurisdictions regulate the activities of all participants in the capital markets. The level of regulation, however, varies dramatically. The emergence of the International Organization of Securities Commissions ("IOSCO") together with the role played in it by the United States is resulting in regulatory convergence. The approach to regulation described above with respect to the United States is a guide to current or future regulatory regimes in other markets.

VII.   SOURCES OF ASSISTANCE

A.   U.S. Law

1.   Statutes

Investment Advisers Act of 1940, 15 U.S.C. §§80b–1 – 80b–21, *as amended.*

Investment Company Act of 1940, 15 U.S.C. §§80a–1 – 80a–52, *as amended.*

Securities Act of 1933, 15 U.S.C. §§77a–77aa, *as amended.*

Securities Exchange Act of 1934, 15 U.S.C. §§78a–78jj, *as amended.*

Trust Indenture Act of 1939, 15 U.S.C. §§77aaa–77bbbb, *as amended.*

2.   Secondary Sources

E. GREENE, *et al.*, U.S. REGULATION OF THE INTERNATIONAL SECURITIES AND DERIVATIVES MARKETS (1996).

L. LOSS & J. SELIGMAN, FUNDAMENTALS OF SECURITIES REGULATION (3d ed. 1995).

L. SODERQUIST, UNDERSTANDING THE SECURITIES LAWS (3d ed. 1994).

PRACTISING LAW INSTITUTE, CORPORATE LAW AND PRACTICE, COURSE HANDBOOK SERIES. (Reproduces materials prepared for educational programs run by PLI on various specialized topics.)

B. *Non-U.S. Law*

1. United Kingdom

a. Statutes

The Prevention of Fraud (Investments) Act 1958, *as amended.*

The Companies Act 1985, *as amended.*

The Financial Services Act 1986.

The Public Offer of Securities Regulations 1995.

The Licensed Dealers (Conduct of Business) Rules 1983 (SI 1983/585).

b. Secondary Sources

BUTTERWORTHS COMPANY LAW HANDBOOK (K. Walmsley ed., 9th ed. 1993). (Includes commentary and text of relevant statutes.)

2. France

Statutes

Regulations No. 91–02 and 92–02 of the Commission des Opérations de Bourse.

3. Germany

a. Statutes

Securities Trading Act of 1994.

Securities Sales Prospectus Act of 1991, *as amended.*

Stock Exchange Act of 1896, *as amended.*

Investment Fund Act of 1970, *as amended.*

Foreign Investment Fund Act of 1969, *as amended.*

b. Secondary Sources

MOHR, GERMAN INSIDER AND STOCK EXCHANGE LAW (1994).

4. Canada

a. Statutes

(i) Province of Ontario: Securities Act R.S.O. 1990, c. S.5, *as amended* by 1992, c. 18, 1993, c. 27, 1994, c. 11, c. 33.

(ii) Province of Quebec: Securities Act R.S.Q., c. V–1.1, *as amended* by 1990, c. 77, 1992, c. 35, 1992, c. 21, 1992, c. 61, 1992, c. 57, 1993, c. 67, 1994, c. 13, c. 23, 1995, c. 33.

b.   Secondary Sources

INTERNATIONAL CAPITAL MARKETS AND SECURITIES REGULATION, VOL. 10A, SECURITIES LAW SERIES (H. Bloomenthal ed. 1982).

INTERNATIONAL SECURITIES REGULATION, VOL. 2 (R. Rosen ed. 1986).

5.   Japan

a.   Statutes

Law concerning Foreign Securities Firms (*Gaikoku Shoken Gyosha ni kannsuru Houritsu*), 1971, Law No. 5, *as amended.*

Law concerning Regulation on Investment Advisory Business pertaining to Securities (*Yuka Shoken ni kakaru Toushi Komongyo no Kisei ni kannsuru Houritsu*), 1986, Law No. 74, *as amended.*

Securities and Exchange Law (*Shoken Torihiki Ho*), 1948, Law No. 25, *as amended.*

Securities Investment Trust Law (*Shoken Toushi Shintaku Ho*), 1951, Law No. 198, *as amended.*

b.   Secondary Sources

JAPAN SECURITIES INSTITUTE, SECURITIES MARKET IN JAPAN (Tokyo: Japanese Securities Institute 1994).

JAPANESE SECURITIES REGULATION (L. Loss, *et al.* eds. 1983).

6.   European Union

a.   Statutes

Investment Services Directive of May 10, 1993 (93/22), O.J. No. L 141, June 11, 1993, p. 11.

Capital Adequacy Directive of March 15, 1993 (93/6), O.J. No. L 141, June 6, 1993, p. 1, *as amended.*

Directive on Listing Conditions of March 5, 1979 (79/279), O.J. No. L 66, March 16, 1979, p. 21, *as amended.*

Directive on Listing Prospectuses of March 17, 1980 (80/390), O.J. No. L 100, April 17, 1980, p. 1, *as amended.*

Directive on On–going Disclosure for Listed Issuers of February 15, 1982 (82/121), O.J. No. L 48, February 20, 1982, p. 26.

Directive on Offering Prospectuses of April 17, 1989 (89/298), April 17, 1989, O.J. No. L 124, May 5, 1989, p. 8, *as amended.*

Insider Trading Directive of November 13, 1989 (89/592), O.J. No. L 334, November 18, 1989, p. 30, *as amended.*

UCITS Directive of December 20, 1985 (85/611), O.J. No. L 375, December 31, 1985, p. 3, *as amended.*

        b.   Secondary Sources

M. VAN EMPEL, FINANCIAL SERVICES AND EEC LAW – MATERIALS AND CASES (1990) (loose leaf).

M. EGAN, *et al.*, EC FINANCIAL SERVICES REGULATION (1994) (loose leaf).

ENDNOTES

[1] Statutes named in the text are cited in full in Section VII, Sources of Assistance.

[2] *See* Chapter 14, *The Foreign Corrupt Practices Act*, for a more detailed discussion of this legislation.

[3] As of this writing (October 1995), the SEC is proposing to raise this threshold to $10 million.

[4] Rule 12g3–2(b) under the Exchange Act. See Section IV.B. for a description of the exchanges and "NASDAQ."

CHAPTER 10

U.S. TAXATION OF INTERNATIONAL TRANSACTIONS

Laurence E. Nemirow, Robert S. Rich and John R. Wilson

I.   INTRODUCTION

Taxes affect most international operations, and tax planning often is an integral part of structuring international business transactions. This chapter presents an overview of the U.S. tax aspects of international business transactions. It is prepared in two parts: the first covers outbound transactions (principally the application of U.S. taxes to foreign operations of U.S. taxpayers); and the second covers inbound transactions (principally the application of U.S. taxes to foreign persons investing or doing business in the United States). The discussion is necessarily general, and taxpayers should consult with their advisors as to their particular circumstances.

United States tax professionals normally advise their clients on the U.S. consequences of international transactions, and often develop a network of foreign tax advisors with whom they consult as to the foreign consequences. As a practical matter, U.S. tax professionals more often become involved in selecting foreign tax advisors in outbound transactions, as inbound investors normally already have foreign tax advisors and look to U.S. tax professionals only for U.S. advice. The type of foreign professional that should be consulted (i.e., a lawyer or accountant) will depend upon the traditions of each foreign country. In some European countries, for example, tax as a specialty of legal practice has not evolved to the degree that it has in the United States, and local accountants or special tax experts (e.g., in France and the Netherlands) may be preferred as sources of tax advice. Tax attorneys have, however, proved to be valuable resources in many areas, including much of Central and South America.

II.   OUTBOUND TRANSACTIONS   ·

A.   *Overview*

In general, a U.S. enterprise with overseas activities seeks to minimize the combined U.S. and foreign taxation of these activities. The means to this end will depend upon the enterprise's specific situation. In the outbound sales context, the goal is often to avoid becoming subject to foreign income taxes altogether, under the rules described in Section II.B, *below*. For outbound investments, some foreign income taxes likely will apply, and the focus shifts to minimizing the total tax burden.

U.S. corporations are subject to U.S. taxation on their worldwide income, whether earned in the U.S. or abroad. At present, the maximum U.S. corporate income tax rate is 35 percent. Similarly, U.S. individual citizens and residents are subject to U.S. taxation on their worldwide income, with a maximum marginal rate of 39.6 percent. "S" corporations and partnerships generally are treated as conduits, meaning that these entities are not directly subject to U.S. tax; rather, their income or loss is taxed to their shareholders or partners. Certain "hybrid" entities, such as U.S. limited liability companies ("LLCs") and similar foreign entities, can be structured as partnerships for U.S. tax purposes.

Unlike the United States, many foreign countries impose their income tax based on the source of income, with full or partial exemptions available for foreign-source income. Many foreign income tax regimes are not as developed as the U.S. system, and some foreign countries have established "tax holidays" or other special tax benefits for foreign investors, especially for major projects or for investments in particular industries or regions. Moreover, in some foreign jurisdictions, income tax rates may be established by negotiation between the taxpayer and the government. This is true especially in developing countries, where contractual assurances from the taxing authority are often indispensable in the absence of a stable and mature tax code.[1]

U.S. enterprises usually become subject to a foreign country's income taxes either by conducting business in a foreign country or by receiving income from a foreign person. In planning an outbound transaction, a threshold question is whether the taxpayer should establish a taxable presence in a foreign jurisdiction, *i.e.*, a foreign office or other fixed place of business. Although nontax considerations often will be decisive in this determination, tax aspects also should be examined. In recent years, U.S. corporate tax rates have been lower than the tax rates of most other industrial nations, so that establishing a taxable presence in another country often will result in more overall tax, even after the U.S. foreign tax credit.

Business income generally is taxed by foreign countries on a net basis, after allowance for deductions. Other foreign-source income (*e.g.*, interest, dividends and royalties from foreign persons) generally is taxed on a flat-rate basis, without allowance for deductions, and the liability for these taxes is often collected through withholding at the source. Such taxes often are effectively offset by the U.S. foreign tax credit, because U.S. tax rates generally exceed applicable withholding tax rates, particularly if the tax rate is reduced by a U.S. income tax treaty.

U.S. persons may obtain relief from foreign income taxes under U.S. income tax treaties with foreign countries. The U.S. currently has bilateral income tax treaties in force with approximately 50 countries. In general, under these treaties a foreign country may tax the business profits of a U.S. enterprise only if the enterprise has a "permanent establishment" in the country, *e.g.*, an office or other fixed place of business. Alternatively, if the U.S. enterprise operates through a local country subsidiary, foreign income tax will be imposed on the subsidiary, and not on the U.S. parent corporation. However, foreign withholding taxes may apply when the subsidiary pays interest, dividends, royalties or other amounts to the U.S. parent. U.S. tax treaties may reduce or eliminate the amount of these foreign withholding taxes.

As a general rule, the profits of a foreign subsidiary are not taxed to the U.S. parent corporation until repatriated as dividends (or the subsidiary makes other payments). There are, however, important exceptions to this rule, most notably the "subpart F" rules applicable to "controlled foreign corporations" ("CFC"s), which can cause all or a portion of the subsidiary's income to be currently taxed to its U.S. shareholders, regardless of whether the income is distributed as dividends.[2]

To prevent "double taxation" of income by both the U.S. and a foreign country, U.S. law allows U.S. taxpayers a foreign tax credit for foreign income taxes paid or accrued.[3] In the case of a foreign subsidiary, the U.S. parent corporation can also claim an indirect or deemed paid credit for foreign taxes paid by the subsidiary. The indirect credit applies only to first, second- and third–tier subsidiaries, and certain ownership thresholds must be met.[4] In theory, the foreign tax credit should result in a U.S. taxpayer paying tax at the higher of the U.S. and foreign tax rates on the earnings attributable to a foreign country; in practice, however, because of numerous limitations on the foreign tax credit, some double taxation often results.[5]

B. *Selling Goods Internationally*

If a U.S. enterprise merely desires to sell its goods internationally, it generally can do so without incurring foreign income taxes. Under applicable tax treaties, foreign income taxes will not apply unless the U.S. enterprise has a "permanent establishment" in the foreign country. A permanent establishment generally includes an office or other fixed place of business, but does not include an independent distributor or an employee who merely refers orders to the home office.[6] However, an employee or agent may give rise to a permanent establishment if he "habitually exercises" the authority to conclude contracts for the enterprise. An enterprise generally can engage in certain sales–related activities (such as the storage or demonstration of goods) without creating a permanent establishment. Thus, if structured properly, many U.S. enterprises can sell goods internationally without concern for foreign income taxes. Similar considerations may apply to the performance of services internationally, provided that no permanent establishment results.

A U.S. enterprise selling its goods internationally should consider whether a foreign sales corporation ("FSC") or domestic international sales corporation ("DISC") would be appropriate. Both FSCs and DISCs can be used to reduce modestly the effective rate of U.S. tax on export sales, but the rules governing these entities are quite complex.[7]

C.   *Branches and Subsidiaries*

The choice between a foreign branch or subsidiary may depend in part upon the U.S. enterprise's current U.S. tax situation. If the U.S. enterprise is a conduit entity such as an "S" corporation, limited liability company or partnership, it may be preferable to operate directly in foreign countries through branches, in order to preserve single taxation of foreign earnings. Using a subsidiary may destroy the desired single tax treatment. If the U.S. enterprise is a corporation, it can establish a U.S. subsidiary with which it files a consolidated return and obtain single tax treatment.

The U.S. enterprise also may desire to operate through a branch or pass–through entity, at least initially, if it expects start–up losses that could be used to shelter U.S. profits. When the foreign branch turns profitable, these tax benefits will be recaptured but the taxpayer should obtain the time value of the deductions.[8] The effectiveness of this strategy can be limited in a number of ways. For example, deductions generally are not allowed until the branch actually begins operations; until then expenditures must be capitalized. Also, certain foreign deductions (*e.g.*, mining exploration or development costs) may be subject to slower write-offs than if incurred domestically.

The choice between branch and subsidiary also can be driven by differing foreign tax rules. The tax rules of a particular country may favor either branches or subsidiaries. In the United Kingdom, for example, branches are subject to a higher effective U.K. tax rate than subsidiaries, after giving effect to the U.S./U.K. tax treaty provisions allowing for partial refund of the advance corporation tax ("ACT") imposed on dividends. Germany, on the other hand, has a "split rate" system wherein distributed profits of a German subsidiary are taxed at a significantly lower rate than undistributed profits. Branch profits are taxed at an intermediate rate.

As discussed above, the foreign branch of a U.S. corporation is subject to U.S. taxation of its worldwide income because no separate legal entity is involved. However, only the activities of the branch (*i.e.*, those attributable to the permanent establishment) will be subject to foreign income taxation. Thus, it will be important to determine what income and deductions are attributable to the branch. Because many foreign tax rates currently are higher than U.S. tax rates, U.S. enterprises often want to minimize the amount of income subject to foreign taxation. This can be done by limiting the income attributable to the branch, in part by setting a favorable (*i.e.*, high) transfer price for goods transferred to the branch. The foreign country, however, can insist upon an "arm's–length" transfer price, under standards similar to those in IRC § 482, to prevent the arbitrary shifting of income.[9] Foreign taxation also can be reduced by attributing deductions (*e.g.*, interest and royalties) to the branch, assuming that these deductions are allowed under foreign law. It is difficult to reduce U.S. income tax through the use of intermediate foreign holding companies created in tax haven countries because of the subpart F rules and the transfer pricing rules.

Foreign subsidiaries of U.S. enterprises face similar issues. For example, if the U.S. enterprise sets up a local sales subsidiary, the U.S. enterprise must either sell the goods to the subsidiary (at an appropriate transfer price) or transfer them on consignment (whereupon the subsidiary should earn a reasonable sales commission). In either case, the subsidiary must deal with the U.S. parent on an arm's-length basis or face potential reallocations of income and deductions by U.S. and foreign tax authorities. In addition, the U.S. parent may fund the subsidiary in part with debt, thereby reducing the subsidiary's income through interest deductions and allowing the tax-free repayment of principal. For this to work, the interest deduction must be allowed in the foreign country (and not disallowed under "thin capitalization" or "earnings stripping" rules) and must offset the tax effect of any foreign withholding taxes on the interest (after application of U.S. tax treaties, which may reduce or eliminate these withholding taxes). The U.S. enterprise also may charge its subsidiary for services it provides, or may license property in return for royalties (subject to local country restrictions or approvals), thereby further reducing the subsidiary's income.

Foreign subsidiaries may give rise to additional U.S. tax issues. First, because the subsidiary is a separate legal entity, transfers to the subsidiary (especially of technology) can raise U.S. tax issues. (*See* section II.F., *below*.) Second, the activities of the subsidiary can cause the U.S. parent to be taxed in the U.S. even before the subsidiary pays dividends. For example, if the subsidiary is a sales or service company for the U.S. parent, activities outside the subsidiary's country of incorporation can generate subpart F income, currently taxable to the U.S. parent.[10] Similar rules may apply to subsidiaries which merely assemble the U.S. parent's products, unless a substantial proportion of the manufacturing actually occurs in the foreign country.

D. *Holding Companies*

For various reasons, U.S. enterprises with operations in a number of foreign countries may desire to have a single holding company for their international operations. For example, a holding company may centralize certain management activities or facilitate financing for the combined international operations.

From a U.S. tax perspective, several issues arise from the holding company structure. First, if the U.S. enterprise has existing subsidiaries, their transfer to a foreign holding company may involve U.S. tax issues, and a "gain recognition agreement" may be required to avoid present taxation.[11] Second, during operations the lower-tier subsidiaries may repatriate profits to the holding company, either through dividends or other payments, such as interest and royalties. These payments may be subpart F income to the holding company, presently taxable to the U.S. parent, unless certain exceptions apply.[12] Finally, the holding company structure should not result in more than three tiers of foreign subsidiaries; the U.S. parent cannot take an indirect foreign tax credit below the third tier.

E.   *Joint Ventures*

U.S. enterprises commonly enter into joint ventures to conduct international business operations. The term "joint venture" has no technical meaning under U.S. tax law, but refers rather to a domestic or foreign corporation, limited liability company, partnership or other entity or arrangement (perhaps even a strategic alliance) between or among two or more persons. As such, a joint venture can give rise to a number of U.S. tax issues, depending upon its tax classification (*e.g.*, whether the venture is treated as a partnership or corporation for U.S. tax purposes), and, in the case of a corporation, whether the corporation is a CFC for U.S. tax purposes.

If the joint venture is structured as a partnership for U.S. tax purposes, each U.S. partner includes its share of income or loss in its U.S. tax returns, much as it would for a branch operation.[13] Similarly, the disposition of joint venture assets is treated like the disposition of a branch.

For foreign corporate joint ventures, the important U.S. tax distinction is whether the corporation is a CFC. Curiously, a 50/50 joint venture between two U.S. enterprises will be a CFC, whereas a 50/50 joint venture with a foreign partner generally will not be. This matters for foreign tax credit purposes because dividends from CFCs usually are treated as general limitation income, whereas dividends from non–CFCs are separately basketed (meaning that, as a practical matter, the foreign tax credit is likely to be less available).[14]

F.   *Formations and Restructurings*

If the U.S. enterprise desires to conduct its international activities through a branch, no U.S. tax issues arise upon formation, because no transfer of assets to a new legal entity occurs. Similarly, if the U.S. enterprise wants to establish a local country subsidiary and fund it with cash, no significant U.S. tax issues arise.[15] If other business assets will be transferred to the foreign subsidiary, however, significant U.S. tax issues can arise.

Under U.S. law, contributions of property to a foreign corporation may be taxable, even if similar transfers to a domestic corporation would have qualified for tax–free treatment, *e.g.*, under IRC § 351.[16] However, IRC § 351 contributions of property for use by the foreign corporation in the "active conduct of a trade or business" outside the U.S. are tax–free, subject to the following exceptions:

- inventory property;

- installment obligations, accounts receivable and similar property;

- foreign currency;

- intangible property (*see below*); and

- leased property, unless the transferee is the lessor.

Moreover, if the taxpayer has an "overall foreign loss" or an aggregate tax loss from the branch, the transfer will cause a recapture of the loss, to the extent of any appreciation in the transferred property.[17]

Transfers of intangible property to foreign corporations are treated quite severely. The transferor is considered to have transferred the property for annual payments contingent upon the use of the property (a "deemed royalty"), which royalty is considered U.S.-source income.[18]

Transfers of appreciated property to foreign partnerships may be subject to a 35 percent excise tax.[19] However, the excise tax does not apply if the taxpayer (before the transfer) elects to treat the transfer under the principles of IRC § 367, although the draconian rules applicable to the transfer of intangible property will apply. The taxpayer also can elect to treat the transfer as fully taxable in lieu of paying the excise tax.[20]

Restructurings of international activities also will give rise to U.S. tax considerations. Certain restructurings (*e.g.*, the combination of two foreign subsidiaries) usually can be accomplished without material U.S. tax consequences, although some adjustments and reporting will be required.[21]

III.   INBOUND TRANSACTIONS

A.   *Overview*

The United States imposes its income tax on the worldwide income of its citizens, residents and domestic corporations. By contrast, nonresident aliens and foreign corporations are subject to tax only on (i) certain types of investment and other nonbusiness income from U.S. sources; and (ii) income effectively connected with a U.S. trade or business. The U.S. tax planning for foreign persons seeks to minimize these two taxes. For foreign individuals, the planning must also take into account the possible impact of U.S. estate and gift taxes, which can apply to transfers of "U.S.-situs" assets.[22] To avoid these taxes, the foreign investor usually interposes a foreign corporation, but this can be more costly for U.S. income tax purposes, and perhaps for foreign tax purposes as well.

Many of the same considerations applicable to outbound transactions are germane in planning inbound activities. For example, the relative U.S. and foreign tax rates will affect various threshold questions, including the net tax effect of establishing a U.S. trade or business and whether to operate in a branch or through a U.S. subsidiary. U.S. branch operations may be desirable if U.S. losses can be utilized to reduce foreign income taxes, while operating through a U.S. subsidiary may defer foreign taxation of operating income until the earnings are distributed. Similarly, the avoidance of double taxation is a principal concern, depending upon the availability of a foreign tax credit or exclusion (in the foreign investor's home jurisdiction) to offset the effect of U.S. taxation. Transfer pricing also can be important, depending upon the effective tax rates in the U.S. and the foreign jurisdiction.

B.   Foreign Persons

An alien individual is classified as a resident for U.S. income tax purposes if he is a lawful permanent resident (green card holder) or satisfies the "substantial presence" test.[23] This test requires the individual to be physically present in the United States for at least (i) 31 days during the current calendar year, and (ii) 183 days on a weighted–average basis during a three–year period, calculated by adding the days of presence in the current year, one-third of the days of presence in the preceding year, and one–sixth of the days of presence in the second preceding year.[24] Even if this test is satisfied, the "closer connection" test still may result in nonresident status, if the individual is in the United States for fewer than 183 days during the current year, has a closer connection with a foreign country and a "tax home" there, and has not taken steps to apply for a green card. In addition, tax treaties may override the determination of U.S. residence, if the individual qualifies as a foreign resident under the "tie–breaker" rules of the treaty.

In general, residence status applies for the entire year. However, the beginning or end of a year can be excluded from U.S. residence, provided that the individual is not in the U.S. during such time (or only for nominal periods not exceeding 10 days), and has a closer connection with a foreign country during such time. These exceptions also require the individual to be a nonresident for the year before or year after, as appropriate. For a "dual–status" year, the foreign person files one return, in which he is taxed as a nonresident for part of the year and as a resident for the remaining portion of the year.[25]

An individual who gives up his U.S. citizenship and moves abroad nevertheless remains subject to federal income tax at graduated rates on his income from U.S. sources for the ten–year period following his loss of citizenship, unless his loss does not have tax avoidance as one of its principal purposes.[26] For this purpose, U.S.–source income is defined to include income from property located in the United States (e.g., equipment) and income from stocks or bonds of domestic corporations.

Compared with the classification of individuals, the classification of corporations is relatively straightforward: a domestic corporation is organized under U.S. law, whereas a foreign corporation is organized under foreign law.[27] The location of business operations or management activities is irrelevant.

C. Nonbusiness Income

Subject to reduction or elimination by an applicable income tax treaty, foreign persons generally are subject to a 30 percent withholding tax on investment and other nonbusiness income from U.S. sources.[28] This category of income, generally referred to as "fixed and determinable annual or periodical" income, or "FDAP," includes dividends, interest, rents, compensation, remunerations, emoluments and royalties – but normally not capital gains. Income constitutes FDAP without regard to whether it is paid in a series of repeated payments or in a single lump sum, although such factors may affect the timing of the tax.

Even if a foreign investor plans to engage in a U.S. trade or business, the FDAP rules may be important. This is because, for various reasons, the investor may form a U.S. corporation to undertake the U.S. business. This corporation will be subject to U.S. corporate tax, mostly like any other U.S. corporation, and the critical U.S. international tax issue will be the repatriation of profits, to which the FDAP rules will apply.[29]

FDAP withholding taxes apply only to U.S.–source income. Dividends and interest usually are sourced to the place of organization of the payor or debtor, respectively.[30] Compensation for services normally is sourced to the place where the services are performed.[31] Rents and royalties are sourced to the location of the underlying property (if the property is tangible), or to the place of use of such property (for patents, copyrights and other intangible property).[32]

U.S. law provides exemptions from withholding tax for interest on deposits with U.S. banks and other financial institutions as well as for "portfolio interest."[33] The latter exemption includes interest paid on an obligation in "registered form" if the U.S. person who would otherwise have to withhold tax receives a statement that the beneficial owner of the obligation is not a U.S. person. Exempt portfolio interest also includes interest on a bearer bond not in registered form if properly directed to non–U.S. holders. A foreign person's ability to utilize the exemption for portfolio interest is limited because various categories of interest are excluded from the exemption, including interest paid to a related foreign person, contingent interest, interest paid to a CFC by a related person, and interest paid to a foreign bank.

U.S. tax treaties typically reduce the withholding tax rates on various types of passive income (e.g., dividends), and sometimes eliminate the withholding tax on other types of income (interest and industrial royalties). However, treaty benefits are subject to certain limitations. For example, newer U.S. treaties contain provisions to prevent "treaty shopping," thereby limiting treaty benefits to residents of the treaty country or other qualified persons. Moreover, the IRS may collapse "back-to-back" conduit financing arrangements with intermediaries resident in treaty countries.[34]

The FDAP rules make "withholding agents" (i.e., persons having control over payment) responsible for the collection and payment of the withholding taxes. Thus, if the tax is not properly withheld, the IRS can pursue its claim against these persons (which, as a practical matter, is usually much easier than collecting from the foreign payee). In arm's-length situations (*e.g.*, a bank loan), there are often detailed contractual provisions as to whether the payor will be required to "gross up" the amount of the payments if FDAP taxes apply.

D.   *Business Income*

The general U.S. income tax (at graduated rates) applies to foreign persons with U.S. business income. This type of income is often referred to as "effectively connected income," or "ECI."[35] The ECI rules apply to foreign persons who directly engage in a U.S. trade or business, or who do so indirectly through a pass-through entity such as a partnership or LLC. As a empirical matter, however, many business activities of foreign persons are conducted through U.S. subsidiary corporations. These corporations, which are subject to U.S. tax on their worldwide income, are not subject to these rules, but instead are subject to the FDAP rules when they make payments (*e.g.*, dividends) to their foreign owners or other foreign persons.

1.   U.S. Trade or Business

Foreign persons often wish to limit their U.S. activities to avoid having a U.S. trade or business. The Code itself does not define the meaning of a U.S. trade or business, except with respect to the performance of personal services and trading in securities and commodities. The performance of personal services within the United States at any time during the taxable year constitutes a U.S. trade or business. There is a limited exception–of little value in practice–for commercial travelers.[36] However, tax treaties often broaden this exception.[37]

Foreign persons are relatively free to trade in stocks, securities and commodities in the United States without being treated as having a U.S. trade or business. In order to encourage the acquisition of U.S. stocks, securities and commodities by foreign persons, the Code provides that trading in securities or commodities through a resident broker, commission agent, custodian or other independent agent does not constitute a U.S. trade or business, unless the taxpayer has an office or other fixed place of business in the United States through which the transactions are effected.[38] Similarly, trading in securities or commodities for the taxpayer's own account does not constitute a U.S. trade or business, as long as the taxpayer is not a dealer or (as to securities) a corporation principally engaged in trading for its own account through its principal office located in the United States. This exemption applies whether transactions are effected by the taxpayer, the taxpayer's employees or other agents, and even if the employee or agent has discretionary authority to make decisions in effecting the transactions.[39]

Outside these specific provisions, a foreign person's activities will constitute a U.S. trade or business if they are sufficiently "regular, continuous and substantial" within the meaning of the case law. The activities of an agent normally are taken into account in making this determination. An isolated transaction usually will not create a U.S. trade or business, and a taxpayer may engage in preparatory activities for a future U.S. trade or business.

If a partnership (whether U.S. or foreign) is engaged in a U.S. trade or business, its partners (whether general or limited) are treated as so engaged.[40] As a consequence, the foreign partners will be taxed on the ECI realized by the partnership. This tax is enforced by a system of withholding, which requires a partnership to withhold tax at the highest marginal rate (without regard to the partner's actual tax rate) on the partnership's ECI, to the extent allocable to foreign partners (even if not distributed).[41] A partner is entitled to a refund of amounts withheld in excess of his tax liability.

2.   Effectively Connected Income

If a foreign person is found to be engaged in a U.S. trade or business, then to determine such person's ECI, income is separated into three categories: (i) U.S.-source FDAP income and capital gains; (ii) other U.S.-source income; and (iii) foreign-source income. Different rules apply to each of these categories.

For the first category, U.S.-source FDAP and capital gains, two rather open-ended tests determine whether such income constitutes ECI:[42]

- whether the income, gain or loss is derived from assets used in, or held for use in, the conduct of the U.S. trade or business (the "asset-use test"); and

- whether the activities of the U.S. trade or business are a material factor in the realization of the income, gain or loss (the "business activities test").

Thus, investment income that would normally be taxed (or exempt, as the case may be, under Code or treaty provisions) under the FDAP rules instead is taxed as ECI if such income is sufficiently related to the foreign person's U.S. trade or business (*e.g.*, income on working capital associated with the business).

Somewhat surprisingly, the second category of income, other U.S.-source income, is treated as ECI without regard to its connection with the U.S. trade or business. This result is known as the "limited force of attraction principle."[43]

As might be expected, only very limited types of the third category of income, foreign-source income, are treated as ECI, and then only if attributable to a U.S. office or other fixed place of business:[44]

- rents or royalties from the use of intangible property (patents, copyrights, secret processes, *etc.*) located outside the United States if derived in the active conduct of a U.S. trade or business;

- dividends or interest from foreign sources derived in the active conduct of a banking, financing or similar business within the United States, or received by a foreign investment company, or received by a corporation the principal business of which is trading in stocks or securities for its own account; or

- income derived from the sale of inventory (outside the U.S.) through a U.S. office or other fixed place of business, unless the inventory property is sold for use, consumption or disposition outside the U.S. and an office or other fixed place of business of the taxpayer in a foreign country participated materially in such sale.[45]

Other foreign-source income is exempt from U.S. tax altogether.

Finally, to prevent circumvention of the ECI rules, two further types of income are treated as ECI even if the taxpayer is not engaged in a U.S. trade or business at any time during the taxable year:[46]

- income attributable to a transaction in another year is treated as ECI if it would have been so treated in that year; and

- gain from the sale of assets formerly used in a U.S. trade or business will be treated as ECI if the assets are sold within 10 years of being used in the U.S. trade or business.

Once the sources of ECI are determined, the foreign person's taxable income must then be calculated. This is done by deducting from the gross income constituting ECI both (i) the expenses, losses and other deductions properly apportioned or allocated thereto, and (ii) a ratable part of any expenses, losses or deductions that cannot definitely be allocated to some item or class of gross income.[47]

3.   Permanent Establishment Rules

Treaties normally narrow U.S. taxation by replacing the concept of ECI with that of income attributable to a U.S. "permanent establishment," and by restricting the graduated tax to "business profits" attributable to the permanent establishment. In general, a permanent establishment is a fixed place of business through which the business is wholly or partly carried on. Treaties also often specify that certain facilities – such as a branch, an office, a workshop, or a place of extraction of natural resources – will constitute a permanent establishment, while certain activities – such as the use of facilities or maintenance of a stock of goods for storage, display or delivery of goods, the purchase of goods or merchandise, the collection of information, advertising, the supply of information, scientific research or similar activities of a preparatory or auxiliary character – will not.

Under many treaties, a principal is not deemed to have a permanent establishment by virtue of carrying on business through a broker, general commission agent, or other "independent agent" acting in the ordinary course of the broker's or agent's business. By contrast, the activities of a "dependent agent" – i.e., someone other than an agent of independent status – will cause the principal to have a U.S. permanent establishment if the agent has, and habitually exercises, an authority to conclude contracts in the name of the principal.

Based upon these rules, if a treaty country resident merely wants to sell its goods in the U.S., it should be able to do so without U.S. tax consequences. Foreign taxpayers also may avoid having a permanent establishment through the activities of a U.S. agent by entering into buy–sell relationships rather than agencies.

4. Branch Taxes

In addition to the regular corporate income tax, a foreign corporation engaged in a U.S. trade or business is subject to a 30 percent "branch profits" tax upon its "dividend equivalent amount" for each taxable year.[48] Foreign corporations may elect to operate in the United States through a domestic subsidiary in order to avoid this tax. Although the branch profits tax is designed to achieve parity between the remittance of branch profits and the distribution of subsidiary earnings (which would be subject to FDAP withholding taxes), it sometimes proves more burdensome. For example, earnings reinvested in nonbusiness assets – such as portfolio investments in excess of working capital needs – generally will add to the dividend equivalent amount and be subject to the branch profits tax, even if not distributed. By contrast, earnings of a U.S. subsidiary are not subject to withholding tax until actually distributed to the foreign parent, whether or not reinvested in the U.S. business. Thus, a foreign corporation subject to the branch profits tax may consider transferring its U.S. activities to a U.S. subsidiary, which it may do without increasing its dividend equivalent amount.[49]

A foreign corporation may consider financing its U.S. branch activities with debt, so that the debt can be repaid in lieu of a repatriation of profits that would attract the branch profits tax. However, interest paid to a foreign person by the U.S. trade or business of a foreign corporation (so-called "branch interest") is treated as if paid by a domestic corporation and is thereby subject to withholding, unless a Code exemption or treaty relief applies.[50]

Both the branch profits tax and the branch-level interest tax may be (and often are) reduced or eliminated by treaties, but only for "qualified residents" of a treaty country.[51] Where treaties do not specify a permissible rate of the branch profits tax, the treaty rate of tax on parent-subsidiary dividends will apply. The rules limiting treaty benefits to qualified residents resemble treaty–shopping provisions of recent U.S. income tax treaties, but these rules apply in addition to limitations imposed by a treaty.

E.   Foreign Investment in U.S. Real Estate

The mere ownership and rental of real property (*e.g.*, under a "triple net lease") generally does not constitute a U.S. trade or business or permanent establishment. However, the absence of a U.S. trade or business can lead to an extremely harsh U.S. tax result: Under the FDAP rules, rental income would be subject to withholding tax of 30 percent of the gross rents, without allowance for deductions (and usually without treaty relief).

To avoid this unfavorable treatment, a foreign person may elect to treat real property income as ECI, and thus subject to the graduated tax.[52] This "net election" is beneficial if the flat tax of 30 percent (or lower treaty rate) on gross income exceeds the graduated tax (imposed at a maximum rate of 35 percent for corporations and 39.6 percent for individuals) on net income. The net election will not cause the electing foreign person to be treated as engaged in a U.S. trade or business for other purposes of the Code, if the foreign person is not otherwise so engaged. Once made, the net election will apply for all subsequent years unless revoked with the consent of the IRS; once revoked, the election cannot be made again for five more years except with the consent of the IRS.

Under the Foreign Investment in Real Property Tax Act ("FIRPTA"), gain on the disposition of U.S. real property interests ("USRPIs") is taxed as ECI (an exception to the general rule that capital gains of foreign investors escape U.S. taxation entirely).[53] USRPIs include interests in real property and interests in "U.S. real property holding corporations" – corporations whose business assets and real property primarily (*i.e.*, 50 percent or more by fair market value) consist of USRPIs. "Interests in real property" include fee interests, co-ownerships, leaseholds, reversionary interests, options to acquire real property interests, interests in mineral deposits and all other forms of ownership in land and improvements except interests solely as a creditor (excluding "equity kickers").[54] The purchaser of a USRPI from a foreign person must withhold 10 percent of the purchase price and pay it in cash to the IRS, unless a party to the transaction submits to the IRS either (i) a notice explaining why the transaction qualifies for nonrecognition treatment (*e.g.*, a like-kind exchange or a tax-free reorganization), or (ii) an application for a withholding certificate on Form 8288–B asking for relief from the withholding requirement (*e.g.*, because the foreign seller will have minimal gain or a loss on the sale).[55] No FIRPTA tax applies on the sale of five percent or less of any class of stock of a corporation that is regularly traded on an established securities market.[56]

F.   Compliance

Foreign persons engaged in a U.S. trade or business must file annual federal income tax returns on Form 1120-F (for foreign corporations) or Form 1040NR (for nonresident aliens). Foreign persons that realize ECI and do not timely file such forms may forfeit deductions and credits otherwise available to reduce their tax liability.[57] Foreign persons who owe tax with respect to FDAP (*e.g.*, because the payor has underwithheld) also must file Form 1120-F or Form 1040NR. Foreign persons who are required to file U.S. income tax returns generally must obtain a U.S. taxpayer identification number from the IRS. Taxpayers must disclose on their tax returns certain "treaty-based return positions," *i.e.*, positions that reduce a taxpayer's tax liability based upon a U.S. income tax treaty.[58] Even if a tax return would not otherwise be required to be filed, a return must nevertheless be filed to disclose such treaty return positions.

Domestic corporations with one or more 25 percent or greater foreign owners must file annual information statements on Form 5472, and must satisfy detailed record keeping requirements with respect to transactions with related foreign persons.[59]

* * *

As noted at the outset, the foregoing is a general summary of the myriad provisions that govern the U.S. tax consequences of both "inbound" and "outbound" investments. These provisions are extraordinarily complex and continuously evolving. Thus, further research and analysis would be required to evaluate the tax aspects of specific situations.

IV. SOURCES OF ASSISTANCE

A. *Institutional*

1. Internal Revenue Service

The Office of the Associate Chief Counsel for International within the Internal Revenue Service provides guidance on a variety of topics related to international tax.

Internal Revenue Service
Associate Chief Counsel (International) (CC:INTL)
Room 3052
1111 Constitution Avenue, N.W.
Washington D.C. 20224
(202) 622-3800

For information and assistance on specific issues relating to international tax, private practitioners may wish to contact IRS personnel listed as "technical contacts" in Vol. 1 "Government Officials" of the TAX DIRECTORY, which is updated quarterly by Tax Analysts. (This IRS roster of contacts is adapted from the Code & Subject Matter Directory published by the IRS as part of its OFFICE OF CHIEF COUNSEL TELEPHONE DIRECTORY.)

2.   The Department of Treasury

The Office of the International Tax Counsel within the Treasury Department also provides guidance on international tax issues.

Department of Treasury
International Tax Counsel
Room 3064
1500 Pennsylvania Ave., N.W.
Washington D.C. 20220
(202) 622-0130

3.   Other Organizations

American Bar Association, Section of Taxation
740 15th Street, N.W.
Washington D.C. 20005
(202) 662-8670; FAX: (202) 662-1032
(Committee on Foreign Activities of U.S. Taxpayers)
(Committee on U.S. Activities of Foreigners & Tax Treaties)

International Fiscal Association Headquarters
World Trade Center
P.O. Box 30215
3001 DE Rotterdam
The Netherlands
(31-10) 4 05 29 90 FAX: (31-10) 4 05 50 31

International Fiscal Association (USA Branch)
Present Chairman J.M. Gonzalez
Coopers & Lybrand
333 Market Street
San Francisco, CA 94105
(415) 957-3185   FAX: 415-957-3394

B.   *Income Tax Treaties*

Actual treaties (published by CCH and others). Also available on line through LEXIS/NEXIS or WESTLAW.

Treasury Department's Model Income Tax Treaty (promulgated June 16, 1981 - a revised Model Treaty is expected soon).

OECD Model Tax Convention on Income and on Capital (1992, Paris).

C. Congressional Reports, Agency Reports, etc.

A Study of Intercompany Pricing Under Section 482 of the Code (the "White Paper"). Notice 88–123, 1988–2 C.B. 458.

Cahiers de Droit Fiscal International ("Studies on International Fiscal Law" – published by the International Fiscal Association).

D. Secondary Sources

1. Books

KUNTZ & PERONI, U.S. INTERNATIONAL TAXATION (1994).

ISENBERG, INTERNATIONAL TAXATION (updated 1994).

POSTLEWAITE & FRANTZEN, INTERNATIONAL TAXATION: CORPORATE AND INDIVIDUAL (1994).

OGLEY, PRINCIPLES OF INTERNATIONAL TAX: A MULTINATIONAL PERSPECTIVE (1994).

WARREN, GORHAM & LAMONT, U.S. TAXATION OF INTERNATIONAL OPERATIONS: TAX IDEAS (1985, updated semimonthly).

LANGER, PRACTICAL INTERNATIONAL TAX PLANNING (PLI, 3d ed. 1985, updated periodically).

RHOADES & LANGER, INCOME TAXATION OF FOREIGN RELATED TRANSACTIONS (1995, updated annually). Volumes 3, 4 and 5 contain text and commentary on U.S. income tax treaties.

BITTKER & EUSTICE, FEDERAL INCOME TAXATION OF CORPORATIONS AND SHAREHOLDERS, Chapter 15 (1994).

BITTKER & LOKKEN, FEDERAL TAXATION OF INCOME, ESTATES AND GIFTS, Part 9, Chapters 65–71 (1988, updated 1995).

MACDONALD, ANNOTATED TOPICAL GUIDE TO U.S. INCOME TAX TREATIES (1989, updated).

BNA TAX MANAGEMENT PORTFOLIOS, *Foreign Income Series* (Portfolios on many subjects, such as FSCs and DISCs, and updated periodically).

CCH HORWATH INTERNATIONAL, INTERNATIONAL TAX HANDBOOK (1994, revised annually).

TILLINGHAST, TAX ASPECTS OF INTERNATIONAL TRANSACTIONS: INTERNATIONAL ECONOMIC LAW (1984).

MCINTYRE, THE INTERNATIONAL INCOME TAX RULES OF THE UNITED STATES (1989).

2.   Periodicals

The following journals are dedicated to international tax issues:

The Journal of International Taxation (Warren, Gorham & Lamont).

International Tax Journal (Aspen Publishers, Inc.).

The BNA Tax Management International Journal.

Tax Notes International (Tax Analysts).

In addition, the ABA Tax Lawyer and the Tax Law Review often include articles on aspects of international taxation.

3.   Selected Articles

Davis & Lainoff, *U.S. Taxation of Foreign Joint Ventures,* 46 TAX L. REV. 165 (1991).

Although somewhat dated, the following articles by Professor Harvey Dale of New York University provide an excellent analysis of certain core areas of U.S. international taxation:

Effectively Connected Income, 42 TAX L. REV. 689 (1988); *Tax Accounting for Foreign Persons,* 37 TAX L. REV. (1982); *Withholding Tax on Payments to Foreign Persons,* 36 TAX L. REV. 49 (1980); *The Reformed Foreign Tax Credit: A Path Through the Maze,* 33 TAX L. REV. 175 (1978).

E.   On-Line Services

LEXIS–NEXIS and WESTLAW both maintain a large collection of U.S. international materials. For instance, the LEXIS FEDTAX library contains the following international tax materials: Tax Notes International, World Tax Report, Journal of International Taxation, IBFD International Tax Treaties, IBFD International Tax News, International Tax Directory, Tax Notes International Magazine. Most of these international tax materials are also contained in the WESTLAW database FTX–ALL.

Subscribers to Tax Notes International may join the Tax Bits International Internet discussion forum (Internet Address: International.group@tax.com).

ENDNOTES

1   Although the following discussion emphasizes income taxation, other types of taxation often play a prominent role in foreign countries. In particular, value added taxes, stamp duties and transfer taxes can surprise U.S. companies that are not accustomed to encountering such taxes domestically. The effect of U.S. or foreign customs duties (which normally run counter to transfer pricing considerations) also need to be taken into account in planning transnational activities.

2   See IRC § 951 et seq. U.S. shareholders of foreign corporations also may be affected by the "foreign personal holding company" rules (IRC § 551 et seq.) and the "passive foreign investment company" or "PFIC" rules (IRC § 1291 et seq.).

3   IRC § 901. The credit is limited to taxes that are substantially similar to U.S. income taxes, or paid in lieu of income taxes. See Treas. Reg. § 1.901-2; IRC § 903.

4   IRC § 902.

5   For example, IRC § 904(a) limits the foreign tax credit to the proportion of U.S. tax (before the credit) as the taxpayer's foreign-source income bears to its total taxable income. (Excess credits can be carried back two years and carried forward five years.) In addition, IRC § 904(d) requires that the foreign tax credit be computed separately for different categories, or "baskets", of foreign-source income, e.g., active business income, passive income and high withholding tax interest.

6   See Section III.D.3, below.

7   See IRC § 921 et seq. (FSC); IRC § 991 et seq. (DISC).

8   See IRC §§ 904(f), 367(a)(3)(C). In addition, the dual consolidated loss regulations under IRC § 1503(d) can prohibit use of the losses or impose further recapture requirements.

9   As in the United States, transfer pricing is becoming increasingly important in most industrial countries. If the foreign country adjusts transfer prices, the U.S. enterprise may need to seek "competent authority" relief to obtain correlative adjustments in the U.S. See Rev. Proc. 91-23, 1991-1 C.B. 534. U.S. taxpayers may enter into "advance pricing agreements" with the IRS (and perhaps also with foreign countries), whereby arm's-length transfer prices are determined in advance (rather than upon audit of the taxpayer's return). See Rev. Proc. 91-22, 1991-1 C.B. 526.

10   IRC § 954(d), (e). Thus, from a U.S. tax perspective, a U.S. enterprise may prefer to have a separate sales or service subsidiary in each country, although this may create additional administrative costs.

11   See IRC § 367; Notice 87-85, 1987-2 C.B. 395; Prop. Reg. § 1.367(a)-3. Under a gain recognition agreement, for some period thereafter, the holding company's transfer of the subsidiary may trigger retroactive recognition of gain on the original transfer.

12   See IRC § 954(b)(4), (c).

13   Special limitations may apply on losses under the dual consolidated loss regulations, particularly if a hybrid entity (taxed as a corporation for foreign country tax

purposes) is used. *See* Treas. Reg. § 1.1503–2.

14   IRC § 904(d)(1)(E), (2)(E).

15   However, U.S. transferors must satisfy certain reporting requirements, *e.g.*, Forms 926 and 5471. *See* IRC §§ 6038, 6038B and 6046.

16   IRC § 367(a)(1).

17   IRC §§ 904(f)(3), 367(a)(3)(C).

18   IRC § 367(d). Because of the sourcing rule, which will limit foreign tax credits, it may be preferable actually to license the intangible property, even though, under IRC § 482, the same "commensurate with income" (or "superroyalty") standard would apply. This may raise issues with a foreign joint venturer.

19   IRC § 1491.

20   IRC § 1057.

21   IRC § 367(b). In addition, caution should be exercised if the surviving entity has a different tax status (*e.g.*, a foreign entity treated as a partnership merging with and into a foreign corporation, or *vice versa*).

22   *See* IRC § 2101 *et seq.* (estate tax on nonresidents); IRC § 2501 *et seq.* (gift tax).

23   IRC § 7701(b). These tests do not apply for estate and gift tax purposes, where residence is determined by the common law test of domicile.

24   Under the "first–year election," an alien individual who is present in the United States for at least 31 consecutive days during the calendar year may elect to be treated as a U.S. resident for the year if he meets the substantial presence test for the following calendar year, does not meet that test for the immediately preceding year, and is present in the United States during the period beginning with the first day of such 31-day period and ending with the year end for at least 75 percent of the number of days in such period. IRC § 7701(b)(4).

25   Treas. Reg. §§ 1.871–13; 1.6012–1(b)(2)(ii).

26   IRC § 877.

27   IRC § 7701(a)(4) and (5). At present, all foreign entities are subject to the classification criteria applicable to domestic partnerships and other unincorporated organizations. The IRS has recently proposed a "check–the–box" system for entity classification, under which the classification of unincorporated entities as partnerships or associations taxable as corporations would become elective. Notice 95–14, 1995–14 I.R.B. 7. It is uncertain whether or how such a system would apply to foreign entities.

28   IRC §§ 871(a) and 1441 (nonresident alien individuals); IRC §§ 881 and 1442 (foreign corporations).

29   Certain issues can arise in the computation of the corporate–level tax because the U.S. corporation is foreign–owned, *e.g.*, the "earnings stripping" limitations on the deductibility of interest. *See* IRC § 163(j).

30   IRC §§ 861(a)(2) and 862(a)(2) (dividends); IRC §§861(a)(1) and 862(a)(1) (interest). Exceptions to these general rules may apply if the domestic payor has mostly active foreign income, or if the foreign payor has U.S. business activities.

31   IRC §§ 861(a)(3), 862(a)(3).

32   IRC §§ 861(a)(4), 862(a)(4).

33   IRC §§ 871(i), 881(d) (bank deposit interest); IRC §§871(h), 881(c) (portfolio interest).

34   IRC § 7701(l); Treas. Reg. § 1.881–3.

35   IRC §§ 871(b) (nonresident aliens) and 882(a) (foreign corporations).

36   IRC § 864(b)(1). *See also* IRC § 861(a)(3).

37   *See, e.g.*, Article XV of the United States–Canada Income Tax Treaty, which grants exemption from U.S. taxation for compensation received by a resident of Canada where either (i) the compensation is not borne by a U.S. resident or by a permanent establishment or fixed base within the United States and the recipient is not present in the United States for more than 183 days, or (ii) the compensation does not exceed $10,000.

38   IRC § 864(b)(2)(A)(i), (B)(i).

39   IRC § 864(b)(2)(A)(ii), (B)(ii) and (B)(iii).

40   IRC § 875. A similar rule applies to beneficiaries of trusts and estates.

41   IRC § 1446.

42   IRC § 864(c)(2); Treas. Reg. § 1.864–4.

43   IRC § 864(c)(3).

44   IRC § 864(c)(4).

45   As a practical matter, by subsequent legislation, such income is now treated as U.S.-source income and thus as ECI under the limited force of attraction principle. *See* IRC §865(e).

46   IRC § 864(c)(6) and (7).

47   IRC § 882(c).

48   IRC § 884(a). The branch profits tax generally replaces the "secondary withhold-ing tax" that applies to a portion of the dividends paid by foreign corporations 25 percent or more of whose income is ECI. However, the secondary withholding tax still applies to foreign corporations that are exempt from the branch profits tax under a treaty (unless the treaty also prohibits the secondary withholding tax). *See* IRC §§884(e)(3), 861(a)(2)(B).

49   *See* Temp. Reg. § 1.884–2T.

50   IRC § 884(f)(1); Treas. Reg. § 1.884–4.

51   *See* IRC § 884(e)(1) (as to branch profits tax); IRC §884(f)(3) (as to branch–level interest tax); IRC § 884(e)(4) and Treas. Reg. § 1.884–5 (defining "qualified resident").

52   IRC §§ 871(d), 882(d); Treas. Reg. § 1.871–10.

53   IRC §§ 897 and 1445.

54   IRC § 897(c); Treas. Reg. § 1.897–1.

55   *See* IRC § 1445; Treas. Reg. §§ 1.1445–2(d)(2) and 1.1445–3. The amount of the with-holding is not necessarily the amount of the tax, and the foreign seller generally must file a U.S. tax return for the year of the transfer.

56   IRC § 897(c)(3).

57   IRC §§ 874 and 882(c)(2); Treas. Reg. §§ 1.874–1; 1.882–4.

58   IRC § 6114; Treas. Reg. § 301.6114–1.

59   IRC § 6038A.

CHAPTER 11

ENVIRONMENTAL LAW

Turner T. Smith, Jr.

I.   INTRODUCTION

Although environmental law has developed more slowly internationally than in the United States, it is an increasingly important factor in transnational practice. National environmental law worldwide is in a state of rapid development. Environmental problems have become a priority as "green" political forces have taken root in a number of countries. A broad range of environmental laws has been enacted in many countries, with widely varying levels of implementation and enforcement. These regulatory laws generally govern the obvious plant-related areas, such as air and water pollution and solid and hazardous wastes. Less frequently, they regulate such other facility-related matters as wetland destruction, asbestos, underground storage tanks (USTs) and polychlorinated biphenyls (PCBs). Increasingly, waste and products transported internationally are also regulated through environmental laws. Further, new laws imposing civil liability for soil and groundwater contamination are being enacted in many countries, or courts are interpreting old laws to the same end. Finally, beyond these developments in national laws, environmental pressures have driven new developments at the international level, such as the negotiation of ozone depletion and hazardous waste transport conventions and an environmental side agreement to NAFTA, and new consideration of trade and environment issues under GATT.

International counsel will meet environmental issues in the regulatory context when dealing with manufacturing operations abroad, as well as with transboundary transport and sale of products (and wastes, with the caution that co-products, by-products, secondary raw materials and returned products may be classified as wastes). The practitioner will also encounter environmental issues in the transactional context, where the impact of regulatory law must be evaluated but where the chief concern is the potential for acquiring, in a business transaction, liability for soil or groundwater contamination or for worker or third-party exposure to hazardous substances from normal operations or accidents. Transnational environmental issues arise much less frequently in the adversarial context at present, chiefly as tort actions, contractual or governmental disputes over soil or groundwater clean-up, or an outgrowth of impasse in the regulatory context.

International practitioners must deal with a number of sources of environmental law. Regulatory and liability law can be found at the national, regional or state (in federal systems), and local levels. National law, of course, is the starting place, and normally applies only within the nation's geographic boundaries rather than extraterritorially. Although it is evolving rapidly everywhere, it is most advanced, outside of the United States, in Europe, from which many of the examples below are drawn. In some countries, regional law is critically important (*e.g.*, Canada, Australia, Belgium, Germany, Spain and Italy). With regard to facility regulation, and in some cases with regard to transboundary transport of wastes, regional and local authorities normally govern implementation (*e.g.*, permitting) and enforcement, and exercise much wider (and largely unreviewable) discretion than is the case in the United States.

Beyond dealing with the impact of national or regional law on operations within each jurisdiction, international practitioners must increasingly cope with the effect of national laws from multiple jurisdictions, when, for example, products or "wastes" travel across borders or plants have transboundary effects. They must also consider the use in some jurisdictions of "voluntary" industry/government agreements (*e.g.*, the Netherlands) and in all jurisdictions of trade-driven forms of "voluntary" requirements (*e.g.*, the developing International Standards Organization's ISO–14000 environmental management and auditing series). European Union (EU) law must be considered in Europe, and it exerts a powerful influence in those Central and Eastern European and other countries hoping to join the EU. Finally, such international institutions as the Organization for Economic Cooperation and Development (OECD) and the World Trade Organization (WTO) are becoming important forums, and some international treaties, such as the Basel Convention (*see* Sources of Assistance), are beginning to affect the international business community. Finally, public and multilateral financing sources frequently have environmental lending procedures and guidelines that are a condition of access to these funding sources.

II.   THE REGULATORY CONTEXT

Environmental regulation can affect a business's facilities, its products, or the company as a whole (*e.g.*, its environmental management structure or its accounting or securities law treatment of environmental issues). It also raises some special issues in the international context.

Although adequate (much less sophisticated or expert) implementation and enforcement is rare outside of Europe and the United States (and spotty at best in much of Europe), most non–U.S. jurisdictions rely heavily, if not exclusively, on administrative or criminal remedies. Officer and director liability is developing apace in Europe; in some civil law jurisdictions, like Germany, it is only the individual, and not the corporate entity, that can be prosecuted.

A.   *Plant Regulation*

Facility regulation will normally be a function of national law, and will govern such matters as air and water pollution and solid and hazardous waste generation. Air and water regulation will generally be less systematic and comprehensive than in the United States. Germany and several other European countries are, however, exceptions. Such regulations will normally be implemented in permits negotiated at the local level, although in civil law countries frequently with local representatives of the central government. Waste regulation is generally less advanced. Germany is also an exception here. In many countries the sheer lack of adequate treatment or disposal facilities may be the most immediate problem. Waste generation, storage, treatment or disposal requirements may apply to on–site or off–site disposal. Transboundary transport of waste provisions (*e.g.*, the Basel Convention; the OECD's decision on shipment of recycled material; the EU Shipment of Waste Regulation; and the U.S./Mexico and U.S./Canada treaties (*see* Sources of Assistance for citations)) must be given special attention, particularly in light of the broad definitions of "waste" involved. Regulatory provisions regarding accidental releases, along with any related reporting requirements, must also be checked (*e.g.*, the EU's "Sevaso" Directive (*see* Sources of Assistance) and related national implementation in Europe).

Facility siting laws may impose siting, construction, operating permit or other requirements. Many foreign jurisdictions, including the EU, have laws analogous to the U.S. National Environmental Policy Act (NEPA).[1] European civil law jurisdictions tend to have more extensive and significant permitting requirements for doing business or building facilities than in the U.S. These provisions may require environmental impact and safety and accident analyses, and the resulting permits may contain important environmental conditions. In English–based common law jurisdictions, similar environmental requirements may be found in land use and land planning permits or approvals. Finally, there is an important trend in Europe, led by the British, to develop integrated permit systems that impose all relevant environmental requirements in a single permit or permit process.

Environmental auditing has long been used in the U.S. as a company management tool to ensure compliance with environmental requirements at the plant level, and is now being adopted by the EU as, in effect, a government–sponsored privately–operated compliance mechanism. This process is being incorporated into a new series of international management standards, ISO–14000.

One of the most important aspects of plant regulation is the law related to clean–up of contaminated soil and groundwater. While clean–up is sometimes a matter of administrative regulatory law, the liability regime is frequently the crucial element here. Both regulatory and liability provisions are developing rapidly in Europe (although not as rapidly elsewhere), and are particularly important and difficult in privatization deals in Central and Eastern Europe, where the prior owner is the government or a public or quasi–public corporation.

B.   Product Regulation

Environmental regulation has traditionally focused more on facilities than on products, with the exception of regulation of certain hazardous chemicals and sprays. Spurred by the need for new solutions to the solid waste problem, important new forms of product regulation are now being developed, particularly in Europe. Many of these laws are new and revolutionary and are spreading rapidly. They include the following:

- Bans on products or components such as asbestos, polyvinylchlorides or heavy metals;

- The direct regulation of the products' features, including their size, shape, volume, weight and recyclability;

- Product "take-back" rules and "producer-responsibility" principles – dealing, for example, with cars, electrical products, tires and batteries, among other products. These are now being developed for the EU and in Germany, France, the Netherlands, Denmark, the United Kingdom, Austria, Sweden, and Switzerland;

- Eco-labelling schemes, proliferating at the EU and at national levels, sometimes using highly problematic "life-cycle analysis;"

- Packaging regulation – including, for example, the EU Packaging Waste Directive, and French, Dutch, Belgian, Austrian, Swedish, and Norwegian packaging programs;

- Eco-taxes, including the Belgian tax on products such as paper, batteries, pesticides, disposable razors, disposable cameras, and various types of product packaging, and the possible EU carbon-energy tax; and

- Traditional regulation relating to existing and new hazardous chemicals – including, for example, regulations on labelling, packaging, pre-market testing, and transport requirements.

Legal provisions that threaten a company's products threaten markets and market shares. They thus cut directly to its bottom line. Product and packaging "take-back" rules will radically reshape the market balance between virgin and recycled materials. These rules can also wreak havoc in international markets as they are put in place, especially when one country acts unilaterally, as Germany did on packaging in the EU. Eco-labels sometimes make arbitrary distinctions, but can affect sales dramatically. Discrimination and trade issues are rife in all forms of product regulation, and rapidly developing green-product advertising claims can be easily abused.

Many jurisdictions fail to differentiate clearly between products – and related by–products, materials for recycling, and taken–back products – and real waste. Yet, if a valuable product is classified as waste, and particularly if it is classified as a hazardous waste, a company's ability to handle, store, transport, recycle, or dispose of it comes under a wholly different, and much more stringent, environmental regulatory regime. As the regulation of trans-boundary waste shipments proliferates, some companies may find that their critical shipments of co–products, by–products, secondary raw materials, and returned products are threatened.

C.   *Company-Wide Issues*

There are several company–wide issues driven by environmental regu-lation that involve special challenges for companies operating internationally. First, the company's environmental management system must be adapted to its international operations, with the need to cope with differing national laws, cultures, languages, and the like, without losing the core values it achieves in the U.S. Second, environmental regulatory requirements and lia-bility risks give rise to accounting and securities law issues that must be con-sidered in the various relevant jurisdictions. Contingent liabilities incurred abroad must be considered, where appropriate, under U.S. securities laws,[2] and foreign accounting bodies and securities laws are beginning to consider the same knotty issues revolving around environmental regulatory and lia-bility risks and clean–ups of past operations that have been dealt with for some years in the U.S.

D.   *Special Aspects of Regulatory Law in the International Context*

National environmental regulatory requirements raise special issues for companies trading or investing across borders. The impact of vertically–lay-ered governmental structures, particularly in the context of federal states, but also in the relationship between EU and member state law, has already been mentioned.

The extraterritorial reach of national environmental laws must also be noted. U.S. law is the chief culprit here, with a long history of U.S. efforts to make various of its regulatory laws (*e.g.*, U.S. antitrust and securities laws) applicable to persons or conduct outside U.S. borders. Although there is a presumption against extraterritorial application, congressional intent governs. Extraterritorial effect is increasingly the subject of litigation under environ-mental laws.[3]

Another topic that must be considered is the developing constraints on national environmental laws stemming from trade agreements. The starting point for analysis is the General Agreement on Tariffs and Trade (GATT), which requires nondiscriminatory treatment of imported products, with exceptions covering some forms of environmental regulation. Much recent

controversy has surrounded the trade/environment interface, and the applicable GATT provisions have been extensively commented on, construed (in
such cases as the "Tuna–dolphin" dispute between the U.S. and Mexico), and
altered and refined in the Uruguay Round Agreement. Where counsel
believes that national environmental regulation has a discriminatory impact
on foreign competitors, careful analysis under GATT may reveal arguments
that can be pursued in the international trade framework, with its wide array
of practical and institutional remedies. (*See* Chapter 16, *Trade Remedies and
Benefits Programs.*)

Another recent international treaty that can have an impact on transnational practice is the North American Free Trade Agreement (NAFTA) and its
accompanying environmental side agreement. (*See* Sources of Assistance for
citation.) NAFTA leaves all three parties free to pursue their own environmental policies but addresses the issue of non–implementation of domestic
law in the side agreement. Articles 14 and 15 of the side agreement allow
nongovernmental organizations (NGOs) and private individuals to initiate
procedures before the North American Commission for Environmental
Cooperation (NACEC) for nonenforcement of national law, a procedure which
counsel may find used against clients by NGOs, or which counsel may use on
behalf of his client where a competitor is the regulated party benefitting
from lax enforcement.

There are a number of other international environmental treaties, of
which the Basel Convention governing transboundary shipment of hazardous waste (*see* Sources of Assistance for citation), the Montreal Protocol
governing production of fluorocarbons, and treaties or conventions governing discharge of pollutants to specific water bodies have the greatest impact
on business currently.

III.   TRANSACTIONAL CONTEXT

Regulatory compliance and liability risks can affect many forms of
international business transactions and can be substantial, even in jurisdictions where the laws are not as stringent as they are in the United States. The
types of deals affected include acquisitions, mergers, joint ventures, construction of new facilities, project financing of new or existing facilities, real estate
transactions, lending transactions, distribution agreements, tolling agreements, and leases. Further, public multilateral bank financing or privatization
transactions also increasingly have an environmental dimension.

As a result, it is critical that any investor contemplating an international
business transaction be familiar with the national and international environmental laws applicable to the transaction. Increasingly, investors must also
consider any public or multilateral bank's environmental guidelines and procedures, with particular attention to the new "appeal" provisions available to
the public and NGOs for "inspection panel" review of a project's environmental effects at the World Bank. Counsel must understand the impact that

these laws and requirements may have on a business deal in order to ensure that environmental risks are adequately identified and managed and that their timing implications are properly taken into account.

A.   Environmental Regulatory Risks

Environmental permit issues must be considered carefully as a transaction is planned, structured and implemented. National permit transfer and notice requirements for existing permits should be carefully reviewed and greater delays anticipated than in U.S. transactions. A letter notifying the appropriate regulatory agencies of the change and requesting permit modification may not technically comply with formal permit modification requirements.

Legal issues and problems related to products must also be considered and can create unforeseen trade barriers and threaten markets if corporate counsel are asleep at the switch during a transaction. Counsel must now also examine the waste shipment patterns of manufacturing facilities and of any product take-back programs.

B.   Environmental Liability Risks

These revolve chiefly around (1) potential soil and groundwater contamination, and (2) tort law hazardous substance risks to workers, to plant neighbors and to customers or consumers. The issues involve essentially: (i) what are the physical (and, derivatively, the legal) risks; and (ii) who bears them? The keys to accommodating these risks in a transaction are, as in domestic deals, to identify and evaluate the physical, and resulting legal, risks in an environmental due diligence investigation, and to allocate them in the transaction documents.

As a practical matter, the exact state of the law on the existence, nature and scope of liability is frequently beside the point in the international context, since the only prudent assumption any place in the world these days is that the law may change during the period of ownership to impose liability for contaminated soil or groundwater on a purchaser who becomes an owner or occupier of real estate.

Some national law provisions (e.g., in France) require seller to notify buyer of contamination. National law should also be checked to see whether it requires that releases of hazardous substances be recorded on the property deed, requires that property be cleaned up before it is transferred, or has other requirements addressed to the transaction itself.

A different range of uncertainties exists for potential tort liability, which will be highly dependent on the nature of the physical risks created by various aspects of the business and on the local legal regime (with an eye to efforts by some tort plaintiffs to sue in U.S. courts for a company's overseas environmental torts).

Although environmental due diligence in the international context has, at its core, many similarities with domestic practice, there are some important additional issues.

First, how does one determine the requirements of the applicable law? In an international transaction, it is frequently very difficult to find, read, and understand the applicable statutory law (much less the regulations, decrees, guidance, etc.) and confidently predict its implementation and application both in the near term and in the future. This is true because of its state of development, implementation and enforcement, because of the differing institutional and cultural contexts in various countries and parts of the world, and because of the simple language problem. One must begin with such basic questions as whether a legal system stems from a civil or a common law tradition, and what its lineage is (usually derived from the colonial heritage of the country concerned, but in any case usually an adaptation of one of the European civil codes or English law). As a practical matter, one must operate by approximation, not at the level of precision and sophistication common in domestic transactions.

Second, where local law is opaque or lacking altogether, one must determine what standards should be looked to. Company policies and multilateral bank standards are frequently used.

Third, how does one find good legal and consulting assistance in a foreign country? Is it best to use local assistance, assistance from large international entities, or some combination of the two? Local talent may be unsophisticated in environmental regulation but may know local conditions and have local contacts. The big international consultants will likely have a broader experience but have less local touch. The approach must be tailor-made for each transaction, although multiple evaluations in different countries on a short time-frame in a large deal may necessitate use, at a minimum, of a coordinating multi-jurisdictional consultant.

Fourth, is an environmental impact assessment required, either under local law or under multilateral bank or U.S. government agency lending guidelines? If so, what is its extent? Where will the money come from to do any required environmental analysis at the pre-feasibility or feasibility stage of a project (normally from the project initiator, which stops many projects in their tracks at the outset)?

Fifth, in a privatization transaction, representations and warranties from the government will be requested by the private investor, but will seldom alone suffice. They can only result in a legal right that must be pursued, after the fact, against a sovereign government, which may or may not be a good credit risk and as to which there may be many practical disincentives or legal impediments to pursuing a recovery action.

The private investor will normally attempt to discount the offering price by an assessment of environmental risk, and will request an indemnity as to risks the investor cannot assess or has not assessed (perhaps due simply to time or other constraints imposed by the government party, as is common in a bidding process). The investor will normally also want to ask for some form of guaranteed or secured funding for the indemnity obligation. He is well-advised to ask for incorporation into the agreement itself of stated clean–up levels and a right to have the government sign–off on a clean–up meeting those levels, with appropriate indemnities for later regulatory developments reflecting government changes in mind.

IV.   SOURCES OF ASSISTANCE

A.   U.S. Statutes and Regulations

Standards Applicable to Generators of Hazardous Waste – Exports of Hazardous Waste, 40 C.F.R. § 262, Subpart E (1995).

Notification Concerning the Basel Convention's Potential Implications for Hazardous Waste Exports and Imports, 57 Fed. Reg. 20602 (1992).

B.   Foreign Statutes and Regulations

Council Regulation 259/93 of 1 February 1993 on the Supervision and Control of Shipments of Waste within, into, and out of the European Community, 1993 O.J. (L 30) 1.

Council Regulation 880/92 of 23 March 1992 on a Community Eco–label Award Scheme, 1992 O.J. (L 99).

Council Regulation 1836/93 of 29 June 1993 Allowing Voluntary Participation by Companies in the Industrial Sector in a Community Eco-management and Audit Scheme, 1993 O.J. (L 168) 1.

Council Directive 578/67 of 27 June 1967 on the Approximation of Laws, Regulations and Administrative Provisions Relating to the Classification, Packaging and Labelling of Dangerous Substances, 1967 O.J. (L 196) 1, particularly as amended by Council Directive 907/76, 1976 O.J. (L 360) 1.

Council Directive 501/82 of 5 August 1982 on the Major Accident Hazards of Certain Industrial Activities, 1982 O.J. (L 230) 1, *as amended by* Council Directive 216/87 of 28 March 1987, 1987 O.J. (L 85) 36 and Council Directive 610/88 of 7 December 1988, 1988 O.J. (L 336) 14.

C.   Treaties and Related Materials

1989 Basel Convention on the Control of Transboundary Movements of Hazardous Wastes and Their Disposal, Mar. 22, 1989, *reprinted in* 28 I.L.M. 649 (1989).

Decision of the Council Concerning the Control of Trans-frontier Movements of Wastes Destined for Recovery Operation, 1992 O.J. (C 92) 39.

Agreement between the United States of America and the United Mexican States on Cooperation for the Protection and Improvement of the Environment in the Border Area, Aug. 14, 1983, U.S.-Mex., T.I.A.S. No. 10827, *as amended by* Annex III, Agreement of Cooperation between the United States of America and the United Mexican States Regarding the Transboundary Shipments of Hazardous Wastes and Hazardous Substances, Nov. 12, 1986, U.S.-Mex., T.I.A.S. No. 11269.

Agreement between the Government of Canada and the Government of the United States of America Concerning the Transboundary Movement of Hazardous Waste, Oct. 28, 1986, Can.-U.S., T.I.A.S. No. 11099.

General Agreement on Tariffs and Trade – Multilateral Trade Negotiations (The Uruguay Round), Dec. 15, 1993, *reprinted in* 33 I.L.M. 1 (1994).

North American Free Trade Agreement between the Government of the United States of America, the Government of Canada, and the Government of the United Mexican States, 1993, U.S.-Can.-Mex., (U.S. Gov't Printing Office No. ISBN 0-16-041960-3, 1993).

North American Agreement on Environmental Cooperation between the Government of the United States of America, the Government of Canada, and the Government of the United Mexican States, Sept. 13, 1993, U.S.-Can.-Mex., (U.S. Gov't Printing Office No. ISBN 0-16-041969-7, 1993). (Also available, with supporting commentary, on CD-ROM from the ABA Section of International Law and Practice.)

D.   *Other Official Documents and Sources*

The Commission on Environmental Law of IUCN – The World Conservation Union, AGENDA 21: EARTH'S ACTION PLAN (Nicholas Robinson ed. 1993).

Sources of Information Concerning Environmental Procedures and Guidelines of U.S. Multilateral Financing Institutions:

Multilateral Development Banks

African Development Bank
Division Chief of the Environment
African Development Bank Headquarters
Avenue Joseph Anoma
01 B.P. 1387
Abidjan 01 Cote d'Ivore
Phone: 22 5 204 444
Fax: 22 5 204 907

Asian Development Bank
Manager, Environment Division
Office of Environment and Social Development
Asian Development Bank
P.O. Box 789
Manila 0980 The Philippines
Phone: 632–632–6883
Fax: 632–636–2444

European Bank for Reconstruction and Development
Head of Unit, Environmental Appraisal
European Bank for Reconstruction and Development
1 Exchange Square
London EC2 A2EH England
Phone: 011 44 171 338 6000
Fax: 011 44 171 338 6848

Inter-American Development Bank
Division Chief, Region I[4]
Division Chief, Region II[5]
Division Chief, Region III[6]
1300 New York Avenue, N.W.
Washington, D.C. 20577
Phone: (202) 623–1000
Fax: (202) 623–3096

The World Bank
Director, Environment Department
The World Bank
Room S–5055
1818 H Street, N.W.
Washington, D.C. 20433
Phone: (202) 477–1234
Fax: (202) 477–0565

U.S. Financing Services

Agency for International Development
Deputy Assistant Administrator,
Center for the Environment
Agency for International Development
320 21st Street, N.W.
Washington, D.C. 20523
Phone: (703) 875–4300
Fax: (703) 875–4639

Export-Import Bank of the U.S.
Environmental Liaison
Export–Import Bank of the United States
811 Vermont Avenue
Washington, D.C. 20571
Phone: (202) 565–3939
Fax: (202) 565–3931

Overseas Private Investment Corporation
Director, Environmental Impact Assessment
Overseas Private Investment Corporation
1100 New York Avenue, N.W.
Washington, D.C. 20527
Phone: (202) 336–8400
Fax: (202) 218–0177

1 GUIDELINES FOR ASSESSING INDUSTRIAL ENVIRONMENTAL IMPACT AND
ENVIRONMENTAL CRITERIA FOR THE SITING OF INDUSTRY, U.N. Environment
Programme, ISBN 92–807–1015–X (1980).

*The following are additional resources for obtaining texts of foreign environmental
statutes and legal documents:*

National Technical Information Service
Springfield, VA 22161
Tel: (703) 487–4650
Fax: (703) 321–8547
(Legal Texts: Central and Eastern Europe, Baltic States, Russia, and the
NIS.) (Texts provided by the U.S. Department of Commerce, Office of General
Counsel.)

ASET Consultants, Inc.
American Services for Eurasian Trade
2009 N. 14th Street, Suite 214
Arlington, VA 22201
Tel: (703) 516–9266
Fax: (703) 516–9269
(List of legal documents from the environmental sectors of Europe and
Asia.)

Environmental Law Institute
Environmental Program for Central & Eastern Europe and for Latin
        America
1616 P Street, N.W.
Washington, D.C. 20036
Tel: (202) 939–3874
Fax: (202) 328–5002

Library of Congress
Western Law Division (the Americas and Western Europe)
Tel: (202) 707–5077
Eastern Law Division (Africa, Eastern Europe, and Asia)
Tel: (202) 707–5085

E.   *Secondary Sources*

1.   Books

CELIA CAMPBELL-MOHN, BARRY BREEN & J. WILLIAM FUTRELL, SUSTAINABLE ENVIRONMENTAL LAW (1993).

DANIEL C. ESTY, GREENING THE GATT – TRADE, ENVIRONMENT, AND THE FUTURE (1994).

DAVID VOGEL, NATIONAL STYLES OF REGULATION: ENVIRONMENTAL POLICY IN GREAT BRITAIN AND THE UNITED STATES (1986).

2 ECKARD REHBINDER & RICHARD STEWART, INTEGRATION THROUGH LAW: EUROPE AND THE AMERICAN FEDERAL EXPERIENCE – ENVIRONMENTAL PROTECTION POLICY (1985).

ENVIRONMENTAL LAW INSTITUTE, EUROPEAN COMMUNITY DESKBOOK (1992) (containing an overview of the European Union environmental legal system and copies of relevant primary legislation).

FRANK FRIEDMAN, PRACTICAL GUIDE TO ENVIRONMENTAL MANAGEMENT (1995).

FRANK P. GRAD, TREATISE ON ENVIRONMENTAL LAW (1973).

Janis L. Kirkland, Nancy G. Simms & Turner T. Smith, Jr., *An International Perspective on Environmental Liability*, in 1 ENVIRONMENTAL DISPUTE HANDBOOK: LIABILITY AND CLAIMS (David A. Carpenter *et al.*, eds. 1991).

LAW OF ENVIRONMENTAL PROTECTION (Sheldon M. Novick *et al.*, eds. 1987).

NAFTA AND THE ENVIRONMENT (Daniel B. Magraw ed. 1995).

THOMAS M. MACMAHON, J. ANDREW SCHLICKMAN & NICOLINE VAN RIEL, INTERNATIONAL ENVIRONMENTAL LAW AND REGULATION (1991).

Turner T. Smith, Jr., *U.S. and European Environmental Legislation*, in ULLMANN ENCYCLOPEDIA OF INDUSTRIAL CHEMISTRY (1995).

TURNER T. SMITH, JR. & PASCALE KROMAREK, UNDERSTANDING U.S. & EUROPEAN ENVIRONMENTAL LAW: A PRACTITIONER'S GUIDE (1989).

E. WEISS, P. SZASZ & D. MAGRAW, INTERNATIONAL ENVRIONMENTAL LAW: BASIC INSTRUMENTS AND REFERENCES (1992).

2.   Periodicals

Environmental Data Services, *ENDS Report* (covering developments in environmental issues in Europe and the U.K. in particular).

Bureau of National Affairs, *International Environment Reporter* (providing reprinted primary source material and reports on current developments).

Cutter Information Corp.,
    Environment Watch - Western Europe
    Environment Watch - Latin America
    Waste Management - Western Europe

3.   Articles

Turner T. Smith, Jr., *Environmental Issues in International Contracts, Joint Ventures, and Project Finance*, Paper Given at the American Law Institute–American Bar Association Course of Study International Environmental Law (May 4–6, 1995) (on file with author).

Turner T. Smith, Jr., *Environmental Regulation on the Rise Worldwide*, National Law Journal, Sept. 19, 1994, at C15.

Turner T. Smith, Jr., *Business — The Environment and Management's Mission*, European Leaders 161 (1994).

Turner T. Smith, Jr. & Roszell D. Hunter, *European Union Environmental Law*, 1994 INTERNATIONAL CORPORATE LAW ENVIRONMENT YEARBOOK 12.

Roszell D. Hunter, *The EU Directive on Integrated Pollution Prevention and Control: A Critical Analysis*, Env't Watch – Western Europe, 18 Aug. 1995.

Roszell D. Hunter, *European Electrical and Electronic Product Take-Back Regulation*, 18 INT'L. ENV'T REP. (BNA) 480 (1995).

Roszell D. Hunter, *The Problematic EU Hazardous Waste List*, 4 EUROPEAN ENVT'L L. REV. 83 (1995).

Roszell D. Hunter, *EU Eco-Management and Auditing Regulation*, 17 INT'L ENV'T REP. (BNA) 142 (1994).

Roszell D. Hunter, *Standardization and the Environment*, 16 INT'L ENV'T REP. (BNA) 185 (1994).

F.   *Offices of the U.S. EPA that Address International Matters*

Office for Enforcement and Compliance Assurance
International Enforcement Programs
U.S. Environmental Protection Agency
401 M Street, S.W.
Washington, D.C. 20460
Tel.:   (202) 260–3217
Fax: (202) 260–9833

Office of General Counsel
International Environmental Law Office
U.S. Environmental Protection Agency
401 M Street, S.W.
Washington, D.C. 20460
Tel.:   (202) 260–1810
Fax: (202) 260–3828

Office of International Activities
U.S. Environmental Protection Agency
401 M Street, S.W.
Washington, D.C. 20460
Tel.:   (202) 260–4870
Fax: (202) 260–4470

Office of International Activities
Eastern Europe, Soviet Union and Technical Assistance
U.S. Environmental Protection Agency
401 M Street, S.W.
Washington, D.C. 20460
Tel.: (202) 260–6154
Fax: (202) 260–4470

Office of International Activities
International Cooperation Division
U.S. Environmental Protection Agency
401 M Street, S.W.
Washington, D.C. 20460
Tel.: (202) 260–4875
Fax: (202) 260–4470

Office of International Activities
International Issues Division
U.S. Environmental Protection Agency
401 M Street, S.W.
Washington, D.C. 20460
Tel.: (202) 260–4878
Fax: (202) 260–8512

Infoterra (EPA's library for international requests)
U.S. Environmental Protection Agency
401 M Street, S.W.
Washington, D.C. 20460
Tel.: (202) 260–5917
Fax: (202) 260–3923

Office of Prevention, Pesticides & Toxic Substances
U.S. Environmental Protection Agency
401 M Street, S.W.
Washington, D.C. 20460
Tel.: (202) 260–2902
Fax: (202) 260–1847

Office of Research and Development
Office of Health Research
National Health Environmental Effects
Research Laboratory
U.S. Environmental Protection Agency
Mail Drop 51–A
Research Triangle Park, NC 27711
Tel.: (919) 541–2537
Fax: (919) 541–4324

Office of Solid Waste and Emergency Response
International and Special Projects Branch
U.S. Environmental Protection Agency
401 M Street, S.W.
Washington, D.C. 20460
Tel.: (202) 260-7944
Fax: (202) 260-0637

ENDNOTES

1   42 U.S.C. § 4321 (1988).

2   This obligation applies to companies that sell securities in the U.S. or are listed on a U.S. stock exchange. But more importantly, it also applies to non-U.S. companies that have 300 or more U.S. stockholders and meet certain other requirements. Such companies must either register their stock under section 12(g) of the Securities Exchange Act of 1934 or establish an exemption by providing information under Securities and Exchange Commission rule 12g3-2(b).

3   *See* Paul E. Hagen, *The Extraterritorial Reach of United States Environmental Laws*, paper given at the American Law Institute–American Bar Association International Environmental Law Conference (May 4-6, 1995); J. Turley, *When in Rome: Multi-lateral Misconduct and the Presumption Against Extraterritoriality*, 84 Nw. U. L. Rev. 598 (1990).

4   Region I is comprised of Brazil, Paraguay, Uruguay, Argentina, Bolivia and Chile.

5   Region II is comprised of Costa Rica, El Salvador, Guatemala, Honduras, Nicaragua, Belize, Dominican Republic, Haiti, Mexico and Panama.

6   Region III is comprised of Colombia, Ecuador, Peru, Venezuela, Bahamas, Barbados, Guyana, Jamaica, Suriname, Trinidad and Tobago.

CHAPTER 12

CUSTOMS LAW

Kenneth G. Weigel*

I.   INTRODUCTION

Customs law has always been important in the commercial context, but the enormous growth of international business has given it particular significance in recent years. Not only are business transactions becoming more international, but cross–border production of merchandise has increased, resulting in greater international movement of materials, parts and finished articles. These cross–border movements are subject to the customs requirements of the countries entered.

Countries regulate the inward flow of goods for various reasons. One is revenue collection; countries impose tariffs and other fees on imports. Another reason is to enforce regulations specific to imported goods, such as quotas, trade restrictions, antidumping orders and country–of–origin marking requirements. Customs services also provide border enforcement of national laws, such as those relating to intellectual property, national health, safety and welfare and public morals. An increasingly important function of customs services is the collection of international trade statistics, which countries require in their international trade negotiations and to deal with trade flows. Customs services are also frequently involved in enforcing export control laws. (See Chapter 13, *Export Controls, Sanctions and Antiboycott Laws.*)

The most obvious reason to consider customs issues in business transactions is the cost arising from import duties. Although tariff rates have been declining for years, generally through multilateral negotiations, rates in excess of 20 percent still exist. Moreover, even at lower levels, duty costs can make the difference between a profit and a loss in a transaction. Another reason to address customs issues thoroughly is to ensure the smooth flow of merchandise across borders. Countries often have detailed documentation and declaration requirements, and minor deviations may result in the detention of goods or penalties. A further consideration may be the existence of quotas or other import requirements (*e.g.,* licenses) that could block or limit imports. Customs planning at an early stage to deal with business transactions or in preparation for investments is essential to address these issues. Planning might result in savings and, at a minimum, should protect the company from unexpected costs and delays.

Customs services have traditionally performed an enforcement function. This enforcement emphasis continues today. The failure to comply with the customs laws of the importing country can result in criminal and civil penalties, seizure and forfeiture of goods or a combination of such penalties. Additionally, importers always face the possibility of time–consuming and costly audits and investigations even where compliance with the laws is ultimately found.

This chapter provides the reader with a basic overview of the more common customs law principles, with a focus on the United States. Customs problems are frequently extremely technical, and their resolution often requires a knowledge of and expertise in a variety of interrelated customs principles. Because of the risk of severe consequences of noncompliance, it is highly recommended that experienced advice be sought to address customs issues early in the planning stage of an international transaction or investment.

II.   INTERNATIONAL FRAMEWORK

The major trading countries have taken steps over many years to harmonize their customs requirements, thereby facilitating international trade. These steps at international harmonization continue. Nonetheless, each country (or association of countries in a customs union such as the European Union) retains responsibility for implementation of the internationally agreed upon principles, and there are still many differences among countries' customs procedures and substantive rules.

There are numerous international agreements and treaties affecting customs. The United States is a party to many of these, such as: the North American Free Trade Agreement ("NAFTA"); the Agreement Establishing The World Trade Organization ("WTO Agreement"), including the General Agreement on Tariffs and Trade (1994) ("GATT 1994") and its other annexes; the Convention Establishing the Customs Cooperation Council (now World Customs Organization) ("WCO"); and the International Convention on the Harmonized Commodity Description and Coding System.[1]

Under the GATT 1994, the United States has agreed to follow an internationally agreed methodology for valuation of imports. This methodology was originally established by the Customs Valuation Code resulting from the Tokyo Round of multilateral trade negotiations concluded in 1979, and it was continued basically unchanged in the recently concluded Uruguay Round of trade negotiations.

The International Convention on the Harmonized Commodity Description and Coding System created the Harmonized Commodity Description and Coding System (known as the "HS"), which is the classification system used by many trading nations, including the United States, for imports and exports. The HS divides all merchandise into categories (known as headings) and subcategories (known as subheadings) and assigns 4–digit numerical codes to the headings and 6-digit numerical codes to the sub-headings (*e.g.*, 7210, "Flat-rolled products of iron or nonalloy steel, of a width of 600 mm. or more, clad, plate or coated," and 7210.90, for those products that are "plated or coated with aluminum"). The HS has general, section and chapter notes and other explanatory principles of interpretation. Countries that adopt the HS classification system also adopt these notes and explanatory language. The WCO has also issued Explanatory Notes[2] to assist in the application of the HS. These Explanatory Notes are generally followed by, but not binding on, each country to the extent they do not conflict with the country's law. Additionally, the WCO meets periodically to interpret and update the HS.

Although the "origin" (*i.e.*, country of origin) of imported merchandise is often important for customs purposes, there is presently little international harmonization on the subject. Origin determinations are required by some countries because their laws mandate that imported merchandise be marked with its country of origin; also, origin is often important in applying trade restrictions (*e.g.*, quotas) as well as obtaining preferential treatment. (Rules of origin for preferential treatment, such as the rules governing what products qualify for duty-free treatment under the NAFTA, are sometimes referred to as "rules of preference" to distinguish them from nonpreferential rules of origin.) Countries frequently have (as does the United States) different origin rules for different import programs. (*See* III.E. *below.*)

The Uruguay Round of multilateral trade negotiations resulted in an Agreement on Rules of Origin ("ARO") in an attempt to harmonize customs country of origin determinations. The ARO's objectives are to obtain harmonization and clarification of nonpreferential rules of origin for goods in trade on the basis of the "substantial transformation" test (*See* III.E.1. *below*); to achieve discipline in the rules' administration; and to provide a framework for notification, review, consultation and dispute settlement on origin issues. The ARO provides that technical work toward these objectives will be undertaken by the WCO. Committees of the WTO and WCO are to be primarily responsible for developing rules of origin that achieve the stated objectives. Eventually, the WTO Ministerial Conference is to establish the results of the harmonization work program in an annex as an integral part of the ARO.

Countries also have bilateral agreements on customs administration. For example, the United States has numerous bilateral agreements with countries regarding cooperation and mutual assistance between the two countries' customs services. Countries with which the United States currently has such agreements include Austria, Belgium, Canada, Finland, Germany, Greece, Korea, Mexico, Norway, Poland, Spain, Sweden, the Russian Federation and the Ukraine.

Overall, although there has been international harmonization of certain customs requirements and procedures among the world's trading partners, significant differences remain in the customs rules and procedures of each country. Nonetheless, the existence of these international agreements and understandings means that importers confront similar general customs principles in many countries, particularly in the United States and its major export markets.

III.   CUSTOMS LAW AND PROCEDURES

This section provides an overview of the common principles and requirements of customs laws. The focus of this section is on U.S. requirements, supplemented with examples from other countries.

A.   *Overview of the U.S. Customs Process*

Merchandise is imported into the United States in a multi-step process by the importer (*i.e.,* the owner, purchaser or in some instances the consignee). Typically, the importer, through its agent, a licensed customs broker, begins the process by filing an "entry" followed by the filing of the "entry summary." In this process, the importer makes certain declarations to the U.S. Customs Service ("U.S. Customs") concerning the nature of the merchandise, as well as the customs classification and value of the merchandise. Once an entry is filed and if the merchandise is admissible, it is generally released by U.S. Customs if not designated for examination. The process ends 90 days after the entry is "liquidated" by U.S. Customs. Liquidation is the final ascertainment by U.S. Customs of duties due on the entry. By statute, entries must be liquidated within one year of the date of entry unless suspended by statute or court order or extended for statutorily specified reasons. Release and even liquidation, however, do not end the process. U.S. Customs frequently conducts post-importation reviews and audits for up to five years after the date of entry.

U.S. Customs is organized into ports and Headquarters in Washington, D.C. For operational purposes, the ports are managed by U.S. Customs Management Centers ("CMCs"); CMCs play no role in decisions concerning imported merchandise. There are also Strategic Trade Centers in five cities in the United States to target, analyze and prioritize use of U.S. Customs' resources.

In addition to overseeing the import process described above, U.S. Customs enforces the laws of many other government agencies, such as the Food & Drug Administration, the Federal Communications Commission, the U.S. Department of Agriculture, U.S. Department of Commerce (*e.g.,* antidumping and countervailing duty orders) as well as export controls, embargoes and other trade actions. It also collects data for trade statistics used by the U.S. government.

Below, the basic elements of the import process are discussed in more detail.

B. Entry[3]

Entry is the administrative process involved in physically bringing merchandise into the customs territory of the United States. All merchandise brought into the United States, except those limited items specifically exempted from customs procedures such as telecommunications transmissions, must be entered.[4] By statute, only certain entities have the right to make entry and to be the importer of record.

There are various types of entry. These include entry for consumption, entry for bonded warehouse and transportation and exportation entry. The type of entry chosen is significant because it determines the amount of duties and when they are due. For example, a warehouse entry does not require the posting of duties.

The most common type of entry is an entry for consumption. An entry for consumption typically involves a two-step process:

1. Filing an entry with U.S. Customs together with the posting of a bond and obtaining a release of the merchandise. The bond is posted as security for compliance with all U.S. laws and requirements.

2. Within 10 business days, the filing of the "entry summary" – a document which provides more information about the imported merchandise and the duties and fees owed – and deposit of estimated duties.

Generally, a licensed customhouse broker is hired by the importer to file the entry as the agent of the importer. As of this writing (October 1995), U.S. Customs is drafting regulations to enable it to switch from paper to paperless, electronically filed entries and entry summaries.

At the time of entry, the importer classifies and values the merchandise. U.S. Customs, generally after release, verifies the accuracy of these representations and then liquidates the entry.[5] Most merchandise is released without being inspected. U.S. Customs does, however, have a right to inspect merchandise as well as to detain merchandise for certain time periods.

In addition to duties, a fee collected for customs processing ("merchandise processing fee"), as well as harbor maintenance fees for merchandise imported by vessel, are collected by U.S. Customs at the time of entry.

C. Classification[6]

Classification is the process of determining where an imported article falls in a country's tariff schedule. There is no single, worldwide tariff schedule. As discussed above, the HS promulgated by the WCO is used by many countries as the basis of their tariff schedules. Each country, however, may interpret the HS differently. Moreover, each country imposes its own rates of duty on imported goods, subject to commitments made under GATT 1994 or other international agreements to set duties at (or not to exceed) certain levels.

In 1989, the United States adopted the Harmonized Tariff Schedule of the United States ("HTSUS"), based on the HS. Although the HS divides classifications to the subheading (6–digit) level, the United States and other countries have created further subdivisions in the HS for duty and statistical purposes. For example, the United States and Canada have each added 8–digit tariff items for tariff rates, and 10–digit classification numbers are maintained for statistical purposes. Similarly, the European Union's integrated tariff has some 10,000 8–digit headings and around 15,000 further subdivisions (usually coded with two extra digits) constituting the basic nomenclature for the Common Customs Tariff as well as for the statistics of external trade of the European Union and the trade between Member States.

All merchandise, unless specifically excepted, imported into the United States is subject to classification under the HTSUS, including U.S. merchandise returning to the United States. Classification of merchandise is an exercise in statutory interpretation. The merchandise is classified in accordance with the rules set forth in the HTSUS, and judicial and administrative precedent. In addition to the normal classifications for merchandise, the HTSUS has special classifications, such as for U.S. goods returned, U.S. goods assembled abroad, temporary importations under bond and temporary tariff provisions.

The U.S. Congress assigns duty rates to these classifications, and the specific duty to be imposed on the merchandise imported into the United States depends on the origin of the imported product. There is a general rate of duty imposed on all imported merchandise, except for that from certain enumerated countries; this is known as the most–favored–nation ("MFN") or column 1 rate. Merchandise from certain countries not eligible for MFN treatment, such as that from North Korea, is subject to the column 2 rate of duty. Special, lower, duties apply to merchandise subject to a preferential trade program or agreement (*e.g.*, the U.S. Generalized System of Preferences ("GSP") or NAFTA). These duty rates are specified in the "Special" column of the HTSUS.

D.   *Valuation*[7]

Most duties set forth in a country's tariff schedule as well as fees are *ad valorem* (*i.e.*, determined as a percentage of the imported article's customs "value"). Therefore, the value of the imported merchandise is necessary to determine the amount of duties and fees owed. To determine the value of imported merchandise, many countries, including the United States, Australia, Canada, Japan, the European Union, China and New Zealand, have adopted the GATT Valuation Code (formally known as the Agreement on Implementation of Article VII of GATT 1994). Again, each country may apply the Code differently. For example, while imports into the United States and Canada are generally valued under the transaction value method (although related-party transactions are subject to greater scrutiny and different valuation methods may apply), the United States and Canada differ in what amounts are included in the dutiable value. For example, some royalties are considered a part of dutiable value by Canada, but not by the United States. Although the European Union also follows the Code, it has a number of specified rules for valuation. For example, European Commission Regulation 334/92 establishes specific unit values for the determination of the customs value of certain perishable goods. The United States has adopted this approach on a very limited basis at some ports (*e.g.*, flowers shipped on consignment at Miami).

The GATT valuation rules, which are reflected in the U.S. customs law, set forth a hierarchy of valuation methodologies. The first of the following applicable methodologies is to be used, except that the importer can elect to use either the third or fourth methods if the first two do not apply:

1. Transaction value ("price paid or payable") of the merchandise. Transaction value is acceptable even in related party transactions under certain circumstances;

2. Transaction value of identical or similar merchandise. For example, a sale of the same merchandise to an importer;

3. Deductive value. This is basically the resale price in the country of importation less post-exportation charges;

4. Computed value. This is basically the cost of production plus expenses and profit; or

5. Any other reasonable basis. This valuation method applies only when none of the above methods are applicable. Value under this method may be determined based on one of the foregoing methods but without satisfying all of the technical requirements of the method.

The application of each of these methods of appraisement is extremely complex and requires detailed knowledge of the law and regulations. Merely using the invoice price is frequently not sufficient. For example, prices in related party transactions can be used only if they meet certain tests. Moreover, U.S. Customs takes an expansive view and, at least initially, will consider all payments made directly or indirectly by the importer to the foreign supplier to be for the merchandise and, therefore, part of the customs value. Another issue in valuing merchandise is the addition for such items as royalties and assists to the invoice price.

E.   *Country of Origin*

As discussed above, origin determinations are important for country of origin marking purposes and for qualifying for preferential duty programs, *e.g.*, GSP and NAFTA. (*See* Chapter 16, *Trade Remedies and Benefits Programs.*) Currently, different criteria are applied by the United States to determine origin depending on the statute and trade program at issue.

1.   Determining the Country of Origin

Determining the country of origin of merchandise produced using parts and components from numerous countries can be extremely difficult. Traditionally, the country of origin of merchandise has been determined as the country in which it was last substantially transformed.[8] A good is substantially transformed when as a result of operations it acquires a new and different name, character or use. The determination of whether a substantial transformation has occurred can be highly subjective.

U.S. Customs has recently begun to use a more objective test based on a change in tariff classification.[9] To apply this test, the classification of the final product determines the specific origin rule for the merchandise, and the rule will specify the change in classification required for there to be a substantial transformation. For preferential duty purposes, there may also be a value-added requirement.

Like the United States, other countries have multiple rules for determining the origin of goods. Canada uses different rules for the determination of origin of goods from NAFTA and non–NAFTA countries. Also, the European Union has various regulations and decisions that apply specific rules of origin with respect to goods and/or countries. The common European Union definition of origin used in nonpreferential arrangements basically provides that the goods originate in the country where wholly obtained or produced, and goods whose production involves more than one country are deemed to originate in the country where they underwent their last substantial, economically justified processing or working in an undertaking equipped for that purpose and resulting in the manufacture of a new product or representing an important stage of manufacture. This rule is similar, but not identical, to the U.S. substantial transformation test. The European Union also has rules of origin defined in the context of preferential agreements, and regulations dealing with special procedures concerning certain countries, such as GSP beneficiaries (*see* below).

2.   Marking[10]

There is no uniformity on country–of–origin marking requirements for imported goods. For example, New Zealand and China do not have country-of-origin marking rules. The European Union does not have country-of-origin rules; it has, however, special import arrangements for goods originating in third countries, including rules relating to the proof of origin.[11] Canada has country–of–origin marking rules, but only for certain merchandise such as wearing apparel, paper products, sporting goods, hardware and household goods. In addition, Canadian Customs has the responsibility for assuring that products imported into Canada, such as textiles, foods and drugs, and consumer products, meet Canadian labelling requirements. Japan has country-of-origin marking rules, generally for all merchandise.

The United States requires that every imported article or its container, with certain specified exceptions, must be marked to indicate its country of origin to the ultimate purchaser in the United States. The country-of-origin marking must be as conspicuous, indelible and legible as possible.

Merchandise imported into the United States not marked with its country of origin is under certain circumstances subject to seizure. In all cases, it is subject to redelivery to U.S. Customs' custody for proper marking and assessment of 10 percent marking duties. Criminal penalties apply for intentional removal or defacement of country of origin markings.

F.   *Fines, Penalties and Forfeitures*

Each country differs in the customs fines, penalties and forfeitures context. Moreover, even the countries of the European Union differ concerning actions against customs fraud and measures prohibiting the release for free circulation of counterfeit goods. In the European Union, the procedures to be followed and the penalties for failure to respect the customs rules are generally contained in national legislation. Such procedures and penalties will, therefore, differ from one Member State to another.

The discussion below is limited to the United States.

1.   Criminal Penalties[12]

Numerous U.S. criminal statutes can apply in the customs law context. An investigation by U.S. Customs may lead to a criminal referral to a U.S. attorney or, if declined, a civil penalty action. There appears to be an increase in criminal prosecutions involving customs law violations, and it is extremely important to treat any customs problem initially as potentially a criminal action.

2.   Civil Penalties

The most frequently used U.S. customs civil penalty statute is Section 592 of the Tariff Act of 1930, as amended.[13] This statute prohibits any person from making, either by negligence, gross negligence or fraud, a false and material statement or act or a material omission in connection with the actual or attempted entry or introduction of merchandise into the United States. Aiders and abettors to such violations are also subject to monetary penalties under the statute. Monetary penalties may be as great as the domestic value of the merchandise. In addition to penalties, any additional duties owed are also assessed. There is a five-year statute of limitations for these penalty actions.

By statute, the amount of penalty assessed under Section 592 can be significantly limited if a prior voluntary disclosure is made of the problem. Note that a prior voluntary disclosure does not affect the ability of the U.S. government to bring criminal charges against the offender. Because of the significant benefits of prior voluntary disclosures, the requirements for making a disclosure are strictly construed.

3.   Seizures

U.S. Customs has two civil seizure statutes.[14] Seizures were formerly used more frequently in connection with the importation of merchandise. Their use is now extremely limited. Typically, seizures are resolved through a petitioning procedure where the seizure is remitted upon payment of some amount, and the merchandise is either allowed to be imported or exported.

4.   Liquidated Damages[15]

For many actions, U.S. Customs requires the posting of a bond to ensure satisfaction of U.S. Customs' requirements. For example, merchandise is released from U.S. Customs' custody subject to certain conditions and performance of these conditions is secured by either a single entry or a continuous bond. If the bond is breached by the principal, it provides for liquidated damages frequently equal to the value of the merchandise.

5.   Mitigation of Claims

By statute, penalties, liquidated damages and other claims are subject to mitigation by U.S. Customs.[16] U.S. Customs has issued guidelines for mitigation of most occurrences.

6.   Offers-in-Compromise[17]

It is possible to settle matters with U.S. Customs through an offer-in-compromise proceeding. Offers-in-compromise are typically decided by U.S. Customs Headquarters, taking into account the probability of success in litigation and the ability of the offender to pay.

7.   Enforcement Trends – Informed Compliance

With passage of the Customs Modernization Act in 1993, the process of importing has changed. We are now in an era of "informed compliance." U.S. Customs informs importers of requirements, and importers must comply. No longer does U.S. Customs classify and value imported merchandise based on the importer's information. Now, the importer must use reasonable care to classify, value and otherwise deal with U.S. Customs or face civil penalties and, in effect, a five-year statute of limitations on duties and interest.[18]

U.S. Customs is revising its entire method of doing business. It will now look at importers as accounts instead of each entry of merchandise as a distinct transaction. It has shifted from review at the time of importation to audits after the fact. It has also begun to use more sophisticated methods to analyze trade and to target certain trade for scrutiny.

Importers must adapt to these requirements or risk serious financial consequences in the future.

G.   U.S. Customs Advice[19]

U.S. Customs provides advice to importers in different forms. Traditionally, importers could request a written ruling from U.S. Customs on a specific issue or transaction. That ruling was binding on that importer for that merchandise and provided guidance to other importers. Additionally, U.S. Customs now has a Pre–Importation Review Program consisting of either pre–approval of an importer's methods and practices or pre–classification of the importer's products. In this era of informed compliance, U.S. Customs will be increasing the information available to educate traders.

H.   Protests[20]

Importers may challenge the liquidation of an entry through the protest procedure. Protests are generally filed on U.S. Customs Form 19 and must be filed within 90 days of the date of liquidation of the entry.

Petitions for refunds of overpayment resulting from a clerical error, mistake of fact or other inadvertence adverse to the importer must be filed within one year of the date of liquidation.

I.   Duty Refund or Deferral Opportunities

There are several methods available for achieving a refund of duties paid or a deferral of duty payment. These include use of a foreign trade zone or subzone; drawback programs (i.e., refund of duties paid on imported merchandise subsequently exported without being used, or used in U.S. manufacture of an article that is exported); bonded warehouses; and temporary importations under bond.[21] Each of these procedures can bring an importer significant duty savings, but their use involves burdens. These burdens include the need for detailed recordkeeping, an increased risk of a customs audit, and the possibility of fines for failure to comply scrupulously with the rules. Consequently, there is a need for cost-benefit analysis before using any of these duty–savings programs.

IV.   SOURCES OF ASSISTANCE

A.   U.S. Statutes and Regulations

Tariff Act of 1930, *as amended,* codified at 19 U.S.C. §§ 1–3624.

19 C.F.R. Parts 1–191.

B. International Agreements and Sources

North American Free Trade Agreement, *done* August 13, 1992, Hein's No. KAV 3417, Temp. State Dep't No. 94–48 (*entered into force* for the United States January 1, 1994). (Hein's is a treaty service available on microfiche. It is available from William S. Hein *&* Co., 1285 Main Street, Buffalo, NY 14209.) (Also available, with supporting commentary, on CD–ROM from the ABA Section of International Law and Practice.)

The Uruguay Round of Multilateral Trade Negotiations on the General Agreement on Tariffs and Trade, *signed* on behalf of the U.S. on April 15, 1994, Hein's No. KAV 4033 (*entered into force* for the United States January 1, 1995).

The Uruguay Round of Multilateral Trade Negotiations on the Agreement Establishing the World Trade Organization, *signed* on behalf of the U.S. on April 15, 1994, Hein's No. KAV 4044 (*entered into force* for the United States January 1, 1995).

Agreement on Implementation of Article VII of the GATT (Customs Valuation Code), *done* on April 12, 1979, 34 U.S.T. 1151–2; T.I.A.S. 10402.

The Convention Establishing the Customs Cooperation Council, *done* on December 15, 1950, 22 U.S.T. 320; T.I.A.S. 7063 (now the World Customs Organization) (*entered into force* for the United States November 5, 1970).

The International Convention on the Harmonized Commodity Description and Coding System, *done* June 14, 1983, Hein's No. KAV 2260, Temp. State Dep't No. 84–45 (*entered into force* for the United States January 1, 1989).

World Customs Organization, EXPLANATORY NOTES TO THE HARMONIZED COMMODITY DESCRIPTION AND CODING SYSTEM (Supp. Feb. 1995).

World Customs Organization, COMPENDIUM OF CLASSIFICATION OPINIONS TO THE HARMONIZED SYSTEM (Supp. Feb. 1995).

World Customs Organization, CUSTOMS VALUATION: COMPENDIUM CONTAINING THE CONVENTION ON CUSTOMS VALUATION, RECOMMENDATIONS, OPINIONS, NOTES AND STUDIES (Supp. July 1992).

C. U.S. Government Publications

Available from the U.S. Government Printing Office:

Office of Commercial Operations, Office of Regulations and Rulings, U.S. Customs Service, Department of Treasury, Customs Valuation Encyclopedia (1980–94).

U.S. Customs Service, Department of Treasury, *Customs Bulletin* (publication containing notices from Customs as well as copies of judicial decisions and significant Customs rulings and other decisions).

U.S. Customs Service, Department of Treasury, Importing into the United States (1995).

U.S. Customs Service, Department of Treasury, Harmonized System Handbook–A Guide to the New U.S. Tariff (August 1986).

U.S. Customs Service, Department of Treasury, Bonded Warehouse Manual for Proprietors, Importers, Customs Officers (1992).

U.S. Customs Service, Department of Treasury, Foreign Trade Zone Manual (1992).

Office of Commercial Operations, U.S. Customs Service, Department of Treasury, Fines, Penalties & Forfeitures Handbook (April 1986 Revision).

U.S. International Trade Commission, Harmonized Tariff Schedule of the United States, USITC Pub. No. 2831 (1995).

Staff of the House Committee on Ways & Means, 104th Cong., 1st Sess., Overview and Compilation of U.S. Trade Statutes (Comm. Print 1995).

D. *Treatises*

R. Sturm, Customs Law and Administration (3d ed. 1993).

S. Sherman, Import Practice: Customs and International Trade Law and a Business Guide to GATT Customs Valuation Code (1980).

E. *Periodicals*

Bureau of National Affairs, International Trade Reporter, *U.S. Import Weekly* (1231 25th St., N.W., Washington, D.C. 20037).

Bureau of National Affairs, *International Trade Reporter* (1231 25th St., N.W., Washington, D.C. 20037).

International Business Reports, *Customs Record* (P.O. Box 1009, Falls Church, VA 22041).

F.   *Electronic Databases*

WESTLAW and LEXIS contain decisions published by Customs.

U.S. Customs notices in the *Federal Register* are also available on–line.

U.S. Customs has an Electronic Bulletin Board to which one may sub–scribe.

ENDNOTES

*The author wishes to thank Nancy Kao of Kirkland & Ellis for her assistance in preparation of the Sources of Assistance as well as Grant Ashby of Trade Consultants, Ltd. (Australia and New Zealand); Glenn Cranker of Stikeman, Elliott (Canada); Ambrose Chua and Nicholas Bromfield of Lovell White Durrant (China and European Union); and Eriko Watanabe and Kenta Tsujimaki of Nagashima & Ohno (Japan) for their assistance on customs laws of their jurisdictions in preparation of the chapter.

1   *See* Section IV, Sources of Assistance, for full citations to agreements, statutes and regulations cited in this chapter.
2   *See* Section IV, Sources of Assistance.
3   *See* 19 U.S.C. § 1481 *et seq.*; 19 C.F.R. Parts 141–144.
4   *See* General Note 16, Harmonized Tariff Schedule of the United States.
5   As a result of the high volume of trade, most entries are not reviewed, but merely liquidated as entered.
6   *See* 19 U.S.C. § 1202.
7   For U.S. value laws and regulations, *see* 19 U.S.C. § 1401a and 19 C.F.R. § 152.100, *et seq.*
8   19 C.F.R. § 134.1(b).
9   19 C.F.R. § 102.20.
10   19 U.S.C. § 1304; 19 C.F.R. Part 134.
11   *See* Articles 22–26 of the Community Customs Code and Articles 35–65 of the implementing Regulation.
12   *See* 18 U.S.C. §§ 1001 – 1033.
13   19 U.S.C. § 1592.
14   19 U.S.C. § 1595a(c); 19 U.S.C. § 1592(b)(6).
15   19 C.F.R. Part 172.
16   19 U.S.C. § 1618.
17   19 U.S.C. § 1617.
18   *See* 19 U.S.C. § 1592(d).
19   19 C.F.R. Part 177.
20   19 U.S.C. §§ 1514 – 1516, 1520(c).
21   19 U.S.C. § 1313; 15 C.F.R. Part 400; 19 C.F.R. Parts 19, 191; and §§ 10.31–10.40, 191, 1313.

CHAPTER 13

EXPORT CONTROLS, SANCTIONS AND ANTIBOYCOTT LAWS

Edward L. Rubinoff

I.   INTRODUCTION

Any company engaged in international trade must contend with export controls imposed by the countries in which it does business. Governments control exports of goods and technology in order to serve their national security, foreign policy, non–proliferation and short supply interests, as well as to carry out their international obligations.

International transactions are subject to U.S. export controls in a variety of ways, some of which are not obvious. An "export" subject to U.S. law includes not only an actual shipment, transfer or transmission of goods or technology out of the United States, but also a transfer within the United States to an embassy or affiliate of a controlled country or to any person within the United States with the knowledge or intent that the goods or technology will be shipped, transferred or transmitted to an unauthorized recipient. The electronic transmission of non–public data abroad, the return of foreign equipment to its country of origin after repair in the United States, the performance of repair work outside the United States, shipments from a U.S. foreign trade zone, and the release of technology to a foreign national in the United States through such means as oral briefings or visual inspection are all deemed "*exports*." Even the hiring of a foreign national in the United States raises export control and licensing issues if the individual will have access to technology.

U.S. export controls can also apply to transactions outside the United States. For example, goods and technology that have been exported from the United States remain subject to control with respect to their reexport from one foreign country to another. (Many such reexports, however, will qualify for an exception from licensing requirements.) The United States also asserts control over certain goods and technology produced abroad using U.S. technology. In some cases, authorization to export technology from the United States will be subject to assurances that items produced abroad that are the direct product of that technology will not be exported to certain destinations without prior authorization. As in the case of direct U.S. exports, the extent of control over a particular foreign transaction will depend on the goods or technology, the destination, the end use and the end user.

This chapter will cover the basics of the U.S. export control system. Other countries maintain similar export control regimes, but none is as complex or as far-reaching as the system administered by the United States. Before transferring goods or technology from one foreign location to another, a company should consider the possible applications of foreign as well as U.S. controls. Even in-country transfers abroad may pose export control issues. Compliance with foreign controls may raise issues under the U.S. antiboycott laws, which are discussed at the end of this chapter.

II.   MULTILATERAL EXPORT CONTROL REGIMES

The United States cooperates with other countries to restrict certain exports through a variety of bilateral and multilateral arrangements. Some of these organizations are formal legal structures, whereas others are simply international conventions. The objectives and mechanisms of these groups differ widely. The key export control regimes are discussed below.

A.   *COCOM and the New Forum*

The Coordinating Committee for Multilateral Export Controls ("COCOM") was an international group consisting of the NATO countries (less Iceland), plus Japan and Australia, established at the outset of the Cold War to coordinate the restrictions on exports of scarce or strategic items to the Soviet Union, the People's Republic of China and their allies. Issuance of a license for export of COCOM-controlled items to a proscribed country involved member-country submission for COCOM approval or compliance with COCOM notification procedures.

The countries participating in COCOM agreed to terminate its operations March 31, 1994. They also agreed, however, to maintain controls on items on the COCOM lists for the time being, without the multilateral review or notification that formerly occurred.

In September 1995, 28 countries, including Russia, the Czech Republic, Hungary, Poland and the Slovak Republic, agreed to establish a new multilateral control system, tentatively named the "New Forum," for the export of conventional weapons and dual-use[1] goods and technology beginning January 1, 1996. Unlike COCOM, the New Forum will not be directed against any state or group of states. However, it will have the ability to single out "regions of concern." Participants in the new regime will implement national export controls relating to goods and technology lists which remain to be agreed upon. The decision to permit or deny the transfer of any item will be solely the responsibility of each member government.

B.   Australia Group

Organized in 1984 and chaired by Australia, this informal group of supplier countries coordinates policies relating to the control of exports of chemical weapons precursors, organisms of biological warfare significance, and related equipment and technology.

C.   Missile Technology Control Regime

Organized in 1987, the Missile Technology Control Regime ("MTCR") is a group of supplier countries concerned over the proliferation of ballistic missiles and other means of air delivery of weapons of mass destruction. Annex I of the MTCR list covers rockets and major missile systems. Annex II contains a number of dual-use items of significance in the construction or guidance of missiles.

D.   Nuclear Suppliers Group

The Nuclear Suppliers Group ("NSG") has long served to coordinate supplier-country policies with respect to safeguards required to prevent the diversion of nuclear fuel to weapons use. The NSG broadened its role by adopting, effective January 1993, a list of nuclear-related dual-use items, together with guidelines for controlling exports of such items. Russia, Argentina and several Central European countries now participate in the NSG along with the founding members from the West.

E.   U.S.-Japan Supercomputer Regime

A 1991 bilateral agreement between the United States and Japan coordinates policies and practices governing exports of supercomputers from both countries. It was originally intended to create rigorous controls on exports of supercomputers to countries outside the COCOM regime. Efforts to include European countries in the agreement have thus far failed.

The agreement requires the parties to define a supercomputer by reference to its performance capacity. A variety of safeguards are mandated for purchasers depending on the country of destination. Each party must provide the other party with 30 days' advance notification of an intent to issue a license to export a supercomputer.

III.   U.S. EXPORT CONTROL PROGRAMS

A.   Export Control Jurisdiction

Export control responsibility in the United States government is vested in numerous federal agencies. Export control responsibilities among agencies may sometimes overlap, because the reasons for controlling exports may differ.

The Department of Commerce's Bureau of Export Administration ("BXA") has the broadest impact on U.S. export activity. BXA exercises licensing jurisdiction over "dual-use" items, meaning goods, technology or software which have civilian uses, but which also have military applications or are deemed to have strategic significance. In 1995, several bills were submitted in Congress proposing to dismantle the Commerce Department and to transfer BXA's export control functions to either a new or an existing government agency.

Defense articles and defense services designed for military purposes are regulated by the Department of State's Office of Defense Trade Controls ("ODTC"). The Treasury Department's Office of Foreign Assets Control ("OFAC") administers trade embargoes and economic sanctions against foreign countries for foreign policy and national security reasons.

The Nuclear Regulatory Commission ("NRC") regulates exports of nuclear reactor vessels, nuclear materials, and commodities for nuclear reactors. The Department of Energy ("DOE") controls exports of technical data related to the production of special nuclear materials. DOE also controls exports of natural gas and electric power.

The Patent and Trademark Office ("PTO") authorizes exports of unclassified technical data in the form of a foreign patent application, amendment or modification. The Drug Enforcement Administration ("DEA") exercises jurisdiction over exports of narcotics and dangerous drugs. The U.S. Maritime Administration controls exports of certain watercraft.

B.   *Dual-Use Export Controls*

1.   **Export Administration Regulations**

BXA administers the Export Administration Regulations ("EAR") under the authority of the Export Administration Act ("EAA").[2] The EAA has lapsed on occasion and has been resurrected by new legislation. During the lapses, the EAR have been kept in force by Presidential Orders issued under the authority of the International Emergency Economic Powers Act ("IEEPA").

2.   **The Commerce Control List**

The items subject to licensing under the EAR are set forth in the EAR's Commerce Control List ("CCL"). Entries on the CCL are identified by an Export Control Classification Number ("ECCN"). For each ECCN, the CCL indicates the country groups for which validated licenses are required, the statutory basis for control, and other important licensing information. Some ECCNs contain "Advisory Notes" that describe the commodities for which licenses are likely to be issued and satisfactory end-users in controlled destinations. The introduction to the CCL provides invaluable guidance for understanding the ECCN numbering system and the structure of the CCL.

3. Country Groups

For EAR export control purposes, foreign countries are separated into various country groups. These designations, used in conjunction with the CCL entries, allow an exporter to determine the licensing requirements applicable to an export of a particular item to a specific destination.

4. Licensing

Under current regulations, all exports subject to the EAR require either a General License or a Validated License. A General License is an authorization in the EAR that permits the export of a good or technology without an application to, or affirmative action by, BXA. If no General License is available, an export must be specifically authorized in writing by BXA on either an individual or multiple basis. Authorization for a particular export transaction is given via an Individual Validated License ("IVL"). Special Licenses, such as the Distribution License, Project License and Service Supply License, may be obtained for bulk shipments of commodities and spare parts that otherwise would require IVLs. License restrictions or denial of license applications generally are not subject to judicial review.

A proposed rewrite of the EAR announced in May 1995 would eliminate the terms *"General"* and *"Validated"* licenses. Instead, the term *"license"* would refer only to an authorization issued by BXA upon application, whereas the numerous General Licenses would be converted into "exceptions" to the obligation to seek a license. A Special Comprehensive License would consolidate the current Distribution, Project and Service Supply Licenses.

Reexporters are required to obtain written authorization for items previously exported from the United States, unless covered by permissive reexport authority, by the reexport provisions of an IVL, or by a Special License.

5. Interagency Review

Many license applications to BXA are subject to review by other agencies. Cases that are referred to other agencies may be discussed in an interagency group. The Department of State chairs separate interagency working groups for the different non-proliferation controls. Cases not handled by one of these groups can be taken to the Commerce-chaired Operating Committee. An agency can escalate a case from one of these groups to the Advisory Committee on Export Policy, chaired by the Assistant Secretary of Commerce for Export Administration, and further escalation is possible to the Export Administration Review Board, chaired by the Secretary of Commerce, or even to the president.

6. Export Control Modalities

National security controls relate to items that are deemed important to the strategic and military capability of "controlled countries." Political changes and the development of the capacity and commitment of these states to safeguard sensitive exports can lead to liberalized export control policies or a change in country group.

Foreign policy controls are additional or parallel controls that are implemented to fulfill U.S. foreign policy objectives and U.S. international obligations. Foreign policy controls relating to nuclear non–proliferation considerations, as well as missile technology control and chemical/biological warfare control, apply in certain instances to items that are not subject to the national security controls, but that the U.S. has deemed to be important to control, either unilaterally or in cooperation with other countries. The United States strengthened these controls in 1991 under the Enhanced Proliferation Control Initiative ("EPCI"). The EPCI controls include the "catch–all" requirement that a license be sought for a wide range of items otherwise eligible for export under General License if the exporter knows that the item will be used in a project involving weapons of mass destruction in a designated country of concern.

For foreign policy reasons, the United States maintains unilateral controls on virtually all items destined for embargoed countries (*i.e.*, North Korea, Iran, Cuba and Libya). Foreign policy controls are also directed at countries where the U.S. is concerned that particular items will be used for terrorism or by the military of a terrorist-supporting country.

7.   Prospective Changes

At the time of this writing (October 1995), significant changes are imminent in the export controls administered by BXA:

- Congress has renewed efforts to revise significantly the EAA.
- BXA has launched a top–to–bottom restructuring and rewriting of the EAR which is expected to be implemented by the beginning of 1996. Proposed new rules were published in May 1995. (*See* 60 Fed. Reg. 25268 (May 11, 1995).)
- The EAR will be revised further to implement whatever new multilateral control procedures are established by the New Forum.
- Pursuant to the September 1993 report to Congress by the statutorily-mandated Trade Policy Coordinating Committee, BXA is considering several important changes in the policies and practices applied to the control of dual-use exports, such as unilateral controls, clarification of the EPCI "catch–all" provisions, and procedures for determining the licensing jurisdiction between the State and Commerce Departments.

C.   *Defense Export Controls*

1.   **International Traffic in Arms Regulations**

The United States maintains a stringent licensing system for the export of conventional arms and other defense articles and services. Within the

Department of State's Bureau of Political–Military Affairs, the Office of Defense Trade Controls ("ODTC") carries out the licensing function for commercial defense exports under the statutory authority of the Arms Export Control Act ("AECA"). The International Traffic in Arms Regulations ("ITAR") implement the AECA. The AECA/ITAR regime is completely separate from the EAA/EAR program.

2.   The U.S. Munitions List

Items subject to export control under the ITAR are found on the U.S. Munitions List ("ML"). Broadly speaking, items are included on the ML when they are designed for military, as opposed to commercial, applications. However, military end–use is not necessarily a determining factor. Dedicated components and related technology are also ITAR–controlled, as are certain items not normally viewed as military (encryption–capable software is a prominent example).

Because the ML lacks detail in comparison with the CCL, many exporters are uncertain whether an item is covered by the ML or the CCL. The Commodity Jurisdiction procedure has been established under the ITAR to alleviate this confusion. In addition, by presidential directive, a process has been under way for several years to transfer export licensing jurisdiction from ODTC to BXA for "dual–use" items over which ODTC has heretofore exercised jurisdiction.

3.   Licensing

U.S. citizens registered with ODTC are eligible to receive licenses for the export of U.S.-origin defense articles and services. Under the ITAR, if an item is controlled on the ML, an ODTC license will be required for export or reexport to any foreign destination, although Canada is exempted from a wide range of licensing requirements. Decisions to approve or deny export license applications are considered on a case–by–case basis and are subject to interagency review. ODTC determinations are made on the basis of U.S. national security requirements and foreign policy interests. As under the EAR, license determinations under the ITAR generally are not subject to judicial review.

License applications that are referred to the Department of Defense are staffed by the Defense Technology Security Administration ("DTSA"), which coordinates positions with the Office of the Secretary of Defense ("OSD") and with the Armed Services. DTSA submits the Defense Department's recommendations and comments to ODTC for consideration in the review process. There are no statutory processing time limits for licensing decisions. However, DTSA has followed a unique procedure whereby it will provide the applicant an informal "day in court" if it decides to recommend denial of an application, to allow the applicant an opportunity to plead his case and try to ascertain the reasons for the denial (if they are not classified). DTSA does not conduct this "day in court" for BXA applicants whose applications are under review; nevertheless, BXA applicants can arrange informal meetings with DTSA licensing and policy officials.

D. *Economic Embargoes and Sanctions*

1. Foreign Assets Control

The Treasury Department's Office of Foreign Assets Control ("OFAC") administers embargoes and economic sanctions against foreign countries and individuals to further U.S. foreign policy and national security goals. OFAC acts under the president's wartime and national emergency powers, as well as under authority granted by specific legislation, to impose controls on transactions with foreign persons.

2. Types of Economic Sanctions

Most OFAC programs impose broad prohibitions on financial and trade transactions with targeted countries. Export restrictions are typically part of a wider set of economic measures.

Economic sanctions programs fall into two broad categories: financial sanctions and asset freezes; and trade and commercial embargoes. Asset freezes prohibit transfers of those foreign assets that are subject to U.S. jurisdiction, or in the possession or control of U.S. persons. Frozen assets cannot be paid out, withdrawn, set off, or transferred in any manner without a Treasury license. Financial sanctions, such as prohibitions on bank lending, may also be imposed. Import embargoes may be selective or all-inclusive. Export embargoes may be product-specific or comprehensive. Commercial embargoes may be extended to include contract performance, travel and transportation prohibitions. Some or all of these options may be combined to effect a comprehensive sanctions program.

OFAC currently administers assets freezes and economic embargoes against Cuba, Iraq, Libya, North Korea, Yugoslavia, and UNITA, and trade and economic sanctions against Iran. OFAC also administers certain residual assets controls involving Cambodia, Iran and Vietnam. OFAC will also implement Executive Orders issued by the president in 1995 prohibiting transactions with certain terrorist organizations that threaten to disrupt the Middle East Peace Process and with members of the Cali drug cartel.

The OFAC regulations vary greatly in their scope and reach. For example, the regulations targeted at North Korea and Cuba prohibit all transactions between U.S. citizens and entities, including foreign subsidiaries of U.S. companies, with these countries regardless of where the transactions take place. By contrast, the regulations directed at Libya, for example, do not generally prohibit transactions of foreign-origin items by U.S. citizens and foreign subsidiaries located abroad. The Iran sanctions prohibit exports to Iran from the United States, reexports from foreign countries of certain U.S.-origin goods and technology, transactions anywhere by a U.S. person involving Iranian-origin goods or services, and the "approval or facilitation" by a U.S. person of a transaction or contract with Iran by a foreign entity owned or controlled by the U.S. person.

3.   Licensing

OFAC's licensing determinations are strongly influenced by the State Department, which reviews all but routine applications to OFAC. OFAC's regulations, while detailed, are also often vague, giving OFAC the flexibility to judge the particular facts of a transaction. License applications that raise policy problems, particularly at State, can take months to process. There is no interagency committee, and no time limits apply.

4.   State Laws

A number of states and localities in the United States enacted sanctions of their own against South Africa during the days of apartheid. Examples were restrictions on investment of state funds in companies that have assets in South Africa and bans on the supply of South African products to public entities in the state. Because of the lifting of U.S. sanctions against South Africa, the status of these laws is unclear. In any event, the existence of these laws indicates the need to bear state and local restrictions in mind when considering an investment or sourcing relationship abroad.

IV.   EXPORT ENFORCEMENT

A.   *Violations of U.S. Export Control Laws*

1.   Export Administration Act

The EAA provides for significant criminal fines and civil penalties for violations of the export control provisions of the Act. A person violating the Act or the regulations may also be denied export privileges. This is a severe penalty – the violator is unable to get or use U.S. export licenses, and it is unlawful for others to engage in export transactions with it. Illegal exports are subject to seizure and forfeiture. Civil penalties and other administrative sanctions are imposed on violators on a strict liability basis (*i.e.,* no requirement of knowledge or intent). BXA and the U.S. Customs service share responsibilities for enforcement of the EAA.

2.   Arms Export Control Act

The AECA provides criminal penalties for willful violations and authorizes civil and administrative sanctions as set out in the EAA. The ITAR provide for debarment of violators from participation in the export of defense articles, technical data or services and for interim suspension pending the final disposition of the debarment proceedings.

3.   Treasury Department Regulations

The embargoes administered by OFAC pursuant to the Trading With the Enemy Act, such as the Cuban Assets Control Regulations, are enforced by criminal penalties only. Other OFAC embargo programs issued under the authority of the International Emergency Economic Powers Act provide for both civil and criminal sanctions.

B.   *Collateral Effects of U.S. Export Control Violations*

One of the greatest problems confronting exporters is the possibility of separate enforcement actions by different U.S. government agencies based on the same factual circumstances. Indeed, there appears to be a growing tendency on the part of U.S. government agencies to cooperate in imposing comprehensive punitive measures against companies and individuals believed to be guilty of export control violations.

The EAA authorizes the Commerce Department to suspend summarily for a period of up to ten years the export privileges of any person or company based upon a criminal conviction of violating other export control statutes, such as the AECA. Similarly, the Commerce Department may temporarily deny export privileges of any person suspected of violating other export control laws.

ODTC will disqualify exporters and deny export privileges for convictions of specified criminal offenses, including violations of the AECA, the EAA and the Foreign Corrupt Practices Act. ODTC may also deny export privileges to persons indicted for violations of these acts. ODTC will also automatically deny export privileges to persons suspended from exporting by other agencies and to any person suspended or debarred from contracting with the U.S. government.

The Federal Acquisition Regulations provide for suspension of the right to contract with the U.S. government upon an indictment, a criminal conviction or civil judgment involving any offense indicating a lack of business integrity or business honesty. Under this authority, the Defense Logistics Agency has shown an inclination to base suspension and debarment proceedings on export control violations. Similarly, the Defense Security Assistance Administration prohibits foreign military sales loan financing to any company whose export privileges have been denied. In addition, the president is authorized to impose restrictions on imports into the United States by any person found to have violated U.S. national security export controls.

C.   *Violations of Multilateral Export Controls*

In addition to enforcing its own laws, the United States government is authorized by Congress to impose sanctions against foreign persons who violate export regulations of foreign countries that are implemented pursuant to multilateral agreements. In most cases, the sanctions are mandatory where a violation occurs.

1.   COCOM Controls

The EAA mandates the imposition of sanctions on foreign persons who have violated foreign export controls established in accordance with the COCOM agreement, where the president determines that the violation has a serious impact on the strategic balance of power. This provision is commonly known as the "Toshiba sanctions" because it was adopted in response to the sale by Toshiba Machine Company of Japan to the former Soviet Union of machinery used to produce submarine propellers. The Toshiba sanctions include a prohibition on contracting with the United States government and a ban on imports of all products produced by the sanctioned person for two to five years. The president is authorized to seek compensation from the foreign person and its government and the Attorney General is authorized to bring an action for damages against the foreign violator. Since COCOM has disbanded and the EAA has lapsed, it is unclear whether these sanctions remain in place. Presumably Congress will address this issue when it considers renewal of the EAA.

2.   Missile Proliferation Controls

The EAA and the AECA direct the president to impose trade sanctions against any foreign person who, without authorization from a country that is a member of the Missile Technology Control Regime ("MTCR"), knowingly exports, transfers or otherwise engages in trade of MTCR Annex Items that contribute to the design, development or production of missiles in a non-MTCR country. The sanctions include two–year bans on export licenses, U.S. government contracts and imports.

3.   Chemical and Biological Proliferation Controls

The EAA and the AECA require the president to impose sanctions on any foreign person who, through exports of controlled goods or technology, "knowingly and materially" contributes to the efforts of a designated foreign country, project or entity to use, develop, produce, stockpile or otherwise acquire chemical or biological weapons. These sanctions include a prohibition on U.S. government contracting and a ban on imports into the United States. The sanctions must be in effect for at least 12 months and may be terminated only if the president determines and certifies to Congress that the sanctioned foreign person has ceased to aid or abet the targeted proliferation efforts.

V.   FOREIGN EMBARGOES AND U.S. ANTIBOYCOTT LAWS

The United States is not alone in imposing economic embargoes. Many countries restrict, for foreign–policy reasons, their trade relations with other countries. The restrictions may take any of a number of different forms, such as a ban on export, import, or supply to governmental entities of products of the sanctioned country. They may be enforced through contract clauses forbidding the use of particular subcontractors affiliated with the sanctioned country, import license procedures, country-of-origin certification requirements under customs laws, and other means. Some of these trade restrictions are consistent with United States policy (*e.g.*, the European Community's embargo of the former Yugoslavia), whereas others are not. The most notable example of a trade restriction at odds with U.S. policy is the Arab League boycott of Israel.

Under the EAA, it is unlawful for any "United States person" to comply with or further, in the interstate or foreign commerce of the United States, "any boycott fostered or imposed by a foreign country against a country which is friendly to the United States" (EAA § 8). "United States persons" are U.S. residents, nationals, legal persons (including U.S. permanent establishments of foreign firms), and foreign subsidiaries and affiliates that are controlled in fact by any of the foregoing.

Section 8 of the EAA is implemented through Part 769 of the EAR (the "Antiboycott Regulations"). BXA's Office of Antiboycott Compliance ("OAC") interprets and enforces the Antiboycott Regulations. Basically the Antiboycott Regulations forbid U.S. persons, in compliance with or in furtherance of "an unsanctioned foreign boycott," to: (1) refuse to do business with or in (or with any national or firm of) a "boycotted country"; (2) discriminate against U.S. persons in employment or otherwise on the basis of race, religion, sex or national origin; (3) furnish information about its business relationships with a "boycotted country" or with any firm believed to be "blacklisted" because of its relationship with the "boycotted country"; (4) furnish information about the race, religion, sex or national origin of any person; or (5) implement letters of credit that contain boycott-related terms. In addition, any U.S. person who receives a request to take any action in furtherance of an "unsanctioned foreign boycott" must report the request to OAC within time deadlines stated in the regulations. There are exceptions to these prohibitions, pertaining to, *inter alia*, compliance with the importing and shipping requirements of a "boycotting country," unilateral selection of specific service providers by "boycotting countries," and a "boycotting country's" immigration and employment laws.

In practice, the Antiboycott Regulations have been directed at actions in support of the Arab League boycott of Israel, but the regulations are broad enough to embrace conduct furthering other foreign trade restrictions that are inconsistent with U.S. policy. In case of doubt as to the applicability of the Antiboycott Regulations to a particular foreign boycott, U.S. exporters and other subject persons operating abroad should consult OAC.

"Furtherance" of a boycott is given a very broad reading in the regulations. For example, receipt of a request from the boycott office of a "boycotting country" for a U.S. corporation's annual report triggers the reporting requirement, and to supply the report would be unlawful, even though the report is a public document.

The Antiboycott Regulations are lengthy, and they draw extremely fine distinctions. For example, it is generally permissible under the regulations to give a "boycotting country" a positive certificate of the origin of a product (*e.g.*, "Product of U.S.A."), but illegal to certify origin in negative terms (*e.g.*, "Not a product of Israel"). The contexts in which violations may occur are numerous: contract bids; establishment of a distribution or agency relationships (which may trigger review of the parties by the local boycott-compliance authorities); and visa applications to "boycotting countries," to name a few.

Noncompliance with the Antiboycott Regulations is punishable by fines and imprisonment. Violators may be subject to the collateral effects discussed in Section IV.B. above. Enforcement has been strict, and it has not been confined to those who comply with an "unsanctioned foreign boycott"; failure to report boycott-related requests within the time limits in the regulations has also resulted in fines for many companies even if the requests were denied.

The Internal Revenue Code ("IRC") also address compliance with foreign boycotts. IRC section 999 requires taxpayers to file reports with the Internal Revenue Service on their operations in any boycotting country identified on a list published annually by the U.S. Department of the Treasury (printed in the Federal Register) and on requests to participate in unsanctioned foreign boycotts. Failures to report are punishable by fine and imprisonment. Section 999 also denies foreign tax credits, limits tax deferral and imposes other tax penalties on companies that comply with such boycotts. Although EAA section 8 and IRC section 999 have similar objectives, they are not identical in their scope, and actions violating the EAA do not necessarily trigger a reporting obligation or a tax penalty under the IRC, and vice versa.

Despite the movement toward peace in the Middle East, the risk of a boycott-related request or other conduct triggering an obligation under the Antiboycott Regulations or the Internal Revenue Code still exists. Other countries (*e.g.*, Germany) also have antiboycott laws. Moreover, the existing law may be interpreted as applying to new foreign boycotts. Thus U.S. exporters and companies operating abroad should bear the U.S. antiboycott laws in mind and maintain internal procedures to comply with them. Because the acts of agents in furtherance of a foreign boycott may be attributed to their U.S. principals, agents should be trained and monitored to ensure they do not cause their principals to violate the antiboycott laws.

VI. SOURCES OF ASSISTANCE

A.   *U.S. Statutes*

Arms Export Control Act, 22 U.S.C. §§ 2751–2796d (1995).

Export Administration Act of 1979, *as amended*, 50 U.S.C. app. §§ 2401–2420 (1995).

Internal Revenue Code, 26 U.S.C. § 999 (1995).

International Emergency Economic Powers Act, 50 U.S.C. §§ 1701–1706 (1995).

National Emergencies Act, 50 U.S.C. §§ 1601–1651 (1995).

Nuclear Non–Proliferation Act of 1978, 42 U.S.C. § 2139a (1995).

Trading with the Enemy Act of 1917, *as amended*, 50 U.S.C. app. §§ 1–44 (1995).

B.   U.S. Regulations

Angolan ("UNITA") Sanctions Regulations, 31 C.F.R. Part 590 (1994).

Cuban Assets Control Regulations, 31 C.F.R. Part 515 (1994).

Export Administration Regulations, 15 C.F.R. Parts 768–799 (1994). (The Antiboycott Regulations are at Part 769. The May 1995 proposed revision and reorganization of the EAR would redesignate those regulations at 15 C.F.R. Parts 730–774.)

Federal Republic of Yugoslavia Sanctions Regulations, 31 C.F.R. Part 585 (1994).

Foreign Assets Control Regulations, 31 C.F.R. Part 500 (1994).

International Traffic in Arms Regulations, 22 C.F.R. Parts 120–128 (1994).

Iranian Assets Control Regulations, 31 C.F.R. Part 535 (1994).

Iranian Transactions Regulations, 31 C.F.R. Part 560 (1994).

Iraqi Sanctions Regulations, 31 C.F.R. Part 575 (1994).

Libyan Sanctions Regulations, 31 C.F.R. Part 550 (1994).

Transaction Control Regulations, 31 C.F.R. Part 505 (1994).

Treasury Regulations (Boycott), 26 C.F.R. § 7. 999–1 (1995); *see also* 43 Fed. Reg. 3,457 (Jan. 25, 1978) (Treasury guidelines).

C. Selected Foreign Statutes and Laws

Germany: Gesetz über die Kontrolle von Kriegswaffen, *Ausführungsgesetz zu Artikel 26 Abs. 2 des 1 Grundgesetzes* vom 20. April 1961 *(Bundesgesetzblatt I*, p. 444 and *Bundesgesetzblatt II 190-1), as amended; Aussenwirtschaftsgesetz* vom 28. April 1961 *(Bundesgesetzblatt I*, p. 481), *as amended.*

EU: Commission of the European Communities, "Proposal for a Council Regulation on the control of exports of certain dual-use goods and technologies and of certain nuclear products and technologies," Brussels, Belgium, COM(92)317 final, August 31, 1992.

France: Decret du 30 novembre 1944, *Journal Officiel*, 1 decembre 1944, pp. 1585–86.

United Kingdom: Import, Export and Customs Powers (Defence) Act of 1939, as amended by Import and Export Act of 1990; Export of Goods (Control) Order, S.I. No. 1191, made April 24, 1994 and coming into force for the purpose of general licenses on May 4, 1994 and for all other purposes on May 25, 1994, as amended by the Export of Goods (Control) Order 1994 (Amendment) Order 1994, S.I. No. 1632, made June 17, 1994 and coming into force June 18, 1994.

Italy: Law No. 185 of 9 July 1990, entitled "New Provisions Governing the Export, Import and Transit of Armaments"; Law No. 222 of 27 February 1993.

Japan: Law of Foreign Exchange and Trade Controls, Law No. 228 of 1949, *as amended.*

D. Treaties

Convention on the Prohibition of Development, Production, Stockpiling and Use of Chemical Weapons, *opened for signature* January 13, 1993, S. Treaty No. 21, 103d Cong., 1st Sess. (1993), *reprinted in* 32 I.L.M. 800 (1993).

Convention on the Prohibition of the Development, Production, and Stockpiling of Bacteriological (Biological) and Toxin Weapons and on their Destruction, *entered into force* March 26, 1975, 26 U.S.T. 583, 1015 U.N.T.S. 163.

Missile Technology Control Regime, revised guidelines 1993, *signed* January 7, 1993, *reprinted in* 32 I.L.M. 1298 (1993).

Treaty on the Non–Proliferation of Nuclear Weapons, *opened for signature* July 1, 1968, 21 U.S.T. 483, 729 U.N.T.S. 45.

E.   *Newsletters and Handbooks*

Defense Trade News
Office of Defense Trade Controls
Bureau of Political–Military Affairs
PM/ODTC, Room 200
U.S. Department of State
Washington, D.C. 20522–0602
(703) 875–5671

The BXA Insider
U.S. Department of Commerce
Bureau of Export Administration
Room 1099D
Post Office Box 273
Washington, D.C. 20044

The Export Practitioner
1920 N Street, N.W.
Suite 750
Washington, D.C. 20036
(202) 463–0904

COPING WITH U.S. EXPORT CONTROLS 1995
Practicing Law Institute
Commercial Law and Practice Course Handbook Series,
No. A733

Boycott Law Bulletin
Post Office Box 73326
Houston, TX 77273
(713) 444–6562.

F.   *Electronic Databases*

The Bureau of Export Administration Library is on the World Wide Web at: http://www.fedworld.gov.
Type ufsbxa at the fedworld main menu.

The Office of Defense Trade Controls maintains the Remote On–Line Bulletin Board (ROBB) which provides information on licensing applications and policy news to registered exporters. To sign up, contact ODTC's Computer Support Staff by mail or fax (703/ 875–5663).

OFAC Federal Register notices are accessible for downloading with charge from Treasury's Electronic Library in the "Business, Trade and Labor Mall" of the FedWorld bulletin board.

G.   *Institutional Assistance*

BXA Office of Exporter Services, Exporter Counseling Division
(202) 482–4811

BXA Office of Antiboycott Compliance
(202) 482–5914

ODTC General Information
(703) 875–6644

OFAC
(202) 622–2510

ENDNOTES

1   *See* Section III.A. for a discussion of this term.

2   See the Sources of Assistance at Section IV of this chapter for citations to the statutes and regulations named in the text.

CHAPTER 14

THE FOREIGN CORRUPT PRACTICES ACT

O. Thomas Johnson, Jr.*

I.   INTRODUCTION

Prohibitions against official bribery are by no means unique to the United States. What is unique to the United States is that its concern with corruption does not stop with its own officials but extends to the corruption of foreign officials as well. By far the most important – and certainly the best known – reflection of this concern is the Foreign Corrupt Practices Act of 1977 (the "FCPA" or the "Act"), which imposes criminal penalties on American enterprises that bribe officials of foreign governments. There are several federal statutes that preceded the FCPA, however, and that bear on the behavior of American enterprises abroad. Although these statutes have largely been eclipsed by the FCPA – at least insofar as they might apply to the bribery of foreign officials – they are part of the legal context within which the FCPA is enforced, and from which the FCPA arose. Moreover, any American enterprise charged with a violation of the FCPA may also be charged with violations of one or more of these other provisions. This chapter first summarizes the more important of these pre–1977 statutes. It then discusses the provisions of the FCPA and various ways in which companies can minimize their chances of getting into trouble under the FCPA.

II.   PRE-1977 STATUTES APPLICABLE TO CORRUPT ACTIVITIES BY AMERICAN ENTERPRISES ABROAD

A.   *The Securities Exchange Act of 1934*

The Securities Exchange Act of 1934, 15 U.S.C. § 78 (the "Exchange Act"), requires that all publicly traded companies in the United States disclose "any material fact necessary in order to make statements made... not misleading." 17 C.F.R. 240.136b2–2. The Securities Exchange Commission ("SEC") long viewed the materiality of information in financial terms. In the mid–1970's, however, the materiality concept was expanded to include not just information that might be financially material, but also information that might be material to an evaluation of the integrity of a company's management.

B.   *The Mail and Wire Fraud Acts*

The Mail and Wire Fraud Acts, 18 U.S.C. §§ 1341 and 1343, prohibit the use of the mails or any means of interstate or international telecommunications for the purpose of executing any scheme to defraud or to obtain money or property by means of false or fraudulent pretenses. Several U.S. companies have been prosecuted for foreign bribery under these statutes on the theory that they knowingly schemed to defraud citizens of a foreign country of the honest and loyal services of government officials. In addition, at least one company has been prosecuted under the Mail and Wire Fraud Acts, not for bribing foreign government officials, but for lying to them in an effort to obtain business.

C.   *The Internal Revenue Code*

Since 1958, section 162(c)(1) of the United States Internal Revenue Code has prohibited the deduction of payments made, directly or indirectly, to foreign government officials if the payments would have been illegal under U.S. law had they been made to U.S. officials. In addition, sections 952 and 964 of the Internal Revenue Code provide that bribes paid by a controlled foreign subsidiary will be treated as a deemed dividend to the U.S. parent, thus increasing the parent's taxable income in the United States whether or not the parent actually received any dividends from the foreign subsidiary.

D.   *The Currency and Foreign Transactions Reporting Act*

The Currency and Foreign Transactions Reporting Act, 31 U.S.C. § 5316, requires that persons transporting or sending over $10,000 in currency into or out of the United States report that fact to the U.S. Customs Service. This requirement applies not only to United States currency, but also to foreign currency, traveler's checks, and checks made payable to cash or to bearer. In the late 1970s there were several prosecutions under this statute involving pre–FCPA bribery of foreign officials.

E.   *False Statements Act*

The False Statements Act, 18 U.S.C. § 1001, imposes criminal penalties on persons or corporations that knowingly make false, fictitious or fraudulent statements, or submit false documents, to any department or agency of the United States government. In the foreign–bribery context, it is potentially applicable in any situation in which a company must make declarations to agencies of the U.S. government, such as the Export–Import Bank or the Agency for International Development, in connection with the financing or authorizing of a foreign sale.

III.   THE FOREIGN CORRUPT PRACTICES ACT OF 1977

The FCPA deals with two separate but related subjects: payments to government officials and corporate accounting and control practices. These subjects are related because, in the past, payments made by U.S. companies to government officials often were made out of funds that were not recorded on the company's books or, if made from recorded funds, were inaccurately described. Thus, the FCPA makes it a crime not only to bribe a foreign official, but also to make false or misleading entries on a company's books for any purpose whatsoever.

A.   *The Anti-Bribery Provisions of the FCPA*

The FCPA's anti-bribery provisions apply to: (1) issuers of securities registered under section 12 of the Exchange Act or companies that are required to file reports under section 15 of the Exchange Act;[1] (2) other legal entities that are organized under the laws of the United States or a U.S. state, or that have their principal place of business in the United States; and (3) natural persons who are citizens, nationals or residents of the United States.[2] Application of the anti-bribery provisions of the Act is subject to five conditions.

1.   Interstate Commerce

The applicability of the Act requires, first, use of the "mails or any means or instrumentality of interstate commerce." As a practical matter, the bribery of a foreign governmental official by a U.S. company will almost always involve the use of some means of interstate commerce (which includes commerce between the United States and a foreign state). For example, an overseas telephone call in which the bribe is discussed or an international trip during which any activity related to the bribe occurs would satisfy this element.

2.   Corrupt Intent

The FCPA prohibits the use of any means or instrumentality of interstate commerce *corruptly in furtherance of* an offer or payment of a bribe. Although the statute itself does not define "corruptly," its legislative history provides helpful guidance. The report of the Senate Committee that considered the FCPA in 1977 defines the term as follows:[3]

> The word 'corruptly' is used in order to make clear that the offer, payment, promise, or gift must be intended to induce the recipient to misuse his official position in order to wrongfully direct business to the payor or his client, or to obtain preferential legislation or a favorable regulation. The word 'corruptly' connotes an evil motive or purpose, an intent to wrongfully influence the recipient.

It does not require that the act be fully consummated, or succeed in producing the desired outcome.

In similar fashion, the report of the House Committee that considered the FCPA states that the "evil purpose" required for a violation is similar to "that required under 18 U.S.C. § 201(b), which prohibits domestic bribery."[4]

The meaning of the term "corruptly" as used in the domestic bribery statute is well-established: A payment or promise has corrupt intent if the payment or promise is knowingly made in exchange for particular conduct on the part of the government official. Where there is no anticipated quid pro quo, there is no corrupt purpose.[5]

The practical significance of the corrupt-intent requirement is rather limited. There are few situations in which all other elements of an FCPA offense are satisfied (i.e., a payment made to a foreign official to influence his performance of his official duties to obtain or retain business) that would not also be corrupt. The most important effect of this element may be to exclude "goodwill gifts" – that is, gifts given to improve relations with a government official that are so small in value that it is unreasonable to believe that the gift would "induce the recipient to misuse his official position." The corrupt-intent requirement also can operate to exclude instances of true extortion – that is, instances in which life or property are threatened.

3.   Offer, Payment, Gift or Promise of Any Money or Thing of Value

The third element of the FCPA's anti-bribery provision is that there must be an "offer, payment, gift or promise" of "money or [a] thing of value." This element presents no interpretive difficulty. Its intent is to sweep broadly to prohibit any offer or promise of a bribe and to make it clear that the bribe itself can consist of "anything of value."

4.   The Recipient of the Offer, Payment, Gift or Promise

The fourth element is that the offer, payment, gift or promise be made to a "foreign official" or to another person "while knowing that some or all of the money offered, given, or promised will be passed on to a foreign official." The FCPA defines a "foreign official" as

> [a]ny officer or employee of a foreign government or any department, agency, or instrumentality thereof, or any person acting in an official capacity for or on behalf of any such government or department, agency, or instrumentality.

This definition includes not only persons employed directly by a foreign government, but also persons employed by commercial enterprises owned or controlled by foreign governments and persons who, while not officers or employees of governmental instrumentalities, nonetheless have responsibilities similar to those of employees.[6] For example, private architects or engineers retained by a government agency to design or supervise the construction of a government building would be "acting in an official capacity for or on behalf of" the government agency responsible for the design and construction of the building.

The most controversial provision of the FCPA prohibits payments to third parties "while knowing" that the recipient will share the payment with a foreign official.[7] The legislative history of the 1988 amendments to the FCPA – which introduced the "knowing" standard – makes it clear that the requisite knowledge may be inferred if a company's management adopts an attitude of "willful blindness," or "unwarranted obliviousness to any action (or inaction), language, or other signalling device that should reasonably alert them of the high probability of an FCPA violation."[8]

5. For the Purpose of Influencing the Foreign Official, in His "Official Capacity," to Assist the Company in "Obtaining or Retaining Business"

The last element presents two issues: (a) when is an official acting in his "official capacity"? and (b) when is a payment related to "obtaining or retaining business"?

The FCPA does not prohibit all payments to government officials for the purpose of obtaining or retaining business. Persons holding government positions may be retained as consultants or commission agents as long as their efforts on behalf of their clients are unrelated to whatever authority or influence they enjoy in their official capacities. Thus, the Justice Department has stated that it would not prosecute specified arrangements between American companies and members of the British and Malaysian Parliaments. In each case, the Member of Parliament held no other government position, and his relationship with the U.S. company complied with local law.[9]

The requirement that a payment be for the purpose of "obtaining or retaining business" has not been interpreted by any U.S. court and has no close parallel in the U.S. domestic bribery statutes. Nonetheless, the Justice Department construes this term broadly, and this view finds support in the legislative history.[10] Thus, payments to government officials to obtain favorable regulatory action, rather than to make a sale, probably fall within this language.

B. Exemptions from the FCPA's Bribery Provisions

1. Facilitating Payments

The FCPA originally prohibited "corrupt" payments made for the purpose of "influencing any act or decision of [a] foreign official in his official capacity" to obtain or retain business. The term "foreign official" was defined to exclude "any employee of a foreign government... whose duties are essen-

tially ministerial or clerical." The legislative history made clear that this definition established an exception for "facilitating" or "grease" payments to lower-
level government employees for routine governmental functions.

The 1988 amendments to the FCPA clarified this exception by focusing
exclusively on the "purpose" of the payments. The amendments replaced the
exclusion of ministerial or clerical employees with an explicit exception for
payments to secure "routine governmental action." This exception permits
payments to *expedite* governmental action; it does not permit payments to
affect the result of a governmental decision–making process.

2.   Affirmative Defenses for Lawful Payments and Promotional Reimbursements

The 1988 FCPA amendments also added two affirmative defenses for
certain types of payments. First, it is an affirmative defense that the payment
at issue "was lawful under the written laws and regulations of the foreign
official's... country." Second, an affirmative defense may also be asserted
where the payment

> "was a reasonable and bona fide expenditure, such as travel and lodg-
> ing expenses, incurred by or on behalf of a foreign official ... and was
> directly related to –
>
> (A) the promotion, demonstration, or explanation of products or ser-
> vices; or
>
> (B) the execution or performance of a contract with a foreign govern-
> ment or agency thereof."

The legislative history of these new affirmative defenses makes clear
that both were intended to be interpreted in a manner consistent with the
basic purposes of the FCPA. A company should rarely need to rely on the
first defense since it will be most unusual for conduct that is *otherwise illegal*
under the FCPA to be *legal* under local law.

The second defense codified Justice Department enforcement policy that
reimbursement to foreign officials for expenses associated with product
demonstrations or tours of company facilities would not be regarded as
unlawful, provided that there was a direct nexus between the expense and
the promotional activity. This new affirmative defense requires that the payment be a bona fide expenditure. This means that the payment cannot be
corruptly made in return for any official act or omission.

3.   Payments Made by Subsidiaries of United States Corporations

As a general rule, the FCPA does not apply to foreign subsidiaries of
U.S. companies.[11] Citizens, nationals, and residents of the United States, how-

ever, are covered by the FCPA as individuals. Moreover, the FCPA prohibits use of the mails or any means or instrumentality of interstate commerce "in furtherance of" a corrupt payment to a foreign official. Thus, should anyone acting on behalf of a U.S. corporation authorize, acquiesce in,[12] or in any way facilitate bribery by a foreign subsidiary, the U.S. corporation would thereby have violated the FCPA. Finally, if a foreign subsidiary can bribe foreign officials without its parent's knowledge or acquiescence, the internal accounting controls that the parent must maintain with respect to all of its assets, including assets located within foreign subsidiaries, may well be inadequate. Thus, even if a foreign subsidiary engages in bribery without the knowledge of any individual associated with its U.S. parent and without the knowledge of any other citizens, nationals or residents of the United States, such bribery might still involve the U.S. parent in a violation of the FCPA's accounting provisions.

C. The Accounting Provisions of the FCPA

The accounting provisions of the FCPA amended section 13(b) of the Exchange Act. There has been only one published judicial opinion interpreting these provisions.[13] Accordingly, their interpretation must be guided by the language of the provisions, their legislative history, and their interpretation by the SEC.

1. Intent

Unlike the anti–bribery provisions, the accounting provisions originally were silent on the level of intent required for criminal liability. This led to a concern that "companies [would be held] criminally liable for minor or inadvertent errors in the creation and maintenance of the general FCPA accounting standards... ."[14] Eventually, the accounting provisions were amended to limit criminal liability to knowing or intentional conduct. Thus, the level of intent necessary to find a criminal violation of the accounting provisions is the same as that for the anti–bribery provisions.

The amendments leave open the possibility of *civil* liability for something less than "knowing" conduct. The SEC has stated, however, that "[t]he accounting provisions principal objective is to reach knowing or reckless conduct."[15] Hence, it is unlikely that an issuer would be held even civilly liable for merely negligent conduct. (*See SEC v. World-Wide Coin Investments, Ltd.*, 567 F. Supp. 724, 740 and 752 (N.D. Ga. 1983).)

2. Liability of Foreign and Domestic Subsidiaries

The accounting provisions apply only to *issuers* that have a "class of securities registered pursuant to section 12 of this title and every issuer which is required to file reports pursuant to section 15(d) of this title."[16] Although an issuer has certain responsibilities for its subsidiaries, the accounting provisions do not apply directly to foreign or domestic subsidiaries of U.S. corporations that are not themselves "issuers."[17]

Generally, domestic subsidiaries have not been named in SEC enforcement actions, even when they were clearly implicated in an alleged accounting violation.[18] This apparent enforcement policy is consistent with the view that the accounting provisions apply only to "issuers." Where a subsidiary has been named in an enforcement action at all, allegations of accounting violations have typically been limited to the parent.[19]

3.   Responsibility of Issuers for Subsidiaries

The FCPA originally was "silent on the issue of the legal responsibility of an issuer for compliance by subsidiaries with the accounting requirements."[20] In 1988, Congress amended the FCPA to address this issue with respect to issuers with 50 percent or less ownership interests in domestic or foreign subsidiaries. The amendments "require only that the issuer proceed in good faith to use its influence, to the extent reasonable under the issuer's circumstances, to cause such domestic or foreign firm to devise and maintain a system of internal accounting controls."[21] This creates a "safe harbor" for issuers with less than a majority interest in a subsidiary, so long as they make good faith efforts to ensure that subsidiaries have adequate controls. The amendments do not address the responsibilities of an issuer with a majority interest in a subsidiary. By implication, however, where an issuer has a majority interest in a domestic or foreign subsidiary, good faith efforts are not sufficient. Rather, the issuer must use its majority position to ensure that the subsidiary has an adequate system of internal accounting controls in place.

IV.   MINIMIZING DIFFICULTIES UNDER THE FOREIGN CORRUPT PRACTICES ACT

A.   Justice Department Review Procedure

Under the current Justice Department Review Procedure, the Justice Department must, upon request, advise an issuer or a domestic concern whether specified future conduct would "violate the Act's anti–bribery provisions and lead the Department of Justice to take enforcement action." This procedure applies only to the anti–bribery provisions of the FCPA; opinions cannot be obtained with respect to the FCPA's record-keeping provisions. Opinions also cannot be obtained with respect to hypothetical conduct.

The Department must issue its opinion within 30 days of receipt of either the request or of any additional information requested by the Department. The Department must seek any additional information that it requires within 30 days of the original request, or within 30 days of an incomplete response to an earlier request for additional information. The Department has, on occasion, issued opinions in a matter of days.

A favorable opinion creates a rebuttable presumption that the proposed conduct is in compliance with the anti–bribery provisions of the FCPA. This presumption may be rebutted by a preponderance of the evidence. The most important factor in determining whether the presumption has been rebutted almost certainly would be the extent to which information supplied to the Department was inaccurate or incomplete.

Information provided to the Department in connection with a request for an FCPA opinion is exempt from disclosure under the Freedom of Information Act. The Department reserves the right, however, to issue a public release describing the identity of the requesting party, "the identity of the country in which the proposed conduct is to take place, the general nature and circumstances of the proposed conduct, and the action taken by the Department of Justice in response to the FCPA Opinion request."

B.   *Policies and Preventive Measures*

Safeguards against FCPA violations may be divided into three categories: policies, procedures and responses.

1.   Policies

In general, policies designed to prevent FCPA violations –

(1) prohibit direct or indirect payments to foreign officials;

(2) prohibit political contributions in countries where corporate contributions are illegal, sometimes requiring authorization of legal contributions by some central authority within the company;

(3) prohibit false entries in the company's books and records;

(4) prohibit the creation of unrecorded funds; and

(5) require compliance with applicable local law.

To be effective, such policies must be widely distributed within a company, including a company's foreign branches or subsidiaries. For foreign operations, policies should be available in the local language.

2.   Procedures Designed to Prevent or Detect Policy Violations

a.   Sales Representative Approval Procedures

Companies that use foreign sales representatives to a substantial degree often have formal approval procedures that must be followed before entering into an agreement with a sales representative. These procedures typically begin with an inquiry into the background of the proposed representative. Such an inquiry might include: (1) obtaining a Dun & Bradstreet report; (2)

obtaining a World Traders Data Report (WTDR) through the Department of Commerce; (3) contacting the relevant country desks at the State and Commerce Departments; (4) contacting the commercial officer at the relevant U.S. embassy; (5) contacting banking and business references (particularly U.S. business references); and, most importantly; (6) interviewing company employees who are familiar with the proposed representative.

Ideally, the initial inquiry should focus on questions such as the follow-ing:

(1) Is there anything in the proposed representative's background that should be a cause of concern?

(2) How did the representative come to the company's attention? Was he recommended by anyone within the customer organization?

(3) What can the representative do to be helpful? Does he have relevant technical expertise? Does he enjoy influence with a customer?

(4) If a representative is being proposed because of his influence with, or access to, a customer, how did he gain that access or influence?

(5) Is the representative's proposed compensation reasonable? What can the representative do that is both legitimate and worth the price charged? Why wouldn't the money be better spent on a price discount?

b.   Internal Audit

Companies with international business also often add to their internal (and external) audit program steps designed to identify corrupt practices. Such steps include:

(1) review of commissions paid for reasonableness and consistency with an approved agreement;

(2) review of agreements to ensure that they were properly approved;

(3) review of selected transactions with governmental customers for indications of corruption, including review of correspondence contained in marketing or sales files; and

(4) review of expenditures for lawyers, advertising, and consultants to be sure that appropriate work product has been received.

If at all possible, audit teams sent to foreign locations should include at least one member who speaks the local language.

Many companies also require key employees periodically to certify that they are unaware of any information indicating a violation of company policy concerning corrupt payments, except as indicated in the certification.

        c.   Training

Anticorruption training programs must be carefully tailored to a company's business. All programs, however, should have certain common elements:

(1) They should be repeated periodically both as refreshers and to catch personnel who are new to the business;

(2) They should be rich in realistic case studies;

(3) They should emphasize the seriousness with which the company views its anticorruption policy;

(4) They should clearly state the penalties for policy violations;

(5) Attendance should be mandatory, and records kept of those attending the sessions; and

(6) Most important, they should aim to teach employees how to spot issues, not how to resolve them. Everyone should leave a training session understanding that any FCPA question should be taken to the general counsel's office, and that there are no stupid FCPA questions.

V.   SOURCES OF ASSISTANCE

A.   *Statutes*

The Foreign Corrupt Practices Act, 15 U.S.C. §§ 78dd-1, 78dd-2, 78ff(a), 78ff(c), 78m(b).

B.   *Regulations*

Justice Department FCPA Review Procedure, 28 C.F.R. Part 80.

C.   *Books*

Donald R. Cruver, Complying With the Foreign Corrupt Practices Act (1994).

D.   Loose -Leaf Services

Foreign Corrupt Practices Act Reporter, Business Laws, Inc.

E.   Articles

Lucinda Low, *The Whats, Whys and How-tos of Compliance Programs*, in ABA SECTION OF INTERNATIONAL LAW AND PRACTICE, II INTERNATIONAL PRACTITIONERS' WORKSHOP SERIES (1993).

Mehren, *Introduction to the Foreign Corrupt Practices Act of 1977 — Law Procedures and Practices*, 10 INST. SEC. REG. 65 (1979).

Note, *Accounting for Corporate Misconduct Abroad: Foreign Corrupt Practices Act of 1977*, 12 CORN. INT'L L.J. 293 (1979).

Note, *Effective Enforcement of the Foreign Corrupt Practices Act*, 32 STAN. L. REV. 561 (1980).

Program, *Practical Implications of the Foreign Corrupt Practices Act of 1977 and Recent Developments*, 35 BUS. LAW. 1713 (1980).

John W. Duncan, *Modifying the Foreign Corrupt Practices Act: The Search for a Practical Standard*, 4 J. INT'L L. & BUS. 203 (1982).

ENDNOTES

The author wishes to thank Michael Danson for his invaluable assistance in preparing this chapter.

1   Note that many foreign corporations are "issuers" and thus covered by the Act.

2   The provisions also apply to certain natural persons – regardless of their nationality – who act on behalf of covered companies. The actions of issuers and certain persons acting on their behalf are regulated under section 103 of the FCPA, 15 U.S.C. §§ 78dd-1, 78ff(a). The actions of other covered entities and natural persons ("domestic concerns") are regulated in substantially identical terms under section 104, 15 U.S.C. § 78dd-2.

3   S. REP. NO. 114, 95th Cong., 1st Sess. 10–11 (1977).

4   H.R. REP. NO. 640, 95th Cong., 1st Sess. 8 (1977).

5   *See, e.g., United States v. Hsieh Hui Mei Chen*, 754 F.2d 817, 822 (9th Cir.), *cert. denied*, 471 U.S. 1139 (1985); *United States v. Strand*, 574 F.2d 993, 995 (9th Cir. 1978).

6   *See* FCPA Review Procedure Release No. 93–1 (Apr. 20, 1993) (quasi-commercial entity "wholly owned and supervised by the government of a former Eastern bloc country… is an instrumentality of the foreign government for purposes of the FCPA").

While no U.S. court has had occasion to construe the term "foreign official" contained in the FCPA, courts have construed the term "public official" in the domestic bribery statute as encompassing payments to private contractors responsible for preparing specifications for construction projects and recommending suppliers for the construction projects. *E.g.*, *United States v. Griffin*, 401 F. Supp. 1222 (S.D. Ind. 1975), *aff'd without opinion*, *United States v. Metro Management Corp.*, 541 F.2d 284 (7th Cir. 1976).

7   Prior to the 1988 amendments, this provision prohibited payments to third parties "while knowing or having reason to know" that some or all of the payment would be used to bribe foreign officials. The amendment of this provision to delete the "having reason to know" language was intended to address concerns that the "reason to know" standard made it possible to prosecute conduct that was merely negligent – *e.g.*, failure to control adequately the actions of agents. *See* S. REP. NO. 100-85, 100th Cong., 1st Sess. (1987).

8   H.R. CONF. REP. NO. 576, 100th Cong., 2d Sess., at 919 (1988).

9   In addition, each Member of Parliament had agreed that he would fully disclose his relationship with the U.S. company and would not use his influence as a Member of Parliament with his government to influence any acts or decisions that would benefit the U.S. company. FCPA Review Procedure Release No. 86-1 (July 18, 1986).

10   *See* H.R. REP. NO. 640, 95th Cong., 1st Sess., at 8 (1977).

11   The only exceptions would be those rare cases in which the subsidiary either has its principal place of business in the United States, and thus qualifies as a "domestic concern," or is itself an "issuer," as that term is used in the Act.

12   Tacit acquiescence by the U.S. corporation is probably sufficient to violate the FCPA.

13   The only judicial decision on the accounting provisions of which the author is aware is *SEC v. World-Wide Coin Investments, Ltd.*, 567 F. Supp. 724 (N.D. Ga. 1983).

14   S. REP. NO. 85, 100th Cong., 1st Sess. 42, 66 (1987) (Additional views of Senators Garn, Heinz, Hecht, Bond, Chafee, and Karnes).

15   Statement of Policy, 46 Fed. Reg. 11,544, 11,547 (Jan. 29, 1981). Apart from the legislative history, the seminal official guidance on these provisions remains an address given by Chairman Harold M. Williams entitled, 'The Accounting Provisions of the Foreign Corrupt Practices Act: An Analysis." Chairman Williams' address "was presented with the concurrence of all members of the Commission and constitutes the Commission's policy." *Statement of Policy*, 46 Fed. Reg. 11,544 (Jan. 28, 1981). This policy remains in effect today. *See* 17 C.F.R. Pt. 241 (1994).

16   15 U.S.C. § 78m(b)(2).

17   Note that the FCPA's accounting provisions, unlike its bribery provisions, apply equally to domestic and foreign activities of "issuers."

18   *See In re Texas Commerce Bancshares, Inc.*, Exchange Act Release No. 24,803 (Aug. 17, 1987); *In re Concord Camera*, Exchange Act Release No. 34,623 (Sept. 1, 1984).

19   *See SEC v. Matthews & Wright Group, Inc.*, Litig. Release No. 12,072 (Apr. 27, 1989); *see also SEC v. Flight Transp. Corp.*, Litig. Release No. 9,736 (Aug. 18, 1982). There have been only two instances in which subsidiaries have been named as parties in injunctive actions and charged with violations of the accounting provision: *SEC v. Gulf Power Co.*, Litig. Release No. 12,678 (Oct. 24, 1990), and *SEC v. Inter-Regional Fin. Group, Inc.*, Litig. Release No. 11,024 (Mar. 13, 1986). In these cases, however, the subsidiaries filed financial statements with the SEC and were themselves "issuers."

20   S. REP. NO. 85, 100th Cong., 1st Sess. 43 (1987).
21   15 U.S.C. § 78m(b)(6).

CHAPTER 15

GOVERNMENT PROCUREMENT

Marshall J. Doke, Jr.

I.   INTRODUCTION

The largest purchasers of goods and services in the world are govern-ments–central, state or provincial, and local. Selling to a government, directly or as a subcontractor, is a different business from selling to a commercial buyer. Perhaps the greatest difference is that the buyer's sovereignty is an inherent aspect of the transaction. Purchases by a government involve more than obtaining the best product or service at the most favorable price. Government contracts are used as a vehicle to achieve socio–economic goals, protect the domestic economy and products, and even implement regulatory and international political policies.

Domestic and foreign government contracts pose special risks because they involve laws, regulations, and policies that are inapplicable to strictly commercial transnational sales. Some of these special laws and practices apply to governmental entities that do not utilize U.S. taxpayer dollars (such as the Army–Air Force Exchange Service) as well as U.S. government–owned entities (such as the Tennessee Valley Authority) and even mixed–ownership government corporations (such as Amtrak). Foreign governments have simi-lar entities and even government–owned commercial entities to which some aspects of sovereignty may apply.

Governments have tended to make their largest procurements from their local firms. Discrimination against "foreign" firms has been a standard practice of many governments. In the United States, this discrimination against nondomestic products exists at the federal, state, and even local gov-ernment levels. At the federal level, the Buy American Act (discussed below)[1] is well–known. Other domestic preferences are less well–known, such as restrictions in annual appropriation acts on the purchase of certain items. Other U.S. domestic preferences are more subtle, such as the Fastener Quality Act, which requires manufacturers of critical fasteners to have samples inspected, tested, and certified by an accredited laboratory in accordance with procedures specified by the Secretary of Commerce. Other countries have similar laws and even more subtle and "invisible" domestic preferences.

Domestic preference laws and practices have created tensions among international trading partners. In view of the increasingly important role that government procurement plays in the global economy, there has been a growing recognition of a need to eliminate or reduce these barriers in order to reduce obstacles to increased international trade as well as to promote economy and efficiency in government procurement of goods and services. This chapter will discuss the international rules and principal U.S. domestic preferences, restrictive procurement laws and policies, and prohibited procurement practices. A description of similar practices by foreign governments also will be provided.

II.   GATT AND GOVERNMENT PROCUREMENT

A.   *The Government Procurement Code*

The General Agreement on Tariffs and Trade ("GATT") originally had limited utility in government procurement. In fact, GATT expressly excluded government contracts from its national treatment rule. The Tokyo Round of the Multilateral Trade Negotiations in 1979 resulted in an Agreement on Government Contracting. The Code does not apply to every procuring agency of the participating countries and excludes certain market areas and types of contracts. For example, service and construction contracts are not covered, nor are procurements by regional and local governments. The purpose of the Code is to eliminate both clearly stated national preferences and the "invisible" devices used to favor domestic products. The Code covers areas such as: notices for proposed purchases; non–preferential specifications; requirements for adequate information and time limits to submit tenders; rules for submission, receipt, and opening of tenders; and nondiscriminatory qualification of suppliers.

The Uruguay Round of trade negotiations, which concluded in 1993, resulted in a new Government Procurement Agreement that requires transparent purchasing procedures and covers sub–central governments and government–owned enterprises. The new agreement requires public notice of procurements, bid deadline rules, preferences for performance rather than design specifications, and effective provisions for bid protests. Offset requirements as a condition to awards will be prohibited unless a specific exception is negotiated. The new code, to which the United States and its major trading partners are signatories, will become effective January 1, 1996 (except that Korea will delay one year).

B.   *United Nations Model Law*

The United Nations Commission on International Trade Law ("UNCI-TRAL") adopted a Model Law on Procurement in 1994 for use by national, state, and local government bodies throughout the world. The key policies in the model law include promoting competition (including foreign suppliers) and promoting fair and equitable treatment among all contractors and suppliers. The model law applies to procurement and construction, with a limited application to related services. The law covers areas including methods of procurement, bid protests and claim, standards of conduct, and record-keeping requirements. It is expected that this model law will be used as a "standard" by trade negotiators to measure compliance with the new Government Procurement Code.

III.   U.S. DOMESTIC PREFERENCES

A.   *Buy American Act*

1.   Background

The Buy American Act dates back to 1933 during the years of the Depression and was enacted to save and create jobs for American workers. The Act states that (with the exceptions discussed below) only such unmanufactured articles mined or produced in the United States, and only such manufactured articles as have been manufactured in the United States substantially from domestic materials, shall be acquired by the federal government for public use. Services are not subject to the preference of the Act. Implementation of the Act in Part 25 of the Federal Acquisition Regulation ("FAR") states that only "domestic end products" may be acquired, which are defined as (a) an *unmanufactured* end product mined or produced in the United States, or (b) an end product *manufactured* in the United States if the cost of components manufactured in the United States exceeds 50 percent of the cost of all its components. Special definitions are provided for construction materials.

2.   Evaluation Preference

One of the exceptions in the Act is where the cost of the items would be "unreasonable," as defined in the FAR. This exception causes the Act actually to operate as an *evaluation preference* for domestic end products. The cost of domestic items is considered "unreasonable" if it exceeds the cost of a foreign item by specified percentages (varying by federal agency and type of supplier).

3.   Domestic End Products

It often is difficult to identify the "end product" being acquired by the government (to which the evaluation percentage is applied). One issue is whether the end product is the "system" delivered to the government or, perhaps, the individual contract line items comprising the system. A determination of the "end product" must be made, of course, before it can be determined what items are "components" (which is critical in determining if the end product is "domestic"). A "domestic end product" must be *manufactured* in the United States, and the cost of components mined, produced, or manufactured in the United States must exceed 50 percent of the cost of all the components.

4.   Exceptions and Waivers

The FAR (§ 25.102) sets forth five exceptions to the Buy American Act's requirements; namely, for items (a) to be used outside the United States, (b) for which the cost would be unreasonable (as determined by the evaluation preference discussed above), (c) for which the agency head determines that domestic preference would be inconsistent with the national interest, (d) that are not mined, produced, or manufactured in the United States in sufficient and reasonably available commercial quantities or of a satisfactory quality, and (e) purchased specifically for commissary resale. The regulations also list over 100 items for which one or more federal agencies have determined that they are not reasonably available in the United States.

Additional exemptions, but with different requirements, are available under various statutes, international agreements, and implementing policies (discussed or cited below), including the Trade Agreements Act, North American Free Trade Agreement, Caribbean Basin Economic Recovery Act, U.S.-Israel Free Trade Agreements Act, and United States memorandum of understanding with the European Union.

B.   Cargo Preference Acts

Several U.S. laws give preference to U.S.-flag vessels when transportation of supplies by ocean vessel is required: the Cargo Preference Act of 1904, 10 U.S.C.A. § 2631 (West Supp. 1995); Merchant Marine Act of 1936, 46 U.S.C.A. § 1101 (West 1975); and the Cargo Preference Act of 1954, 46 App. U.S.C. § 1241(b) (West Supp. 1995). These provisions are implemented for civilian agencies in FAR Part 47.5 and the Department of Defense FAR Supplement (DFARS), Subpart 247.5, for Department of Defense agencies.

C.   Exceptions to Competition

The Competition in Contracting Act of 1984 requires "full and open" competition in government contracting, meaning that all responsible sources (including foreign sources) are permitted to submit sealed bids or competitive proposals. There are, however, a number of exceptions to the requirement for full and open competition which can, effectively, exclude foreign sources. For example, contracts may be awarded without competition to maintain the availability of a domestic facility, producer, or supplier or when disclosure of the government's needs would compromise national security. Other exceptions allow preferences to small business concerns and previously approved or qualified sources. Purchase under these exceptions would be called "selective" tendering or "single" tendering under certain international agreements.

IV. OTHER INTERNATIONAL PROCUREMENT AGREEMENTS

A. *Trade Agreements Act*

The primary exception to the Buy American Act is provided by the Trade Agreements Act of 1979 ("TAA"). To qualify for a TAA exemption to the Buy American Act, the procurement must exceed a dollar amount designated by the U.S. Trade Representative ($182,000 in 1995). In addition, the procurement must be by one of the over 50 government agencies listed in FAR § 25.406 and not be one of the types of contracts excepted from the TAA under FAR § 25.403 (such as contracts essential for national defense, construction contracts, and service contracts). The exemption also requires that the product be from one of the nearly 50 "designated countries" listed in FAR § 25.401 and satisfy a rule of origin test (a "substantial transformation," customs-law-type test) that the product originated in a designated country. The practical effect of a TAA exemption is that the product is evaluated on an equal basis with U.S. products (*i.e.*, no domestic preference is applied).

B. *NAFTA*

The North American Free Trade Agreement ("NAFTA") was implemented by Congress in the NAFTA Implementation Act. NAFTA has its own provisions on government procurement and requires Canada, Mexico, and the United States to eliminate domestic preferences with respect to most nondefense purchases by North American suppliers. NAFTA is somewhat broader in scope than the GATT Procurement Code and applies to procurements by specified federal agencies of goods, services, and construction above certain monetary thresholds. Under FAR § 25.402, certain offers of NAFTA country end products are evaluated without regard to Buy American Act restrictions. The regulations also utilize a "substantial transformation" type test to determine the country of origin of products that are not wholly the growth, product, or manufacture of Canada or Mexico.

C. *Memoranda of Understanding*

In certain reciprocal memoranda of understanding with foreign governments described in DFARS § 225.872, the Department of Defense has determined it inconsistent with the public interest to apply restrictions of the Buy American Act to the acquisition of defense equipment from certain "qualifying countries." The provisions do not apply to construction contracts or to certain other exempted transactions.

V. RESTRICTIVE PROCUREMENT LAWS AND POLICIES

A. Communist and Other Country Source Restrictions

There are various restrictions on the acquisition of supplies and services by the government, or for use in performing U.S. government contracts, described in FAR Subpart 25.7. These include supplies or services originating from, or transported from or through, sources within the Communist areas of North Korea, Vietnam, Cambodia, or Cuba. Supplies or services also may not be acquired from Iraq. These restrictions are implemented by a mandatory contract clause in FAR § 52.225-11, which also requires the restrictions be included in all subcontracts.

B. Transactions with Terrorist Countries

Section 843 of the 1994 National Defense Authorization Act requires prospective government contractors for goods or services exceeding $5 million to report each commercial transaction with the government of a "terrorist country" during the past three years or the period after November 30, 1993, whichever is shorter. As initially implemented in DFARS § 252.209-7004, terrorist countries included Cuba, Iran, Iraq, Libya, North Korea, Sudan, and Syria.

C. Other Restrictions

There are a number of other U.S. laws that have special application to sales to foreign governments. Export controls are covered in Chapter 13. Special attention must be paid to the munitions list included in the International Traffic in Arms Regulations ("ITAR"), 22 C.F.R. Parts 120–130, administered by the Office of Defense Trade Controls ("ODTC") in the Department of State. The Foreign Corrupt Practices Act (see Chapter 14), of course, is relevant to sales to foreign governments. In addition, there are import restrictions governing defense items which are regulated by the U.S. Department of the Treasury under 27 C.F.R. Parts 47, 178, and 179, and the ODTC under the ITAR.

VI. PROHIBITED PRACTICES

A. Introduction

Selling to the U.S. government is a specialized business requiring familiarity with numerous special laws, regulations, policies, and practices. Even a summary of all these requirements could not be attempted in this chapter. There are certain laws, however, that are so counter to practices in foreign countries that they deserve special mention. Foreign companies desiring government contracts in the United States should be advised of several of these laws when they first consider the market.

B. *Procurement Integrity Law*

A federal law, commonly called the Procurement Integrity Act, prohibits certain actions "during the conduct of any federal procurement" (which, generally speaking, begins with the government's drafting the specifications and ends when a contract is awarded). The prohibitions (which have criminal penalties) apply to all competing contractors and their employees or agents and preclude offers, or even discussions, of future employment or business opportunities with any procurement official. Another section prohibits giving or offering any gratuity or "other thing of value" to any procurement official. These are common types of prohibitions in the U.S., but a third precludes actions some marketing personnel believe are within their job descriptions. This prohibition precludes soliciting or obtaining any "proprietary or source selection information" regarding a procurement. *"Propriety information"* is anything a competitor submits to the Government. *"Source selection information"* includes government information that, if disclosed, would jeopardize the integrity of the procurement (*e.g.,* competitors' prices, technical evaluations of proposals, and ranking of proposals). Competitors must certify that their employees are familiar with these provisions and will report any violations or possible violations immediately.

C. *Kickbacks*

The Anti-Kickback Act of 1986 was passed to deter subcontractors from making, and contractors from accepting, payments for the purpose of improperly obtaining or rewarding favorable treatment in connection with a government contract or subcontract. The Act prohibits any person from offering, soliciting, or accepting any *"kickback"* (defined to include any money, fee, gift, gratuity, or anything of value). The Copeland (Anti-Kickback) Act also prohibits construction contractors from inducing employees to give up any part of their compensation.

D. *Independent Pricing*

A mandatory solicitation provision for fixed-price-type contracts contained in FAR § 52.203-2 requires offerors to certify that the prices in the offer have been arrived at independently without any communications with other offerors for the purpose of restricting competition. Offerors also must certify that they will not disclose their prices to any competitor. There are also criminal penalties for making false certifications.

E.　*Contingent Fees*

Another prohibited practice involves "contingent fee" arrangements. Federal law (at 10 U.S.C. § 2306(b) and 41 U.S.C. § 254(a)) precludes arrangements to pay contingent fees for soliciting or obtaining government contracts. A *"contingent fee"* means any commission, percentage, brokerage, or other fee that is contingent upon the success that a person has in securing a government contract. An exception is provided for fees to bona fide employees and bona fide commercial agencies. Prospective contractors generally are required to disclose contingent fee arrangements in order to permit the government to evaluate the arrangement before award, and a mandatory solicitation provision is provided for this purpose.

F.　*Gratuities*

Another mandatory government contract clause in FAR § 52.203-3, entitled *"Gratuities,"* provides that government contracts may be terminated if the contractor or any employee or representative offers or gives any government employee any gift or entertainment. In addition to termination, the clause provides for "exemplary damages" of not more than 10 times the amount of the gratuity. Government termination actions under this clause have been pursued even for drinks and meals for government employees.

VII.　FOREIGN GOVERNMENT PROCUREMENTS

A.　*Overview*

The procurement systems of other governments vary widely in form, partly due to differences in institutions and local conditions. Historically, there have been two major differences between U.S. and foreign government procurement practices. First, the long tradition of "full and open competition" in the U.S. permitting virtually everyone, domestic and foreign (albeit with preferences favoring domestic products), to compete for government contracts has not been commonly practiced in foreign countries. The general rule elsewhere has been for governments to invite only "selected" companies to participate. Second, foreign government procurements generally have not employed transparent systems; *i.e.,* written and readily available laws, regulations, purchasing information, and evidence of the practices employed in awarding contracts. This is in sharp contrast to the system under which the U.S. not only publishes virtually all procurement policies and practices but also allows competitors to enforce the rules under a "bid protest" system. These two major differences have discriminated against U.S. suppliers and long have been the subject of negotiation with our trading partners.

B.   Opportunity to Participate

Under the U.S. system, virtually everyone has a legally enforceable right to compete for most government contracts. In other countries, foreign suppliers may simply never be invited to participate in the procurement. In international practice, a bid or offer now is generally called a *"tender."* Open (or public) tendering procedures are the least frequently utilized by foreign governments. More commonly, "selective" tendering procedures are followed under which the purchasing authority only invites certain suppliers, usually from a pre-established list, to submit a bid. The criteria for being included among those invited to tender often are vague and frequently discriminatory against foreign suppliers. When only one supplier is considered, this "sole source" negotiation is called the *"single tendering"* procedure.

C.   Obstacles for Foreign Suppliers

As opposed to the published policies and practices in the United States, there are a number of "invisible" practices of foreign governments that discriminate against U.S. suppliers. The first is simply not to make information regarding proposed purchases (such as time limits, addresses, product or service descriptions) readily available. The deadlines for submission of tenders may be too short to permit an adequate response by foreign suppliers. The notice often fails to include essential criteria for acceptance, such as quality and delivery conditions. Some requirements are much more difficult for foreign suppliers, such as residence, registration, local representation, and financial guarantees. Technical specifications may favor domestic suppliers. Some purchasing authorities even are permitted to open tenders in secret, and the evaluation criteria may be sufficiently vague to permit local suppliers to have an advantage. Remedies for improper evaluation and award of contracts usually are inadequate or nonexistent.

D.   Offset Agreements

Many foreign governments purchasing military goods and services from U.S. companies (often with U.S. financing) require the U.S. sellers to compensate the foreign buyer in some manner, including co-production, licensed production, subcontract production, countertrade, overseas investments, technology transfer, barter, counter-purchases, and buy-back arrangements. These are collectively known as *"offset agreements."* Section 123 of the U.S. Defense Production Act Amendments of 1992 generally discourages offset agreements, stating that they are inefficient and market-distorting. Any U.S. firm that enters into a contract for sale of a weapon system or defense-related item to a foreign country or foreign firm must report any offset agreement exceeding $5 million in value to the government. The Bureau of Export Administration of the Department of Commerce has regulations covering the collection of information on offset agreements. The DOD also has regulations establishing policies relating to offset agreements.

VIII.   SOURCES OF ASSISTANCE

A.   *U.S. Statutes and Regulations*

Anti-Kickback Act of 1986, 41 U.S.C.A. §§ 51–58 (West 1987 & Supp. 1995).

Buy American Act, 41 U.S.C.A. § 10a–10d (West 1987 & Supp. 1995).

Cargo Preference Act of 1954, 46 U.S.C.A. § 1241(b) (West Supp. 1995).

Cargo Preference Act of 1904, 10 U.S.C.A. § 2631 (West Supp. 1995).

Carribbean Basin Economic Recovery Act, 19 U.S.C.A. § 2701 (West Supp. 1995).

Competition in Contracting Act of 1984, Title VII of the Deficit Reduction Act of 1984, Pub. L. No. 98–369, 98 Stat. 494, 1175 (1984) (codified as amended in scattered sections of 10 and 41 U.S.C.A.).

Copeland (Anti-Kickback) Act, 18 U.S.C.A. § 874 (West Supp. 1995).

Fastener Quality Act, 15 U.S.C.A. § 5401 (West Supp. 1995).

Merchant Marine Act of 1936, 46 U.S.C.A. § 1101 (West 1975).

NAFTA Implementation Act, Pub. L. No. 103–182, 107 Stat. 2057 (1993) (codified in scattered sections of U.S.C.A.).

National Defense Authorization Act for Fiscal Year 1994, Pub. L. No. 103–160, 107 Stat. 1547 (1993).

Procurement Integrity Act, 41 U.S.C.A. § 423 (West Supp. 1995).

Trade Agreements Act of 1979, 19 U.S.C.A. §§ 2501–2582 (West 1980).

Federal Acquisition Regulation, 48 C.F.R. Parts 1–53 (1994).

Department of Defense Federal Acquisition Regulation Supplement, 48 C.F.R. Parts 201–253 (1994).

B. *Treaties and Agreements*

Agreement on Government Procurement, GATT Tokyo Round (Apr. 12, 1979), H.R. Doc. No. 153, 96th Cong., 1st Sess., pt. I (1979).

North American Free Trade Agreement, U.S. Govt. Printing Office: 1992–330–817/70635 (1992). (Also available, with supporting commentary, on CD-ROM from the ABA Section of International Law and Practice.)

United States Memorandum of Understanding with the European Union, Executive Order No. 12849, 59 Fed. Reg. 30931 (May 27, 1993).

Uruguay Round Trade Agreements, Office of the U.S. Trade Representative, Final Act Embodying the Results of the Uruguay Round of Multilateral Trade Negotiations (Dec. 15, 1993).

C. *Secondary Sources*

1. Books

J. CIBINIC, JR. & R. NASH, JR., FORMATION OF GOVERNMENT CONTRACTS (1982).

J. CIBINIC, JR. & R. NASH, JR., ADMINISTRATION OF GOVERNMENT CONTRACTS (3d ed. 1995).

P. FELLER, SPECIAL SUPPLEMENT, U.S. CUSTOMS AND INTERNATIONAL TRADE GUIDE (Matthew Bender 1994).

2. Periodicals

Adler & Metzger, *Government Contractor Teaming Arrangements and the Antitrust Laws*, 61 FED. CONT. REP. (BNA) 416 (March 28, 1994).

Anthony & Hagerty, *Cautious Optimism as a Guide to Foreign Government Procurement*, 12 PUB. CONT. L.J. 1 (1981).

Astor, *The EC Source Selection Regime: Quick Introduction*, 26 PUB. CONT. NEWSLETTER No. 4 (Summer 1991).

Cao, *Government Procurement Policies: An Invisible Barrier to U.S. Exports in the 1980's*, 15 NAT'L CONT. MGT. J. 68 (1981).

Capio, *The International Government Procurement Code*, 13 NAT'L CONT. MGT. J. 107 (1979).

Doke, *Competition Requirements in Public Contracting: The Myth of Full and Open Competition*, 64 FED. CONT. REP. (BNA) No. 3 (Supp. July 17, 1995).

Dyer, *A Primer on Export Controls*, 35 CONT. MGT. 23 (Aug. 1995).

de Graff & King, *Towards A More Global Government Procurement Market: The Expansion of the GATT Government Procurement Agreement in the Context of the Uruguay Round*, 29 INT'L LAW. 435 (Summer 1995).

Gallatin & Ramo, *Acquisition of Foreign Products—A Warning to Commercial Contractors*, 28 CONT. MGT. 12 (July 1988).

Green, *European Community Procurement—Part II*, 91–6 BRIEFING PAPERS (Fed. Pub. Inc., 1991).

Janik & McConville, *The Buy American Act*, 2 ACQUISITION ISSUES NO. 9 (Holbrook & Kellogg Inc., Sept. 1992).

Joelson, *World Trade: U.S. Implementing Legislation*, 23 INT'L BUS. LAW. 291 (July/Aug. 1995).

Kenney *et al.*, *Domestic Preference Provisions/Edition II*, 94–3 BRIEFING PAPERS (Fed. Pub. Inc., Feb. 1994).

Kuckelman, *Contracting with the North Atlantic Treaty Organization*, 20 GEO. WASH. J. INT'L. LAW & ECON. 527 (1987).

Marvel, *International Offsets: An International Trade Development Tool*, 35 CONT. MGT. 4 (Oct. 1995).

Murphy, *Exporting Goods and Services Under the NAFTA*, 6 INT'L QUARTERLY 1 (1994).

Myers, *The New UNCITRAL Model Law on Procurement*, 23 PUB. CONT. L.J. 267 (1994).

Russin, *Offsets in International Military Procurement*, 24 PUB. CONT. L.J. 65 (Fall 1994).

Sampliner & O'Shea, *Rules of Origin for Foreign Acquisitions Under the Trade Agreements Act of 1979, NAFTA, and the New GATT Accords*, 23 PUB. CONT. L.J. 207 (1994).

Stamps, *The Department of Defense Balance of Payments Program: A Brief History and Critique*, 18 PUB. CONT. L.J. 528 (1989).

3. Current Developments: Domestic and International Procurement

The Government Contractor (Fed. Pub. Inc.).

Federal Contracts Report (BNA).

Government Contractor Reporter (CCH).

ENDNOTES

[1] Statutes and regulations named in the text are cited in full in the Sources of Assistance (Section VIII).

CHAPTER 16

TRADE REMEDIES AND BENEFITS PROGRAMS

Judith H. Bello and Alan F. Holmer

I.   INTRODUCTION

In today's global economy, producers of all nations find themselves in competition with one another, often in both their home and third country markets. In light of increasing transnational competition, proliferating international trade agreements and national trade regulatory regimes offer both promise and peril to producers, importers and exporters.

For example, a U.S. producer sharply losing U.S. market share to increasing imports may wish to consider the panoply of U.S. laws providing relief against import competition. Major factors in selecting among those remedies include: whether the imports are from one, a few, or many countries; the rate at which they are increasing; the terms on which they are being sold; and how and to what extent such imports are affecting the U.S. industry concerned. If the prices being charged for imports are unfairly low, U.S. producers may perceive a competitive opportunity to reduce foreign competition lawfully by filing an antidumping petition. The possible issuance of an antidumping order and imposition of additional duties would be to their advantage and, of course, the disadvantage of importers. However, the same producers, when they export their products to a foreign market, may find themselves the object of an antidumping proceeding brought by local producers under that country's laws.

Some understanding of the types of trade remedies under the laws of many countries is, therefore, necessary to assess the benefits and risks of international trade transactions. This chapter reviews some of the key U.S. remedies, most of which have parallels under the national laws of other countries. In particular, many nations have antidumping duty and countervailing duty programs for relief against unfairly traded imports, and safeguard or escape clause trade remedies for relief against significantly increasing imports. Foreign enforcement of antidumping remedies is vigorous and ensnares a significant volume of export trade. Likewise, many countries are part of a regional free trade agreement or customs union that provides preferential access to their markets. Also, the European Union has a commercial instrument policy similar to (but also different from) the U.S. section 301 remedy used mainly to open markets abroad and induce foreign governments to better protect intellectual property.

Some, but not all, of these trade remedies have legal bases in international trade agreements. The original multilateral umbrella trade agreement was the General Agreement on Tariffs and Trade ("GATT"), established in 1947. Through the original GATT and six subsequent rounds of tariff negotiations, the GATT succeeded dramatically in reducing tariff levels in the markets of member nations. As the tariffs declined, however, nontariff barriers sprang up in their place. Over the years, the GATT was supplemented by optional codes establishing discipline on many of these nontariff practices, such as subsidies, dumping, government procurement, customs valuation, and standards. However, not all GATT members adopted these agreements.

These pioneering initiatives in regulating nontariff barriers were supplemented in turn by the eighth round of GATT negotiations, the so-called Uruguay Round. These culminated in December 1993 with the conclusion of the negotiation of an Agreement Establishing the World Trade Organization ("WTO"). This Agreement not only improves the former GATT and optional GATT codes, but unites them into a single undertaking and establishes multilateral rules for the first time for trade in services, trade-related investment measures, and the protection of intellectual property. The WTO umbrella agreement, with many annexed agreements, entered into force on January 1, 1995, and will replace the GATT (which was continued temporarily as a transition measure, because many developing countries were unable to implement the new WTO Agreement by the time of its entry into force).

The WTO agreements establish rules that bind member nations, including the U.S., and that serve as parameters for the application of national trade remedies or programs such as the antidumping and countervailing duty laws, safeguard or escape clause measures, regional free trade agreements and customs unions, and unilateral trade benefit programs. The WTO Agreement also includes an Understanding on Dispute Settlement, establishing a system for resolving disputes among member governments about the application of any WTO rules. Although private parties have no access to this regime, any WTO member government may challenge the manner in which another member government administers any trade remedy or program subject to WTO rules.

II.   SECTION 301 OF THE TRADE ACT OF 1974

Although the U.S. has many legal remedies for relief against imports, it has one preeminent tool for use in opening foreign markets, inducing foreign governments to better protect intellectual property, and protecting U.S. foreign direct investment from discrimination: section 301 of the Trade Act of 1974, as amended ("Trade Act").[1]

Based on a more limited remedy provided in the Trade Expansion Act of 1962, section 301 of the 1974 act provides for complaints about foreign government trade practices and policies to be filed with the Office of the U.S. Trade Representative. The Trade Representative is authorized, but not required, to initiate an investigation.

On the basis of an investigation, the Trade Representative is required to determine whether the foreign governmental practices or policies complained of violate a trade agreement or nullify or impair benefits to the U.S. under a trade agreement. If not, the Trade Representative alternatively must determine whether those acts are unjustifiable, unreasonable or discriminatory *and* a burden or restriction on U.S. commerce.

If the Trade Representative finds a violation of a trade agreement or an unjustifiable and burdensome practice, he is required to take appropriate action in response (subject to rather generous exceptions). Otherwise, he is authorized, but not required, to take action.

Where the section 301 investigation involves a trade agreement, such as the Agreement Establishing the World Trade Organization, the Trade Representative is required to invoke the applicable dispute settlement procedures of that agreement. If the investigation does not involve a trade agreement, he essentially conducts a negotiation with the foreign government concerned.

The action authorized under section 301 (which is actually sections 301–309) includes tariff increases, the imposition of quotas, restrictions on service sector access authorizations, and all other action within the power of the president. Where the Trade Representative concludes an agreement resolving a section 301 case, he is required to monitor its implementation.

The aim of section 301 is not to effect sanctions, but rather to increase the leverage of U.S. trade negotiators and thus the prospects for a trade–liberalizing outcome. Its successful use in opening markets and obtaining better protection of intellectual property in the late 1980s spawned a series of clones, including: Special 301, a variant aimed at intellectual property; Super 301, a variant aimed at identifying the greatest trade expansion opportunities by focusing on the most egregious impediments to trade; section 301–style telecommunications provisions; and a section 301–style approach to government procurement.

The use of section 301 measures, other than through WTO or other agreed dispute settlement procedures, is controversial in the post–Uruguay Round era. Any increase in a tariff beyond a "bound" rate is likely to be found to violate article II of the WTO's GATT 1994; any trade restriction applied to products of some WTO Members, but not others, is likely to be found to violate article I of GATT 1994, which provides for most–favored-nation treatment.

III.   THE ANTIDUMPING LAW

A.   *Background*

The U.S. antidumping law dates back to the early twentieth century, when U.S. steel producers urged the Congress to provide a means through which they could seek relief from unfairly low priced steel imported from Canada. Amended many times since, the antidumping law is set forth in Title VII of the Tariff Act of 1930, as amended ("Tariff Act").

The U.S. antidumping law is applied in the context of internationally negotiated rules on antidumping proceedings and measures. From its establishment in 1947, the GATT established rules on antidumping proceedings in article VI. Those rules were supplemented and amplified considerably in the Tokyo Round multilateral trade negotiations by an Agreement on Implementation of article VI of the General Agreement on Tariffs and Trade. An amended antidumping agreement is one of many WTO agreements that entered into force in 1995.

B.   *Principal Issues*

There are two overarching legal issues in any antidumping investigation: (1) Are imports of subject merchandise sold at prices below their "normal value"? (2) Are imports causing or threatening material injury to a U.S. industry, or materially retarding the establishment of a U.S. industry? These fact-intensive issues, each of which is an umbrella for a plethora of sub-issues, are determined in separate but parallel investigations by, respectively, the administering authority, currently the Department of Commerce ("Department"), and the International Trade Commission ("Commission").

C.   *Parallel Investigations*

An investigation normally is initiated in response to a petition filed by U.S. producers, a trade association of producers or a union. (The Department may also self-initiate an investigation.) In addition to having standing, the petitioners must demonstrate that they represent the U.S. industry. If so, and if they allege both sales at less than "normal value" and injury or threat of injury, the Department and the Commission each initiates an investigation. The Commission first makes a preliminary determination on injury; if affirmative, the investigations proceed. The Department then makes first a preliminary and then a final determination as to the extent of dumping; its final investigation proceeds whether or not its preliminary finding is affirmative. However, the Commission proceeds to issue a final determination only if the Department's final determination is affirmative.

D.   *The Commerce Department's Normal Value Investigation*

In its investigation, the Department normally compares sales in the U.S. market (the export price or constructed export price) with sales in the home market ("normal value"). If there are insufficient sales in the home market, the Department generally bases "normal value" on sales in a third country market. If there are no sales in the home (or third-country) market in the ordinary course of trade made at prices above the cost of production, the Department instead constructs a value based upon: the cost of materials and fabrication; general and administrative expenses; profit; and the costs of containers or coverings required to place the subject merchandise in a condition packed ready for shipment to the U.S.

In making these comparisons, the Department calculates the price of the subject merchandise in each market concerned on an *ex factory*, packed ready for shipment, basis. It does so by subtracting from the sales price various charges or costs incurred in the movement and sale of the merchandise from the factory to its ultimate destination. Where the merchandise is first sold to the U.S. to an affiliated company, the Department generally constructs an export price to avoid reliance on the internal transfer price. In these circumstances, the Department additionally subtracts from the sales price (1) the affiliated U.S. purchaser's selling expenses in the U.S., (2) the cost of any further manufacture or assembly in the U.S., and (3) the profit allocated to such U.S. activities.

The Department subtracts similar costs and charges from the sales price in the home (or third country) market. Moreover, it increases or decreases the "normal value" to adjust for differences in the merchandise sold in the U.S. and home (or third-country) markets with respect to quantities, physical characteristics, circumstances of sale, or level of trade. However, the Department generally disregards any sales in the home (or third-country) market determined to be made at prices below the cost of production. If there are no prices above the cost of production, as noted above, the Department disregards the sales prices altogether and instead constructs a value for use as "normal value."

E.   *The International Trade Commission's Injury Investigation*

In its investigation, the Commission defines the "like" product or products under investigation, and determines whether a U.S. industry (that is, the U.S. producers of a like product) is injured, or threatened with injury, by reason of imports of the subject merchandise. The Commission's determination is based on a broad range of factors, including the absolute and relative volume of imports, any price depressing or suppressing effects of imports, any underselling of U.S. like products by the subject imports, and any economic factors relating to the condition of the U.S. industry (*e.g.,* actual and potential declines in output, sales, market share, profits, productivity, return on investments and utilization of capacity; factors affecting domestic prices; and actual and potential negative effects on cash flow, inventories, employment, wages, growth, ability to raise capital, and investment, research and development).

F.   Orders and Reviews of Orders

If the Department and Commission issue final affirmative determinations, the Department automatically issues an antidumping order, requiring importers to pay cash deposits in the amount of estimated antidumping duties (which are in addition to normal customs duties). In narrowly prescribed circumstances, the Department may suspend its investigation based upon undertakings by the exporters concerned relating to the price and/or quantities of subject merchandise exported to the U.S. Suspension agreements are exceptional. Following the anniversary date of the order's issuance, the Department, upon request, conducts an administrative review in which, based on more recent information, it assesses duties on past entries and establishes a new estimated cash deposit rate.

Every five years, the Commission conducts a review to determine whether revocation of an order would result in resumption or continuance of injury to a U.S. industry. The Commission additionally may conduct a review based on changed circumstances.

G.   Judicial Review

The antidumping law provides a right to appeal final actions to the U.S. Court of International Trade, and thereafter to the Court of Appeals for the Federal Circuit in Washington, D.C. Under the North American Free Trade Agreement, appeals in cases involving imports from Canada or Mexico generally are heard instead by binational panels of experts established under Chapter 19 of that agreement.

IV.   THE COUNTERVAILING DUTY LAW

A.   Background

The first countervailing duty law was enacted in 1890, in response to complaints by U.S. beet and cane sugar producers about subsidized sugar imported from Russia. Amended many times since, the law applies to all imports and to domestic as well as export subsidies.

The U.S. countervailing duty acquired an international legal basis in 1947 with the conclusion of the GATT, articles VI and XVI of which address countervailing measures and subsidies. These provisions were variously amended and, in 1980, succeeded by the Subsidies Code for GATT Contracting Parties that elected to adhere to its provisions. That code, whose application was optional, has been replaced by the WTO Agreement on Subsidies and Countervailing Measures, applicable to all WTO members.

B.   Principal Issues

Like an antidumping investigation, a countervailing duty investigation is defined by two overarching legal issues: Are imports of subject merchandise subsidized? Do such imports cause or threaten material injury to a U.S. industry, or materially retard the establishment of an industry? These fact-intensive issues are answered by, respectively, the administering authority (currently the Department) and the Commission in separate but parallel investigations.

Normally an investigation is initiated in response to a petition filed by an interested party (producers, a trade association of producers or a union) on behalf of a U.S. industry. (The Department of Commerce may also self-initiate an investigation.) If the petitioners represent the U.S. industry, make allegations of both subsidies and injury, and provide information reasonably available to them in support of those allegations, the Department initiates an investigation.

C.   Parallel Investigations

Once initiated, a countervailing duty investigation proceeds in the same sequence as an antidumping investigation: a preliminary determination by the Commission, followed by a preliminary and then final determination by the Department, concluding with a final determination by the Commission. The investigation is terminated if there is a negative determination at any stage except the Department's preliminary determination, which proceeds to the Department's final determination even if it is negative.

D.   The Department's Subsidies Investigation

The Department begins its investigation by presenting questionnaires to the government concerned, inquiring about alleged subsidy practices. Any export subsidies found are allocated over the total value of exports of the subject merchandise (or the total value of exports to the U.S., as appropriate).

In addition, the Department identifies and quantifies domestic subsidies. These include governmental financial contributions, certain forms of income or price support, or payments to a funding mechanism, when they are made to a specific person and confer a benefit. Specific examples include equity infusions on terms inconsistent with the investment practice of the country in which the equity infusion is made, loans or loan guarantees on terms incomparable with the commercial terms for loans available on the market, and the provision of goods or services for less than adequate remuneration (or, where goods are purchased, for more than adequate remuneration).

As agreed in the Uruguay Round negotiations resulting in the WTO Agreement, certain domestic subsidies are not countervailable: certain subsidies to fund research or to benefit the environment or disadvantaged regions. Previously these subsidies were subject to countervailing duties under U.S. law.

E. *The Commission's Injury Investigation*

Parallel to the Department's investigation to identify and quantify export and domestic subsidies is the Commission's investigation to determine whether a U.S. industry is injured, or threatened with injury, by subsidized imports. The criteria compiled, analyzed and assessed by the Commission are virtually identical to those used in an antidumping injury investigation: volume of imports; any price depressing or suppressing effects of imports; any underselling of U.S. like products by subject imports; and any economic factors relating to the condition of the U.S. industry (*e.g.*, actual and potential declines in output, sales, market share, profits, productivity, return on investments and utilization of capacity; factors affecting domestic prices; and actual and potential negative effects on cash flow, inventories, employment, wages, growth, ability to raise capital, and investment, research, and development).

F. *Orders and Reviews of Orders*

If both agencies issue final affirmative determinations, the Department automatically issues a countervailing duty order, requiring importers to pay cash deposits in the amount of estimated countervailing duties, in addition to other duties. In narrowly prescribed circumstances, the Department is authorized to suspend its investigation based upon undertakings by the government and exporters concerned. Suspension agreements are exceptional; normally countervailing duty orders are issued. The order is then subject to review annually by the Department upon request. In each such review, the Department, based upon more recent information about U.S. imports of subject merchandise in the period of review, assesses countervailing duties on past entries and establishes a new cash deposit for estimated countervailing duties.

The Commission does not undertake analogous annual reviews, but is required to revoke a countervailing duty order after five years unless it determines that revocation would result in resumption or continuance of injury (or threat of injury) to a U.S. industry. The Commission also may conduct reviews at other intervals based upon changed circumstances.

G. *Judicial Review*

Like the antidumping law, the countervailing duty law provides a right to appeal final actions to the U.S. Court of International Trade, and thereafter to the Court of Appeals for the Federal Circuit in Washington, D.C. Under the North American Free Trade Agreement, appeals in cases involving imports from Canada or Mexico generally are heard instead by binational panels of experts established under Chapter 19 of that agreement.

V.   SECTION 201 OF THE TRADE ACT OF 1974 (ESCAPE CLAUSE)

In addition to many trade remedies designed to provide relief against unfair trade practices, the "escape clause" provides relief against increasing imports causing or threatening serious injury, regardless of whether they are fairly traded. Section 201 of the Trade Act of 1974, as amended, authorizes petitions to be filed with the International Trade Commission, complaining that imports of a particular product are increasing and that such increasing imports are a substantial cause of serious injury to a U.S. industry.

Section 201 is often called the *"escape clause,"* because its application enables the U.S. temporarily to escape its obligations under the GATT/WTO that generally prohibit quotas and tariff increases beyond bound rates. It is based upon article XIX of the original GATT and now GATT 1994, which authorizes the temporary imposition of import restrictions to facilitate continued support for freer trade and the GATT generally. Internationally, these types of measures are called "safeguard actions."

Unlike antidumping or countervailing duty proceedings, a section 201 investigation pertains to imports globally rather than from a specific country. However, under the North American Free Trade Agreement, there are special provisions (in article 802) regarding the inclusion of imports from Canada and Mexico in any escape clause proceeding.

In response to a petition supported by information reasonably available to the petitioner(s), the Commission initiates an investigation. It obtains information through questionnaires submitted to U.S. producers and importers and other affected parties, and generally from interested parties. The Commission holds a hearing, in which interested parties may participate, and considers briefs filed in the proceeding.

On the basis of the record, the Commission makes its determination of any injury and causation. If its finding is affirmative, the president is required to take

> all appropriate and feasible action within his power which the President determines will facilitate efforts by the domestic industry to make a positive adjustment to import competition and provide greater economic and social benefits than costs.

19 U.S.C. § 2253(a)(1). Relief may be provided initially for up to four years, and extended for up to four years if the Commission determines, following public proceedings, that measures continue to be required and that the domestic industry is adjusting to import competition. (When import relief is afforded

for more than one year, it must be phased down at regular intervals.) Relief may be afforded through tariff increases, the imposition of quotas or tariff rate quotas, appropriate adjustment measures, the negotiation of orderly marketing agreements or other agreements, legislative proposals, or any other action within the authority of the president.

VI.   SECTION 337 OF THE TARIFF ACT OF 1930

Section 337 of the Tariff Act of 1930, as amended, provides a remedy against imports that are unfairly traded. It declares unlawful unfair methods of competition and unfair acts in the importation or sale of articles if the threat or effect of such importation or sale is to (1) destroy or substantially injure an industry in the U.S., (2) prevent the establishment of such an industry, or (3) restrain or monopolize trade and commerce in the U.S.

Although broadly drafted, the remedy is applied most often when imports are found to infringe a valid and enforceable U.S. patent, registered trademark, or registered mask work of a semiconductor chip product. The importation or sale of infringing articles is unlawful if an industry in the U.S. relating to the articles protected exists or is in the process of being established. Where infringement occurs, importation or sale is actionable under section 337 without any demonstration of injury or threat of injury.

The International Trade Commission administers section 337 by conducting investigations subject to the Administrative Procedure Act. An administrative law judge conducts the proceeding, and issues a recommendation upon which the Commission votes. If the Commission finds a violation, it may issue an order excluding imports or a cease and desist order, either of which is subject to presidential disapproval. The exclusion order is enforced at the U.S. border by the U.S. Customs Service.

Following a determination of a violation by the Commission, the president may, within 60 days of his notification by the Commission, disapprove the determination for "policy reasons." Presidential disapproval deprives the Commission determination and order of any effect. If the president instead takes no action or approves the determination and order, they become final.

Any person adversely affected by a Commission determination under section 337 may appeal to the U.S. Court of Appeals for the Federal Circuit.

VII.   REGIONAL FREE TRADE AGREEMENTS (FTAS) AND NONRECIP-
ROCAL TRADE BENEFIT PROGRAMS

Article XXIV of the original GATT, GATT 1947, and the same provisions of GATT 1994 as amended by the WTO Agreement permit preferential trade arrangements within free trade areas or customs unions under certain conditions. The best known customs union is the European Union ("EU"), established originally as the European Community under the Treaty of Rome of

1957. The EU has grown from the original five member countries to fifteen, and many other countries have applied for membership.

In the last decade, more and more countries have entered into one or more free trade agreements. Whereas a customs union entails common external tariffs (and in the case of the EU, many non-trade measures such as plans for a common currency), a free trade area does not. Members of free trade agreements maintain the sovereign right to establish different external tariffs, but generally agree to eliminate (or substantially reduce) tariff and nontariff barriers in trade within the free trade area.

The United States negotiated its first FTA with Israel in 1984–85, followed by an FTA with Canada that entered into force in 1989. The U.S.–Canada bilateral FTA was succeeded by the trilateral North American Free Trade Agreement ("NAFTA") with Mexico, which entered into force in 1994. Currently the U.S., Canada and Mexico are negotiating with Chile regarding the latter's proposed accession to the NAFTA.

In addition, the U.S. and its Western Hemisphere trading partners have established the goal of achieving free trade throughout the Americas by 2005; and the U.S. and member nations of the Asia Pacific Economic Cooperation forum have established the same goal for achievement by 2010 for developed countries and 2020 for developing countries. Regional free trade agreements not including the United States as a member also have proliferated in many regions. These FTAs or customs unions can affect transactions substantially by lowering barriers to trade for goods or services of the participating members, but not for those of nonmembers.

In addition to its free trade agreements, the United States has several programs of nonreciprocal trade benefits intended to benefit developing countries. The broadest of these is, as the name suggests, the Generalized System of Preferences ("GSP"). This program entitles eligible products of beneficiary countries to enter the U.S. free of duty.

Similar, but more limited, programs are provided under the Caribbean Basin Economic Recovery Act and Andean Trade Preference Act. Under these programs, eligible products of certain Caribbean and Andean countries may enter the U.S. duty-free.

Each of these programs is established through legislation that results in revenue reductions. Under the congressional "pay-as-you-go" rules, the extension of any such program requires identification of offsetting revenue. In an era of budget restraint, it is becoming increasingly difficult to fund such programs, despite their benefits.

VIII. SOURCES OF ASSISTANCE

A. *U.S. Statutes and Regulations*

Trade Act of 1974, §§ 301–309 ("Trade Act"), *as amended*, 19 U.S.C. §§ 2411–2420.

Super 301: Trade Act, § 310, 19 U.S.C. § 2420.

Special 301: Trade Act, § 182, 19 U.S.C. § 2242.

Antidumping law: Tariff Act of 1930, §§ 731 *et seq.* ("Tariff Act"), *as amended,* 19 U.S.C. §§ 1673 *et seq.*

Countervailing duty law: Tariff Act, §§ 701 *et seq.*, 19 U.S.C. §§ 1671 *et seq.*

Section 201: Trade Act, §§ 201–204, 19 U.S.C. §§ 2251–2254.

ATPA: Andean Trade Preference Act, 19 U.S.C. §§ 3201–3206.

CBERA: Caribbean Basin Economic Recovery Act, *as amended,* 19 U.S.C. §§ 2701–2707.

GSP: Trade Act, Title V, 19 U.S.C. §§ 2461–2466.

Section 337: Tariff Act, § 337, 19 U.S.C. § 1337.

USTR section 301 regulations, 15 C.F.R. Part 2006.

Department of Commerce antidumping duty and countervailing duty regulations, 19 C.F.R. Parts 353–355; 60 Fed. Reg. 25,130 (1995) (interim regulations; request for comments).

International Trade Commission antidumping duty and countervailing duty regulations, 19 C.F.R. Part 207; 60 Fed. Reg. 18 (1995) (interim rules with request for comments).

International Trade Commission regulations implementing sections 201 and 337, respectively, 19 C.F.R. Parts 206, 210.

USTR GSP regulations, 15 C.F.R. Part 2007.

B.   *International Agreements*

General Agreement on Tariffs and Trade, October 30, 1947, T.I.A.S. 1700, 4 Bevans 639.

Agreement Establishing the World Trade Organization and Accompanying Agreements, H.R. DOC. NO. 316, 1 URUGUAY ROUND TRADE AGREEMENTS, TEXTS OF AGREEMENTS, IMPLEMENTING BILL, STATEMENT OF ADMINISTRATIVE ACTION, AND REQUIRED SUPPORTING STATEMENTS, 103d Cong., 2d Sess. (1994); *see also* 33 I.L.M. 1144.

The North American Free Trade Agreement, H.R. Doc. No. 159, 1 North American Free Trade Agreement, Texts of Agreement, Implementing Bill, Statement of Administrative Action, and Required Supporting Statements, 103d Cong., 1st Sess. (1993). (Also available, with supporting commentary, on CD-ROM from the ABA Section of International Law and Practice.)

C. Other Official Documents

House Comm. on Ways and Means, 104th Cong., 1st Sess., Overview and Compilation of U.S. Trade Statutes (Comm. Print 1995).

Import Administration, International Trade Administration, Department of Commerce, Antidumping Manual (July 1994).

Office of the United States Trade Representative, 1995 Trade Policy Agenda and 1994 Annual Report of the President of the United States on the Trade Agreements Program (1995).

Office of the United States Trade Representative, A Guide to the U.S. Generalized System of Preferences (GSP) (Aug. 1991).

GAO Report to Congressional Requestors, International Trade: Assessment of the Generalized System of Preferences Program, GAO/GGD-95-9 (Nov. 1994).

D. Secondary Sources

Aggressive Unilateralism: American Section 301 Trade Policy and the World Trading System (J. Bhagwati & H. Patrick eds. 1990).

Antidumping Law and Practice: A Comparative Study (J. Jackson & E. Vermulst eds. 1990).

T. Bayard & K. Elliott, Reciprocity and Retaliation in U.S. Trade Policy (1994).

Bello & Holmer, *GATT Dispute Settlement Agreement: Internationalization or Elimination of Section 301?*, 26 Int'l Law. 795 (1992).

Fed-track Guide to Antidumping Findings and Orders (updated monthly).

Fed-track Guide to Countervailing Duty Cases (updated monthly).

Holmer, Horlick & Stewart, *Enacted and Rejected Amendments to the Antidumping Law: In Implementation or Contravention of the Antidumping Agreement?*, 29 Int'l Law. 483 (1995).

Maruyama, *The Evolution of the Escape Clause -Section 201 of the Trade Act of 1974 as Amended by the Omnibus Trade and Competitiveness Act of 1988*, 1989 B.Y.U. L. REV. 393.

J. PATTISON, ANTIDUMPING AND COUNTERVAILING DUTY LAWS (1995, updated annually).

Symposium on Countervailing Duty Law, 21 LAW & POL'Y INT'L BUS. 503 (1990), including *Antidumping and Countervailing Duty Law: A Selected Bibliography*.

Winham & Grant, *Antidumping and Countervailing Duties in Regional Trade Agreements: Canada-U.S. FTA, NAFTA and Beyond*, 3 MINN. J. GLOBAL TRADE 1 (1994).

"WTO" (THE WORLD TRADE ORGANIZATION) – THE MULTILATERAL TRADE FRAMEWORK FOR THE 21ST CENTURY AND U.S. IMPLEMENTING LEGISLATION (Terence P. Stewart ed., forthcoming 1996).

Zeitler, *Federal Unfair Competition Actions: Practice and Procedure Under Section 337 of the Tariff Act of 1930*, 86 AM. J. INT'L L. 238 (1992).

E.   On-Line Services

For antidumping duty information, call FedWorld BBS at (703) 321–8020, or access the Internet at: FTP://FTP.FEDWORLD.GOV/PUB/IMPORT/IMPORT.HTM.

Relevant for various trade laws and their implementation, the U.S. Code, the Code of Federal Regulations, and *Federal Register* notices since July 1980 can be found using WESTLAW and LEXIS/NEXIS.

F.   Telephone Hot Line

USTR Section 301 hot line, (202) 395–3871.

Commerce Department hot line reporting information on new antidumping duty and countervailing duty petitions filed, (202) 482–0430.

G.   Government Offices Providing Small Business Assistance Regarding Antidumping Duty/Countervailing Duty Proceedings

United States Trade Commission
The Trade Remedy Assistance Office
500 E Street, S.W.
Washington, D.C. 20436

Special Assistant to the Deputy Assistant Secretary for Investigations
Office of Investigations
Import Administration
U.S. Department of Commerce
Pennsylvania Avenue and 14th Street, N.W.
Room 3099
Washington, D.C. 20230

ENDNOTES

1   See the Sources of Assistance in Section VIII of this chapter for full citations to the statutes, regulations and international agreements cited in the text.

CHAPTER 17

LEGALIZATION OF DOCUMENTS FOR USE ABROAD

Peter H. Pfund[1]

Numerous types of documents originating in one country may need to be used or submitted in another country. Such documents include: company by-laws; powers of attorney; affidavits; birth, marriage and death certificates; divorce decrees; incorporation papers; deeds to real property; documents related to education and degrees received; home studies in connection with adoptions; true copies; patent applications; and judgments and other legal papers. Documents that are in a form that makes them admissible in the country in which they originated generally need additional certifications in order to make them usable or admissible in a foreign country where they are to be used. This chapter describes the certification – or legalization – process, first, for U.S.-origin documents intended for use abroad and second, for foreign documents intended for use in the United States.

I. INTRODUCTION

It is necessary for the person seeking certification of a document to specify in which country or countries the document is to be used. How the document is certified will depend on whether the country of intended use is or is not a party to the 1961 Hague Convention Abolishing the Requirement of Legalisation for Foreign Public Documents (the "Hague Legalization Convention").[2]

A. *Traditional Legalization*

U.S. documents intended for use abroad traditionally require certification up the line, *e.g.*, for documents executed before a notary public, by the court clerk of the jurisdiction in which the notary public serves, and finally by the office of the state's secretary of state or his counterpart. What sequence of certifications is required for different types of documents and documents that have been notarized or originated with different state or local authorities depends on the laws and procedures of the individual U.S. states or other jurisdictions. The final certification at the state level by the state secretary of state is followed by a certification called an *"authentication"* by the Authentications Officer of the U.S. Department of State, acting under delegated authority from the U.S. Secretary of State in Washington, D.C. In order to bridge the chain of certifications within the United States over to a certification that makes the documents usable or admissible in another country, the documents require "legalization" by the embassy or a consulate in the United States of the country in which the documents are to be used, if legalization is a requirement for use in that country. In some countries, the embassy or consular legalization must be certified by that country's foreign ministry to make the document usable or admissible in that country. Other countries may require authentication of the seal of the U.S. Department of State by the U.S. embassy in the foreign country.

Authentication of the documents by the U.S. Secretary of State, *i.e.*, the Authentications Officer of the Department of State on behalf of the Secretary of State, is more than a certification that the documents appear to be the subject of a valid immediately previous certification by someone whose signature and seal have every appearance of matching the signature and seal of a person notified to the State Department's Authentications Office as authorized to certify documents from that U.S. jurisdiction. In accordance with 22 C.F.R. Part 131.2, it is the duty of the Authentications Officer to examine not only the most recent document that is to be authenticated, but also the basic document to which previous certifications have been affixed by other authorities. The Authentications Office also has the duty to refuse authentication when there is good reason to believe that the certification is for an unlawful or improper purpose[3] or the requested authentication would be contrary to public policy. Authentication may also be refused if any previous certification appears to have been improperly issued, *e.g.*, if a mere photocopy of a notarized document has been certified as if it were the original. Documents in a foreign language must be accompanied by an English translation that has been certified by the translator and notarized.

For authentication of documents previously certified by the appropriate state government certification, a check or money order made out to the United States Department of State for $4.00 (fee as of September 1995) per document, and an indication in which country the document is to be used, should be sent or may be brought to:

Authentications Office
Department of State
2400 M Street, N.W. – Room 101
Washington, D.C. 20520

Over-the-counter service for up to three documents per person is available on weekdays (except holidays) from 8:00 a.m. to 12:00 noon. The Authentications Office's recorded detailed information on all requirements may be reached by phoning (202) 647-5002. The caller may leave a message and request a return call if the recorded message has not answered his or her question. A pamphlet entitled *"Authentication Services"*[4] may be requested by writing or phoning the Authentications Office or leaving a message at the above phone number.

Unless otherwise instructed, the State Department will return-mail the authenticated documents to the customer after about one week. However, the customer may request that the State Department, after authentication, transmit the documents for legalization directly to the embassy or consulate of the country in which the documents are to be used. If that is requested, the documents should include a transmittal letter addressed to the embassy/consulate, the proper fee for legalization charged by the embassy/consulate, and a pre-addressed, stamped envelope for the embassy's or consulate's return of the documents to the customer.

The cost for foreign embassy legalization varies from embassy to embassy, and it is up to the requestor to determine from the respective embassy what the cost for legalization is and to whom the check should be made out. The telephone number of any embassy or consulate located in Washington can be determined from the Washington telephone directory. It is usually the consular section of the embassy that performs legalizations.

The documents can be hand-carried to the State Department for authentication, and from the State Department to the embassy/consulate for legalization in order to expedite the process. Otherwise, it is advisable to assume that the process will take two or more weeks from the time that the document to be authenticated and legalized is received by the State Department's Authentications Office before the document is received back from the embassy or consulate that has subsequently legalized it.

The legalized document should be acceptable/admissible as to its certified and legalized form for every official purpose throughout the country of intended use.

For further information, *Authentication of Documents for Use Abroad* may be requested from the U.S. Department of State, by telephoning the Department's autofax system at (202) 647-3000 from a fax machine telephone, following the prompts, and requesting document number 1046. Requests to have the documents mailed can be made by calling (202) 647-5225.

B.   *Streamlined Certification of Documents for Use in Hague Convention Countries*

The Hague Legalization Convention entered into force for the United States in October 1981. This Convention, as implemented in the United States, dispenses not only with the need for legalization of a document by the embassy/consulate of the country where it is to be used, but also with the need for prior authentication of the document by the U.S. Department of State. The Hague Convention saves considerable time and money by empowering state secretaries of state to certify documents intended for use in other countries that are parties to the Hague Convention by a prescribed form – the Convention "*apostille*" – that directly entitles the documents to acceptance in those countries. The document requires no certification in the United States beyond the *apostille*. In fact, the Convention exempts the certification by Convention *apostille* from any further certification or legalization and discourages any further certification or legalization.

The Convention benefits are available to all documents that qualify as "*public documents*". The term "*public document*" encompasses not only documents issued by public or governmental authorities but also all private documents (wills, powers of attorney, attestations, affidavits, etc.) that have been sworn to before a notary public and subsequently certified in accordance with the procedures applicable in the particular U.S. state or other jurisdiction.

The Hague Legalization Convention entitles a document covered by *apostille* to acceptance/admission/recognition by all authorities – national, regional and local – in any other country that has become a party to the Convention. As of November 1, 1995, there are 51 countries besides the United States that have become parties to this Convention.[5]

In the United States, all states and all other parts of the United States with the exception of the Territory of the Virgin Islands have named their respective Secretaries of State and/or the Deputy or Assistant Secretaries of State to complete and sign Hague Convention *apostilles*. The U.S. State Department Authentications Office issues *apostilles* for documents certified by the issuing federal agencies, such as patents and accreditations of academic institutions. In addition, the clerk of each federal court has been empowered to issue the *apostilles* for documents originating in that court or contained in the records of cases before that court. Documents originating in state courts or from their files are subject to certification by the court clerk for those courts and by the Hague Convention *apostille* issued by a competent person in the Office of the state Secretary of State.

Competent state officials, the State Department's Authentications Officer and the clerks of federal courts have been notified, by their functional titles, to the Netherlands Ministry of Foreign Affairs – the depositary under the Convention – as competent to issue *apostilles* for documents originating in the United States within their jurisdiction. The Ministry regularly passes such information to other Hague Convention party countries.

It is up to the person or office seeking an *apostille* to specify in which country or countries party to the Convention the document is to be used. The requesting party should ensure that the document is certified by the Convention *apostille* that refers in French to the Convention at the top of the *apostille* form – "(Convention de La Haye du 5 octobre 1961)." If a document is to be used in both a Hague Convention country and a non–Hague Convention country, it is best that it be issued in duplicate, with one copy certified in the traditional way requiring State Department authentication and embassy/consulate legalization, and the other copy certified with the Hague Convention *apostille*.

For further information, a document entitled *Hague Convention Abolishing the Requirement of Legalisation for Foreign Public Documents* may be requested from the U.S. Department of State by calling the Department's autofax system at (202) 647–3000 from a fax machine telephone, following the prompts, and requesting document number 1053. Requests to have the document mailed can be made by calling (202) 647–5225.[6]

C.   Non-Acceptance of Document Covered by Hague Convention Apostille

If a document certified by *apostille* should not be accepted by authorities in the country of its intended use and that country is a party to the Hague Convention, the Authentications Office of the Department of State should be notified of the circumstances, time, and place, including the name of the official who refused to accept the document, together with a copy of the *apostille* in question. When appropriate, the Department will seek to have the country of intended use of the document ensure that its authorities are made aware of their treaty obligation to accept *apostille*–certified documents from the United States. The most complete information that can be obtained will be needed to help the Department and the foreign government involved correct the situation.

II.   DOCUMENTS FROM ABROAD INTENDED FOR USE IN THE UNITED STATES

A.   Traditional Legalization ("Authentication")

If documents originating abroad are to be used in the United States, the process is the mirror–image of the process described above. In order for such documents to be made admissible in court in the United States or to be in an acceptable form for registration or other uses, the documents must have been legalized ("authenticated" in the usage of U.S. embassies/consulates) by the U.S. embassy or consulate in the country in which the document originated. Before such legalization is possible, the document must have been authenticated or certified by the foreign ministry of the country of origin.

Legalization of the document through attachment to it of the completed and signed appropriate authentication form (by grommet and ribbon fastened by a seal that has been impressed by the U.S. embassy/consulate), makes the document usable throughout the United States.[7]

B.   *Documents Covered by Hague Convention Apostille*

In order to be usable or admissible in the United States, documents from other countries that are parties to the Hague Convention and their prior certification(s) need only be covered by a completed *apostille* issued by the authority of the country of origin that has been notified to the Ministry of Foreign Affairs of the Netherlands, the Convention's depositary, as competent to issue the *apostille* for documents originating in that country. The competent authority is notified by functional title, not by the name of the person holding that title at any one time.

The documents certified by *apostille* do not require legalization by the U.S. embassy or a U.S. consulate in the country where the document originated. Since the Hague Convention entered into force for the United States in 1981, the U.S. embassy and consulates in every country that is a party to the Hague Convention are under instructions no longer to legalize documents originating in that country because such documents are capable of certification by that country's authorities with a Hague Convention *apostille* to make them admissible in the United States. The United States, by becoming a party to the Hague Convention, has a treaty obligation to all other party countries for documents so certified to be accepted as to their certified form at all levels of government – federal, state and local.[8] Failure by such a governmental authority in the United States to accept such a document is likely to be brought to the attention of the U.S. Department of State.

U.S. embassies and consulates abroad are, however, still able to provide notarial services (services normally performed by a notary public in the United States) for *anyone* wishing to execute a document *for use in the United States*, such as acknowledgements, oaths on affidavits, and powers of attorney.

The Hague Convention is silent about the manner in which the *apostille* may be attached to the document it certifies. Thus, rather than being grommeted and ribboned to the underlying document, with the ribbon ends fastened under a seal, the manner of attachment was not deemed important (a staple is adequate) because the first four numbered spaces of the completed *apostille* identify the underlying document by identifying its country of origin, who signed the previous certification, in what capacity and with what seal or stamp.

Only if there is some specific and fully explained and apparently justified reason for doubt whether the underlying document has in fact been certified by the *apostille* will there be grounds for questioning the issuing country authorities about the specific *apostille* and underlying document and asking that country for confirmation that there is a record of the issuance of the *apostille* – a record that Article 7 of the Hague Convention requires every authority issuing *apostilles* in countries party to the Hague Convention to maintain. Countries parties to the Hague Convention have an obligation to maintain for an unspecified period of time accessible records of the issuance of every *apostille*. Such records may be and are being maintained on paper, micro- and ultra-fiche and by computer.

III.   SOURCES OF ASSISTANCE

A.   *U.S. Statutes and Other Sources of Federal Law*

22 U.S.C. §§ 4215 (notarial acts, oaths, affirmations, affidavits, and depositions; fees), 4221 (depositions and notarial acts; validity; perjury; admissibility; forgery).

28 U.S.C. §§ 1740 (admissibility of authenticated copies of consular papers), 1741 (authenticated copies of foreign official documents as evidence).

22 C.F.R. Part 92 – Notarial and Related Services.

22 C.F.R. § 131.1 – Certification of documents.

22 C.F.R. § 131.2 – Refusal of certification for unlawful purpose.

Rule 44(a)(2), Fed. R. Civ. P., 28 U.S.C. Appendix – proof of official record; authentication of foreign record.

Rule 902(3), Fed. R. Evid., 28 U.S.C. Appendix – self-authentication – foreign public documents. (There is no amendment to Rule 902(3) corresponding to the 1991 amendment of Rule 44(a)(2), Fed. R. Civ. P., to take account of the fact that the Hague Convention is in force for the United States.)

B.   *Treaties*

1961 Hague Convention Abolishing the Requirement of Legalisation for Foreign Public Documents, T.I.A.S. 10072; 33 U.S.T. 883; 527 U.N.T.S. 189; 28 U.S.C.A., appended to Rule 44 (with lists of party countries and authorities in the United States competent to issue *apostilles*).

U.S. Senate Executive L., 94th Cong., 2d Sess. (1976), with message and report, and text of Hague Convention.

C.   *Other Official Documents*

Authentication of Documents for Use Abroad, 6 pages, a general briefing paper for the public prepared by the Bureau of Consular Affairs of the Department of State, available by mail upon request by phone to (202) 647–5225; request via phone–equipped fax machine from Department of State autofax system by calling (202) 647–3000 and seeking document number 1046.

Hague Convention Abolishing the Requirement of Legalisation for Foreign Public Documents, a briefing paper for the public prepared by the Bureau of Consular

Affairs of the Department of State, available by mail upon request by phone to (202) 647–5225; request via phone–equipped fax machine from Department of State autofax system by calling (202) 647–3000 and seeking document number 1053. This paper lists countries party to the Hague Convention, includes a sample *apostille* and a diagram of the process, lists who can issue *apostilles* at what cost in the federal government and the individual U.S. states and other jurisdictions, and provides information on authorities competent in other party countries to issue *apostilles* for documents originating in those countries.

Addendum (Section 4, paragraphs 304.1–304.7) to *Guide to Judiciary Policies and Procedures* (Vol. IV, Ch. 3), by Administrative Office of the United States Courts.

CLERKS MANUAL, United States District Courts, Vol. I, Section 17.06 – [Hague Convention] *Apostilles*

Opinion of George Deukmejian, Attorney General of the State of California, on the Hague Convention Abolishing the Requirement of Legalization for Foreign Public Documents, 65 Ops. Cal. Atty. Gen. 205 (1982); 21 I.L.M. 357 (1982).

Opinion of John K. van de Kamp, Attorney General of the State of California, 71 Ops. Cal. Atty. Gen. 362 (1989).

Document Authentication; two pages, undated, available from the U.S. State Department (describing the Department's policy against the authentication of documents relating to unsanctioned foreign boycotts).

D. Secondary Sources

1. Books

B. RISTAU, 1 INTERNATIONAL JUDICIAL ASSISTANCE (CIVIL AND COMMERCIAL), 241–254 (1990).

II BASIC DOCUMENTS OF INTERNATIONAL ECONOMIC LAW, 845–854 (S. Zamora & R. A. Brand eds. 1990).

J.P. SINNOTT, A PRACTICAL GUIDE TO DOCUMENT AUTHENTICATION: LEGALIZATION OF NOTARIZED AND CERTIFIED DOCUMENTS, 3–4, 11–30 (1985).

2. Law Review Articles

Amram, *Toward Easier Legalisation of Foreign Public Documents*, 60 A.B.A.J. 310 (1974).

Griew, *Hague Draft Convention on the Legalisation of Foreign Documents and the Form of Wills*, 8 INT'L & COMP. L. Q. 559 (1959).

Harvey, *The United States and the Hague Convention Abolishing the Requirement of Legalisation for Foreign Public Documents*, 11 HARV. INT'L. L. J. 476 (1970).

The Hague Convention Abolishing the Requirement of Legalisation for Foreign Public Documents (Report of the Committee on the International Unification of Private Law, with Action by the ABA Section of International Law and the House of Delegates), 9 INT'L LAW. 755 (1975).

ENDNOTES

[1]   The views expressed in this chapter are those of the author and not necessarily those of the Department of State.

[2]   T.I.A.S. 10072; 33 U.S.T. 883; 527 U.N.T.S. 189; *entered into force* for the United States on October 15, 1981, *reprinted in* 20 I.L.M. 1405 (1981).

[3]   *E.g.*, compliance with an unsanctioned foreign boycott. For a discussion of U.S. legal prohibitions on such compliance, see Chapter 13, *Export Controls, Sanctions and Antiboycott Laws*. The State Department's longstanding policy is to refuse to authenticate documents relating to unsanctioned foreign boycotts. *See* Sources of Assistance, Section III, for reference.

[4]   Department of State Publication 9518.

[5]   Antigua & Barbuda, Argentina, Armenia, Australia, Austria, The Bahamas, Barbados, Belarus, Belgium, Belize, Bosnia–Herzegovina, Botswana, Brunei, Croatia, Cyprus, El Salvador, Fiji, Finland,   France, Germany, Greece, Hungary, Israel, Italy, Japan, Lesotho, Liechtenstein, Luxembourg, Former Yugoslav Republic of Macedonia, Malawi, Malta, Marshall Islands, Mauritius, Mexico, Netherlands, Norway, Panama, Portugal, Russian Federation, Saint Kitts and Nevis, San Marino, Seychelles, Slovenia, South Africa, Spain, Suriname, Swaziland, Switzerland, Tonga, Turkey, United Kingdom. Those seeking certification of documents for use in the Russian Federation or the part of the former Yugoslavia that calls itself Yugoslavia may wish to check with the Office of Citizens Consular Services (CA/OCS/CCS), U.S. Department of State, phone: (202) 647-3666, for advice on how to ensure that they have documents that are likely to be accepted in those countries.

[6]   For information on what that 23–page document contains, *see* the Sources of Assistance in Section III of this chapter.

[7]   Rule 44(a)(2), Fed. R. Civ. P., 28 U.S.C. Appendix; Rule 902(3), Fed. R. Evid., 28 U.S.C. Appendix.

[8]   *See* Opinion of California Attorney General in 1982 which takes the position that a California requirement inconsistent with this obligation was preempted by the treaty-based obligation, 21 I.L.M. 357 (1982). For a further such opinion by a subsequent California Attorney General, see 71 Ops. Cal. Atty. Gen. 362 (1989).

CHAPTER 18

INTERNATIONAL LITIGATION

Gary B. Born

I.   INTRODUCTION

This chapter[1] deals with the distinctive issues that arise in U.S. civil law suits involving parties from foreign countries or conduct occurring outside the United States. International civil litigations also involve purely domestic issues (for example, procedural issues arising under the Federal Rules of Civil Procedure or substantive issues arising under state tort or contract law). In this chapter, however, we are concerned solely with the peculiarly international issues that recur in international civil litigations in U.S. courts.

International civil litigation is of relevance at almost every stage of a dispute. At the outset of any international litigation (or arbitration), counsel must consider issues of international jurisdiction and forum selection. Shortly thereafter, questions of service of process and taking of evidence must be addressed. In cases involving foreign states, or state-owned companies, counsel must consider issues of sovereign immunity under the Foreign Sovereign Immunities Act, 28 U.S.C. §§ 1601 *et seq.* ("FSIA"), and the potential applicability of the act of state doctrine. Almost any international litigation will also present choice of law questions, either under traditional conflicts rules or under federal doctrines relating to the extraterritorial application of U.S. law. And, finally, even if a U.S. judgment is successfully obtained, an international litigant must also consider whether and how that judgment can be enforced.

International civil litigation often intersects with other areas of international practice. In many international disputes, one or more international commercial arbitration agreements may arguably be applicable. Counsel must decide whether the client's interests are served by invoking such arbitration agreements, and if not, whether and how the dispute may be structured to permit litigation. (*See* Chapter 19, *International Commercial Arbitration.*)

Virtually any sort of international dispute can be the subject of international litigation in U.S. courts. When international commercial transactions go sour, international litigation is frequently the result. Indeed, this possibility must be borne in mind when drafting international contracts, as well as when counselling clients after difficulties have arisen.

Similarly, international export control, customs, financing, intellectual property, securities, trade, and creditors' rights issues often arise in U.S. international litigation. (*See* the chapters on these topics elsewhere in this book.) In each such context, the basic principles of international litigation outlined here provide the starting point (and, often, the ending point) for resolving most issues.

II.   INTERNATIONAL CIVIL LITIGATION IN U.S. COURTS

This section summarizes the principal areas within the field of international civil litigation that are of importance to U.S. practitioners. All arise principally in U.S. courts during adversarial civil litigation.[2]

A.   *Personal Jurisdiction*

1.   Introduction

A threshold issue in any international civil litigation in U.S. courts is whether the defendant is properly subject to the personal jurisdiction of the court. Personal jurisdiction over foreign parties is subject to the same basic principles that govern jurisdiction over domestic parties. In both cases, personal jurisdiction requires both an affirmative jurisdictional grant by a state or federal statute and the absence of any constitutional prohibition.

It is also important to consider at the outset the possibility that a U.S. judgment against a foreign defendant may need to be enforced outside the United States. The United States is not party to any mutual recognition of judgments treaty; as a consequence, the enforcement of U.S. judgments abroad is a question of foreign law, which varies from nation to nation. In general, however, most foreign states will refuse to enforce U.S. judgments unless they are based upon assertions of jurisdiction that satisfy either local requirements or local views of international requirements. Even if U.S. jurisdictional requirements can be satisfied, counsel should, therefore, consider the effect of such requirements upon enforcement of a U.S. judgment.

2.   State and Federal Long–Arm Statutes

All U.S. states have enacted long–arm statutes that define the circumstances in which state courts may assert personal jurisdiction over non–resident defendants. Although a number of such statutes simply incorporate, and extend to the limits of, the due process clause of the 14th Amendment to the U.S. Constitution, others contain general formulae defining when non-residents are subject to personal jurisdiction. A state court will generally be unable to hear an international litigation unless the applicable state long–arm statute grants it jurisdiction.

Congress has not enacted a general federal long–arm statute. The personal jurisdiction of federal courts is defined, in the first instance, by Rule 4 of the Federal Rules of Civil Procedure. Under Rule 4, federal courts are authorized to assert personal jurisdiction in: (a) those circumstances permitted by the local state long–arm statute where the federal district court is located; (b) those circumstances permitted by any specialized federal long–arm statute; or (c) under new Rule 4(k)(2), in federal question cases to the limits of the U.S. Constitution, provided that the defendant is not subject to jurisdiction in any other state.

Congress has enacted a number of specialized long–arm statutes, which grant federal courts jurisdiction in specific statutory contexts. Examples include the federal antitrust laws and the federal securities laws. These federal jurisdictional grants can be invoked under Rule 4 of the Federal Rules of Civil Procedure. (Personal jurisdiction over foreign states and their state-owned companies and agencies is defined by the FSIA, as discussed in section II.E.)

3.   Due Process Clause

Even if a state or federal long–arm statute grants personal jurisdiction, that jurisdiction cannot be exercised unless applicable due process standards are satisfied. The same general due process standards apply to assertions of jurisdiction over foreign defendants as to the exercise of jurisdiction domestically.

a.   General Jurisdiction

The Supreme Court has distinguished between "general" and "specific" jurisdiction. (*Helicopteros Nationales de Colombia v. Hall*, 466 U.S. 408 (1984).) General jurisdiction permits the forum court to exercise jurisdiction over the defendant in suits involving *any* claims, whether or not they have a relationship to the forum. The principal bases that are recognized as sustaining general jurisdiction are: (i) nationality or domicile; (ii) incorporation; (iii) in some jurisdictions, registration to do business; (iv) "continuous and systematic" business activities sufficient to make the defendant "present" in the forum; and (v) tag service within the forum's territory.

b.   Specific Jurisdiction

Specific jurisdiction permits the forum court to exercise jurisdiction over the defendant *only* as to claims that "arise out of" or "relate to" the defendant's contacts with the forum. Moreover, the defendant must have "minimum contacts" with the forum sufficient to justify the assertion of specific jurisdiction. That standard is generally understood to require a showing that the defendant "purposefully" engaged in conduct in the forum, or affecting the forum, sufficient to create "minimum contacts." (*World-Wide Volkswagen Corp. v. Woodson*, 444 U.S. 286 (1980).) In addition, any assertion of jurisdiction must be "reasonable." (*Burger King Corp. v. Rudzewicz*, 471 U.S. 462 (1985).) The Supreme Court has indicated that, in international cases, special attention must be given to the distinctive difficulties and costs that foreign defendants may encounter in defending a lawsuit in the United States. (*Asahi Metal Indus. Co. v. Superior Court of California*, 480 U.S. 102 (1987).)

c.   National Contacts and State Contacts

The due process clause of the 14th Amendment has long been held to apply to the exercise of jurisdiction by a state court. U.S. courts have almost always concluded that the 14th Amendment requires that the defendant have "minimum contacts" with the state in question.

Most lower federal courts have concluded that, in cases where jurisdiction is based upon a federal long-arm statute, the due process clause of the 5th Amendment applies. They have generally concluded that the 5th Amendment permits consideration of the defendant's contacts with the entire United States, rather than merely with the state in which the federal district court is located. Lower federal courts are divided in cases involving state law claims within a federal court's diversity jurisdiction, or federal substantive claims where personal jurisdiction is based upon a borrowed state long-arm statute.

B.   *Service of Process*

1.   Introduction

Service of process in international cases can raise troublesome issues. Serving process on defendants located in foreign nations requires determining whether the United States is party to a treaty or international convention that affects service, as well as whether local law in the place where service is to be effected permits particular mechanisms of service. In addition, service on foreign states and their agencies, instrumentalities, and majority-owned corporations must generally be effected in accordance with the FSIA.

As with personal jurisdiction, U.S. practitioners must consider at the outset of any litigation whether a resulting U.S. judgment may require enforcement abroad. If so, foreign law advice on the service of U.S. process may be appropriate; in many countries, a foreign judgment will be unenforceable if service of process was not effected in accordance with local requirements.

2.   Federal Rule of Civil Procedure

Rule 4 of the Federal Rules of Civil Procedure governs the service of process outside the United States in civil actions in federal district courts. Rule 4 was extensively revised in 1993.[3]

a.   Service within the United States

Service of process on a foreign defendant can sometimes be made within the United States pursuant to the otherwise applicable provisions of Rule 4 governing domestic service. Examples of such service include cases where an individual defendant is physically present in the United States, where a foreign person has appointed an agent within the United States for receipt of service of process, and where a foreign person is deemed, by operation of U.S. law, to have an agent in the United States (for example, by virtue of an alter ego relationship).

b.   Rule 4(f) and International Agreements

New Rule 4(f) provides that service outside the United States should be made "(1) by any internationally agreed means reasonably calculated to give notice," such as those means authorized by the Hague Convention on the Service Abroad of Judicial and Extrajudicial Documents ("Hague Service Convention").[4] The United States is party to the Hague Service Convention, together with most European nations, Japan, Canada, China, Egypt, Israel, and Turkey.

Under Rule 4(f)(1), U.S. litigants are required to resort to the mechanisms set forth in the Hague Service Convention if service is made in a signatory state. Beyond Rule 4(f)(1), the Supreme Court has said that the Hague Service Convention provides the exclusive means for effecting service on the territory of a signatory state. (*Volkswagenwerk AG v. Schlunk*, 486 U.S. 694 (1988).) The Court has also held, however, that, if U.S. law permits service on a foreign party to be effected in the United States without the need for service abroad, the Convention is not applicable. (*Id.*)

The Hague Service Convention sets forth multiple possible avenues for the service of process. Most notably, under Article 5 a "Letter of Request" may be dispatched to the "Central Authority" in the requested state. The Convention appends a model letter of request, which must be complied with. The U.S. Marshal's Service provides a pre–printed form (USM–94) which may be used. Rule 4(f)(1) was specifically intended to permit the use of Article 5's Central Authority mechanism.

The Convention also permits, provided that the state of destination does not object: (i) service under Article 10(a) by ordinary post; (ii) service under Article 10(b) by "judicial officers, officials, or other competent persons of the state of origin"; (iii) service under Article 10(c) "directly through the judicial officers, officials or other competent persons of the State of destination"; and (iv) service under Article 19 in a manner authorized by the laws of the state of destination. The available avenues for service under the Convention in any particular case depend upon the reservations and service rules of the destination state.[5] Rule 4(f)(1) apparently authorizes use of these alternatives, as well as the Central Authority mechanism, where the receiving state has not objected.

The United States is also party to the Inter–American Convention on Letters Rogatory.[6] Other parties currently include Argentina, Chile, Ecuador, Guatemala, Mexico, Panama, Paraguay, Peru, Uruguay, and Venezuela. At least one lower court has held that the Inter–American Convention is not exclusive.[7]

c.   Rule 4(f)(2)'s Alternative Means of Service

Rule 4(f)(2) also provides alternatives mechanisms of service, which may be used "if there is no internationally agreed means of service or the applicable international agreement allows other means of service." The additional alternatives are:

(A) in the manner prescribed by the law of the foreign country for service in that country...; or

(B) as directed by the foreign authority in response to a letter rogatory or letter of request; or

(C) unless prohibited by the law of the foreign country, by

(i) delivery to the individual personally of a copy of the summons and the complaint; or

(ii) any form of mail requiring a signed receipt, to be addressed and dispatched by the clerk of the court to the party to be served.

These mechanisms may only be used if they are, in a particular case, "reasonably calculated to give notice."

If an avenue prescribed in Rule 4(f)(2) is used, foreign counsel may need to be consulted. Under Rule 4(f)(2)(A), service must be made in a manner permitted by foreign law; it is not settled whether this provision refers to foreign law regulating service in cases in foreign courts or foreign law regulating service from abroad.[8]

Service by letter rogatory under Rule 4(f)(2)(b) involves the expense, delay and uncertainty traditionally associated with such mechanisms. In some nations (e.g., Switzerland), however, the only form of foreign service that may be effected is via letter rogatory. Local counsel can provide definitive advice on local law constraints.

d.   Rule 4(f)(3)

Rule 4(f)(3) permits service of process as ordered by a district court. Unlike Rule 4(f)(2), there is no express prohibition against court-ordered service in a manner not permitted by the law of the place of service. It does not, however, permit service in violation of an applicable international agreement.

e.   Foreign Sovereign Immunities Act

Service upon "foreign states" is required by Rule 4(j)(1) to be effected pursuant to 28 U.S.C. § 1606. Section 1608 of the FSIA sets forth the exclusive means for service of process on foreign states. Section 1608(a) deals with service upon the foreign state itself (*e.g.*, the Republic of France). Section 1608(b) deals with service upon foreign states' "agencies and instrumentalities," a term that includes corporations owned more than 50% by a foreign state. Both sections set forth hierarchies of means of service, and counsel must use the preferred mechanisms if available.

f.   Waiver of Service of Process

New Rule 4 of the Federal Rules of Civil Procedure provides a mechanism for requesting "waivers" of service of process. Rule 4(d) permits plaintiffs to request waivers of formal service by sending a complaint, summons, request for waiver, and other information by first class mail or "other reliable means." If the defendant refuses to waive service, he can be sanctioned for the costs. The sanction provision of Rule 4(d)(2), however, applies only to a "defendant located within the United States."

C.   *Forum Selection*

Forum selection is extremely important in international litigation. In many cases, different national legal systems provide dramatically different resolutions of the same dispute. These differences arise from variations in substantive laws, procedural rules, and the character of decision makers. There are a variety of "forum selection" issues that arise in U.S. courts.

1.   Forum Selection Clauses

International commercial and financial agreements routinely include forum selection clauses designating the forum in which disputes relating to the agreement can (or must) be resolved. These clauses raise issues of both interpretation and enforcement.

a.   Interpretation of Forum Selection Clauses

Forum selection clauses come in countless forms, all of which raise issues of interpretation. One of the most significant interpretative issues is whether a forum selection clause is "permissive" or "mandatory." A permissive forum selection clause allows the parties to litigate their disputes in the contractual forum (and generally functions also as a submission by both parties to the personal jurisdiction of the forum), but does not require that disputes be resolved there; litigation can also be pursued in other fora that may have jurisdiction over the parties and the dispute. In contrast, a mandatory (or exclusive) forum selection clause requires that the parties' disputes be resolved solely in the contractual forum. Before concluding that a particular forum selection agreement is exclusive, U.S. courts generally require a relatively clear indication that this was the parties' intent.

Another significant interpretative issue concerns the scope of forum selection clauses. Most such agreements encompass all disputes that "arise out of," that "relate to," or that are "in connection with" the parties' underlying agreement. Whatever formulation is used, disputes can arise concerning the clause's application to non–contractual claims, such as tort claims or claims based on statutory rights. Most U.S. courts apply general principles of contract interpretation to resolve such disputes (usually without considering whether these principles are dictated by state or federal law).

b.   Enforceability of Forum Selection Clauses

Forum selection clauses are not infrequently challenged on grounds of enforceability. In federal courts, the enforceability of forum selection clauses choosing foreign fora is generally governed by federal common law.[9] The same is arguably true of forum selection clauses choosing U.S. fora in international disputes, although 28 U.S.C. § 1404(a) is probably applicable in such cases.

State courts have generally not considered in detail whether state law or federal law governs the enforceability of forum selection clauses. Most state court decisions have been consistent with the federal law principles discussed below. Nevertheless, in some states, forum selection agreements continue to be regarded as contrary to public policy. A few states have enacted forum selection legislation.[10]

Federal common law rules governing the enforceability of forum selection agreements are derived from *Bremen v. Zapata Off-Shore Co.*, 407 U.S. 1 (1972). There, the Supreme Court held that forum selection clauses in international admiralty disputes were presumptively enforceable, subject only to limited exceptions. These exceptions exist where the party resisting enforcement can clearly show that (i) enforcement would be "unreasonable or unjust," (ii) the "clause was invalid for such reasons as fraud or overreaching," or (iii) the clause violates a fundamental "public policy" of the forum.[11]

2. *Forum Non Conveniens*

Even if a U.S. court can exercise personal jurisdiction over a foreign defendant, and even if venue is proper, the doctrine of *forum non conveniens* permits dismissal of the action in some circumstances. *Forum non conveniens* is a common law doctrine that allows trial courts discretion to dismiss actions on the grounds that the plaintiff's chosen forum is disproportionately inconvenient and an alternative forum for hearing the claims exists.

The leading contemporary *forum non conveniens* decision is *Piper Aircraft Co. v. Reyno*, 454 U.S. 235 (1981), where the Court held that a U.S. plaintiff's selection of a U.S. forum is entitled to great deference, and that this choice may only be displaced upon a weighing of public interest and private interest factors that clearly point towards dismissal. The Court held that a non–U.S. plaintiff's choice of a U.S. forum was not entitled to similar deference. The Court also held that the fact that a foreign forum might provide a less favorable legal regime for the plaintiff was not a factor entitled to significant weight in *forum non conveniens* analysis, unless the foreign forum would effectively provide no remedy at all.

Lower federal courts have generally held that *Piper's* statement of the *forum non conveniens* doctrine is a rule of federal law, applicable in federal courts in both diversity and federal question cases.[12] Although the *forum non conveniens* doctrine has generally been applied to federal securities claims, it has been held inapplicable to federal antitrust claims.[13]

State courts have generally, but not always, applied the *Piper* rule, most often without considering whether it is a rule of federal or state law. A few states have, by judicial decision or statute, significantly modified or curtailed the *Piper* rule.

3.   *Lis Alibi Pendens* and Antisuit Injunctions

U.S. litigants sometimes find themselves enmeshed in parallel proceedings in which the same (or an overlapping) dispute is simultaneously litigated in both U.S. and one or more foreign courts. In general, U.S. courts have held that there is no prohibition against such parallel proceedings, reasoning that each action should proceed to judgment, at which point rules regarding the recognition of foreign judgments can come into force.[14]

Notwithstanding this general rule, the *lis alibi pendens* doctrine permits U.S courts to stay U.S. actions pending the outcome of identical or closely related foreign proceedings. Application of the doctrine is left largely to the discretion of the trial judge.

Antisuit injunctions are injunctions forbidding parties from commencing or participating in litigation in a foreign forum. They are rarely issued by U.S. courts because of concerns about interfering with foreign judicial jurisdiction and notions of international comity. U.S. courts generally issue antisuit injunctions only where necessary to prevent vexatious and oppressive litigation, to protect their jurisdiction, or to prevent the circumvention of local public policy. Nevertheless, some courts have taken a more vigorous approach, issuing antisuit injunctions merely in order to halt duplicative litigation that is viewed as unduly expensive.[15]

4.   Venue

Venue over non–U.S. defendants is generally not a significant issue in U.S. federal court actions. The Alien Venue Statute provides that "[a]n alien may be sued in any district." The FSIA, 28 U.S.C. § 1391(t), provides a specialized venue regime for actions against foreign states, which is more restrictive than the Alien Venue Statute.

5.   Federal Subject Matter Jurisdiction

A federal court cannot adjudicate a dispute unless it has subject matter jurisdiction under both the U.S. Constitution and a federal statute. The two most significant areas of federal subject matter jurisdiction in domestic matters – federal question and diversity jurisdiction – are also frequently invoked in international disputes. Federal question issues in the international context can be complex.[16]

In addition, there are several bases of federal subject matter jurisdiction that are specifically applicable in international matters. First, Article III of the Constitution provides federal courts with subject matter jurisdiction in all cases "between a State, or the Citizens thereof, and foreign States, Citizens or Subjects." This provision, granting so–called "alienage" jurisdiction, is implemented by 28 U.S.C. §§ 1332(a)(2) and 1332(a)(3). These provisions provide U.S. federal courts with subject matter jurisdiction over cases in which U.S. citizens litigate against foreign citizens and where two diverse U.S. citizens litigate against one another and a foreign citizen is joined on one side or the other. Neither section, nor Article III, grants jurisdiction where two aliens litigate against one another. Cases involving multiple parties can present difficult issues and lower courts have reached divergent results.[17]

Second, the Alien Tort Statute, 28 U.S.C. § 1350, provides federal subject matter jurisdiction over "all causes where an alien sues for a tort only, [committed] in violation of the law of nations." In recent years, section 1350 has been used with increased frequency, particularly in so–called "human rights" litigation. It is applicable (if at all) principally in cases involving claims of atrocious behaviour by foreign government officials (such as torture and slavery).[18]

D.   *Discovery of Materials Located Abroad*

International litigation often requires U.S. parties to seek discovery of materials located outside the United States. The Federal Rules of Civil Procedure (and most state discovery rules) permit direct U.S. discovery of materials located outside U.S. territory. Thus, applying Rules 26 and 34, U.S. courts have held that a party to U.S. litigation subject to the personal jurisdiction of the U.S. court can be ordered to produce documents located outside the United States. The determinative issue is whether the documents are in the "control" of the party from whom discovery is sought – not where the documents are located.[19]

Compliance with U.S. discovery orders seeking documents located outside the United States is sometimes forbidden by foreign law. A number of foreign states have enacted so–called "blocking statutes" or have legislation mandating bank or other secrecy. The existence and content of such statutes can be ascertained by consulting local counsel abroad, or by contacting the U.S. Department of State, Office of American Citizens Services.

U.S. courts have held that they have the power to order discovery of materials located abroad, notwithstanding the existence of foreign laws prohibiting compliance with U.S. discovery requests. (*See Société Internationale v. Rogers*, 357 U.S. 197 (1958).) Where foreign law prohibits compliance with a U.S. discovery order, however, U.S. courts, in determining whether to order discovery and what sanctions to impose if discovery is not made, will often apply a balancing test weighing U.S. and foreign national interests and private concerns.[20]

The Federal Rules of Civil Procedure have also been held to permit U.S. courts to order individuals residing abroad to travel to the United States to attend depositions. U.S. trial courts have substantial discretion in ordering U.S. depositions (or in selecting a foreign situs). In the latter case, the court and counsel must ascertain whether local foreign law permits depositions and under what conditions. Foreign governmental officials must often be notified, and/or participate in, U.S. depositions conducted on foreign territory.[21] U.S. courts will generally not order depositions to be conducted abroad in violation of foreign law, although they may order foreign persons to travel to the United States to attend a deposition, notwithstanding foreign prohibitions.

Rule 45 of the Federal Rules of Civil Procedure permits, in some cases, discovery of materials located outside the United States from non-party witnesses. In general, a subpoena can be served under Rule 45 only within the territorial jurisdiction of the district court issuing the subpoena. That makes it impossible, in many cases, to subpoena foreign witnesses unless they have a place of business within the United States where they can be served. Even if such service can be effected, some U.S. courts have displayed reluctance to order foreign witnesses to produce foreign documents in U.S. court.[22] Under 28 U.S.C. § 1783, subpoenas can, in certain circumstances, be served outside the United States on U.S. nationals or residents.

The United States is a party to the Hague Convention on the Taking of Evidence Abroad in Civil or Commercial Matters ("Hague Evidence Convention").[23] The Convention provides mechanisms by which courts in one signatory state can obtain evidence located in other signatory states.

It is important to consult the reservations and declarations of states that have acceded to the Hague Evidence Convention. Under Article 23 of the Convention, member states can declare that they will not execute letters of request for the purposes of pretrial discovery of documents. Virtually all signatories to the Convention have made such declarations, thus significantly limiting the efficacy of the Convention's mechanisms for U.S. litigants.

In *Société Nationale Industrielle-Aerospatiale v. U.S. District Court*, 482 U.S. 522 (1987), the Supreme Court rejected the argument that the Hague Evidence Convention was the exclusive mechanism for obtaining evidence located within the territory of a signatory state. The Court held that the Convention merely provided alternatives that supplemented the discovery mechanisms under the Federal Rules of Civil Procedure (and state discovery rules). The Court also held, however, that the doctrine of international comity had to be applied on an ad hoc, case-by-case basis, to determine whether in particular circumstances the Convention's mechanisms should to be used instead of direct U.S. discovery. Most U.S. lower courts applying this comity-based balancing test have concluded that use of the Convention is not necessary in order to obtain discovery from parties to a U.S. litigation.

There may be circumstances in which direct U.S. discovery from a foreign entity is not possible because the entity is not a party to the U.S. litigation and because it is not subject to Rule 45 subpoena service or to other U.S. discovery mechanisms.

E.   Foreign Sovereign Immunity

Much international commerce involves foreign states or state–owned corporations or departments. Litigation against such entities raises questions of sovereign immunity under U.S. (and foreign) law.

The FSIA, 28 U.S.C. §§ 1601 *et seq.*, provides a comprehensive statutory regime that defines the jurisdiction of U.S. courts over foreign states and their agencies and instrumentalities, the immunities of such entities, and the procedures in cases against such entities.

The FSIA applies to foreign states proper (such as the Federal Republic of Germany); to political subdivisions of foreign states (such as provinces or states); and to "agencies or instrumentalities" of foreign states (defined by section 1603 as corporations more than 50 percent–owned by foreign states). Section 1604 provides foreign states with a general grant of immunity from the jurisdiction of U.S. courts, but section 1605 goes on to enumerate a number of specific exceptions to that immunity. The exceptions, which have generated substantial litigation, include provisions regarding waivers of immunity (§ 1605(a)(1)); commercial activity with a U.S. nexus (§ 1605(a)(2)); non–commercial torts within the United States (§ 1605(a)(5)); and arbitration (§ 1605(a)(6)). [24]

Where the FSIA denies a foreign state immunity, section 1330(b) provides an affirmative grant of personal jurisdiction to U.S. federal courts. Section 1330(a) provides a similar grant of subject matter jurisdiction. Actions against foreign states in federal courts are non–jury actions. (28 U.S.C. § 1330(a).)

Section 1609 of the FSIA provides that foreign state property located within the United States is generally immune from the enforcement jurisdiction of U.S. courts. Section 1610 goes on, however, to provide a number of exceptions to this immunity. The exceptions generally parallel those under section 1605, with some limitations.

F.   Act of State Doctrine

The act of state doctrine is a common law doctrine that provides that U.S. courts will not sit in judgment on the validity (and perhaps the legality) of foreign acts of state consummated on foreign territory. The seminal modern statement of the doctrine was *Banco Nacional de Cuba v. Sabbatino*, 376 U.S. 398 (1964), where the Supreme Court refused to consider the validity of a Cuban expropriation of sugar, owned by a foreign party, within Cuba. The Court held in *Sabbatino* that the act of state doctrine is a rule of federal common law that both state and federal courts are obliged to apply, notwithstanding contrary state law rules.

The act of state doctrine is subject to a variety of vaguely–defined exceptions and limitations.[25] First, the doctrine only applies when a U.S. court is asked to hold a foreign act of state invalid (or, perhaps, illegal), and not when a U.S. action merely involves inquiry into the motives of foreign acts of state. (*W.S. Kirkpatrick & Co. v. Environmental Tectonics Corp.*, 110 S.Ct. 701 (1990).)

Second, a divided Supreme Court has suggested (but not held) that a formal letter from the Department of State (a "Bernstein letter") stating that the act of state doctrine should not be applied will render the doctrine inapplicable. (*First National City Bank v. Banco Nacional de Cuba*, 406 U.S. 759 (1972).) Lower courts are divided as to the status of the so–called Bernstein exception. In litigation where the amount in dispute warrants the effort, and where the act of state doctrine is arguably applicable, counsel should consider the advisability of attempting to obtain a Bernstein letter (or prevent the obtaining of a Bernstein letter) from the Department of State.

Third, a divided Supreme Court has also suggested (but again not held) that the act of state doctrine does not apply to purely commercial conduct of foreign states. (*Alfred Dunhill of London Inc. v. Republic of Cuba*, 425 U.S. 682 (1976).)

Fourth, the act of state doctrine only applies to acts of state that are made on the territory of the foreign state whose act is at issue. This "situs" requirement has produced difficult questions in cases involving intangible property rights.

Fifth, the act of state doctrine is generally held to apply only in the absence of a treaty obligation. Lower courts have generally refused to apply the doctrine if the act of the foreign state violates its treaty obligations to the United States.[26]

Sixth, Congress has partially repealed or overridden the act of state doctrine in the Second Hickenlooper Amendment. 22 U.S.C. § 2370(e)(1)–(2). The Amendment makes the act of state doctrine inapplicable where a foreign state expropriates property of U.S. nationals in violation of international law.

G.   *Applicable Law*

1.   **Extraterritorial Application of Federal Statutes**

Federal regulatory regimes play an important role in many international commercial disputes. This is particularly true of the antitrust and securities laws, RICO, and federal civil rights legislation.

Where a federal statute expressly applies to conduct occurring outside U.S. territory, U.S. courts will apply the statute as drafted. It is possible that due process objections could be raised to legislative efforts to regulate conduct having no contacts with the United States, but there is no meaningful precedent on the possibility.

Where a federal statute is silent as to its extraterritorial application, U.S. courts apply a so–called "territoriality presumption." (*See EEOC v. Aramco*, 111 S.Ct. 1227 (1991).) This presumption holds that no extraterritorial application will be inferred unless Congress has expressly and affirmatively stated that federal legislation is applicable to conduct occurring outside the United States.

U.S. courts have nevertheless applied both the federal antitrust and federal securities laws extraterritorially. The precise standards for extraterritorial application vary from statute to statute, but in general federal legislation will be applied to conduct outside the United States that has sufficiently direct and foreseeable consequences in the United States.[27]

2. Choice of Law

The choice of applicable law in U.S. courts is generally (but not exclusively) a matter of state choice–of–law rules. (*Klaxon Co. v. Stentor Elec. Mfg. Co.*, 313 U.S. 487 (1941); *Day & Zimmerman, Inc. v. Challoner*, 423 U.S. 3 (1975).) Federal common law choice–of–law rules have been applied in a few contexts, for example, under the FSIA (by some courts) and under other federal regulatory regimes.

Different states have adopted different choice of law rules. Some states adhere to the strictly territorial rules of the *Restatement (First) Conflict of Laws*; others have adopted the "most significant contacts" analysis of the *Restatement (Second) Conflict of Laws*; while yet other jurisdictions have adopted variations of contemporary academic "interest analysis."[28]

H. *Enforcement of Foreign Judgments*

The recognition and enforcement of foreign judgments in the United States is generally governed by state law. About 20 states have enacted some version of the Uniform Foreign Money Judgments Recognition Act (the "UFMJRA") (reproduced in 13 *Uniform Laws Ann.* 263 (1980)). The remaining states generally have adopted a common law approach, based upon principles of international comity, to the recognition and enforcement of foreign judgments.

Under both common law and the UFMJRA, U.S. courts will presumptively give effect to final civil judgments of foreign courts. (*Hilton v. Guyot*, 159 U.S. 113 (1895); *Restatement (Second) Conflict of Laws* § 98 (1971).) This presumptive validity is subject to a number of significant exceptions, which vary according to state law. (*See* UFMJRA §4; *Restatement (Third) Foreign Relations Law of the United States* § 482.) (*See also* Chapter 21, *Creditors' Rights and Bankruptcy*.)[29]

III. SOURCES OF ASSISTANCE

A. *U.S. Statutes, Regulations and Case Law*

Most international law statutes and cases are accessible through generally available research sources, including West reporters, WESTLAW, LEXIS-NEXIS, United States Code and U.S.C.A.

B. Foreign Statutes and Laws

B. RISTAU, INTERNATIONAL JUDICIAL ASSISTANCE (1990) (foreign statutes relating to service and discovery).

U.S. Department of State, Office of American Citizens Services, Room 4711, Washington D.C., telephone: 202–647–5226.

Szalidits, *Foreign Law in English*, 34 AM. J. COMP. L. 180 (1986).

C. Treaties

Convention on the Service Abroad of Judicial and Extrajudicial Documents in Civil or Commercial Matters, *done* at The Hague November 15, 1965; *entered into force* February 10, 1969; 20 U.S.T. 361; 658 U.N.T.S. 163.

Convention on the Taking of Evidence Abroad in Civil or Commercial Matters, *done* at The Hague March 18, 1970; *entered into force* October 7, 1972; 23 U.S.T. 2555; 847 U.N.T.S. 231.

Inter–American Convention on Letters Rogatory, *done* at Panama City January 30, 1975, OAS Treaty Series No. 43; *reprinted in* 14 I.L.M. 329 (1975); Additional Protocol, *done* at Montevideo May 8, 1979, OAS Treaty Series No. 56, *reprinted in* 18 I.L.M. 1238 (1979). Both entered into force for the United States July 28, 1988.

U.S. DEPARTMENT OF STATE, UNITED STATES TREATIES AND OTHER INTERNATIONAL AGREEMENTS (ANNUAL).

WESTLAW (USTREATIES) AND LEXIS–NEXIS (INTLAW/USTRTY).

D. Secondary Sources

G. BORN & D. WESTIN, INTERNATIONAL CIVIL LITIGATION IN UNITED STATES COURTS (2d ed. 1992).

G. BORN, INTERNATIONAL COMMERCIAL ARBITRATION IN THE UNITED STATES (1994).

A. LOWENFELD, INTERNATIONAL LITIGATION AND ARBITRATION (1993).

B. RISTAU, INTERNATIONAL JUDICIAL ASSISTANCE (1990, 2 Vols.).

AMERICAN LAW INSTITUTE, RESTATEMENT (THIRD) FOREIGN RELATIONS LAW OF THE UNITED STATES (1986).

AMERICAN LAW INSTITUTE, RESTATEMENT (SECOND) CONFLICT OF LAWS (1971 AND 1986 REV.).

CASAD, JURISDICTION IN CIVIL ACTIONS (1991).

WILLIAM W. PARK, INTERNATIONAL FORUM SELECTION (1995).

VED P. NANDA & DAVID K. PANSIUS, LITIGATION OF INTERNATIONAL DISPUTES IN U.S. COURTS (LOOSELEAF, 1995).

ENFORCEMENT OF FOREIGN MONEY JUDGMENTS ABROAD (LOOSELEAF, Philip R. Weems ed. 1994, 2 Vols.).

ENFORCING FOREIGN JUDGMENTS IN THE UNITED STATES AND UNITED STATES JUDGMENTS ABROAD (Ronald Brand ed. 1992).

E.   *Periodicals*

The International Lawyer (American Bar Association, Section of International Law and Practice).

American Journal of Comparative Law.

International Legal Materials (American Society of International Law).

International & Comparative Law Quarterly.

ENDNOTES

1   This chapter draws from GARY BORN & DAVID WESTIN, INTERNATIONAL CIVIL LITIGATION IN UNITED STATES COURTS (2d ed. 1992) (hereafter "BORN & WESTIN").

2   The one exception concerns the enforcement of U.S. judgments in foreign courts.

3   Born & Vollmer, *The Effect of the Revised Federal Rules of Civil Procedure on Personal Jurisdiction, Service and Discovery in International Cases,* 150 F.R.D. 221 (1993).

4   *Done* at The Hague, November 15, 1965; *entered into force* February 10, 1969; 20 U.S.T. 361; 658 U.N.T.S. 163; *reprinted in* 28 U.S.C.A. Federal Rules of Civil Procedure Rule 4.

5   The reservations are reprinted at 28 U.S.C.A. Federal Rules of Civil Procedure 4, and are also available from the U.S. Department of State, Office of American Citizens Services (formerly, the Office of Consular Services), Room 4711, Washington, D.C. 20520 (telephone 202-647-5226). Advice on foreign law relating to service can be obtained from local counsel or, in summary and not always accurate fashion, from the Office of American Citizens Services.

6   *Done* at Panama City January 30, 1975, OAS Treaty Series No. 43, *reprinted in* 14 I.L.M. 329 (1975). Additional Protocol, *done* at Montivideo May 8, 1979, *reprinted in* 18 I.L.M. 1238 (1979). Both entered into force for the United States on July 28, 1988.

7   *Pizzabiocche v. Vinelli*, 772 F. Supp. 1245 (M.D. Fla. 1991).

8   *E.g., Grand Entertainment Group, Ltd v. Star Media Sales, Inc.*, 988 F.2d 476 (3d Cir. 1993) (interpreting old Rule 4(i)(A) to require compliance with foreign law regarding service from abroad).

9   *E.g., TAAG Linhas Aereas v. Transamerica Airlines, Inc.*, 915 F.2d 1351 (9th Cir. 1990).

10   E.g., N.Y. General Obligation Law § 5-1402 (Consol. 1978).

11   For a more detailed discussion, *see* BORN & WESTIN *at* 223-74.

12   *In re Air Crash Disaster Near New Orleans*, 821 F.2d 1147, 1154-59 (5th Cir. 1987), *reinstated in part*, 883 F.2d 17 (5th Cir. 1989); *Sibaja v. Dow Chemical Co.*, 757 F.2d 1215 (11th Cir.), *cert. denied*, 474 U.S. 948 (1985).

13   *See* BORN & WESTIN at 305-06 (citing authorities).

14   *Laker Airways v. Sabena, Belgian World Airlines*, 731 F.2d 909 (D.C. Cir. 1984).

15   For a more complete discussion, *see* BORN & WESTIN at 320-21.

16   *See, e.g., Republic of the Philippines v. Marcos*, 806 F.2d 334 (2d Cir. 1986).

17   *See* BORN & WESTIN at 542-56.

18   *E.g., Filartiga v. Peña-Irala*, 630 F.2d 876 (2d Cir. 1980).

19   *E.g., In re Uranium Antitrust Litigation*, 480 F. Supp. 1138 (N.D. Ill. 1979).

20   *See* RESTATEMENT (THIRD) FOREIGN RELATIONS LAW OF THE UNITED STATES § 442 (1986); *Reinsurance Co. of America v. Administratia Asigurarilor de Stat*, 902 F.2d 1275 (7th Cir. 1990).

21   BORN & WESTIN 360-66; B. RISTAU, I INTERNATIONAL JUDICIAL ASSISTANCE 76-91 (1990).

22   *E.g., Laker Airways v. Pan American World Airways*, 607 F. Supp. 324 (S.D.N.Y. 1985).

23   *Done* at The Hague March 18, 1970; *entered into force* October 7, 1972; 23 U.S.T. 2555; 847 U.N.T.S. 231; *reprinted in* 28 U.S.C.A. Federal Rules of Civil Procedure, Rule 26.

24   For more detailed discussion of the substantial case law under each of these provisions *see* J. DELLAPENNA, SUING FOREIGN GOVERNMENTS AND THEIR CORPORATIONS (1988); BORN & WESTIN at 449-540.

25   These exceptions are more fully discussed in BORN & WESTIN at 647-738.

26   *E.g., Kalamazoo Spice Extraction Co. v. Provisional Military Government of Socialist Ethiopia*, 729 F.2d 422 (6th Cir. 1984).

27   *See* RESTATEMENT (THIRD) FOREIGN RELATIONS LAW OF THE UNITED STATES § 403 (1986); BORN & WESTIN at 590-645.

28   *See* Smith, *Choice of Law in the United States*, 38 HASTINGS L. J. 1041 (1987); RESTATEMENT (SECOND) CONFLICT OF LAWS (1971).

29   *See also*, BORN & WESTIN at 767-69.

CHAPTER 19

INTERNATIONAL COMMERCIAL ARBITRATION

James H. Carter

I.   INTRODUCTION

Commercial arbitration is now the primary method of dispute resolution in international commerce. The main advantages of international arbitration over litigation are: (1) relatively greater predictability, since any dispute generally will be handled in a single place rather than by competing proceedings in two or more court systems and by arbitrators in whose selection the parties may participate; and (2) reasonable assurance that the decision will be enforceable, since there is an international treaty providing for enforceability of international arbitral awards in most countries of the world but no such agreement for court judgments. The process can be imperfect and complicated, but it is usually better than the alternatives.

In addition, parties increasingly include in their arbitration clause arrangements for formal negotiation and/or mediation as non–binding dispute resolution steps, to be followed by binding arbitration if the other methods fail. Such multi–step clauses are not yet the norm internationally but are worth consideration because mediation has a surprisingly high success rate.

II.   DRAFTING ARBITRATION CLAUSES

Arbitration clauses in international agreements can provide either for *administered* arbitration, with the assistance of an international arbitration organization, or *non-administered* arbitration before arbitrators selected by the parties (ad hoc) and without any administrative services. Administered arbitration offers the advantage of a "brand name" imprimatur on the award, which aids in its enforcement and therefore strengthens the likelihood that the award will be paid without need for judicial enforcement. On the other hand, an agency will charge administrative fees which might be avoided (at least in part) in non–administered arbitration.

The leading international arbitration organizations are: the International Chamber of Commerce's Court of International Arbitration ("ICC"), which is based in Paris but administers proceedings worldwide; the American Arbitration Association, which is based in New York but operates nationwide and, through cooperation arrangements with other institutions, internationally; and the London Court of International Arbitration, active in England and elsewhere, principally in or among Commonwealth countries. There are significant national arbitration organizations in a number of other countries, such as Sweden, Hong Kong and Austria, which entertain international cases to be heard there, and Switzerland is an important site for non–administered and many ICC arbitrations. Many arbitrations with Chinese parties also now occur in China under the rules of the China International Economic Trade Arbitration Commission.

International transactions sometimes involve governments or government–owned entities as parties, and they are regular arbitration participants. The International Centre for the Settlement of Investment Disputes ("ICSID") is a specialized arbitration organization, operated by the World Bank, for disputes arising from investment agreements between private investors and foreign governments. U.S. bilateral investment treaties with various countries commit their trading entities to arbitration of disputes with private parties, and the North American Free Trade Agreement contains similar provisions for investment disputes. The new European Energy Charter Treaty[1] also authorizes private parties to bring arbitrations against host governments for disputes arising out of energy–related investments.

All of the principal administering organizations now have generally similar rules and provide roughly equivalent types of services, although there are differences, and the agencies with greater experience generally are preferred. In the case of non–administered arbitration, it is usual for the clause to specify a governing set of rules, the most common of which is the United Nations Commission on International Trade Law ("UNCITRAL") Arbitration Rules. These rules specify, for example, how arbitrators will be selected and otherwise provide a framework to make sure that the arbitration will go forward.

The national laws of leading arbitration jurisdictions generally support arbitration and limit judicial intervention. Many of these laws are based on the UNCITRAL Model Law on International Commercial Arbitration. However, there are significant differences among national laws.

The most important factor in drafting an arbitration clause is to analyze the transaction and determine where it should be arbitrated. Consider, for example, the nationalities of the parties, the governing law of the contract and the principal language of the transaction. Where will the events that might likely to lead to a dispute occur? What would be the most likely place of enforcement? Such factors may incline the decision naturally toward a particular venue or limited set of venues. Once the governing law and language are identified and a logical site for the arbitration is chosen, the parties generally either designate the leading local arbitral organization or one of the internationally active organizations or select non-administered arbitration under the UNCITRAL or a similar set of rules.

Often parties will choose a venue in a country other than the home of either of the parties in order to assure neutrality. This is not, however, universally the case. It is very expensive to hold an arbitration in a "neutral" country far distant from both parties' home bases, and this is a particularly relevant consideration at the drafting stage for the party most likely to find itself in the position of the claimant if something goes wrong.

It also is important that the country selected as the site of the arbitration be a party to the U.N. Convention on the Recognition and Enforcement of Foreign Arbitral Awards (the "New York Convention").[2] More than 100 countries are now parties to this treaty, which obligates each of them to enforce an arbitral award rendered in another Convention country, subject only to specified defenses based on gross abuses of procedural rights or violation of public policy. A few South American countries not yet parties to the New York Convention are parties to the similar Inter-American Convention on International Commercial Arbitration,[3] which the U.S. has also ratified.

Arbitration clauses may be simple, and the rules of various organizations and the UNCITRAL Rules typically include examples of such "bare bones" clauses. These may, however, be altered or expanded. The scope of the clause may vary, for example, and drafters should determine whether they wish all matters that arise out of or relate to the contract to be subject to arbitration or whether they prefer that some matters be left for resolution in another way (for example, by expert evaluation). If the clause does not specify that disputes "relating to" the transaction are subject to arbitration, there is some risk that contract claims may be arbitrable but tort claims may not be. In addition to the scope and place of arbitration, a properly drafted clause should identify the language in which the arbitration is to be held and whether there will be a sole arbitrator or three arbitrators. In international matters, the norm is to select three arbitrators, with one named by each side and the third chosen by agreement or by the administering agency. All of the relevant rules discuss in detail how this is to be done. A sole arbitrator is cheaper, but parties often feel that a three-arbitrator tribunal gives them greater assurance that errors will be avoided.

Arbitration clauses also sometimes provide expressly for ancillary relief in the courts of any country having jurisdiction. This may be important because time usually passes while an arbitration tribunal is organized and before it is in a position to make binding preliminary decisions. Only courts are able to provide necessary emergency relief, such as attachment of funds, avoidance of the deterioration of merchandise or prevention of infringement of intellectual property rights. The laws of many countries acknowledge that parties are free to ask courts to act in aid of arbitration in these circumstances, but arbitration clauses often specify the availability of access to such relief to avoid confusion.

Parties may wish to exclude certain remedies, such as consequential or punitive damages, and to provide waivers of immunity when dealing with sovereign entities. For U.S. enforcement purposes, the arbitration clause usually specifies that judgment may be entered on the award by any court having jurisdiction.

Clauses for agreements involving more than two parties present special drafting problems and should be reviewed with a knowledgeable arbitration practitioner.

Arbitration clauses may include provisions for non–binding negotiation, mediation, conciliation or mini– trials, to be followed by a binding arbitration if the non–binding stage is unsuccessful. Various organizations estimate that from 60 to 85 percent of such non–binding procedures lead to settlement, but it is sometimes difficult to agree on such a procedure once a dispute has arisen. It may therefore be useful to provide for a non–binding alternative dispute resolution stage in the clause. On the other hand, time (and some expense, although not much) necessarily will be consumed by the non–binding ADR activity before the claiming party can move the dispute into binding arbitration. Some drafters therefore do not wish to tie themselves in advance to such a procedure in a situation where their client is likely to be the party seeking recovery of funds or enforcement of other rights in the event of a dispute.

III.   INTERNATIONAL ARBITRATION IN PRACTICE

International commercial arbitration typically involves an interplay between the law governing the transaction, the laws of the countries where parties are located and the law of the place where an arbitration will be held.

When a dispute arises, arbitration typically can be initiated with a relatively simple demand. However, under some rules a party initiating arbitration must designate its arbitrator at this point. In such a case, time will be consumed while the claimant selects an appropriate person. Although some administering authorities have procedures to expedite arbitrations in emergencies, normally a period of several weeks or even months will elapse while the respondent answers the arbitration demand and designates another arbitrator, following which the parties will seek to agree on a third arbitrator or proceed with the selection processes of an arbitration organization. Usually no one actually goes to the physical site of arbitration for quite some time.

Arbitration proceedings tend to be episodic rather than continuous in the manner of an American trial. The arbitration tribunal typically will meet with the parties' representatives at an early stage to learn about the case and set out a schedule. Usually there will be much less "discovery" than would be typical of a U.S. court proceeding. Documents will be exchanged, but they may be limited to those on which each side wishes to rely. There may be requests for production of other documents, and in unusual circumstances there may be depositions. The latter, however, are quite rare in international proceedings. If witnesses are to be heard, they normally are summoned before the tribunal. In practice, much of the case tends to be presented in written form, through detailed factual submissions and briefs or other materials discussing them. The arbitrators can study these matters separately without need to come together again until it is time to hear argument from the parties and hear witnesses on such matters as may be appropriate.

If the arbitration proceeding takes place in a common law country and under the chairmanship of a common law arbitrator, it normally will feature some live testimony with cross-examination. If it takes place in a civil law country and under the chairmanship of a civil law arbitrator, the hearing procedure may consist largely of dialogue between the arbitrators and counsel, with limited witness participation. If there are live witnesses, civil law arbitrators typically will take a more active role in questioning them than would be the case in common law proceedings, and there is likely to be only limited cross-examination. When the parties are from different systems and the arbitrators also represent separate legal traditions, some form of "blended" procedure is likely to be adopted.

At the end of the process, the arbitrators (or a majority of them) issue an award. The prevailing party may ask the court at the place of arbitration to give effect to the award by turning it into a local judgment, and the losing party may ask the court at that place to set the award aside on the basis of any irregularities under relevant law. Because of the New York Convention, however, it is not necessary to obtain any such local judicial imprimatur before proceeding to enforcement. Rather, the prevailing party may take the award to any Convention country where the loser's assets are to be found and ask a court there to enforce the award. Most awards that go to court are enforced, since the basis for resisting enforcement are quite limited. This is true, for example, in the United States.

International arbitration proceedings are not necessarily cheaper nor speedier than litigation. Arbitrators, unlike courts, must be paid by the parties. If there are three arbitrators, their schedules must be accommodated in arranging for hearings. It is therefore unusual for international commercial arbitrations to be concluded in less than a year.

IV.   SOURCES OF ASSISTANCE

A.   *Published Sources*

1.   **U.S. Statutes**

Federal Arbitration Act ("FAA"), 9 U.S.C. §§ 1 *et seq.*

State international arbitration statutes (may supplement the FAA for international transactions in areas not covered by federal statute but may not be inconsistent), *e.g.*, Cal. Div. Proc. Code §§ 1297.11–1297.432.

State domestic arbitration statutes (same), *e.g.*, N.Y. Civ. Prac. Law §§ 7501 *et seq.*

Foreign Sovereign Immunities Act of 1976, 28 U.S.C. §§ 1330, 1332(a)(2)–(4), 1391(f), 1441(d) and 1602–1611.

2. Foreign Statutes

Relevant statutes of the major nations are collected in Chapter IV of the American Arbitration Association's INTERNATIONAL ARBITRATION KIT (4th ed. 1993). More detailed country–by–country legal surveys appear in:

HANS SMIT & VRATISLAV PECHOTA, WORLD ARBITRATION REPORTER (1990).

INTERNATIONAL COUNCIL FOR COMMERCIAL ARBITRATION, INTERNATIONAL HANDBOOK ON COMMERCIAL ARBITRATION (Albert Jan van den Berg & Pieter Sanders eds., 1990).

3. Treaties

Convention on the Recognition and Enforcement of Foreign Arbitral Awards, 21 U.S.T. 2517, 330 U.N.T.S. 38 (1958), no. 4739, *reprinted in* INTERNATIONAL ARBITRATION KIT, *supra*, at 15.

Inter–American Convention on International Commercial Arbitration, OAS Treaty Series No. 42 (1975), *reprinted in* INTERNATIONAL ARBITRATION KIT, *supra*, at 63, *and* 14 I.L.M. 336 (1975).

4. Other Official Documents

UNCITRAL Arbitration Rules, G.A. Res. 31/98, *reprinted in* 15 I.L.M. 701 (1976).

UNCITRAL Model Law on International Commercial Arbitration, U.N. GAOR, 40th Sess., Supp. No. 17, Annex I, at 81–93, U.N. Doc. A/40/17 (1985), *reprinted in* 24 I.L.M. 1302 (1985).

5. Secondary Sources

a. Books

GARY B. BORN, INTERNATIONAL COMMERCIAL ARBITRATION IN THE UNITED STATES (1994).

W. LAURENCE CRAIG *et al.*, INTERNATIONAL CHAMBER OF COMMERCE ARBITRATION (2d ed. 1990).

ALAN REDFERN & MARTIN HUNTER, LAW AND PRACTICE OF INTERNATIONAL COMMERCIAL ARBITRATION (2d ed. 1991).

b. Periodicals

Arbitration International, affiliated with the London Court of International Arbitration.

The International Court of Arbitration Bulletin, affiliated with the ICC.

Journal of International Arbitration, published in Switzerland.

The American Review of International Arbitration, affiliated with the Parker School of Foreign and Comparative Law at Columbia University.

INTERNATIONAL COUNCIL FOR COMMERCIAL ARBITRATION, YEARBOOK OF COMMERCIAL ARBITRATION (A. van den Berg ed., annual).

c. Specific articles – drafting arbitration clauses

American Arbitration Association, *Drafting Dispute Resolution Clauses: A Practical Guide* (1993).

Ball, *Just Do It – Drafting the Arbitration Clause in an International Agreement*, 10(4) J. INT'L ARB. 29 (1993).

Blessing, *Drafting Arbitration Clauses*, WORLDWIDE FORUM ON THE ARBITRATION OF INTELLECTUAL PROPERTY DISPUTES 95 (World Intellectual Property Organization 1994).

Bond, *How to Draft an Arbitration Clause (Revisited)*, 7 ICSID REV.–FOR. INVEST. L.J. 153 (1992).

Delaume, *How to Draft an ICSID Arbitration Clause*, 7 ICSID REV.–FOR. INVEST. L.J. 168 (1992).

Hoellering, *How to Draft an AAA Arbitration Clause*, 7 ICSID REV.–FOR. INVEST. L.J. 141 (1992).

Hunter, *et al.*, THE FRESHFIELDS GUIDE TO ARBITRATION AND ADR CLAUSES IN INTERNATIONAL CONTRACTS (Kluwer 1993).

International Centre for Settlement of Investment Disputes, ICSID MODEL CLAUSES, Doc. ICSID/5/Rev. 2 (1993).

Murphy, *How to Draft a Transnational Arbitration Clause: The Four Languages of Charles V*, CORPORATE COUNSEL'S GUIDE TO INTERNATIONAL ALTERNATIVE DISPUTE RESOLUTION 3.001 (Business Laws, Inc. 1993).

B. *Institutional Assistance*

1. American Arbitration Association: 140 West 51st Street, New York, NY 10020–1203; telephone (212) 484–4000; fax (212) 765–4874.

2. U.S. Council for International Business (U.S. affiliate of ICC): 1212 Avenue of the Americas, New York, NY 10036–1689; telephone (212) 354–4480; fax (212) 575–0327.

3. London Court of International Arbitration: 12 Carthusian Street, London EC1M 6EB, England; telephone (011–44–171) 417–8228; fax (011–44–171) 417–8404.

4. International Chamber of Commerce: International Court of Arbitration, 38, Cours Albert 1er, 75008 Paris, France; telephone 33-1-49 532828 (fax 33-1-49-53-2833).

5. International Centre for Settlement of Investment Disputes, 1818 H Street, N.W., Washington, D.C. 20433; telephone (202) 477–1234.

ENDNOTES

1   *Done* at Lisbon, December 17, 1994, not yet in force. *Reprinted in* 34 I.L.M. 382 (1995).

2   *Done* at New York June 10, 1958; *entered into force* June 7, 1959; for the United States December 29, 1970; 21 U.S.T. 2517, 330 U.N.T.S. 38 (1958).

3   *Done* at Panama January 30, 1975; *entered into force* June 16, 1976; for the United States October 27, 1990; OAS, Treaty Series, No. 42, *reprinted in* 14 I.L.M. 336 (1975).

CHAPTER 20

CREDITORS' RIGHTS AND BANKRUPTCY

Don S. DeAmicis

I.   INTRODUCTION

International creditors' rights consist of rights and remedies available under applicable law to a creditor of one nation in the event a debtor of, or with assets in, another nation is unable or unwilling to pay a debt or satisfy an obligation. They are critical to a creditor seeking to use multiple legal systems to compel a debtor to pay a debt. The nature and scope of available rights and remedies are frequently delineated in a private agreement between the debtor and creditor, which may contain provisions dealing with the granting of security interests, choice of law, and choice of forum or arbitration. Remedies available to unsecured creditors to compel payment will differ greatly from remedies available to creditors who have been granted security for the payment obligation. A creditor will be required to commence a proceeding before a court or arbitration panel, or if the applicable law permits, to begin the process of realizing on the collateral without court involvement. Once a judgment or arbitral award is rendered, a creditor will still be confronted with the need to enforce the money judgment or arbitral award against the debtor or its assets, often in jurisdictions other than that of the court rendering judgment.

Bankruptcy is, in part, a specialized area of creditors' rights where a court is required to intervene because a debtor is insolvent and unable to pay its creditors. However, because bankruptcy is a collective action involving numerous creditors as well as employees, suppliers, government authorities and others with a stake in the debtor, it is often a more complex multidimensional proceeding than a creditor lawsuit. In an international bankruptcy, an insolvent debtor with assets and creditors located in more than one country either voluntarily (or as required by law) commences a bankruptcy proceeding or is forced into one by its creditors and thereby implicates the laws of at least two nations. With property, employees and creditors located in several nations, each nation has important concerns about the administration of the insolvent estate, the supervision of management of the debtor, the identification and allowance of creditor claims, and the distribution of assets according to certain priority rules.

The practice of international creditors' rights and bankruptcy routinely involves litigation or arbitration, and therefore it is essential that a legal adviser understand the legal framework and procedures under which international commercial litigation and arbitration are conducted. U.S. creditors seeking recovery of debts from foreign debtors are often confronted with complicated issues involving service of process abroad, as well as discovery and the taking of evidence abroad. A more detailed analysis of issues arising in the international litigation and arbitration contexts may be found in Chapter 18, *International Litigation* and Chapter 19, *International Commercial Arbitration*.

II.   SECURED AND UNSECURED CREDITORS

A.   *Secured Creditors*

The laws of each country where property is located will generally govern whether and how a creditor may obtain a security interest or mortgage in specified tangible or intangible assets or a guarantee of a debtor's obligations by a third party.[1] There are wide variations among countries on the precise type of property that can be used, the nature of the security interest that can be obtained by a creditor, and formalities required for validity and enforceability. The creation, perfection, and on-going maintenance of security interests will entail numerous costs, which may include filing fees, notarial fees and stamp taxes.

Virtually all countries permit business debts to be secured by a mortgage on real property, as well as by a security interest in personal property, although types of available personal property security interests vary greatly. A pledge of personal property is a customary form of security in personal property, and generally requires the creditor or its agent to take possession of the pledged property. Other types of security interests include conditional sales agreements, title retention agreements under which title remains with the seller of goods until the full purchase price has been paid, chattel mortgages, trust deeds, floating and fixed charges, leases and assignments of accounts receivable. The laws of most foreign countries are significantly less flexible than Article 9 of the Uniform Commercial Code in the U.S., which applies to security transactions without regard to form or the person who has title to the collateral. In many countries, security interests in accounts receivable are often quite cumbersome to perfect, and security interests in after-acquired property are not enforceable.

Formalities imposed by local law must be strictly observed for the mortgage or personal property security interest to be valid, and these often include specific content requirements, as well as requirements that documents be executed before a notary public and recorded with a real estate or commercial registry. There are usually no limitations on foreigners taking security, although some countries prohibit foreigners from owning certain real property (near country borders) or exercising control over certain companies (*e.g.*, broadcasting), and therefore enforcement of security interests in such assets will be problematic. In addition, exchange control regulations may subject enforcement of security interests by a foreign creditor to prior authorization or completion of certain formalities.

The remedies available to a creditor to enforce a mortgage or personal property security interest vary substantially among nations. In some jurisdictions, a creditor can undertake enforcement of its security interest without court or judicial involvement. A holder of a real estate mortgage may be able to exercise a power of sale or appoint a receiver without filing any court action. Similarly, a creditor with a personal property security interest may be entitled to take possession of the collateral and effect a sale, or appoint a receiver, over the debtor's assets. Many countries, however, require the institution of judicial proceedings by a creditor seeking to realize on its collateral, which lead to a public auction with the creditor receiving the cash proceeds. Before commencing a court action, a U.S. creditor should carefully consider the estimated time for recovery, anticipated costs and the need to post court bonds. Some countries require non-residents to post bonds sufficient to guarantee that the opposing party's court costs and attorney's fees are paid. (For a more detailed discussion of secured transactions, *see* Chapter 6, *Secured Transactions.*)

B.   *Unsecured Creditors*

An unsecured foreign creditor seeking repayment should avail itself of all out-of-court recovery possibilities because court proceedings are typically lengthy and costly. Judicial prejudgment remedies, such as attachments, garnishments, liens or injunctions, are often available to unsecured creditors seeking to compel payment of a debt. These remedies serve to prevent a debtor from disposing of assets during the proceeding. Many of these prejudgment remedies are available on an *ex parte* basis and their availability will often persuade the debtor to make payment.

If exercise of prejudgment remedies does not result in payment, an unsecured creditor will be forced to commence a court proceeding or seek the institution of a bankruptcy proceeding against the debtor. Different, and perhaps summary, procedures may apply depending on the type of instrument evidencing the debt.

C.   *Other Issues*

1.   **Attorneys' Fees**

Whether a successful creditor can recover attorneys' fees in a foreign proceeding will be determined by the foreign country law. Unlike the U.S., where attorney's fees are not typically recoverable unless specifically provided for by statute or pursuant to contract, many foreign countries provide that the prevailing party in a lawsuit must be paid its court costs and attorneys' fees.

2.   Currency Exchange

Creditors should evaluate whether a foreign court may render a judgment in a currency other than its local currency if the parties have specified the applicable currency by private contract. In addition, foreign exchange controls may prevent a creditor that is successful in enforcing its rights from remitting proceeds outside the foreign country.

3.   Personal Jurisdiction

A creditor, by commencing a lawsuit in a foreign country, will give the foreign court *in personam* jurisdiction over it. Possible counterclaims should be evaluated prior to commencing a foreign action.

III.   RECOGNITION AND ENFORCEMENT OF FOREIGN COUNTRY MONEY-JUDGMENTS

A.   *In the United States*

1.   Comity

There is no international treaty or federal legislation in the U.S. governing the recognition and enforcement of foreign judgments, and the matter typically is regulated under state law, subject to limitations imposed by the U.S. Constitution and international law. U.S. courts are generally thought to be receptive to recognizing foreign judgments, based on the principle of comity articulated by the Supreme Court in *Hilton v. Guyot*, 159 U.S. 113, 163–64 (1885):

> "Comity," in the legal sense, is neither a matter of absolute obligation, on the one hand, nor or mere courtesy and good will, upon the other. But it is the recognition which one nation allows within its territory to the legislative, executive or judicial acts of another nation, having due regard both to international duty and convenience, and to the rights of its own citizens or of other persons who are under the protection of its laws.

2.   Uniform Foreign Money–Judgments Recognition Act; Non–Uniform States

Approximately 20 states, including the major commercial states of California, New York and Texas, have adopted the Uniform Foreign Money-Judgments Recognition Act ("UFMJRA"), although some have done so with considerable variation and amendment.[2] The UFMJRA, which is limited to money judgments, codifies state rules establishing conditions for recognition and grounds for non-recognition of foreign money judgments that had long been applied by courts in the United States. The balance of the states are non-uniform states where the law on recognition and enforcement of foreign money judgments has not been codified, but rather has developed through decisions of state and federal courts applying state law. These non-uniform states typically apply factors comparable to those followed by uniform states. The *Restatement*, which sets forth the prevailing common and statutory law principles concerning the recognition and enforcement of foreign country judgments, closely parallels much of the UFMJRA. (*See Restatement (Third) of the Foreign Relations Law of the United States*, §§ 481, 482 (1987).)

The traditional rule in the U.S. is that recognition of a judgment is a pre-requisite to its enforcement. Accordingly, a creditor seeking to enforce a foreign judgment typically commences a new lawsuit for recognition in a U.S. court.

Under the UFMJRA and the *Restatement*, a court is required to deny recognition if:

(1) The judgment was rendered under a system which does not provide impartial tribunals or procedures compatible with the requirements of due process of law;
(2) The foreign court did not have personal jurisdiction over the defendant; or
(3) The foreign court did not have jurisdiction over the subject matter.

Courts in the United States have rarely denied recognition based on the first ground for mandatory non-recognition – that the rendering system's procedures were unfair or not compatible with due process. The second ground for mandatory non-recognition arises when the rendering court did not have personal jurisdiction over the defendant. The UFMJRA lists six factors through which personal jurisdiction can be established, including domicile, personal service, consent, voluntary appearance and substantial contacts. It further provides that other bases for jurisdiction may be recognized by the court. UFMJRA, § 5. The *Restatement* sets forth the same factors, but it includes additional grounds for a foreign court to assert personal jurisdiction. (*Restatement* § 482(1)(b).)

In addition to mandatory non-recognition, there are numerous other grounds a court may consider in determining whether or not to accord recognition: insufficient notice, judgment obtained by fraud, cause of action or judgment repugnant to public policy, the existence of conflicting judgments entitled to recognition, lack of finality of the judgment, proceedings contrary to agreement between parties regarding forum where dispute was to be settled, and inconvenient foreign forum. In some states, lack of reciprocity remains a ground for non-recognition. (*See generally*, UFMJRA Section 4(b)(1)–(6); *Restatement*, § 482.)

3.   Enforcement

The principal way of enforcing a foreign money judgment is to bring a new lawsuit based on the original foreign judgment, which results in a U.S. judgment that is then enforced under traditional procedures. It is unlikely in most states that a foreign country money judgment can be enforced under the provisions of the Uniform Enforcement of Foreign Judgments Act, 13 U.L.A. 173 (1964), by registering the foreign judgment without filing an action to obtain recognition.

4.   Currency Exchange

U.S. courts typically set the exchange rate for a foreign judgment as of the date of the U.S. judgment granting enforcement, although courts may set the exchange rate on the date of breach.

B.   In Foreign Countries

Recognition and enforcement of a U.S. judgment in a foreign country is determined by the foreign country's domestic law.[3] Although specific requirements will vary from country to country, many of the requirements for recognition and enforcement are virtually identical. Generally, a foreign court will enforce a judgment only if the court rendering the judgment gave the debtor proper notice and possessed jurisdiction over both the debtor and the subject matter. Foreign courts also will enforce only judgments that are final and comply with the public policy of the enforcing jurisdiction. These requirements are identical to those applied by U.S. courts. In addition, there is often a requirement that the country where the judgment was rendered grants reciprocity by recognizing judgments of the foreign country. To ensure recognition and enforcement, it is essential to comply with very technical procedural requirements dealing with the transmission of the judgment, signature authentication and notarization requirements, and translation of documents into the official language of the receiving country.

Foreign courts have refused to grant recognition and enforcement of U.S. judgments on several grounds. First, courts will deny recognition and enforcement where there was failure to serve the defendant in accordance with the laws of the foreign country. This problem has been ameliorated by the entry into force of the Hague Service Convention,[4] but remains a problem where a foreign nation is not a party to the Convention. Second, if the foreign court where enforcement is sought lacks jurisdiction over the defendant, it may refuse to enforce a money judgment. This is often an insurmountable difficulty when a defendant owns property in a country where enforcement is sought, but otherwise has no connection. Third, the exercise of long-arm jurisdiction by the U.S. court will lead a foreign court to deny enforcement if its policy is not to enforce a judgment against a national unless there is a clear indication that the national intended to submit to the rendering court's jurisdiction. Finally, some courts may determine that reciprocity does not exist due to the lack of uniformity among U.S. states regarding recognition and enforcement of foreign judgments. (For further discussion of these topics see Chapter 18, *International Litigation*.)

IV.   INTERNATIONAL BANKRUPTCY

No international consensus exists on the appropriate goals of bankruptcy. Although most countries agree in principle that when a debtor is liquidated there should be an equitable distribution of assets among creditors, fundamental differences remain regarding the avoidance of pre–bankruptcy transactions and the priority of creditors in distributions from insolvent estates. More significantly, the goal of enabling an insolvent debtor to reorganize itself, often against the wishes of its creditors, in an effort to preserve "going concern" value is still not widely accepted. Widely divergent economic and social values concerning a debtor are, in part, the cause of the conflict and inefficiencies in administration that characterize international bankruptcies. Major recent transnational insolvencies such as Maxwell Communications Corporation, Bank of Commerce and Credit International, and Olympia & York have highlighted many of the shortcomings of the existing system in dealing with complex multinational organizations with operations, assets, and creditors located in numerous countries. These problems arise because the credit, security and insolvency laws of nations often diverge widely, and because there exist no uniform rules of private international law applicable to transactional insolvencies. The fundamental issue that is confronted in every instance is which nation's laws and courts will be used to divide the assets of the debtor, or to decide whether, and on what terms, the debtor can reorganize.

A.   *U.S. Bankruptcy Proceedings Involving U.S. Debtors with Foreign Assets*

1.   Universal Jurisdiction

The U.S. Bankruptcy Code, 11 U.S.C. §§ 101–1330, purports to exercise exclusive jurisdiction over all property of the U.S. debtor located throughout the world. In theory, all domestic and foreign creditors of the U.S. debtor are stayed from further action against the debtor and its property during the pendency of the bankruptcy proceedings. The effectiveness of this claim of extraterritorial power in foreign countries where assets are located depends on the cooperation of foreign courts.

The basis for U.S. jurisdiction is the doctrine of "universality," which presumes full international effect of local bankruptcy adjudications and is supported by the goals of unifying the debtor's estate, treating creditors equally, and administering the bankruptcy efficiently. For many other countries, however, jurisdiction is based on the doctrine of "territoriality," which rejects any extraterritorial effect of bankruptcy adjudication and requires institution of bankruptcy proceedings in every jurisdiction where assets of the debtor are located. This doctrine is supported by goals of protection of local creditors, variations in bankruptcy laws of each jurisdiction, and simplicity and certainty of local proceedings.

Given the conflicting jurisdictional principles underlying legal systems, it is not surprising that U.S. bankruptcy courts are often unable to exercise their power extraterritorially. Several factors account for this phenomenon. First, lack of *in personam* jurisdiction over a non–U.S. creditor may prevent a U.S. court from enforcing its jurisdiction over the debtor's worldwide assets. This often occurs when foreign creditors seize foreign assets or continue to enforce judgments against the debtor in violation of the automatic stay. Second, foreign laws often permit a local insolvency proceeding to be instituted when assets are located in the jurisdiction, even when the principal site of the debtor's assets and operations is in the United States. These concurrent bankruptcies permit the courts of multiple countries to administer assets found within their jurisdictions. Finally, the universal jurisdiction asserted by the U.S. courts conflicts with notions of jurisdiction applied in other countries and is simply not recognized.

2. Protecting Foreign Assets

Legal proceedings by foreign creditors or by a U.S. debtor (or its representatives) with respect to foreign assets are often initiated in a foreign jurisdiction coincident with the filing of a bankruptcy petition in the U.S. The existence of the automatic stay normally prevents a U.S. creditor from commencing such proceedings due to the possibility of imposition of court sanctions. However, a foreign creditor with no substantial connection to the U.S. often has the ability under local law to commence a local bankruptcy proceeding and seize or attach assets without fear of sanction, and will do so if it believes such action will maximize its recovery.

A U.S. debtor must take prompt action if it is to protect its foreign assets. The precise procedures to be followed will differ from country to country. Foreign courts may recognize the authority of the U.S. bankruptcy representative and permit it to sue to recover assets in the foreign jurisdiction or to obtain discovery in aid of the administration of the estate. The U.S. representative may be able to petition foreign courts to commence a local bankruptcy proceeding, which may be ancillary to the main U.S. proceedings. The commencement of a local bankruptcy proceeding may benefit the U.S. debtor by bringing all of its local assets and creditors before the foreign court, and also may serve to invalidate existing attachments obtained by creditors. Concurrent bankruptcy proceedings also give rise to conflict–of–law issues, frequently with respect to the applicable law for use of avoiding powers. Given the prospect that foreign creditors may seize assets located abroad, U.S. debtors in Chapter 11 reorganization often seek "first day payment orders" from U.S. bankruptcy courts, permitting a debtor to pay off foreign creditors while domestic creditors remain unpaid. If a creditor has succeeded in receiving a distribution in a foreign proceeding, it is not entitled to receive a distribution in the U.S. bankruptcy proceedings until U.S. creditors have received an equivalent distribution. (*See* 11 U.S.C. § 508(a).)

B.   Foreign Bankruptcy Proceedings

1.   Nature of Relief Available

U.S. creditors are increasingly involved in the foreign bankruptcy proceedings of non-U.S. debtors. The local bankruptcy law will determine the rights available to the creditor and there are many variations in bankruptcy laws.[5] Virtually all bankruptcy systems provide that a debtor or creditor may seek to have the debtor declared bankrupt, which leads to liquidation of the debtor's business. Various countries also provide for a composition or amicable agreement where creditors waive a percentage of their claims and the debtor continues in business. Some countries also provide for a "suspension of payments," which involves a moratorium on payments to assist a debtor in temporary financial difficulty. The U.S. is unusual in permitting the debtor in a Chapter 11 reorganization proceeding a wide degree of latitude to seek to reorganize over the objections of secured creditors.

2.   Management of the Debtor's Business

Most foreign countries require the appointment by the court or the creditors of a trustee or administrator to manage or supervise the debtor's business. Legal systems differ significantly as to whether creditors are permitted to play a significant role in the bankruptcy administration.

3.   Personal Liability of Directors

Many foreign countries impose personal liability on directors of a debtor for actions taken that contributed to the debtor's insolvency or increased the loss to creditors. In cases where a multinational corporation is financially distressed, this often leads to tensions between the directors of a foreign subsidiary and the U.S. parent regarding the conduct of the subsidiary's business and finances.

4.   Rights of Secured Creditors

The rights of secured parties are often much stronger in foreign countries than they are in the U.S. Many foreign countries, for instance, permit a secured creditor to commence proceedings to realize upon its security, notwithstanding the commencement of a bankruptcy proceeding. Moreover, most foreign jurisdictions do not permit a secured creditor's collateral to be used to fund bankruptcy administration and reorganization expenses absent its consent. Creditors should also consider whether rights of set-off or recoupment exist which could improve their recovery.

5. Avoiding Pre–Bankruptcy Transactions

Most bankruptcy laws contain provisions directed at avoiding pre-bankruptcy transactions that involve fraudulent conveyances. A more contentious issue involves the ability of the debtor to recover from a creditor money that was paid on account of a valid antecedent debt. The U.S., in pursuing the goal of equality of treatment for creditors, has established time periods for the recovery of payments as preferences without regard to whether the transfer was fraudulent. Many other countries require that a debtor's intent to defraud other creditors be established prior to any recovery.

6. Priorities of Distribution

Each nation's bankruptcy code contains its own unique set of payment preferences and priorities for distributions made to creditors. The bankruptcy systems of virtually all countries, including major industrialized countries, grant a priority to creditors who possess a valid security interest in the debtor's property. In many countries, unlike the U.S., no automatic stay is applicable, and a secured creditor is permitted to proceed to foreclose on its collateral. Most nations will also grant a priority to unsecured claims arising from expenses of the administration of the bankruptcy proceeding, including fees of the trustee and professionals. However, priority schemes for distributions with respect to unsecured claims arising prior to the bankruptcy proceeding vary greatly among the following types of claims: employee and wage claims, retiree or social security claims, consumer claims, and tax and other governmental claims.

7. Filing a Claim

A U.S. creditor with a claim against a debtor in a foreign bankruptcy proceeding should ensure that it has complied with the formalities of the claims preparation and submission process. Unlike U.S. laws which establish a bar date after which claims submitted are disallowed, many foreign bankruptcy laws allow a claim to be filed at any time. Numerous countries do not require that notice of the bankruptcy proceeding be sent by mail to creditors, instead providing only for publication in an official publication.

C. Foreign Debtors with U.S. Assets — Section 304 of the U.S. Bankruptcy Code

The U.S. Bankruptcy Code provides a flexible statutory scheme to facilitate cooperation by U.S. courts in the bankruptcy of a foreign debtor with assets in the United States. Section 304 of the Bankruptcy Code authorizes a foreign representative of a foreign debtor appointed in a foreign proceeding to commence a case ancillary to the foreign proceeding in the U.S. bankruptcy courts. Its purpose is to provide a mechanism whereby the foreign representative can receive the aid of a U.S. court in a pending foreign insolvency proceeding which is governed by non–U.S. insolvency law. Section 305 authorizes a U.S. bankruptcy court to suspend or dismiss a U.S. bankruptcy proceeding in deference to a pending foreign insolvency proceeding. In addition to ancillary relief, a foreign representative of a foreign debtor may file an involuntary bankruptcy petition under Section 303(b)(4) and commence a plenary bankruptcy proceeding in the United States. Section 306 provides that the appearance of a foreign representative under Sections 303, 304, or 305 does not submit the foreign representative to U.S. jurisdiction for any other purpose.

1. Eligibility for Relief

Section 304 sets forth no specific eligibility requirements other than the limitation that only the foreign representative selected in the foreign insolvency proceeding may commence a Section 304 proceeding. There is no requirement that the foreign debtor be eligible to be a debtor in a plenary U.S. bankruptcy proceeding or that the foreign debtor have assets in the judicial district where the Section 304 petition is brought.

2. Relief Available Under Section 304

Relief under Section 304 is not automatic. A Section 304 ancillary proceeding is commenced with the filing of both a Section 304 petition and a complaint requesting the bankruptcy court to grant specified relief. A court is authorized, in its discretion and at the request of the foreign representative, to: (1) enjoin the commencement or continuation of actions against the non–U.S. debtor and its property; (2) order the turnover of property of the non–U.S. debtor to the foreign representative; and (3) order other appropriate relief. A Section 304 proceeding is an ancillary proceeding and, unlike a plenary bankruptcy proceeding, does not impose an automatic stay or create a bankruptcy estate.

The bankruptcy court in an ancillary proceeding commenced under Section 304 has the broad discretion to grant appropriate relief in near blank–check fashion. Relief may be granted to the foreign representative in aid of the foreign proceeding and to prevent individual U.S. creditors from seizing and realizing upon property belonging to creditors as a group. Foreign representatives have successfully used a Section 304 ancillary proceeding to obtain injunctive relief staying actions and judgments against the debtor and its U.S. property, the creation and enforcement of liens, and setoffs. Section 304 has also been used by foreign representatives to obtain property of the non–U.S. debtor located in the U.S., to challenge allegedly fraudulent or preferential transfers, and to pursue discovery. U.S. bankruptcy courts have refused to grant relief when it conflicts with other legal principles and could not be obtained in a plenary bankruptcy case, such as a request by a foreign representative to enjoin payment of a letter of credit or a request to enjoin forfeiture of assets to the U.S. pursuant to the Racketeer

Influenced and Corrupt Organizations Act. Courts will also refuse to issue an order compelling turnover of assets until there has been a preliminary determination of ownership rights under local law. (*In re Koreag, Controle et Revision S.A.*, 961 F.2d 341 (2d Cir.), *cert. denied*, 113 S.Ct. 188 (1992).)

3. Factors for Section 304 Relief

In determining whether or not to grant relief, Section 304(c) provides that a bankruptcy court is to be guided by what will best assure an economical and expeditious administration of the estate of the non–U.S. debtor, consistent with the following factors:

(1) just treatment of all holders of claims against or interests in the estate;

(2) protection of claim holders in the United States against prejudice and inconvenience in the processing of claims in such foreign proceeding;

(3) prevention of preferential or fraudulent dispositions of property of the estate;

(4) distribution of proceeds of the estate substantially in accordance with the order prescribed by the Bankruptcy Code;

(5) comity; and

(6) if appropriate, the provision of an opportunity for a fresh start for the individual whom the foreign proceeding concerns.

The breadth of these factors, ranging from protective provisions to comity, give U.S. bankruptcy courts a great measure of flexibility. Courts recognize that the non–U.S. insolvency law need not be identical to that of the U.S.; however, "it must be of a nature that it is not repugnant to the American laws and policies...." (*In re Gee*, 53 B.R. 891 (Bankr. S.D.N.Y. 1985).) A court is more likely to defer to the non–U.S. proceeding if the U.S. creditors are institutions and if it believes the non–U.S. court will treat U.S. creditors substantially as they would be treated in the U.S. However, there is still a great deal of debate regarding the proper weight to be accorded the various factors, and this issue is often a hotly contested matter in Section 304 proceedings.

4. Plenary Bankruptcy Proceeding Under Section 303(b)(4)

In addition to ancillary proceedings, a foreign representative may institute an involuntary U.S. bankruptcy case against its debtor under Section 303(b)(4) of the Bankruptcy Code. If the petition is granted, the foreign representative obtains the full relief available under U.S. bankruptcy law. The foreign debtor must meet certain eligibility requirements: It must have assets or a residence in the U.S. and cannot be a foreign bank or insurance company. Because the requirements for Section 304 relief are less stringent, a foreign representative may qualify for ancillary relief even though the debtor would not have been eligible for plenary relief.

V.   SOURCES OF ASSISTANCE

A.   *U.S. Statutes and Regulations*

Bankruptcy Code: 11 U.S.C. §§ 101 *et seq.*

Federal Rules of Bankruptcy Procedure.

Judiciary and Judicial Procedure – 28 U.S.C. §§ 157, 158, 455, 586, 959, 1334, 1408, 1409, 1410, 1411, 1412, 1452, 1927, 1930, 2075.

Uniform Foreign Money Judgments Recognition Act, 13 U.L.A. 261 (West 1962 & Supp. 1994).

B.   *Foreign Laws*

P. WOOD & P. TOTTY, BUTTERSWORTH'S INTERNATIONAL INSOLVENCY LAWS (1994) (contains English translations of laws of Belgium, France, Germany, Italy, Luxembourg, Netherlands, Switzerland, Japan, Spain).

C.   *Treaties*

Arbitration

Inter–American Convention on International Commercial Arbitration, Jan. 30, 1975, OAS Treaty Series No. 44, *reprinted in* 14 I.L.M. 328 (1975); *codified* at 9 U.S.C. § 301. Additional Protocol, May 24, 1984, OAS Treaty Series No. 65, *reprinted in* 24 I.L.M. 472 (1985).

Convention on the Recognition and Enforcement of Foreign Arbitral Awards, June 10, 1958, 21 U.S.T. 2517, T.I.A.S. No. 6997, 330 U.N.T.S. 3, *codified* at 9 U.S.C. § 201.

Judicial Procedure

Convention on the Service Abroad of Judicial and Extrajudicial Documents in Civil or Commercial Matters, *done* at The Hague, November 15,

1965, *entered into force*, February 10, 1969; 20 U.S.T. 361, T.I.A.S. 6638, 658 U.N.T.S. 163.

Convention on the Taking of Evidence Abroad in Civil or Commercial Matters, *done* at The Hague, March 18, 1970, *entered into force* October 7, 1972; 23 U.S.T. 2555, T.I.A.S. 7444; 87 U.N.T.S. 231.

Convention Abolishing the Requirement of Legalisation for Foreign Public Documents, *done* at The Hague, October 5, 1961, *entered into force* October 15, 1982; T.I.A.S. 10072; 527 U.N.T.S. 189.

Inter-American Convention on Letters Rogatory, *done* at Panama City Jan. 30, 1975, OAS Treaty Series No. 43; *reprinted in* 14 I.L.M. 329 (1975), *entered into force* for the U.S. July 28, 1988.

Additional Protocol to the Inter-American Convention on Letters Rogatory, *done* at Montevideo May 8, 1979, OAS Treaty Series No. 56, *reprinted in* 18 I.L.M. 1238 (1979), *entered into force* for the U.S. July 28, 1988.

Protocol on Uniformity of Powers of Attorney which Are to Be Utilized Abroad, April 16, 1942, 161 U.N.T.S. 229.

D. *Secondary Sources*

1. Books

AMERICAN LAW INSTITUTE, RESTATEMENT (THIRD) OF THE FOREIGN RELATIONS LAW OF THE UNITED STATES (1987).

AMERICAN BAR ASSOCIATION, NAT'L INST. ON MULTINATIONAL COMMERCIAL INSOLVENCY (1993).

CURRENT DEVELOPMENTS IN INTERNATIONAL AND COMPARATIVE CORPORATE INSOLVENCY LAW (J. Ziegel ed. 1994).

CURRENT ISSUES ON CROSS-BORDER INSOLVENCY AND REORGANIZATION (E. Leonard & C. Besant eds. 1994).

J. DALHUISEN, DALHUISEN ON INTERNATIONAL INSOLVENCY AND BANKRUPTCY (1984).

INSOLVENCY LAW: THEORY AND PRACTICE (H. Rajak ed. 1993).

INTERNATIONAL EXECUTION AGAINST JUDGMENT DEBTORS (D. Campbell ed. 1993).

INTERNATIONAL LOAN WORKOUTS AND BANKRUPTCIES (D. Gitlin & R. Mears eds. 1989).

2.   Bibliography

American Bar Ass'n, International Bankruptcy Subcommittee, Section of Business Law, *Bibliography of International Insolvency* (October 6, 1994).

3.   Periodicals

International Bar Association: Section on Business Law, *International Insolvency and Creditors' Rights Report, Newsletter of Committee J: Insolvency and Creditors' Rights.*

ENDNOTES

1   For a detailed country-by-country description of types of security interests available in foreign countries, and how they are created and enforced, see AMERICAN BAR ASSOCIATION NAT'L INSTITUTE ON MULTINATIONAL COMMERCIAL INSOLVENCY (1993) (twenty-three countries); INTERNATIONAL LOAN WORKOUTS AND BANKRUPTCIES (R. Gitlin & R. Mears eds., 1989) (fifteen countries).

2   Uniform Foreign Money-Judgments Recognition Act, §§ 1-9, 13 U.L.A. 261 (West 1962 & Supp. 1994). The following states have adopted the UFMJRA: Alaska, California, Colorado, Connecticut, Georgia, Idaho, Illinois, Iowa, Maryland, Massachusetts, Michigan, Minnesota, Missouri, New York, Ohio, Oklahoma, Oregon, Texas, Virginia and Washington.

3   For a detailed country-by-country analysis of the recognition and enforceability of U.S. judgments in foreign countries, see NATIONAL INSTITUTE, *supra* note 1, GITLIN & MEARS, *supra* note 1.

4   Convention on the Service Abroad of Judicial and Extrajudicial Documents in Civil or Commercial Matters, *done* at The Hague, November 15, 1965; *entered into force* February 10, 1969; 20 U.S.T. 361, T.I.A.S. 6638, 658 U.N.T.S. 163.

5   For English translations of the insolvency laws of Belgium, France, Germany, Italy, Luxembourg, Netherlands, Switzerland, Japan and Spain, see P. WOOD & P. TOTTY, BUTTERWORTH'S INTERNATIONAL INSOLVENCY LAWS (1994).

CHAPTER 21

FOREIGN INVESTMENT IN THE UNITED STATES

Steven B. Pfeiffer*

I.   INTRODUCTION

The United States has a long history of favoring foreign investment. In 1791 Alexander Hamilton expressed what would become the predominant, although not always universal, sentiment of the country:[1]

> [T]here may be persons disposed to look with a jeal-
> ous eye on the introduction of foreign Capital, as if it were an
> instrument to deprive our own citizens of the profits of our
> own industry; but, perhaps, there never could be a more
> unreasonable jealousy. Instead of being viewed as a rival, it
> ought to be considered as a most valuable auxiliary, conduc-
> ing to put in Motion a greater Quantity of productive labour,
> and a greater portion of useful enterprise, than could exist
> without it.

Despite this general perspective, the U.S., from time to time, has adopted legislation restricting or regulating foreign investment, usually in specific industries. Currently, the federal government limits or regulates foreign investment in the fields of communications, aviation, shipping, power generation, fishing, mineral leasing, and banking. The U.S. requires foreign parties investing in agricultural land or in U.S. companies to make reports to the federal government, and the executive branch is authorized to block acquisitions of U.S. businesses that threaten to impair national security. Individual states also restrict foreign investment in such areas as insurance, banking, and real estate.

The following is a summary of these restrictions and reporting requirements. Federal restrictions on foreign investment are discussed in section II; federal reporting requirements are listed in section III; and section IV is a brief discussion of state laws that can affect foreign investment. These restrictions and reporting requirements most frequently arise in the transactional context, when a foreign party acquires an interest in a business or assets located in the U.S. They can also be important, however, in a litigation context when, for example, a U.S. company seeks to prove that a foreign competitor is operating in the U.S. in violation of a particular regulation.

This chapter is not intended to provide a comprehensive treatment of all regulations that might apply to a particular foreign investment in the United States. Certain regulations and reporting requirements that might be imposed upon foreign investors or the officers and directors of companies investing in the U.S. are discussed elsewhere in this book (including antitrust, export control, immigration, securities, and tax requirements). In many instances, these substantive laws are significantly different from, and often more demanding than, those in the foreign investor's home jurisdiction. Other aspects of U.S. law, such as environmental statutes and regulations or the U.S. common law of products liability, are not directed toward foreign investors specifically but can have a significant, adverse impact on an acquisition by a foreign party or that party's ability to conduct business.

It is likely that U.S. regulation in these areas is more burdensome than the regulations in the foreign investor's home country, making it necessary on occasion to educate a foreign client to the risks of a proposed venture under U.S. law. In many cases, particularly those involving state law issues or relating to heavily regulated areas such as securities or banking, the practitioner should consult local counsel or a specialist in the field before advising a client.

II.   FEDERAL RESTRICTIONS ON FOREIGN INVESTMENT

A.   *General Limitations*

In considering any of the restrictions on foreign investment listed below or any other restrictions imposed in a specific case, a practitioner should consider, first, whether there are limitations on the government's authority to impose those restrictions. The government could be limited by the U.S. Constitution (*e.g.*, the equal protection clause of the 14th Amendment as applied to resident aliens) or by treaties or trade agreements between the U.S. and the country in which the foreign investor is domiciled. The North American Free Trade Agreement ("NAFTA"), for example, eliminates certain barriers to investment in the U.S., Canada, and Mexico by individuals and enterprises with substantial business activities in a NAFTA country and provides a dispute settlement mechanism by which issues involving NAFTA compliance can be arbitrated.

B.   *Communications*

Foreign investment in radio and television stations located in the U.S. and in the Communications Satellite Corporation is strictly limited by federal statute, and certain state and local restrictions limit foreign ownership of telephone and telegraph services.

1.   Radio and Broadcast Television

Under the Communications Act of 1934, ch. 652, 48 Stat. 1064 (codified as amended in scattered sections of 47 U.S.C.), foreign ownership, operation, or control of radio and broadcast television stations in the U.S. is restricted. The Communications Act requires any person transmitting communications by radio (which includes radio and television broadcasts) to obtain a license from the Federal Communications Commission (the "FCC"). Such licenses may be issued only to persons who are found by the FCC to be qualified and who are eligible for employment in the United States. Unless an exception is made by the FCC, these licenses may not be issued to: (i) a foreign government or its representative; (ii) an alien individual or foreign corporation; (iii) a corporation of which any officer or director is an alien or of which more than one-fifth of the stock is owned by aliens; or (iv) a corporation controlled by another corporation of which any officer or more than one-fourth of the directors are aliens or of which more than one-fourth of the stock is owned by aliens.

These restrictions were adopted in the protectionist atmosphere of the Great Depression and have been challenged recently. As a consequence, a relaxation of the restrictions is currently under consideration in Congress.

2.   COMSAT

In 1962 Congress authorized the formation of a private corporation, the Communications Satellite Corporation, or COMSAT, to establish a commercial communications satellite system. (*See* Communications Satellite Act of 1962, 47 U.S.C. §§ 701-757 (1988).) The legislation provides that COMSAT's directors and officers must be U.S. citizens. Not more than 20 percent of the shares of the portion of its stock held by parties other than common carriers may be held by the types of alien entities listed in the discussion of radio and television licenses above.

3.   Telephone and Telegraph

The federal government does not prohibit foreign ownership of wire communications. All parties (including foreign parties) are, however, prohibited from constructing, extending, acquiring, or operating any telecommunications line without obtaining a certificate from the FCC that confirms that public convenience and necessity require, or will require, the construction or operation of the line. There are also restrictions on the control and operation of telephone and telegraph services at the state and local level, including, in some states, prohibitions on ownership of local telephone and telegraph companies by persons who are not domiciled in the state.

C. *Aviation*

Under the Federal Aviation Act of 1958, Pub. L. No. 85–726, 72 Stat. 731 (codified as amended in scattered sections of 49 U.S.C.), foreign air carriers generally may not provide domestic air transportation in the U.S., but may, under permit from the Department of Transportation, operate international air routes that serve the U.S. The Federal Aviation Act limits foreign investment in aviation by restricting alien control or ownership of U.S. domestic air carriers. An air carrier may provide air transportation services to the public only if it possesses a valid certificate of public convenience and necessity, which may only be issued to "citizens" of the United States. For these purposes, a partnership qualifies as a U.S. citizen if all of its members are citizens. A corporation or association is a citizen if: (i) it is created or organized under the laws of the U.S., a state, or a territory or possession of the U.S.; (ii) its president is a citizen; (iii) at least two-thirds of its directors and managing officers are citizens; and (iv) at least 75 percent of its voting interest is owned or controlled by citizens.

Aircraft operating in the U.S. must generally be registered with the Federal Aviation Administration, and aircraft owned by parties who are not U.S. citizens are eligible for registration only under limited circumstances. An individual alien, for example, may register an aircraft only if he or she is a permanent resident of the U.S. A corporation not qualifying as a U.S. citizen under the requirements described in the previous paragraph may register an aircraft only if the corporation is lawfully organized and doing business under U.S. law and the aircraft is based and primarily used in the U.S.

Under federal regulations, noncitizens are allowed, however, to act as air freight forwarders and foreign charter operators.

D. *Fisheries and Maritime Industries*

1. **Fisheries**

The principal limitations on foreign investment in the U.S. fishing industry are the restrictions on foreign ownership of United States–flag vessels. Under the Magnuson Fishery Conservation and Management Act, 16 U.S.C. §§ 1801–1882 (1988 & Supp. V 1993), foreign vessels are not permitted to fish commercially within the boundaries of any state. Foreign vessels may fish within the Exclusive Economic Zone ("EEZ"), an area that is contiguous to the United States' territorial sea and extends two hundred miles from shore, but only upon issuance of a permit by the Secretary of Commerce. Foreign vessel fishing within the EEZ is subject to annual quotas, which reflect preferences for U.S. vessels.

A vessel may only be registered as a United States–flag vessel if it has not been registered under the laws of a foreign country and is owned by: (i) the U.S. or a U.S. state; (ii) an individual citizen of the U.S.; (iii) an association or similar entity in which all members are citizens of the U.S.; (iv) a partnership in which all general partners are citizens of the U.S. and a controlling interest in the partnership is owned by citizens of the U.S.; or (v) a corporation established under the laws of the U.S. or of a U.S. state, in which both the chief executive and the chairman of the board are citizens of the U.S. and no more of its directors are noncitizens than a minority of the number necessary to constitute a quorum.

A U.S. vessel may only engage in commercial fishing activities in the navigable waters of the United States or the EEZ upon receipt of a fisheries endorsement. In order to qualify for a fisheries endorsement, a vessel must meet the ownership requirements listed above and have been built in the U.S., unless subject to a limited exception. In addition, if a vessel seeking a fisheries endorsement is owned by a corporation, citizens of the U.S. must own a controlling interest in the corporation, including more than 50 percent of the stock and of the voting shares.

2. Maritime Industries

Federal maritime laws generally prohibit foreign vessels from transporting passengers or merchandise between points in the U.S. but allow them to participate in shipping operations conducted between the U.S. and foreign ports.

Under the Merchant Marine Act of 1920, ch. 250, 41 Stat. 988 (codified as amended in scattered sections of 46 U.S.C.), the shipping of cargo between points in the U.S. is generally limited to U.S.-flag vessels that are built in the U.S. and owned by U.S. citizens. A corporation, partnership, or association will only qualify as a citizen for these purposes if 75 percent of the entity is owned by U.S. citizens. In addition, a corporation will not qualify as a U.S. citizen unless: (i) its chief executive and chairman of the board are citizens of the U.S.; (ii) "no more of its directors than a minority of the number necessary to constitute a quorum are noncitizens"; and (iii) the corporation is organized under the laws of the U.S. or one of the states.

Federal law also provides that, with some exceptions, only U.S. vessels are eligible for certain federal assistance programs and that only U.S. vessels may engage in certain towing and salvage operations.

The Shipping Act of 1916, 46 U.S.C. app. §§ 801–842 (1988 & Supp. V 1993), prohibits the sale or transfer of U.S. vessels to noncitizens, absent approval by the Maritime Administration. It is equally unlawful to place a U.S. vessel under foreign registry or to operate the vessel under a foreign country's authority without the prior approval of the Maritime Administration.

E. Energy

The Atomic Energy Act of 1954, 42 U.S.C. §§ 2011–2286 (1988), requires that any facility utilizing or producing nuclear materials be licensed by the Nuclear Regulatory Commission and prohibits the issuance of such a license to an alien or any corporation owned, controlled, or dominated by an alien, foreign corporation, or foreign government. The Nuclear Regulatory Commission is also responsible for licensing all persons who transfer, deliver, receive possession of or title to, or import into or export from the U.S. nuclear source material, and is forbidden from licensing any party to take these actions upon a determination that it would be inimical to the common defense and security or the health and safety of the public to do so.

The Federal Energy Regulatory Commission is authorized by statute to issue licenses for constructing, operating, and maintaining dams and reservoirs for hydroelectric power generation. Similarly, the Geothermal Steam Act of 1970 authorizes the Secretary of the Interior to issue leases for developing geothermal steam resources on certain lands administered by the Department of the Interior or the Department of Agriculture. These licenses and leases may not be issued to foreign entities, but foreign parties are not prohibited from owning stock of U.S. corporations that hold them.

F.   *Mineral Leases*

Several federal statutes limit the ability of foreign parties to invest directly in mineral deposits on federal land. Section 1 of the Mining Law of 1872, 30 U.S.C. § 22 (1988), limits the exploration for mineral deposits on government-owned lands to U.S. citizens and those who have declared their intention to become citizens. The Mineral Leasing Act of 1920, Pub. L. No. 66-146, 41 Stat. 437 (codified as amended in scattered sections of 30 U.S.C.), authorizes the Secretary of the Interior to lease interests in deposits of coal, oil, oil shale, and gas, but prohibits the issuance of such leases to foreign parties. The Outer Continental Shelf Lands Act, 43 U.S.C. §§ 1331–1356 (1988 & Supp. V 1993), and regulations promulgated thereunder, 30 C.F.R. pt. 260 (1994), provide for comparable mineral leases in the subsoil and seabed of the outer continental shelf. These restrictions on ownership of mineral leases apply only to direct ownership by alien entities. A foreign party may hold such leases or other interests indirectly through a U.S. corporation. For a foreign party to qualify for such indirect ownership under the Minerals Leasing Act, however, that party's home country must provide similar mineral leasing privileges to U.S. citizens or corporations.

Also, some states, such as Alaska and California, limit the right of foreign parties to explore for and mine minerals on state-owned land.

G.   *Banking*

Banking is one of the most heavily regulated sectors of the U.S. economy for both domestic and foreign participants. Banks must comply with a complex array of sometimes overlapping federal and state statutes and regulations. At the federal level, banks are monitored by the Federal Reserve Board (the "FRB"), the Office of the Comptroller of the Currency (the "OCC"), and the Federal Deposit Insurance Corporation. Each state also has a banking superintendent to whom a bank chartered by that state must report.

Before engaging in the banking business in the U.S., a foreign entity must obtain approval from the FRB and a license from the appropriate regulatory agency (the OCC for national banks and for nationally chartered branches and agencies of foreign banks; the state superintendent of banking for state banks, branches, agencies, or representative offices). To obtain a license, a foreign investor is required to provide extensive information, including financial information and the names of its shareholders, directors, and officers. The application process includes an investigation of certain key individuals by regulatory and law enforcement agencies. Generally, the information included in a license application is available for public inspection.

The International Banking Act of 1978, Pub. L. No. 95–369, 92 Stat. 607 (codified as amended in scattered sections of 12 U.S.C.), establishes the principle of national treatment as the basis for the regulation of foreign banking activities in the U.S. Therefore, as a general rule, foreign banks operating in the U.S. are subject to the same restrictions and opportunities as domestic banks. After the failure of the Bank of Credit and Commerce International and the scandal involving improper lending practices at the Atlanta branch of Banca Nazionale del Lavoro, however, Congress enacted the Foreign Bank Supervision Enhancement Act of 1991, which expanded the authority of the FRB to regulate the activities of foreign banks in the U.S.[2] A foreign investor must now obtain approval from the FRB before opening a U.S. banking subsidiary, branch, agency, or commercial lending company. The FRB is prohibited from approving a license for such activities unless the foreign bank is "subject to comprehensive supervision or regulation on a consolidated basis by the appropriate authorities in its home country." The FRB also has broad authority to conduct examinations of the domestic banking operations of foreign banks, whether chartered by federal or state authorities. Each U.S. banking office of a foreign bank must now be examined on site every 12 months.

The federal government does not restrict foreign ownership or control of national banks but does require that all directors and CEOs of national banks be U.S. citizens and that a majority of the directors reside in the state where the bank is located or within 100 miles of the bank. The OCC has authority to waive the citizenship requirement for the CEO and a minority of the directors of a national bank that is a subsidiary or affiliate of a foreign bank. Some states prohibit and other states limit the foreign ownership of a bank organized under state law. States also have citizenship and residency requirements for directors of state chartered banks.

Banks operating in the U.S. until recently have been limited by state and federal law in their ability to conduct banking activities in more than one state. The Riegle–Neal Interstate Banking and Branching Efficiency Act of 1994, Pub. L. No. 103–328, 108 Stat. 2338, however, authorized the FRB to approve an acquisition by a Bank Holding Company ("BHC") of a bank located outside the BHC's home state regardless of state law, provided the BHC is adequately capitalized and managed. The Act authorizes the appropriate agencies to approve mergers between insured banks with different home states if the states involved have not prohibited interstate mergers. The Act also allows foreign banks, upon approval of the OCC and FRB, to establish, acquire, or operate branches to the same extent national or state banks are allowed to do so.

As a general rule, like domestic banks, foreign banks conducting banking activities in the U.S. are prohibited by the Glass–Steagall Act, 12 U.S.C. §§ 24 (Seventh), 78, 377, 378 (1988 & Supp. V 1993), from underwriting, selling, or distributing securities. There are exceptions to this rule, however, and limited involvement in securities underwriting is possible. This issue is also the subject of debate in the banking industry and the government, so it is possible that the ability of banks to conduct securities underwriting activities could be liberalized in the future.

H. *Real Property*

Although the primary restrictions on alien ownership of real property are found in state law, federal statutes restrict the ownership of land by persons from countries with which the U.S. is at war (Trading with the Enemy Act, 50 U.S.C. app. §§ 1–6, 7–39, 41–44 (1988)), and persons from countries subject to U.S. travel and trade restrictions. (See, e.g., Cuban Assets Control Regulations, 31 C.F.R. Part 515 (1994), Iranian Assets Control Regulations, 31 C.F.R. Part 535 (1994).) Also, alien individuals may not obtain grazing rights on public lands under the Taylor Grazing Act, 43 U.S.C. §§ 315 to 315n, 315o-1, 485, 1171 (1988), although foreign companies authorized to do business under the laws of the state in which the grazing rights would be exercised are eligible for such rights.

In summary, while it must be said the U.S. restricts foreign investment in certain areas, it should be apparent that these restrictions only cover limited segments of the economy. Also, in only a very few cases is the restriction an outright prohibition on foreign participation. Frequently, an investment can be made in a regulated industry by a foreign investor, provided the investment is made in a manner permitted by the relevant statutes and regulations.

III. FEDERAL REPORTING REQUIREMENTS

The following is a summary of federal reporting requirements that relate to foreign investment. As stated in the introduction, this discussion does not include reporting requirements of general application. For example, the premerger notification and waiting period requirements under the Hart-Scott-Rodino Antitrust Improvements Act of 1976 frequently affect foreign investments in the U.S., but these requirements apply to domestic as well as foreign concerns. (*See* Chapter 8, *International Antitrust*.)

A.   National Security Review: Exon-Florio

The Exon–Florio Amendment to the Defense Production Act of 1950, 50 U.S.C. app. § 2170 (1988 & Supp. V 1993), authorizes the President, following a review by the inter–agency Committee on Foreign Investment in the United States ("CFIUS"), to block an acquisition of a U.S. business by a foreign person if the acquisition threatens to impair the national security of the United States. CFIUS includes representatives from the State, Treasury, Defense, and Commerce Departments.

In most instances the filing of a report under Exon–Florio is technically voluntary. CFIUS can, however, compel disclosure of the terms of any trans-action under its subpoena power, and the President may block a transaction or order divestment after the fact, regardless of whether a notice was filed. Under the National Defense Authorization Act for Fiscal Year 1993, 50 U.S.C. app. § 2170a (Supp. V 1993), a filing is required before any entity controlled by a foreign government may acquire a U.S. company that is performing or has been awarded certain contracts with the Department of Defense or the Department of Energy. The filing may be made jointly by the foreign entity and the U.S. target company and may be made at any time. Also, a member of CFIUS may file "agency notice" if that member has reason to believe that an acquisition may have an adverse impact on national security.

Upon receipt of the notification, CFIUS must make a decision within 30 days whether to investigate the transaction further. CFIUS is required to advise the parties to an acquisition promptly of a determination not to investigate. This determination concludes action under the Exon–Florio Amendment. An investigation is mandatory in any case in which an entity controlled by or acting on behalf of a foreign government seeks to acquire a U.S. company and the transaction could affect U.S. national security. When CFIUS undertakes an investigation, it must be completed no later than 45 days after the decision to investigate is made, and the President must take action no later than 15 days after the completion of the investigation.

Certain acquisitions are exempt from filing, such as an acquisition of voting securities pursuant to a stock split or pro rata dividend or an acquisi-tion between two subsidiaries of the same parent entity. Also, any transaction not reasonably related to U.S. national security is exempt from filing. The statute and regulations do not define "national security," however, and the examples in the regulations are far from exhaustive. (The regulations only list the acquisition of a toy maker, a producer of food products, a hotel, a restau-rant, or a legal services firm as not threatening national security.) It is more useful to review the contents of voluntary notice (31 C.F.R. § 800.402) to get an idea of the types of factors CFIUS will find most important (e.g., acquisition of facilities that manufacture classified products, target companies having con-tracts with the Department of Defense, etc.). The CFIUS staff is also available to discuss specific cases and does not encourage filing if a case is not reason-ably related to national security.

Various foreign and domestic parties have expressed concern over the potential scope of Exon–Florio. In general, however, these concerns have not proved to be warranted. As of Spring 1995, 918 notifications had been submitted to CFIUS. Of these, only fifteen had been investigated. Five of those were withdrawn, ten were submitted to the President for decision, and in only one case was divestment ordered.

These statistics indicate that for the vast majority of transactions Exon–Florio should not be a significant hindrance. To some extent the statistics obscure, however, the full impact of Exon–Florio, particularly on acquisitions of defense contractors. For example, the statistics do not reflect potential foreign investment transactions that were abandoned because of Exon–Florio concerns prior to notification. Nor do they reflect the number of cases in which deals have been modified to satisfy government concerns. Nonetheless, it should be apparent that most acquisitions of U.S. businesses by foreign parties should not be significantly impeded by Exon–Florio.

B.   *Foreign Investment Surveys*

In the mid–1970s, a confluence of factors caused an unprecedented amount of foreign capital to be invested in the U.S., resulting in a general alarm that some of the country's finest assets were being acquired by foreign investors. As Congress attempted to respond to these concerns, it became apparent that the existing records of foreign investment were inadequate. To fill this information gap, Congress passed the International Investment and Trade in Services Survey Act of 1976, 22 U.S.C. §§ 3101–3108 (1988), which requires reporting of all investments in U.S. business enterprises by which a foreign person comes to own directly or indirectly 10 percent or more of the voting securities of any such enterprise.

The reporting requirements consist of: (i) initial investment reports required upon the acquisition of a U.S. business enterprise; (ii) quarterly reports; (iii) annual reports; and (iv) five-year benchmark surveys. All such reports must be filed with the Department of Commerce, Bureau of Economic Analysis.

1.   Initial Investment Reports

a.   Form BE–13

A Form BE–13 must be filed within 45 days after any investment in a U.S. business enterprise resulting in the foreign ownership of 10 percent or more of the voting interest in the enterprise. All ownership of real estate that is not for personal use must also be reported. The BE–13 must be filed by either the U.S. business enterprise in which a foreign person obtains 10 percent or more of the voting interest or the U.S. affiliate of a foreign person when it acquires a U.S. business enterprise.

A total exemption is available only for purchases of real estate exclusively for personal use. A partial exemption is available if: (i) the newly acquired or established U.S. business has total assets of $1 million or less and owns less than 200 acres of U.S. land; or (ii) an existing U.S. affiliate acquires and merges into its own operations a U.S. business or segment at a total acquisition cost of $1 million or less, provided the acquisition does not involve the purchase of 200 acres or more of U.S. land. To take advantage of either of these partial exemptions, a Supplement C, "Exemption Claim, Form BE-13," must be filed.

b.   Form BE-14

Form BE-14 applies to the same type of transaction as a BE-13 but must be filed by a U.S. person acting as an intermediary (such as a real estate broker, business broker, brokerage house, CPA, or attorney) in the transaction or a U.S. person who enters into a joint venture with a foreign person to create a U.S. business enterprise. This report must be filed no later than 45 days after the transaction.

Form BE-14 need not be filed if: (i) the U.S. intermediary knows that a Form BE-13 is being filed; (ii) the real estate is being acquired by the foreign person exclusively for personal use and not for profit-making purposes; or (iii) the business has total assets or the joint venture has a capitalization of $1 million or less and the enterprise owns less than 200 acres of U.S. land.

2.   Quarterly Report: Form BE-605

Form BE-605 is a quarterly update of the initial, annual, and five-year reports. This report is required for every U.S. business enterprise exceeding the $20 million exemption level discussed below, in which a foreign person had a direct or indirect ownership interest of at least 10 percent anytime during the quarter. The form must be filed within 30 days after the close of each calendar (or fiscal) quarter, except for the final quarter of the calendar (or fiscal) year, when reports should be filed within 45 days.

A complete report is not required if the foreign ownership is indirect and the U.S. affiliate has had no direct transactions with the foreign parent and has no accounts (debt balances) with the parent, provided the portion of the report form constituting a claim for exemption is filed. A U.S. affiliate is also exempt from filing a complete report if each of the following three items for the U.S. affiliate (not the foreign parent's share) is $20 million or less, either positive or negative: (i) total assets, (ii) annual sales or gross operating revenues, excluding sales taxes (not gross margin), and (iii) annual net income (loss) after provision for U.S. income taxes.

3.   Annual Report: Form BE-15

Form BE-15 must be filed each year if a foreign person owns or controls, directly or indirectly, 10 percent or more of the voting securities of a U.S. affiliate. The form is generally due on May 31, approximately 60 days after the form for a given year is distributed or made available. A U.S. affiliate classified as a bank is exempt from filing the BE–15. Also, a U.S. affiliate with (i) total assets, (ii) annual sales or gross operating revenues, excluding sales taxes, and (iii) annual net income after provision for U.S. income taxes, of $10 million or less is not required to file this form. The BE–15 is not required to be filed for a year covered by the BE–12 Benchmark Survey (*e.g.*, 1992, 1997, etc.).

4.   Five–Year Report: Form BE–12

This report must be filed by a U.S. affiliate if, at the end of a designated Benchmark Survey year, a foreign person directly or indirectly owns or controls 10 percent or more of the beneficial interest in the affiliate. This survey is conducted once every five years, the last Benchmark Survey year being 1992. A U.S. affiliate is exempt from filing a Benchmark Survey form if each of the following do not exceed $1 million: (i) total assets, (ii) sales, or gross operating revenues, excluding sales tax, and (iii) net income after provision for U.S. income taxes. If this exemption applies, a Form BE–12(X) (Claim for Exemption) must be filed by the U.S. affiliate.

C.   *Banking*

A foreign bank holding company ("BHC") and any company controlling a BHC are required to make periodic reports to the Federal Reserve Board. These include semi–annual reports on financial transactions with affiliates (Form FR Y–8f) and annual reports that include financial statements of the foreign bank and related U.S. nonbanking companies and information regarding shareholders, directors, and officers (Form FR Y–7). These reports are generally available to the public. Foreign banks are also required to file an annual report (Form FR 2068) that includes the foreign holdings of the bank and certain financial information related thereto. This form is not available to the public.

D.   *Agricultural Land*

Pursuant to the Agricultural Foreign Investment Disclosure Act of 1978, 7 U.S.C. §§ 3501–3508 (1994), Form CFSA–153 must be filed upon the acquisition or transfer of any interest in U.S. agricultural land by a foreign person. The term "foreign person" includes all foreign entities and U.S. corporations in which a foreign person or group of related foreign persons has a 10 percent or greater interest or in which unrelated foreign persons hold interests aggregating 50 percent or more.

Form CFSA–153 must be filed with the county office of the Agricultural Stabilization and Conservation Service within 90 days after the acquisition or disposition of agricultural land by a foreign person. These reports are open to public inspection.

For purposes of Form CFSA–153, the term *"any interest"* does not include: (i) security interests; (ii) leaseholds of less than 10 years; (iii) contingent future interests; (iv) noncontingent future interests that do not become possessory upon the termination of the present possessory estate; (v) surface or subsurface easements unrelated to agricultural production; or (vi) an interest in mineral rights. The term *"agricultural land"* does not include land of less than 10 acres with annual gross receipts from the sale of farm, ranch, forestry, or timber products of $1,000 or less.

IV.   STATE LAWS

In addition to the federal requirements discussed above, a foreign investor may be subject to state and local government reporting requirements and other regulations. Distinctions exist from state to state, making it impractical to describe all of the potential requirements here. The following is a discussion of the reports and filings that typically may be required.

A.   *Qualification to Do Business*

A company that conducts business in any state other than the state in which it is incorporated generally must "qualify" with the Secretary of State (or equivalent officer) of the other state by filing the appropriate forms and paying annual fees. Companies failing to qualify are typically precluded from enforcing contracts in the courts of the state.

B.   *Inheritance by Foreign Persons*

A nonresident alien investing in the U.S. might want to consider his or her ability to bequeath or devise the investment to a foreign person through a will. Under the law of several states if a local court determines that the country in which the legatee or devisee is domiciled would deprive him or her of the bequest or devise (*e.g.*, if it is a communist country), or if the country would not allow a U.S. person to receive property bequeathed or devised by a domiciliary of that country, the grant will not be honored.

C.   *State Insurance Laws*

The sale of insurance and the ownership of insurance companies are governed by state law. Each state requires licensing of an insurer by the state insurance commission, and such licensing depends on the insurer's ability to meet rigorous financial requirements, including, in some cases, contributions to funds designed to ensure that policy holders' claims are satisfied. The financial requirements imposed upon a foreign insurer in some cases exceed the requirements for in-state companies. Many states require notice to, and approval from, the state insurance commissioner prior to acquisition of control over a local insurance company by a foreign entity. Some states restrict such acquisitions if the acquiring party is controlled by a foreign government.

D.   Ownership of Land

Many states restrict foreign ownership of land, and some require that such ownership be reported to the state. As with other state laws, this ownership restriction varies significantly from state to state. Some states, for example, restrict ownership of land by "enemy" aliens, while others allow ownership of land by aliens but limit the acreage that can be owned. Some focus on agricultural land, while others restrict only the acquisition of state-owned land.

V.   SOURCES OF ASSISTANCE

A.   U.S. Statutes and Regulations

Agriculture: 7 U.S.C. §§ 3501–3508 (1994); 7 C.F.R. § 781 (1995).

Aviation: Federal Aviation Act of 1958, Pub. L. No. 85–726, 72 Stat. 731 (codified, *as amended*, in scattered sections of 49 U.S.C.); 14 C.F.R. §§ 211, 297, 380 (1995).

Banking: International Banking Act of 1978, Pub. L. No. 95–369, 92 Stat. 607 (codified, *as amended*, in scattered sections of 12 U.S.C.); Foreign Bank Supervision Enhancement Act, which consists of sections 201–215 of the Federal Deposit Insurance Corporation Improvement Act of 1991, Pub. L. No. 102–242, 105 Stat. 2236 (codified in scattered sections of 12 U.S.C.); Riegle–Neal Interstate Banking and Branching Efficiency Act of 1994, Pub. L. No. 103–328, 108 Stat. 2338; Glass–Steagall Act, 12 U.S.C. §§ 24 (Seventh), 78, 377, 378 (1988 & Supp. V 1993).

Communications: Communications Act of 1934, ch. 652, 48 Stat. 1064 (codified, *as amended*, in scattered sections of 47 U.S.C.); Communications Satellite Act of 1962, 47 U.S.C. §§ 701–757 (1988).

Energy: 42 U.S.C. § 2133 (1988) (atomic); Federal Power Act, 16 U.S.C. §§ 791–825 (1988); Department of Energy Organization Act, 42 U.S.C. §§ 7151(b), 7172(a) (1988) (hydroelectric); 30 U.S.C. §§ 1001–1027 (1988) (geothermal steam).

Fisheries: Magnuson Fishery Conservation and Management Act, 16 U.S.C. §§ 1801–1882 (1988 & Supp. V 1993); 46 U.S.C. §§ 12101–12108 (1988 & Supp. V 1993); 46 C.F.R. § 67.39 (1994).

Investment Surveys: International Investment and Trade in Services Survey Act of 1976, 22 U.S.C. § § 3101–3108 (1988); 15 C.F.R. §§ 806.1–.18 (1995). Some of the filing requirements are specified only on the Investment Survey forms themselves (*e.g,* Form BE-13, BE-14, etc.) These are available from the Bureau of Economic Analysis: (202) 606-5577.

Maritime: Merchant Marine Act of 1920, ch. 250, 41 Stat. 988 (codified, *as amended,* in scattered sections of 46 U.S.C.); Shipping Act of 1916, 46 U.S.C. app. §§ 801–842 (1988 & Supp. V 1993); Merchant Marine Act of 1936, ch. 858, 49 Stat. 1985 (codified, *as amended,* in scattered sections of 46 U.S.C.); 46 U.S.C. app. §§ 289, 316 (1988); 46 U.S.C. §§ 12101–12108 (1988 & Supp. V 1993); 46 C.F.R. § 221.11 (1994).

Minerals: Mining Law of 1872 §1, 30 U.S.C. § 22 (1988); Mineral Leasing Act of 1920, Pub. L. No. 66–146, 41 Stat. 437 (codified, *as amended,* in scattered sections of 30 U.S.C.); Outer Continental Shelf Lands Act, 43 U.S.C. §§ 1331–1356 (1988 & Supp. V 1993); 30 C.F.R. pt. 260 (1994).

National Security (Exon–Florio): 50 U.S.C. app. § 2170 (1988 & Supp. V 1993); 31 C.F.R. Part 800 (1994).

Real Property: Trading with the Enemy Act, 50 U.S.C. app. §§ 1–6, 739, 41–44 (1988); Taylor Grazing Act, 43 U.S.C. §§ 315 to 315n, 315o-1, 485, 1171 (1988); 31 C.F.R. Parts 515, 535 (1994).

B. Books

BUREAU OF NATIONAL AFFAIRS, FOREIGN INVESTMENT IN THE U.S. (John I. Forry ed., 3d ed. 1989).

EDWARD M. GRAHAM & PAUL R. KRUGMAN, FOREIGN DIRECT INVESTMENT IN THE UNITED STATES (2d ed. 1991).

MANUAL OF FOREIGN INVESTMENT IN THE UNITED STATES (J. Eugene Marans, *et al.* eds., 2d ed. 1993).

REVIEW OF FOREIGN ACQUISITIONS UNDER THE EXON–FLORIO PROVISION (Lawrence R. Fullerton, *et al.* eds., 1992).

C. Periodicals

Direct Investment in North America (Bureau of National Affairs).

D.   Articles

John Barrett, *Existing Legal Restrictions on Foreign Investment in Specific Industries*, in A.B.A. INSTITUTE ON FOREIGN DIRECT INVESTMENT IN THE UNITED STATES 21 (1988).

Patrick M. Norton, *Foreign Investment: Restrictions and Reporting Requirements*, in A.B.A. INSTITUTE ON COUNSELING FOREIGN–OWNED U.S. ENTERPRISES (1992).

Christopher F. Corr, *A Survey of United States Controls on Foreign Investment and Operations: How Much is Enough?* 9 AM. U.J. INT'L L. & POL'Y 417 (1994).

John A. Cottingham *et al.*, *Regulatory Hurdles to Foreign Direct Investment in the United States*, CURRENTS, Spring 1994, at 3.

E.   Institutional Assistance

Exon–Florio: Committee on Foreign Investment in the U.S.: (202) 622–1860.

Investment Surveys: Department of Commerce, Bureau of Economic Analysis: (202) 606–5577.

ENDNOTES

*The author wishes to thank his colleagues John A. Cottingham and John D. Taylor for their assistance in drafting this chapter.

1   Alexander Hamilton, *Report on Manufactures*, in THE REPORTS OF ALEXANDER HAMILTON 148 (JACOB E. COOKE ed. 1964).

2   The Foreign Bank Supervision Enhancement Act consists of sections 201–215 of the Federal Deposit Insurance Corporation Improvement Act of 1991, Pub. L. No. 102–242, 105 Stat. 2236 (codified in scattered sections of 12 U.S.C.).

CHAPTER 22

IMMIGRATION AND NATIONALITY

Angelo A. Paparelli and J. Ira Burkemper

I. INTRODUCTION

In serving individuals and entities with global business interests, the international lawyer will likely encounter a wide range of legal issues affected by the rapidly–changing immigration laws of the United States and foreign countries. Multinational corporations frequently transfer their managers, executives, and employees possessing specialized knowledge of the corporation's products or procedures to the United States for temporary assignments. When smaller businesses abroad wish to expand their markets to the United States, the international lawyer may be asked to assist in the establishment and staffing of a branch or subsidiary in this country. Immigration issues thus arise in the planning context, in the transactional context, and in the regulatory context (as approval or enforcement matters). They arise less frequently in the context of private disputes.

This chapter discusses immigration issues in these different contexts, with emphasis placed on the employment–based visa categories under U.S. law most often utilized by corporations engaged in the international transfer of personnel on a temporary and permanent basis. An overview of other visa categories available to aliens, for example, those based on family relationships or asylum, is beyond the scope of this chapter[1]; Section V, however, lists a number of sources of assistance for the interested practitioner.

II. U.S. IMMIGRATION LAW

A central theme throughout the history of employment–related U.S. immigration law is the conflict between promotion of U.S. business interests (both domestic and international) and protection of the domestic labor market. The framework of statutes and regulations governing employment–based visas attempts to strike a balance between these two goals. The challenge for the immigration lawyer is to accomplish the purposes of the international business client through (a) careful selection of the appropriate employment–based visa category, and (b) meticulous documentation demonstrating that the chosen employee and the sponsoring employer are each qualified for the desired visa category.

In recent years, Congress has enacted stringent employment verification and reporting requirements for alien employers and sanctions for failure to comply with those requirements and, in particular, for knowingly employing unauthorized aliens. Lawyers must be attentive to their clients' compliance with these laws. In corporate acquisitions, the purchaser can also succeed to the acquired company's liabilities in this area, and attention to compliance with these employment rules has, as a consequence, become an important aspect of due diligence.

Congress has delegated primary administrative and enforcement authority for the laws pertaining to U.S. immigration to three federal agencies: the Immigration and Naturalization Service ("INS"), the Department of State ("DOS"), and the Department of Labor ("DOL"). Other agencies, such as the U.S. Public Health Service, play more limited roles in immigration rule-making, administration, and enforcement. The visa categories regulated by these agencies are of two basic types: immigrant and non-immigrant.

III. EMPLOYMENT-BASED IMMIGRATION LAW IN THE UNITED STATES

Foreign nationals seek to enter the United States for a variety of business reasons. The lawyer's job is to determine the most appropriate strategy for obtaining authorization to enter the country, based on client needs and such business circumstances as cross-border ownership structures, market-expansion plans, and human-resource strategies.

U.S. immigration laws present the attorney with a wide variety of options that can be implemented concurrently or sequentially to achieve the client's objectives. However, practitioners should proceed with extreme caution in this area; immigration law in the United States is a maze of often confusing statutes, regulations, and agency operating instructions that must be integrated with other areas of the law, such as taxation, estate planning, export controls, and general employment law. For example, U.S. export control laws prohibit any release of technology to foreign nationals unless a general license authorizes the transfer or the company has obtained a specific license from the appropriate licensing agency. (*See* Chapter 13, *Export Controls, Sanctions and Antiboycott Laws*.) Permanent residents or foreign persons who are present for extended periods of time in the United States on a visitor or another nonimmigrant visa status may also be subject to U.S. tax laws as tax residents or domiciliaries. If the law classifies them as U.S. "tax residents" for U.S. income tax purposes, they will be taxed on their worldwide income in generally the same manner as are U.S. citizens. (*See* Chapter 10, *U.S. Taxation of International Transactions*.)

Frequent changes in immigration laws and procedures, and the overlapping jurisdiction of several federal agencies, require lawyers to commit substantial time maintaining the requisite level of knowledge and competence. The increasing complexity of this area of the law has led a number of states to create specialty certifications for practitioners with a documented measure of expertise in U.S. immigration law.

A. *Immigrant Visas*

U.S. immigration law includes five major categories ("preferences") of employment-based, numerically-limited immigrant visas. Beneficiaries of these visas are eligible for lawful permanent resident ("LPR") status in the United States.[2] The primary advantage of immigrant visas, as opposed to nonimmigrant visas, is that they have an unlimited validity period and can, therefore, lead to U.S. citizenship.

The first preference is reserved for "priority workers," a category that is subdivided to include: (1) aliens at the top of their field of endeavor who possess "extraordinary ability" and may be sponsored for this immigrant visa category by an employer or be self-sponsored; (2) outstanding professors and researchers in qualified academic or private institutions of research; and (3) certain multinational executives and managers who meet the requirements for intracompany transferees (discussed below in the L-1 visa category).

The second preference provides for admission of individuals holding advanced degrees (master's or higher) or. the equivalent (a baccalaureate and five years of progressively responsible work experience), or who, because of their "exceptional ability" (a less burdensome standard than the first-preference term "extraordinary") in the sciences, arts, or business, will substantially benefit the national economy, cultural or educational interests, or welfare of the United States. If admission of such an individual can be shown to be "in the national interest" (a concept of broad and flexible scope), the requirement of a sponsoring employer with an existing job offer may be waived; hence, this category likewise allows self-sponsorship.

The third preference is reserved for professionals who possess only baccalaureate degrees, and for skilled workers (those in jobs requiring at least two years' experience) and "other" (unskilled) workers who fill positions for which there is shown (by a process of government-monitored recruitment known as labor certification) to be a shortage of U.S. workers.

The fourth preference is available for certain "special immigrants," a miscellaneous provision covering such individuals as employees of international organizations and religious workers.

Finally, the fifth preference is for investors who will create a new business employing at least 10 U.S. workers through an investment of $1 million or more (or $500,000 if invested in a rural area or an area of high unemployment). This category – promulgated with much fanfare and designed to compete with investor-visa provisions in Australia and Canada – has proven to be an under-utilized disappointment because of its two-stage grant of permanent residence (spaced over a two-year period) and its burdensome documentary requirements (*e.g.*, copies of the applicant's last five years of world-wide tax returns and documents on any civil, administrative or criminal proceedings involving the applicant for the last 10 years).

B. *Nonimmigrant Visas*

There are currently over 40 classes of nonimmigrant visas available, four of which are used primarily in the employment context.

1. B–1 Visas

The nonimmigrant visa category most frequently used for commercial purposes is the B–1 (business visitor) category, used to gain entry for brief business trips, typically lasting less than three months. Citizens of many designated countries may enter the United States without a visa on B–1 business visits for less than 90 days.[3] This category offers the advantage of simplicity; no petition need be filed in advance with the INS, and there is no entanglement with the DOL (as occurs with other categories described below). But the B–1 category also carries with it certain disadvantages: The B–1 visitor (1) may not engage in prohibited forms of employment that compete with the domestic labor market; (2) may not receive a salary from any U.S. source (although U.S.-source reimbursement of reasonable and customary expenses is permitted); (3) may not remain for prolonged periods (initial entry is theoretically allowed for up to one year and extensions permitted in six-month increments); and (4) must prove to sometimes skeptical consular officers or INS inspectors that he or she will return to an unrelinquished foreign permanent residence when the temporary purpose of entry is concluded.

Three of the most common nonimmigrant visa categories to facilitate the entry of foreign workers into the United States for longer periods are the E, H–1B, and L–1 categories. Unlike the B–1 visa, these categories allow the employment of foreign workers in the United States and the payment of U.S.-source salary, and also allow the worker's spouse and minor children to accompany him or her to the United States and engage in study, volunteer activities, or recreation (but not in employment).

2. E Treaty Visas

Most of the Friendship, Commerce and Navigation Treaties and Bilateral Investment Treaties between the United States and other countries (*see* Chapter 1, *The International Practice of Law,* Sources of Assistance) confer on a foreign entity the authority to employ selected categories of personnel in its U.S. subsidiaries and affiliates. Congress has implemented this treaty right by enacting Section 101(a)(15)(E) of the Immigration and Nationality Act (INA), which allows the issuance of visas under one of two work–authorized classifications (E–1 Treaty *Trader* and E–2 Treaty *Investor*). E visas may be issued to nationals of a particular treaty country who are or will become owners or qualifying employees in a U.S.-based treaty enterprise.

E-1 treaty *trading* entities (or individual traders) must engage in trade conducted principally between the United States entity and the treaty country. E-2 treaty *investment* entities (or individual investors) must prove that an individual or entity possessing the nationality of a treaty country has invested or is in the active process of investing a substantial amount of capital in a U.S.-based commercial enterprise.

As authorized in regulations promulgated by the U.S. DOS, and more extensively described in the *Foreign Affairs Manual* ("*FAM*"), E-1 or E-2 visas may be issued to citizens of a treaty country who will be engaged at the U.S. treaty enterprise in positions that are (a) "executive" or "supervisory", or (b) "if... in a minor capacity," in a position requiring the visa applicant to possess special qualifications that make the services to be rendered "essential to the efficient operation of the business" (so-called "essential-skills" personnel).

The essential-skills subcategory is further divided into (a) individuals with technical or specialized skills required by the U.S. treaty enterprise for a prolonged, typically indefinite, period, and (b) subordinate personnel in the E-2 (but not E-1) category, such as highly trained technicians or start-up workers, who will train U.S. workers and then leave the United States within a relatively brief period, usually not more than one or two years after entry.

E-1 and E-2 visas are issued directly at U.S. embassies and consular posts outside the United States upon submission of: (a) satisfactory evidence of the required trading or investment activity by a qualifying treaty enterprise or individual; and (b) proof of the visa applicant's treaty nationality and personal qualifications for employment in the U.S. as an executive, a supervisor or a person with essential skills. Subject to rules of reciprocity involving the length of visa validity for Americans seeking employment in the treaty country, E visas are usually issued for multiple entry and are valid for up to five years. Since applicants for E visas need not prove that they possess an unrelinquished foreign residence, E visas are usually renewable indefinitely, and thus are typically considered long-term nonimmigrant visas.

3. H-1B Visas

The H-1B category is reserved for aliens who (1) enter the U.S. to perform services in a "specialty occupation," i.e., an occupation which requires the theoretical and practical application of a body of highly specialized knowledge, and for which attainment of a baccalaureate or higher degree (or its equivalent) is a minimum requirement for entry into the occupation in the United States, and (2) are qualified to perform services in the specialty occupation because they have attained a baccalaureate or higher degree, or its equivalent, in the specialty occupation. Common examples of specialty occupations include architects, engineers, and accountants, and professionals in the fields of mathematics, physical sciences, social sciences, computer sciences, education and the arts.

The primary appeal of H–1B classification is that aliens in this category need not possess any prior work experience. In addition, an H–1B visa may be granted for an initial three–year period, and an additional three–year extension in H–1B classification may be obtained.

In spite of these benefits, the H–1B visa has become a less attractive visa option in recent years due to a new requirement for the employer to apply to the DOL for certification of a Labor Condition Application ("LCA") prior to filing a petition with the INS for H–1B visa classification on behalf of the prospective foreign worker. In filing the LCA with the DOL, the employer must attest that for the entire period of authorized employment:

1.   The employer will pay all H–1B aliens at least the higher of:

   a. the *actual* wage level paid by the employer to all other individuals with similar experience and qualifications for the specific position in question; *or*

   b. the *prevailing* wage level for that specific occupational classification by all employers in the geographic area of intended employment;

2.   The employment of the H–1B alien will not adversely affect the working conditions of workers similarly employed in the area of intended employment (working conditions include hours, shifts, vacation periods, and fringe benefits);

3.   There was not a strike, lockout, or work stoppage in the course of a labor dispute in the relevant occupation at the place of employment on the date the LCA is signed and submitted. (Moreover, no H–1B worker may be employed if a strike or other labor action should arise in the future.); and

4.   Notice of the application was posted in two conspicuous locations in the employer's establishment (or was provided to a collective bargaining representative in the occupational classification in which the H–1B nonimmigrant will be employed) on or before the date the employer files the LCA with the DOL.

The employer must also satisfy public access requirements that it make available for public inspection certain documentation regarding the LCA. In addition, the employer must retain certain supporting documentation for inspection by DOL in the event of a complaint.

The employer's wage practices and LCA procedures may be investigated by the DOL on its own initiative or on the filing of a complaint by any aggrieved party. If a complaint is filed or if the DOL initiates its own inquiry, the DOL Wage and Hour Administrator will investigate and determine whether the employer failed to meet a condition specified in the LCA or misrepresented a material fact. In the event that the Administrator determines that the employer made a misrepresentation of a material fact in the application, or that the employer does not meet the applicable standard regarding each of the attestation elements, the Administrator may (1) impose a $1,000 fine per violation, (2) bar the employer from obtaining future immigrant and nonimmigrant work visas for a period of at least one year, and (3) order the employer to provide for payment of back wages.

4.   L–1 Visas

The L–1 visa category can be used to bring foreign employees into the United States by U.S. entities with a qualifying foreign parent, subsidiary, or affiliate. The INS L–1 regulations state that one entity must effectively control the other (typically through ownership of a 50% or greater interest), or a third entity must effectively control both of the affiliated entities. Unlike the E visa category, the L–1 visa holder need not be a citizen of the same country as the foreign entity.

An L–1 visa may be issued to an employee of the foreign entity who has been employed abroad (for a minimum of one year out of the three years immediately prior to entry into the United States) in an "executive", "managerial" or "specialized knowledge" position, and who is coming to the U.S. to work in one of these three types of positions. L–1 visas may be obtained on an individual basis, or on a "blanket" basis for those entities which are frequent users of the L–1 visa category. The blanket procedures allow an entity to make one application and receive approval for virtually all L–1 transferees over a three–year period.

The L–1 category is divided into two subcategories: L–1A visas are issued to qualified employees who will be working in executive or managerial capacities; L–1B visas are issued to those who will be working in a specialized knowledge capacity.

Recent changes in the law and regulations have expanded the definitions of executive and manager. "Executive capacity" now includes assignments within an organization in which the executive need not direct the organization as a whole, but may direct a major component or function of the organization. Similarly, "managerial capacity" includes assignments within an organization in which the employee primarily manages an essential function, or department or subdivision of the organization, notwithstanding that the individual does not directly manage people.

"Specialized knowledge" means special knowledge possessed by an individual of the petitioning organization's products, services, research, equipment, techniques, management, or other interests and its application in international markets, or an advanced level of knowledge or expertise in the organization's processes and procedures.

Both L–1A and L–1B visas may be issued for an initial three–year period, unless the U.S. entity is a "new office", i.e., has been open for less than one year. Extensions of stay may be granted, up to a maximum five–year stay in the L-1B category, and a seven-year stay in the L-1A category. In the case of a "new office," the initial period of authorized stay is one year, and at the end of this period additional information confirming the commercial viability of the U.S. entity must be provided in the documentation supporting the petition extension request.

In addition to the longer (seven-year) period allowed for the L-1A visa holder, a key benefit of obtaining an L-1A visa over the L-1B is that a determination of L-1A eligibility mirrors the determination of eligibility for the first preference priority workers immigrant visa category (discussed above). If permanent residency (i.e., obtaining the so-called "green card") is contemplated for the future, demonstrating a prior INS determination of L-1A nonimmigrant visa eligibility will aid in obtaining the immigrant visa and will obviate the need for labor certification.

C.   The Administrative Process of U.S. Immigration Laws

The agency charged with primary enforcement of U.S. immigration laws is the INS, which is a branch of the U.S. Department of Justice. The INS's operational programs are varied and include the following: border patrol to detect and prevent the smuggling and illegal entry of aliens into the United States; detention and deportation of aliens from the United States who are found to be deportable or excludable; inspections at land, sea, and air ports of entry; adjudications of petitions and applications for immigration benefits, including asylum; and dissemination of information regarding immigration laws and procedures. Most adverse decisions of the INS are appealable in accordance with the Administrative Procedures Act, INA and INS regulations.

IV.   IMMIGRATION LAWS OUTSIDE THE UNITED STATES

U.S. immigration laws and regulations, though labyrinthine in nature, provide a wide array of choices for multinational businesses that require the services of foreign workers. Recent developments in the U.S. Congress portend that the immigration laws will become more restrictive and challenging.

This same trend is apparent in developed and developing countries worldwide, as historic tensions between global trade-promotion and the parochial protection of domestic labor markets become ever more pronounced. A detailed discussion of the rapidly evolving business-related immigration laws of other nations is beyond the scope of this chapter (indeed, the topic, if treated comprehensively, would surpass the length of this book). The trend, however, is for other nations' immigration laws to mirror the general U.S. approach, with emphasis on the need to establish the anticipated economic contribution and credentials of the business- or work-visa applicant and his or her sponsoring employer.

Companies establishing a business or engaging in other business activity abroad that will be staffed at least in part by expatriates will need to understand the immigration law and regulations of the forum country. Limited sources of international immigration law are available and listed in the Sources of Assistance.

As global business expands and the transfer of skilled professionals over national boundaries inevitably increases in the months and years to come, the need for sophisticated legal advice on employment-based immigration law will likewise grow more pressing. Predictably, therefore, the lawyer specializing in immigration law (currently, a peculiarly U.S. phenomenon) will become a key participant in the cast of advisors to multinational businesses and global investors, even if the transactions in question have no U.S. component.

V.   SOURCES OF ASSISTANCE

A.   *Primary Sources*

1.   Statutory Materials

8 U.S.C.A., *Aliens and Nationality* (§§ 1–1434).

BENDER'S IMMIGRATION AND NATIONALITY PAMPHLET (1992).

FEDERAL IMMIGRATION LAWS & REGULATIONS (1995 ed.).

U.S. HOUSE OF REPRESENTATIVES, FEDERAL IMMIGRATION LAWS & REGULATIONS (1994 ed.) (Print Serial No. 2).

U.S. HOUSE OF REPRESENTATIVES, IMMIGRATION AND NATIONALITY ACT WITH AMENDMENTS AND NOTES ON RELATED LAWS (9th ed. 1992).

2.   Administrative Materials

Superintendent of Documents, Code of Federal Regulations (C.F.R.): Title 8, Aliens and Nationality (1994); Title 20, Employees' Benefits (1993); Title 22, Foreign Relations (1992); Title 28, Judicial Administration (1992); and Title 42, Public Health (1992).

IMMIGRATION AND NATURALIZATION SERVICE, INS OPERATIONS INSTRUCTIONS, REGULATIONS AND INTERPRETATIONS (1992).

STATE DEPARTMENT, FOREIGN AFFAIRS MANUAL (FAM), Vol. 9 – Visas (1987).

3. Legislative Materials

J. BAILY, LEGISLATIVE HISTORY OF IMMIGRATION AND NATIONALITY ACTS. LEGISLATIVE HISTORY AND RELATED DOCUMENTS (1977–1986).

B. *Essential Reference Materials*

BOUCHARD, IMMIGRATION LAW SERVICE (Phone: 800–323–1336) (Comprehensive eight–volume looseleaf treatise).

C. GORDON, S. MAILMAN & S. YALE-LOEHR, IMMIGRATION LAW & PROCEDURE (1995) (available as multi–volume set and CD–ROM) (highly recommended).

Interpreter Releases (Washington, D.C.: Federal Publications, Inc., weekly) (Phone: 615/377–3532; fax: 202/659–2233) (absolutely essential, highly recommended).

Immigration Briefings (Washington, D.C.: Federal Publications, Inc., monthly) (Phone: 615/377–3532; fax: 202/659–2233).

Immigration Resource Information Service ("IRIS") (Washington, D.C.: Federal Publications, Inc., a CD–ROM database which incorporates the two immediately preceding publications, the Kurzban book noted below, and other useful resource materials) (Phone: 615/377–3532; fax: 202/659–2233) (highly recommended).

Immigration Policy & Law (Alexandria, VA: Buraff Publications, weekly) (Phone: 800/333–1291; fax: 703/739–8505) (a useful newsletter).

C. *Treatises, Casebooks, and Other Resources*

FRAGOMEN, IMMIGRATION PROCEDURES HANDBOOK: A HOW-TO GUIDE FOR LEGAL AND BUSINESS PROFESSIONALS (1993).

ALEINIKOFF, IMMIGRATION PROCESS AND POLICY (2d ed. 1991).

GORDON, IMMIGRATION LAW AND PROCEDURE (revised ed. 1993).

KURZBAN, KURZBAN'S IMMIGRATION LAW SOURCEBOOK (1994).

MURPHY, 1993–94 IMMIGRATION AND NATIONALITY LAW HANDBOOK (1993).

PATEL, PATEL'S IMMIGRATION LAW DIGEST (1992).

STEEL, STEEL ON IMMIGRATION LAW (1992).

WEISSBRODT, IMMIGRATION LAW AND PROCEDURE IN A NUTSHELL (3rd ed. 1992).

D.   *Government Publications and Directories*

U.S. DEPARTMENT OF LABOR, BALCA DESKBOOK (2d ed.).

U.S. DEPARTMENT OF LABOR, DICTIONARY OF OCCUPATIONAL TITLES (4th ed. 1991).

U.S. DEPARTMENT OF LABOR, OCCUPATIONAL OUTLOOK HANDBOOK (1992/1993 ed.).

U.S. DEPARTMENT OF STATE, FOREIGN AFFAIRS MANUAL (Publication 2FAM –1).

IMMIGRATION AND NATURALIZATION SERVICE, HANDBOOK FOR EMPLOYERS (1991) (Publication M–274).

IMMIGRATION AND NATURALIZATION SERVICE, IMMIGRATION OFFICER'S FIELD MANUAL FOR EMPLOYER SANCTIONS (1988).

IMMIGRATION JUDGES' BENCHBOOK (1988).

E.   *Publications Dealing Primarily with Business and Employment-Based Immigration*

FRAGOMEN, IMMIGRATION LAW AND BUSINESS (1992).

GOLDBLUM, AILA'S LABOR DEPARTMENT DIRECTORY FOR IMMIGRATION LAWYERS (2d ed. 1994).

LAWLER, PROFESSIONALS: A MATTER OF DEGREE (1993).

SIMON, ECONOMIC CONSEQUENCES OF IMMIGRATION (1990).

STEEL, EMPLOYMENT–BASED IMMIGRATION: NEW LAW AND NEW STRATEGIES (1993).

UNDERSTANDING IMMIGRATION UNDER NAFTA (Washington, D.C.: Federal Publications Inc., 1994).

F.   Foreign Immigration Laws

CAMPBELL, INTERNATIONAL IMMIGRATION AND NATIONALITY LAW (1994).

MARTINDALE-HUBBELL LAW DIGEST, CANADIAN AND INTERNATIONAL LAW DIGEST (annual).

G.   Useful Addresses and Telephone Numbers

American Immigration Lawyers Association, 1400 I Street, N.W., Suite 1200, Washington, D.C., 20005, tel. (202) 371-9377.

Immigration and Naturalization Service, 425 I Street, N.W., Washington, D.C. 20536, tel. (202) 514-2000.

Department of State, Visa Office, 2401 E Street, N.W., Washington, D.C. 20522, tel. (202) 634-3600.

Department of Labor, 200 Constitution Avenue, N.W., Washington, D.C. 20522, tel. (202) 219-5000.

ENDNOTES

1   Immigration Reform and Control Act of 1986 ("IRCA"), Pub. L. No. 99-603, 100 Stat. 3359 (Nov. 6, 1986).
2   LPRs are also referred to as "Green Card" holders, although the card that evidences a foreign national's LPR status is no longer green.
3   According to the provisions of the Visa Waiver Pilot Program, persons from certain countries applying as visitors for business or pleasure for a period not in excess of 90 days with a nonrefundable ticket may enter the United States without a visa. INA § 217, 8 U.S.C. § 1187; 8 C.F.R. § 217; 22 C.F.R. § 41.2. At present, citizens of the following countries may utilize this program: Andorra, Austria, Belgium, Brunei, Denmark, Finland, France, Germany, Iceland, Italy, Ireland, Japan, Liechtenstein, Luxembourg, Monaco, Netherlands, New Zealand, Norway, San Marino, Spain, Sweden, Switzerland, and U.K. 8 C.F.R. §§ 212.1(i), 217. Ireland has been added as a probationary country under new procedures established by the Immigration and Nationality Technical Corrections Act of 1994. 8 C.F.R. § 217.5(a)(2).

CHAPTER 23

INTERNATIONAL LABOR AND EMPLOYMENT LAW

Donald C. Dowling, Jr.

Employment costs drive many foreign deals, and many other overseas ventures succeed or fail depending on how the parties handle employment considerations. The overseas workplace tends to be much more heavily regulated than is common under the U.S. "employment–at–will" regime. Even low–wage countries like Mexico impose onerous employment regulations that far surpass their U.S. counterparts; U.S. companies unaware of these laws sometimes see their wage savings disappear in compliance costs. Radical differences in employment laws can trip up the unwary U.S. international transactional lawyer, and can prove expensive to clients.

I.   INTRODUCTION

"International employment law," from a U.S. business's point of view, means the legal issues involved in employing people outside the U.S. International employment issues arise from the employment of expatriates (nationals of the employer's home state sent abroad), foreign country nationals (citizens of the foreign state in which the workers are employed), and third–country nationals (citizens of a country other than the employer's home nation and the place of employment). "International *labor* law" speaks specifically to labor union issues in the international context. To a U.S.–based business, international labor and employment law involves foreign regulations and practices, treaties, and U.S. laws with an extraterritorial reach. International labor and employment law arises in both the transactional and domestic contexts.

II.   FOREIGN LAW AND PRACTICE

The most important aspect of international labor and employment law is *foreign* employment law and practice – the local rules governing employment in a U.S. business's overseas workplaces.

A.   *Foreign Law*

U.S. employers often complain about burdensome domestic U.S. employment laws, and about high jury verdicts in U.S. discrimination cases. U.S. businesses and their lawyers are, therefore, often surprised to learn that foreign countries' employment laws tend to be radically more employer-restrictive than U.S. laws. Although U.S. *discrimination* laws are by far the most stringent, the U.S. leaves much of the rest of the employment relationship relatively unregulated. U.S. employment law chiefly protects specific groups of workers from discrimination; foreign countries' employment laws typically protect everybody.

In the U.S. we often hear about the erosion of the employment–at–will doctrine, but employment–at–will remains the starting point of U.S. non-union employment relationships. U.S. workers can still quit at any time and be fired at any time for any reason (other than for a discriminatory reason). The U.S. generally does not regulate non–discriminatory firings, no U.S. law requires severance pay, no U.S. law requires notice before individual termi-nations,[1] no U.S. law caps how many hours in general workers can work, and no U.S. law requires paid (or unpaid) vacations, paid sick leave, or paid maternity leave.

By contrast, other countries' laws deem employment to be "indefinite" or "unlimited." Millions of overseas employees have concrete, statutorily-mandated rights to generous pre–firing notice and severance pay. For exam-ple, a fired 35–year–old Spaniard with 15 years on the job is legally entitled to, on average, $56,000; a fired 45–year–old Italian with 20 years' service gets $130,000.[2] These figures are for *average* workers; severance costs for long–term, highly–compensated executives soar higher. And some foreign countries (*e.g.,* Belgium) require long notice periods before firings can be effective.

Foreign countries' extensive employment regulation goes beyond termi-nation protections. For example, many countries require long paid vacations (sometimes at premium pay) and impose caps on work hours above which overtime is flatly illegal. A European Union directive requires employers to provide at least 14 weeks *paid* maternity leave,[3] and most European countries go beyond this – Danish women get 28 weeks maternity leave paid at 90 percent of salary, and many countries require sick pay. Venezuelan women are entitled to 8 months' *paid* leave following births and adoptions, and Venezuela prohibits most discharges during pregnancy and for one year thereafter. Businesses in Venezuela with more than 20 employees even have to provide child care centers.[4] By contrast, the recently–enacted and widely-heralded U.S. "Family and Medical Leave Act" – which followed and was inspired by these other countries' more progressive laws – grants childbear-ing women only 12 weeks' *unpaid* leave, and has no childcare provisions.[5]

A U.S.–based business that sets up overseas operations must account for the heavy costs which foreign laws like these impose. For example, the pub-licity blitz surrounding the North American Free Trade Agreement ("NAFTA") included many citations to Mexico's low wages. A number of U.S. companies opened Mexican operations on the basis of these reports, only to learn that Mexico imposes hefty non-wage employment costs – including substantial Christmas bonuses, premium-pay vacations, and severance pay. Mexico's very constitution creates rights to employee profit participation (10 percent of corporate profits), paid maternity leave, and a right to strike without being replaced. And contrary to stateside myth, large companies' compliance rate with Mexican employment laws pushes 90 percent.[6] The fact that Mexican employees cost far more than their wage rates suggest has forced some U.S. companies to shut down their Mexican operations and return to the U.S.[7] A similar example is China, where wages may be low, but where government officials sometimes require foreign companies to hire several times more workers than they need.

B.   Individual Employment Contracts

In the U.S., typically only labor union members and top executives are parties to comprehensive written employment agreements that confer substantive benefits. But in civil law countries, individual workers hold written contractual documents spelling out startlingly-specific rights to employer-provided benefits and policies. For example, U.S.-based multinational law firms employ associate lawyers in the U.S. under oral terminable-at-will employment arrangements – but most of these firms' European office receptionists and secretaries hold binding written contracts guaranteeing employment with generous benefits. Foreign laws often require these written contracts, and they often prohibit employers from unilaterally changing terms in them.[8] Foreign laws also bind acquiring companies to their predecessors' labor and employment agreements.[9]

C.   Labor Unions

Only a little over 10 percent of the U.S. non-government workforce is unionized, which is one of the world's lowest unionization rates. U.S. businesses operating abroad therefore must be prepared for the statistical reality that they are far more likely to run into unions overseas. Companies in industries not typically unionized in the U.S., such as high technology, are often shocked when they meet union organizers abroad.

The good news is that in foreign countries the *effect* of having a union is less drastic than in the United States. Abroad, master multiemployer collective bargaining agreements often set wages for entire industries – for union and non-union shops alike. (The effect is analogous to a non-union U.S. construction company paying "prevailing wages" on a state job.) Therefore, union representation abroad can have little connection to a workplace's wage levels.

Foreign unions tend to be less adversarial than is traditional under the U.S. model; as a consequence, in the foreign workplace there is less of an "us-versus–them" mentality and more genuine cooperation. Conversely, foreign unions expect to play a broader role in determining management issues. Some nations, *e.g.*, Germany, have "worker participation" laws that require empowering employee representatives with a management voice.

Strikes abroad can be crippling. As AFL–CIO lobbyists in the U.S. have been stressing for years, foreign laws usually prohibit hiring strike replacements. Foreign unions seem to call more strikes, but often their walk–outs last just a day or a week. Yet, while foreign strikes tend not to rival the drawn out, violent disputes historically seen in the U.S., there have been prolonged and devastating labor stoppages abroad.

III. TREATIES AND THE INTERNATIONAL LABOR ORGANIZATION

A. *The EU, NAFTA, and Other Trade Blocs*

When the U.S. founding fathers drafted the U.S. Constitution, they realized they needed to cover "interstate commerce" – which is now understood to include interstate employment. *Not* to regulate interstate employment would have left the states free to compete against one another, impeding any true single market. The same philosophy applies to trade blocs among sovereign states. In fact, a real push is now afoot to harmonize labor standards in the global economy via multilateral trade agreements.[10]

The European Union treaty, for example, contains a chapter expressly on employment (in Euro–speak, "social") law, which allows for European-wide employment regulation,[11] and which expressly guarantees "that men and women should receive equal pay for equal work."[12] Most European Union employment law takes the form of "directives" that each member state incorporates through its domestic legislation.[13] For example, a U.S. company opening a factory in Greece, therefore, can focus on Greek employment law without worrying about the body of European Union social directives. U.S. companies with European–wide operations, however, need to study European-level social law in order to fashion their transnational employment policies. European directives also give employers in Europe a peek at the future of domestic member state legislation: There is often a years–long lag between Brussels' promulgation of a directive and each member state's adoption and enforcement of its implementing law.

NAFTA addresses trade in services, but like most other trade bloc treaties, NAFTA does not regulate substantive employment law to the extent the European Union does. The much–publicized NAFTA "labor side agreement" contains a procedure by which signatory nations can bring charges against other signatory countries for not enforcing their own internal employment laws.[14] Because the side agreement creates legal obligations only between governments under public international law, it has little effect on the practice of private international employment law – although labor unions have begun using it as a political tool.

B. *GATT, GATS and WTO*

The General Agreement on Tariffs and Trade ("GATT") (phasing into the World Trade Organization ("WTO") and the General Agreement on Trade in Services ("GATS")) do not yet substantively regulate signatory countries' internal employment laws. However, a trend seems to be emerging toward "harmonizing" employment laws internationally. The United States, in fact, is the world's leader in injecting employment issues into the free trade debate.[15] Therefore, these international trade agreements may come to have more practical effect on international employment law and practice than they do now.

C. *Friendship, Commerce and Navigation Treaties*

The United States is a party to more than 130 mostly bilateral "Friendship, Commerce, and Navigation" ("FCN") treaties, by which the U.S. and each FCN signatory encourage commerce with the other.[16] These treaties tend to allow businesses from signatory nations to set up shop in each other's country and to install key management personnel of their choice. Although U.S. practitioners most often encounter FCN employment provisions as a defense to U.S. discrimination lawsuits against foreign employers operating in the U.S., lawyers advising United States clients on their overseas employment operations should take full advantage of whatever affirmative employment and immigration rights any applicable FCN treaty may grant.[17]

D. *The International Labor Organization*

The Geneva-based International Labor Organization ("ILO") has no direct effect on the day-to-day practice of private international employment law. The ILO's work binds nations, not businesses, and its treaties (of which the U.S. has ratified notoriously few) are not self-executing. To this extent the ILO is akin to the Organisation for Economic Cooperation and Development ("OECD"): These organizations focus on global macropolitical or macroeconomic strategy, not on issues relating to specific private international deals.

IV. THE EXTRATERRITORIAL EFFECT OF U.S. EMPLOYMENT LAW

Although foreign employment laws and international treaties are by far the most important sources of law regulating U.S.-based companies' overseas workplaces, another notable area is the extraterritorial reach of *U.S.* employment law itself.

A.   Discrimination Law

Alone among the countries of the world, the United States presumes to apply its employment discrimination laws overseas.[18] Yet the extraterritorial reach of U.S. discrimination law is much less important than it may at first appear, because the United States extends its discrimination laws (Title VII, the Americans with Disabilities Act, and the Age Discrimination in Employment Act) only to U.S.-passport-carrying citizens who work overseas for U.S.-controlled entities.[19] Because U.S. businesses' overseas workplaces tend to be populated predominantly by local employees (foreign nationals), U.S. discrimination laws cover only a small percentage of American businesses' overseas workforce.

If, for example, the McDonald's on the Champs-Elysées decided to fire everyone over 40, the only workers with standing under the U.S. Age Discrimination in Employment Act would be those U.S. citizens, if any, who had conquered French immigration law and landed a job there. U.S. law leaves American companies free to discriminate overseas against foreigners.[20]

An important issue in an overseas-context employment lawsuit is whether the foreign employer is legally under the "control" of a U.S.-based entity. Although the concept of "control" in U.S. discrimination law extends beyond wholly-owned subsidiaries and reaches majority-owned foreign incorporated entities, many overseas ventures with U.S. participation do not rise to the level of being under U.S. "control." For this reason, the extraterritorial reach of U.S. employment laws can be a factor persuading a U.S. entity *not* to insist on majority control of an overseas joint venture.

The U.S. discrimination laws are somewhat more complex regarding overseas *recruitment*. Foreign employers – including the overseas operations of U.S. employers – typically impose age limits and other discriminatory conditions in their job-wanted ads. Theoretically, a U.S.-controlled entity overseas cannot discriminate against a U.S. citizen who applies for a job, even if that American fails to meet the discriminatory conditions. However, as a practical matter this rarely occurs, because foreign countries' immigration laws restrict Americans' overseas job hunts. (*See* Chapter 22, *Immigration and Nationality*.)

B.   Labor Union Law

Another extraterritorial employment issue is the reach of *labor union* law. The U.S. Wagner and Taft-Hartley Acts[21] do not apply abroad *per se*, but in today's increasingly international economy domestic disputes under these laws often take on international aspects. Courts take a case-by-case approach to determine whether an issue is a domestic U.S. labor dispute in a foreign context (to which U.S. labor law applies), or whether it is a foreign labor problem (to which U.S. labor law does not apply). Outcomes in specific cases are difficult to predict.[22]

V.   CONTEXT: HOW INTERNATIONAL LABOR AND EMPLOYMENT ISSUES ARISE IN PRACTICE

U.S. businesses operating abroad too often encounter more expensive labor problems and more extensive labor court litigation than do their local competitors. Civil law lawyers tend to see employment law as a branch of corporate law. U.S. attorneys working on international deals must themselves adopt this mindset, to keep aware of the integral role that foreign employment law plays in the very structure of overseas business. Because U.S. employment law (outside the discrimination area) is by international standards largely unregulated, U.S.-trained lawyers must be especially careful to remain alert to the employment law ramifications of their international advice.

A.   Transactional Context

International lawyers who structure transnational deals regularly look into the tax, environmental, and antitrust (competition) aspects of their proposed business plans. Yet too often U.S. businesses – even Fortune 500 companies – and their lawyers all but ignore the labor and employment side of international transactions, leaving these issues to be cleaned up after the closing. This can have disastrous effects.

For example, one U.S. company that opened a factory in Canada forgot to inquire into Canadian labor law. A month after start–up, a union representative appeared and announced he represented the workforce and wanted to schedule meetings to negotiate a collective bargaining agreement. Canadian labor law, the company quickly learned, certifies unions as soon as most employees sign assent forms – there need not be an election. Had the company's transactional lawyers advised on this in advance, the company would have put on a "no union" campaign as soon as it opened. It might have stayed union–free.

As another example, one U.S. Fortune 50 company kicked off a giant project in France by recruiting 200 French citizens and soliciting another 200 U.S. employees to work in France as expatriates. To attract this 400–employee force, the company stressed the generous employee benefits packages for which it was famous. After the 400 signed on but before they started work, the company learned that French benefit-vesting law prohibits employers from unilaterally rolling back any benefit a company once offers. With the fate of its French venture uncertain, the company cut out most of the promised benefits, touching off a human relations crisis – one which would have been averted had the transactional lawyers offered comparative employment law advice in the deal's early stages.

Foreign countries' onerous employment laws raise important transactional issues that U.S. lawyers need to account for when they structure foreign deals. For example, when a U.S. business takes over a European competitor, the EU's "acquired rights directive" binds the acquiror to the predecessor's labor and employment contracts and strictly limits freedom to streamline the new workforce.[23] And lawyers who advise on international deals have to understand foreign "worker participation" laws, because how an entity gets structured will dictate what employee involvement obligations it has. (As examples, choice of corporate form in Germany – AG versus GmbH – determines worker participation obligations, and companies can avoid the European Union's new "Works Council Directive"[24] if they structure their European operations a certain way.)

Another employment topic that raises international transaction issues for U.S. businesses is the generous levels of employee benefits common abroad. International deals have gone awry when a U.S. CEO realized that his European branch manager would get better benefits – such as country club memberships and off-shore payment of income – than he got.

Of course, in ironing out the details of any specific foreign deal, U.S. lawyers will often need foreign counsel's advice to understand the target country's employment laws. Because in foreign practice employment law dovetails into corporate law, foreign transactional lawyers will often prove to be competent employment law advisors. Increasingly, however, in European and common law countries employment law is developing into a specialty in its own right; lawyers who practice employment law exclusively are becoming more and more common abroad.

B.   *Adversarial Context*

In foreign countries, as in the U.S., employment disputes (especially those arising out of firings) often end up in court. Civil law countries usually have special-jurisdiction labor courts that handle these matters exclusively. To stay out of labor court, U.S. businesses abroad must – before firing (and, better, before *hiring*) an overseas employee – understand what foreign employment law and procedure which will apply.

The application of foreign employment laws and the jurisdiction of foreign labor courts tend to be mandatory at the place of employment. In this, foreign countries really are no different from the United States. If, for example, Brazil's Varig Airlines tried to save costs at its U.S. reservations offices by transferring to the U.S. low–wage Brazilian reservation agents, Varig (assuming it procured all the proper visas) could not bind these Brazilians to employment contracts calling for wages below the U.S. federal minimum, or to overtime rules, union representation policies, discrimination provisions, or other terms violating U.S. law. Once legally working in the U.S., any Brazilian can of course call upon the U.S. courts and labor agencies to enforce U.S. statutory protections for employees.

Other countries operate the same way. A U.S. employer usually cannot bind either its U.S. expatriates or foreign nationals to employment agreements that call for substantive employment law or procedure contrary to that of the place of employment. This tends to be true regardless of the parties' citizenship, and regardless of what the text of any employment contract might say.

A fired U.S. expatriate is therefore in the best of all possible worlds: He or she simultaneously can sue in the U.S. for violation of U.S. discrimination laws, and can file charges abroad to collect statutory severance pay and to redress any violations of the host country's local worker-friendly employment laws. Increasingly, expatriates are getting more savvy and are doing just this. Lawyers representing multinational employers must keep one step ahead, and plan for these situations before they arise.

VI.   SOURCES OF ASSISTANCE

A.   *Foreign Employment Laws and International Employment Practice*

1.   Secondary Sources

a.   Books

COMPARATIVE LABOUR LAW AND INDUSTRIAL RELATIONS (Roger Blanpain ed. 1982) (overview of comparative labor law).

EUROPEAN LABOUR COURTS: CURRENT ISSUES (Werner Blenk ed. 1989) (summarizes labor court and termination law systems of eight European countries plus Israel).

BNA TAX MANAGEMENT FOREIGN INCOME PORTFOLIO series (various dates) (series of individual–country legal reports, each of which contains a summary of its subject's employment laws).

INTERNATIONAL EMPLOYMENT LAW (Dennis Campbell ed. 1996) (forthcoming) (summarizes employment law systems of various countries and of the European Union).

LABOR LAW COMMITTEE ON BUSINESS LAW OF THE INTERNATIONAL BAR ASS'N, INTERNATIONAL HANDBOOK ON CONTRACTS OF EMPLOYMENT (2 vols., 1988 & Supp. 1994) (each chapter summarizes employment laws of a different county).

ORGANISATION FOR ECONOMIC COOPERATION AND DEVELOPMENT, TRADE AND LABOR STANDARDS: A REVIEW OF THE ISSUES (Paris: OECD 1995) (summarizes role of labor issues in free trade agreements).

BEVERLY SPRINGER, THE SOCIAL DIMENSION OF 1992: EUROPE FACES A NEW EC (New York: Greenwood Press 1992) (summarizes EU social agenda).

EUROPEAN EMPLOYMENT AND INDUSTRIAL RELATIONS GLOSSARIES (Tiziano Trev & Michael Terr eds. 1991–95) (series of books summarizing EU member states' employment regimes).

b.   Periodicals

Canadian Employment Law for U.S. Companies (Nashville, monthly) (published by M. Lee Smith, Publishers and Printers).

Comparative Labor Law Journal (Philadelphia, quarterly) (published by Univ. of Pennsylvania).

International Labour Review (Geneva, quarterly) (published by ILO).

Social Europe (Luxembourg, 3 times per year) (published by Commission of the European Communities).

c.   Specific Articles

Donald C. Dowling, Jr., *Preparing for the Internationalization of U.S. Employment Law Practice*, 43 LAB. L.J. 350 (1992), *reprinted in* 5 INT'L Q. 16 (1993).

Nancy E. Honig & Donald C. Dowling, Jr., *How to Handle Employment Issues in European Deals*, 13 PREV. L. REP. 3 (1994).

Nobuhisa Ishizada, *Subsidiary Assertion of Foreign Parent Corporation Rights Under Commercial Treaties to Hire Employees "Of Their Choice,"* 86 COLUM. L. REV. 139 (1986).

Stephen A. Mazurak, *Comparative Labor and Employment Law and the American Labor Lawyer*, 70 UNIV. DETROIT MERCY L. REV. 531 (1993).

Erika de Wet, *Labor Standards in the Globalized Economy: The Inclusion of a Social Clause in the GATT/WTO*, 17 HUM. RTS. Q. 443 (1995).

B.   *The Extraterritorial Effect of U.S. Employment Law*

1.   Statutes and Regulations

29 U.S.C. §§ 623(h), 630(f) (ADEA abroad).

42 U.S.C. §§ 2000e–1(a), (c), 2000e–5(f)(3) (Title VII abroad).

42 U.S.C. §§ 12111(4), 12112(c) (ADA abroad).

2.   Other Official Documents

EEOC Policy N–915.002, "Enforcement Guidance on Application of Title VII and the Americans with Disabilities Act to Conduct Overseas and to Foreign Employers Discriminating in the U.S." (10/20/93), *reprinted in* CCH, *EEOC Compliance Manual* ¶ 2169.

EEOC Policy N–915.039, "Application of the Age Discrimination in Employment Act and the Equal Pay Act to American Firms Overseas, Their Overseas Subsidiaries, and Foreign Firms" (3/3/89), *reprinted in* CCH, *EEOC Compliance Manual* ¶ 2165.

3.   Secondary Sources

a.   Books

JAMES M. ZIMMERMAN, EXTRATERRITORIAL EMPLOYMENT STANDARDS OF THE U.S. (1992).

b.   Specific Articles

Frank Balzano, *Extraterritorial Application of the National Labor Relations Act,* 62 UNIV. CIN. L. REV. 573 (1993) (Comment).

Janice R. Bellace, *The International Dimension of Title VII,* 24 CORN. INT'L L.J. 1 (1991).

Mary Claire St. John, *Extraterritorial Application of Title VII: The Foreign Compulsion Defense and Principles of International Comity,* 27 VAND. J. TRANSNAT'L L. 869 (1994).

Lairold M. Street, *Extraterritoriality: Conflict of Laws,* NAT'L B. A. J. (July/August 1995, at 16).

James M. Zimmerman, *International Dimension of U.S. Fair Employment Laws: Protection or Interference?,* 131 INT'L LAB. REV. 217 (1992).

C.   *Institutional Assistance*

Delegation of the European Commission, Washington Office (for assistance with European Union employment law), 2300 M Street, N.W., 3rd Floor, Washington, D.C. 20037; tel.: 202/862–9500, fax: 202/429/1766.

International Labor Organization Branch Office, Washington, 1828 L Street, N.W., Suite 801, Washington, D.C. 20036; tel.: 202/653–7652, fax: 202/653–7687.

United States Equal Employment Opportunity Commission, New York District Office (has initial responsibility for administering overseas EEOC issues worldwide), 7 World Trade Center, 18th Floor, New York, NY 10048–0948; tel.: 212/748–8500, fax: 212/748–8464.

ENDNOTES

1   *But cf.* 29 U.S.C. §§ 2101 *et seq.* (under U.S. statute inspired by earlier European Union directive, large U.S. employers must give 60 days' notice before certain mass layoffs). *Compare Council Directive on the Approximation of the Laws of the Member States Relating to Collective Redundancies,* Directive 75/129, O.J. Eur. Comm. (No. L 48) p. 29 (Feb. 17, 1995) (European Union).

2   BNA INDIVIDUAL EMPLOYMENT RIGHTS REP., Mar. 10, 1992, at 4.

3   *Council Directive Concerning the Protection at Work of Pregnant Women, or Women Who Have Recently Given Birth,* Directive 92/85, O.J. EUR. COMM. (No. L 348) p. 1 (Oct. 11, 1992) (European Union).

4   Venezuela Labor Law, *Venezuelan Official Gazette,* Dec. 20, 1990.

5   *Codified* at 29 U.S.C. §§ 2601 *et seq.* (enacted Feb. 5, 1993). The 12–week leave requirement appears at 29 U.S.C. § 2612(a)(1).

6   *Wall St. J.,* Apr. 13, 1993, at A11, col. 4.

7   *See, e.g., Wall St. J.,* Sept. 22, 1993, at A1, col. 6.

8   *See, e.g. Council Directive on an Employer's Obligation to Inform Employees of the Conditions Applicable to the Contract or Employment Relationship,* Directive 91/533, O.J. EUR. COMM. (No. L 288), p. 32 (Oct. 14, 1991) (European Union).

9   *See, e.g., Council Directive on the Approximation of the Laws of the Member States Relating to the Safeguarding of Employees' Rights in the Event of Transfers of Undertakings, Businesses, or Parts of Businesses,* Directive 77/187, O.J. EUR. COMM. (No. L 061), p. 26 (Feb. 14, 1977), *modified by* O.J. Eur. Comm. (No. L 001), p. 484 (Mar. 1, 1994) (European Union).

10   *See, e.g.,* ORGANISATION FOR ECONOMIC COOPERATION AND DEVELOPMENT, TRADE AND LABOR STANDARDS: A REVIEW OF THE ISSUES (1995); Erika de Wet, *Labor Standards in the Globalized Economy: The Inclusion of a Social Clause in the GATT/WTO,* 17 HUM. RTS. Q. 443 (1995).

11   Treaty Establishing the European Economic Community, Mar. 25, 1957, 298 U.N.T.S. 11, *as amended,* at arts. 117–27 and at "Protocol on Social Policy."

12   *Id.* at art. 119.

13   *Id.* at art. 189.

14   North American Free Trade Agreement, North American Agreement on Labor Cooperation, Sept. 16, 1993.

15   *Cf.* ORGANISATION FOR ECONOMIC COOPERATION AND DEVELOPMENT, TRADE AND LABOR STANDARDS: A REVIEW OF THE ISSUES (1995).

16   Lairold M. Street, *Korean Air Lines: The Future Interpretation of "Executive" and "Engage" in Friendship, Commerce, and Navigation Treaties,* 14 HASTINGS INT'L & COMP. L. REV. 93, 94 (1990), *citing* Walker, *Provisions on Companies in United States Commercial Treaties,* 50 AM. J. INT'L. L. 373, 374 (1956).

[17] For sources of FCN treaties, see Chapter 1, Section II, "Sources of Assistance,"

[18] The United States Equal Employment Opportunity Commission administers federal anti-discrimination laws in the first instance, but after exhausting administrative remedies, complainants gain a right to sue on their own.

[19] 29 U.S.C. §§ 623(h), 630(f) (ADEA abroad); 42 U.S.C. §§ 2000 e-1(a), (c), 2000e-5(f)(3) (Title VII abroad); 42 U.S.C. §§ 12111(4), 12112(c) (ADA abroad).

[20] U.S. state laws operate similarly. Many states have anti-discrimination laws which parallel the federal statutes; these state laws at most apply only to state "citizens" working abroad.

[21] *Codified* at 29 U.S.C. §§ 151 *et seq.*

[22] *See, e.g., Int'l Longshoremen's Ass'n AFL-CIO v. NLRB,* 56 F. 3d 205 (D.C. Cir. 1995) (U.S. union's request that Japanese union wage secondary boycott against two non-union Florida stevedoring companies which loaded fruit sent to Japan held not subject to U.S. labor law); *NLRB v. Dredge Operators,* 19 F. 3d 2217 (5th Cir. 1994) (U.S. shipowner must bargain with NLRB-certified union representing employees on board ships operating in Hong Kong waters); *Van Blaricom v. Burlington Northern RR Co.,* 17 F. 3d 1224 (9th Cir. 1994) (U.S. collective bargaining agreement not enforced in favor of Canadian employer). *See generally* Frank Balzano, *Extraterritorial Application of the National Labor Relations Act,* 62 U. CIN. L. REV. 573 (1993) (Comment).

[23] *See* note 9 *supra.*

[24] *Council Directive on the Establishment of a European Works Council or a Procedure in Community-Scale Undertakings for the Purposes of Informing and Consulting Employees,* Directive 94/45, O.J. EUR. COMM. (No. L 254), p. 64 (Sept. 22, 1994) (European Union).

CHAPTER 24

WILLS, TRUSTS, ESTATES AND RELATED TAXES

Barbara R. Hauser

I.   INTRODUCTION

Issues relating to personal "estate planning" are particularly complex when more than one country is involved. Different countries vary considerably in laws relating to wills, rights of succession, the validity of trusts, administration of estates and, of great importance, all related taxes. They also vary considerably in attitudes and preferences in relation to any of these subjects. The United States has a particularly broad scope of estate and gift taxation. Instances of double (and triple) taxation are becoming increasingly common. Professional advisors on this issue may also differ from United States practice. In civil law countries, for example, this personal planning is often handled by *notaires*, not lawyers. It is important to consult with a professional who is familiar with the local law. (*See* Chapter 26, *Selecting and Working with Foreign Counsel.*) Although bilateral treaties play a role in this area, local law remains the most important source of rules governing the disposition of property.

Typical contexts in which these issues arise are as follows:

- Citizen of A owns assets in country of B
- Citizen of A works (and lives) in country of B
- Citizen of A is married to citizen of B
- Citizen of A lives in country of B and owns assets in country of C and dies while in country of D, and so on.

II.   GENERAL ISSUES

A.   *Property Rights*

Prior to examining a particular will, the lawyer must first understand the property rights that may apply. There are many instances when there is not the complete testamentary freedom of disposition that we are accustomed to in the United States. Even in the United States, of course, a surviving spouse almost always has the right to contest a will that does not leave a specified minimum amount to the spouse. In many European countries, a married couple will have entered into a property agreement or will otherwise own property more in a community property manner, which means that one individual will not have the right to dispose of all of the property that the individual had acquired. In addition, in most civil law jurisdictions children have enforceable rights to inherit specified amounts. The location of the assets, the place of the marriage, and the nationality and residency of the individuals can all be critical factors in resolving the threshold question of which country's law will apply with respect to a particular issue.

B. *Multiple Wills*

In some cases of property in multiple jurisdictions, it may be efficient to have more than one will in effect at the same time, with the additional will restricted to the disposition of property located within that country. Any time multiple wills are used, the drafting must be done extremely carefully – especially with the tax payment provisions. A local professional should either prepare or review the will that will be intended to be used in a particular country.

C. *Powers of Attorney*

In the United States, we often use additional documents such as powers of attorney that are "durable," *i.e.*, that can be effectively used while the individual, although alive, is under a temporary or permanent disability and is unable to manage his or her financial affairs. These are often used also for convenience purposes, even without the existence of a disability. Increasingly common are powers of attorney that are directed toward health care decisions, sometimes known as "advance directives for health care." Very prevalent are "living wills," which set out the individual's wishes relating to medical care when a terminal, hopeless illness has been diagnosed. Documents such as these are quite uncommon outside of the United States and probably would be very difficult, and often impossible, to enforce in another country.

D. *Revocable Trusts*

Revocable trusts are often used in the United States for the purpose of avoiding the probate process. A lawyer should be very careful, however, about deciding to transfer any non–United States assets into a United States revocable trust. Many countries do not have the probate process we have in the United States, and the transfers would, therefore, not provide any particular benefit. More seriously, the mere act of the transfer of ownership to a revocable trust will often cause a current tax under the laws of another country. For example, the transfer of property located in Canada to a United States revocable trust would cause a current Canadian income tax on the amount of gain. Many civil law jurisdictions are also not familiar with the concept of a trust and would refuse to recognize the trust for any purpose. In those cases, the transfer could be treated as a transfer to the individual or institution serving as trustee for all purposes. On the other hand, a non-resident owner of United States real property should consider using a revocable trust to avoid U.S. probate.

E.   *Marital Trusts*

Marital trusts, which are often used in the United States as part of a testamentary plan, would have the above difficulties. This is mentioned separately to highlight the quandary we have in the United States because of the tax code provision disallowing a United States marital deduction for any property passing to a surviving spouse who is not a United States citizen. The marital deduction can be regained, albeit on a temporary basis, only by transferring the property to a Qualified Domestic Trust (QDOT). Thus, it is impossible as a practical matter to satisfy the United States estate tax marital deduction requirement and a civil law country's non-recognition of trusts when the assets to be transferred are located in the civil law country.

F.   *Asset Protection Trusts*

Somewhat popular in the United States are trusts located in "tax-haven" jurisdictions, which are designed solely to protect the assets from United States creditors. The transfers are subject to the United States gift tax. If control is retained, the assets are subject to United States estate tax. All income earned is subject to United States income tax.

G.   *Death*

The death of a U.S. citizen outside of the United States should be reported to the United States embassy. As discussed later in more detail, the full United States estate tax applies at the death of a U.S. citizen regardless of residence and regardless of the location of assets. If the total fair market value of the estate is in excess of $600,000 (the current unified credit equivalent), a United States Estate Tax Return (Form 706) must also be filed.

III.   TAX ISSUES

Whether by travel, work, marriage or growing multinational investing, the greater incidence of ties to two (or more) countries is creating a growing interest in understanding the effects of taxes imposed at death on one's holdings, or at the time of lifetime gifts. Most countries that have substantial death tax systems also have added some form of transfer tax for lifetime gifts. These gift tax systems vary considerably, however, and will not be discussed in any detail.

The first stage of coordinating several legal systems is the analysis of the current situation. It is usually best to concentrate on one country at a time. The first country's death tax effect on a particular situation should be fully understood before inquiring as to the effect, if any, of the next country with which there are contacts, and so on. When there appear to be overlapping taxes, the analysis moves up a level, to analyze the effect of any treaty.

A. National Taxes

The logical place for a tax advisor to begin is with the tax rules of his or her own country. For this purpose, the initial focus will be on the imposition of taxes at death (since that is an inevitable event, whereas lifetime gifts are an optional and voluntary act). There are several aspects to consider.

1. Tax Jurisdiction

One must first determine the relevant tax jurisdictions. For example, within the United States it is important to consider the particular state, which may have its own taxes, in addition to the federal tax. In Switzerland, there is no national death tax, and the death tax will be determined solely by the separate cantons, some of which have none and some of which also permit their municipalities to add a death tax, etc.

2. Existence of a Tax Upon Death

The next question is whether or not the relevant jurisdictions have a tax that is imposed at the time of death. There are several countries where there is no tax that results from a death (for example, Israel).

3. Nature of the Tax

If the jurisdiction has a tax upon death, the next question is the nature of the tax. It could be an "inheritance" tax, an "estate" tax, an "income" tax, or yet another type.

a. Inheritance Tax

An inheritance tax is a tax imposed on funds received by beneficiaries. It may often make a difference in the amount of the tax, or in the tax rate, if the recipient is closely related to the deceased person. There may be a focus on the location of the recipient as well. Most, but not all, civil law countries have an inheritance tax system. Japan also has an inheritance tax system. It should be noted that the term "inheritance tax" is sometimes used to refer to a tax on the assets of the deceased person (which would normally be thought of as an "estate" tax), so it is sometimes necessary to inquire past the term that is used.

b.   Estate Tax

An estate tax, such as the United States federal tax, refers to a tax imposed on the aggregate assets owned by a person at death. Generally, but not always, the relationship of the recipient to the decedent does not affect the amount of the tax or the rate of the tax. Similarly, the location of the recipient is generally not a relevant factor. It is possible for a jurisdiction to have both an inheritance tax and an estate tax.

c.   Income Tax

An income tax generally taxes income received during the decedent's lifetime, from wages or investments, but in the case of Canada it also covers the "deemed disposition" (similar to a sale) of assets that occurs at death. Australia also imposes a tax at death on the income tax gain for certain assets.

d.   Other Taxes

Other taxes may also apply at death. For example, the United States has a complete chapter of its tax code relating to the Estate Tax (Chapter 11) (as well as a chapter on the Gift Tax (Chapter 12), but additional taxes can occur at death. There may be a tax imposed at death under the Generation-Skipping Transfer Tax chapter (Chapter 13), relating to the separate and additional tax imposed on transfers that "skip" a generation. In the Income Tax chapter (Chapter 1), there is also a separate excise tax on "excess" retirement benefits imposed at death.

4.   Jurisdictional Basis and Scope

If there is a tax imposed as the result of a death, the next inquiry is the jurisdictional basis of the tax–in other words, to whom and/or to which property does the tax apply. More specifically, the question is which contacts are considered critical enough by a country in order to assert its jurisdiction for tax purposes.

A related question is the territorial scope of the tax. Does the tax apply only to assets located within the tax jurisdiction, or to other assets as well? For example, the United States imposes its death taxes on all assets, worldwide, owned by a United States citizen.

a.   Status of the Person

Most systems focus on the deceased person. A critical question is usually whether or not the person was *"domiciled"* in that country/ jurisdiction at the time of death. With respect to the United States, nationality is also a critical concept. There are instances, however, where the relevant person is the recipient of the transferred assets. In other cases, the tax will be imposed on either basis: the domicile of the deceased person or of the recipient. When the jurisdictional base is the person, it is often, but not always, true that the assets are considered on a worldwide basis.

(1) **Domicile/Residency.** The definition of domicile or residency can vary considerably from country to country. For historical reasons there are also countries, *e.g.*, England, where a person can be considered to be domiciled for several years after having in fact left on a permanent basis.

For death tax purposes a person is domiciled in the United States at death if (1) he was living there, even briefly, with (2) no definite present intention of later moving. It is usually assumed that holders of "green cards" (for immigration purposes) would be considered domiciled for these purposes.

The complexity and lack of uniformity of domicile tests is quite unfortunate. It is increasingly common to have individuals with multiple domiciles or, in some cases, with no domicile.

(2) **Nationality.** The United States takes an unusual approach. In addition to domicile, it uses the fact of citizenship as a complete jurisdictional basis for death taxes. This applies even when a person is a citizen of another country as well, *i.e.*, a dual citizen. This jurisdictional basis generates multiple instances of double taxation. Any United States citizen domiciled in another country is automatically subject to potential world–wide taxation by both countries. (The United States has estate tax treaties, intended to ameliorate double taxation, with only 16 countries.)

b.   Property

Another separate jurisdictional basis is often property, distinct from the person. In other words, the location of property within a tax jurisdiction may be a sufficient basis upon which to impose a death tax. This is another area in which double taxation is quite possible. For example, the United States treats as located within the United States any stock issued by a corporation organized under the laws of one of the states within the United States. Most jurisdictions will tax land/real property that is physically located within the country.

5.   Items That Are Taxed

Although many countries include all assets or interests owned by the deceased person as taxable, this is not always true. Some countries exclude certain types of assets from the tax.

For example, the United States will not tax United States bank deposits (or certain other investments) owned by a non–resident alien, even though the account is located within the United States. It also does not tax certain interests in trusts and other life interests or annuities. Life insurance payable on the death of the deceased person is not taxed if it is owned, in a qualifying manner, by another person or entity (unless it was transferred within three years prior to death). However, assets that were in fact given away during lifetime are often included in the estate when the person kept some continuing rights over the property. Many countries exclude different categories of assets.

6.   Definitions of Property

Another variable is the definition of a property interest. This can also vary considerably by country. Even the category of "real property"/immovables is not consistent. Within the United States there can be one or more of the following involving real property: land owned outright, condominiums, cooperatives, mineral interests, air rights, conservation easements, growing crops, leases, options, mortgages, partnerships, corporations, trusts, joint ventures, underlying fee interests owned by states (*e.g.*, in Hawaii) or park jurisdictions, etc. In other jurisdictions, the interest may be the right of usufruct.

In addition, the deceased person may or may not be treated as the "owner" for these purposes of property that would otherwise seem to have been owned by that person. For example, if there are "forced heirship" rights, or automatic spousal rights, in some countries the deceased person is treated as having owned only that portion as to which there was a legal right to dispose freely of the property. Under conflicts of laws rules, then, it is often critical to determine which law determines the nature and extent of the property interest.

7.   Valuation of Assets

Many countries have specific approaches to valuation for death tax purposes. The valuation rules may also vary by category of asset. For example, local real estate, family businesses, forest land, and farm lands are often valued at a lower rate. When there are two (or more) tax jurisdictions, each will use its own method of valuation.

8.   Tax Rates

Tax rates vary considerably. There are Swiss Canton rates of three percent; the United States rates are as much as 55 percent; in Japan the rates are as much as 70 percent; and so on. The applicability of a particular rate often depends on two variables: the size of the transfer and the relationship of the recipient to the deceased. Generally there are higher tax rates as the size of the transfer increases and higher rates as the degree of relationship becomes more remote. Occasionally different rates apply to a non–resident, as used to be true in the United States.

9.   Exempt Amounts

There is often an initial amount that is excluded from the tax. That amount is sometimes referred to as an exemption or a personal allowance. This can be an amount per recipient or one amount in total. The amounts can also vary based on the recipient's relationship to the deceased. In the United States there is technically no such concept, but in practice the availability of a tax credit (currently $192,800) means that there is no tax on the initial $600,000 (sometimes referred to as an exemption equivalent).

10. Deductions

There are several ways in which deductions arise. One is at the initial analysis of either the "net" value of particular assets, or of the total of assets. Certain debts, claims, expenses, etc. may be allowed in arriving at the taxable amount. There is an additional possibility of having further "deductions" from the amount that in the end results in a tax. For example, in the United States after the net value of the estate is determined there is an additional deduction for assets passing to a spouse (in a qualifying manner). There is no limit on the amount of that deduction.

a. Spouse

There are often substantial deductions for transfers to a spouse. In some cases there may also be different definitions of "spouse" for these purposes (such as common-law marriages, for example). The United States now makes a distinction between spouses who are United States citizens and spouses who are not United States citizens (who no longer receive the regular marital deduction).

b. Children

An initial question is to determine whether the person is treated as a legal child for these purposes. In most jurisdictions, legal adoption has the effect of conferring the status of a legal child (and usually of removing it from the initial parent). There are still many instances where girls have different (lesser) inheritance rights than do boys.

c. Charities

The treatment of transfers for charitable purposes varies considerably. In the United States there is a full deduction for qualifying charitable transfers. Other countries do not provide a full deduction for charitable gifts. The definition of a "charity" for these purposes also varies significantly by country.

d. Foreign Taxes as Debts

In some cases it is not possible to receive a tax credit for death taxes imposed by other jurisdictions. It may be possible in those cases to subtract them as debts, so they are treated as additional deductions.

11. Credits

Tax credits are often available. More common types include credits for foreign taxes, gift taxes, and previously-taxed property.

12. Post–Death Tax Reduction Methods

In some cases, it is possible to alter the death tax by certain post–death transfers or agreements. In some countries, the heirs can re–divide the inheritances by agreement among themselves as a group. In many non–probate jurisdictions, the heirs have the option of refusing the inheritance. In the United States a properly filed disclaimer can result in the transfer to other beneficiaries without the gift tax that would otherwise be imposed.

13. Person(s) Responsible for the Payment

In probate jurisdictions (the United Kingdom and the United States), the appointed executor is responsible for the payment of the tax. (There is usually a secondary liability of the recipient if the executor has not made the payment.) In civil law jurisdictions, it is usually the recipient who is responsible for the payment of the tax.

14. Deadline for Payment

The deadlines for payment of the tax also vary. In the United States payment is generally due nine months after the date of death. France permits a longer time for non–residents.

B. *Analysis for Additional Countries*

The same thorough analysis must be done for any additional countries with which the deceased person, or the recipient person, or the property, had sufficient contacts.

C. *Application of Treaties*

After there has been a determination that two (or more) jurisdictions would apply a tax to the same property or person, the analysis moves up one level, to the international treaty level. The death tax treaties are intended to eliminate or minimize double taxation. If there is a treaty between the two relevant countries, those provisions (which can change many of the regular tax rules) control. It is usually possible, however, to choose not to take advantage of a treaty.

Most of the death tax treaties are based on one of the Model Treaties proposed by the Organization for Economic Cooperation and Development ("OECD"). Although any particular treaty may have significant changes from the Model Treaty, it may be helpful to refer to the Commentaries on the Model Treaties since the treaties tend to be quite difficult to understand. Real property can generally be taxed by the country in which it is located. In general, the older treaties tend to focus on particular assets, and assign them to one (and only one) of the tax jurisdictions. The newer treaties tend to focus on the deceased person's domicile as the prevailing tax jurisdiction. They include provisions to determine which of the two domicile claims will be the one chosen for treaty purposes. They also deal with credits/exemption amounts, deductions for marital transfers, and foreign death tax credits. Each treaty must be read with particular attention. Some countries have many estate tax treaties: France currently has 35, Ireland, 24. Others have fewer: Sweden, 17; the United States, 16; the United Kingdom, 10; Switzerland, 10; Austria, 7; and Italy, 6. Norway has 3, Belgium and Spain have 2, and Japan has only 1 (with the United States).

IV.   SOURCES OF ASSISTANCE

A.   Periodicals

European Taxation, Comparative Study of Inheritance and Gift Taxes, Volume 34, Number 10–11, International Bureau of Fiscal Documentation, Amsterdam, The Netherlands, 1994.

B.   Books

INTERNATIONAL TRUST LAWS (John Glasson ed. 1992) (with continuous updates).

MARSHALL LANGER, PRACTICAL INTERNATIONAL TAX PLANNING (3d ed. 1995).

TIMOTHY J. LYONS, CAPITAL TAXES AND ESTATE PLANNING IN EUROPE (1994).

WILLIAM H. NEWTON III, INTERNATIONAL INCOME TAX AND ESTATE PLANNING (1994).

AMERICAN BAR ASSOCIATION, PRACTICAL INTERNATIONAL ESTATE PLANNING (1994).

HOWARD M. ZARITSKY, TAX MANAGEMENT, FOREIGN TRUSTS, ESTATES AND BENEFICIARIES (1989).

C.   Treaties

For citations to bilateral treaties to which the U.S. is party affecting estate and gift taxes, see WORLDWIDE TAX TREATY INDEX (Marion Marshall ed. 1994 ed.), Part II.

D.   Hague Conventions

Hague Convention on the Law Applicable to Trusts and on their Recognition, *done* at The Hague on October 20, 1984, *reprinted in* 23 I.L.M. at 1388 (1984).

Hague Convention on the Law Applicable to Matrimonial Property Regimes, *done* at The Hague on October 4, 1976, *reprinted in* 25 Am J. Comp. L. 394 (1977).

Hague Convention Concerning the International Administration of the Estate of Deceased Persons, *done* at The Hague on October 2, 1972, *reprinted in* 11 I.L.M. at 1277 (1972).

Hague Convention on the Conflicts of Laws Relating to the Form of Testamentary Dispositions, *done* at The Hague on 5 October 1961, 51 U.N.T.S. 175.

E.   Organizational Assistance

ABA Section of International Law and Practice, Committee on International Property, Estate and Trust Law; tel.: (202) 662–1660; fax: (202) 662–1669.

International Academy of Trusts and Estates Counsel; tel.: (415) 442–1379; fax: (415) 896–5245.

International Fiscal Association; tel.: (415) 957–3185; fax: (415) 957–3394.

Union Internationale Des Avocats Committee on International Laws of Succession; tel.: (33) 1–45 08 82 34; fax: (33) 1–45 08 82 31.

CHAPTER 25

FAMILY LAW

Gloria F. DeHart

I.   INTRODUCTION

The expansion of communication facilities, access to information, exchange of goods and services, and personal mobility have resulted in the increased interdependence of people and nations and a corresponding increase in the involvement of all practitioners in problems with international aspects. Family law, an area of law with perhaps the most firmly entrenched local and state foundation, is no exception as men, women and children cross international boundaries in the creation – and sometimes the breakup – of relationships and families. In a single short chapter, it is not possible even to mention, much less summarize, all of the potential problems and law that may have international relevance. Marriage and divorce, family (spousal and child) support, custody, including parental abduction, and adoption are reviewed briefly in this chapter, with particular emphasis on conventions and bilateral treaties to which the United States is or may become a party. Important issues relating to trusts and estates are discussed in chapter 24.

The United States has become a party to only four of the conventions developed by the Hague Conference on Private International Law. The only family law convention in this group, that on international parental child abduction, is one of the most important and successful of the Hague family law conventions and will be discussed in section IV below. Since becoming a party to this Convention in 1988, the United States has become more active in family law issues, including participating in the preparation and negotiation of additional conventions by the Hague Conference and the Organization of American States.

Although not directly related nor applicable only to family law, the three procedural Hague Conventions which the United States has ratified, discussed elsewhere in this publication, are important for family law litigation involving parties present or resident in or documents available in foreign countries. (*See* Chapter 1, *The International Practice of Law*, for a general discussion; Chapter 18, *International Litigation*, for a more detailed discussion of the Hague Service Convention and the Hague Evidence Convention; and Chapter 17, *Legalization of Documents for Use Abroad*, for a discussion of the Hague Legalisation Convention.)[1]

In the absence of a convention, the effect given in a country to a judicial or official act taken in another country is based on the concept of comity. Recognition may or may not be conditioned on the granting of reciprocity. The terms of existing conventions, whether or not in force in the country, may give some indication of consensus in the basic approach taken to such problems generally and in applying comity. For that reason this chapter identifies certain conventions to which the United States is not a party.

II. MARRIAGE AND DIVORCE

A. *The Hague Conventions*

The Hague Conference on Private International Law has developed three conventions related to marriage and divorce: Convention of 1978 on Celebration and Recognition of Marriages (three party States as of 3 February 1995);[2] Convention of 1978 on the Law Applicable to Matrimonial Property Regimes (three party States as of 3 February 1995);[3] Convention of 1970 on the Recognition of Divorces and Legal Separations (15 party States as of 3 February 1995).[4] The United States is not a party to any of the three and it appears unlikely at this time that it will become a party.

The marriage and marital property regime Conventions require the Contracting State to apply the rules of the Conventions to all marriages, not just those celebrated in other Contracting States. The divorce recognition Convention, on the other hand, applies only to divorces and legal separations occurring in another Contracting State. Although recognition of a divorce or separation decreed in a non–Contracting State is not required, it is possible, perhaps likely, that the same rules will be applied to all cases. Because these and other conventions on this subject are not in force in many countries, these countries will use their own conflict–of–law rules to govern recognition. The variation is considerable, and there is no comprehensive compilation of the systems that exist.

B. *Marriage*

In the usual case, the validity of a marriage in the country where celebrated will depend on the law of the place of celebration. That law will include rules governing capacity to marry, requirements for residence or domicile, and procedures for entering into a marriage in effect in that country. In some cases, however, the country of celebration may apply not only its own internal rules, but its rules on conflict of laws. That is, some countries may apply the law of the country of the nationality of the parties or of their pre–marital domicile. Some countries may not recognize a marriage valid in the place of celebration if it violates their public policy. In general, the Hague Convention sets out commonly used and accepted rules, and does not prevent the application of rules more favorable to recognition. Only reference to the laws of the countries involved in a validity or recognition question can resolve the issue.

In the United States, state law must be consulted. Perhaps the most common approach is that taken by the *Restatement (Second) of Conflict of Laws*[5] which establishes as a general principle that the law of the state with the most significant relation to the marriage and the parties with respect to the particular issue should govern, and a rebuttable presumption that the state of celebration has the most significant relationship.

C.   *Divorce*

1.   Recognition of Foreign Divorces in the United States

Problems in the recognition of a divorce most commonly arise in the United States in the context of remarriage when U.S. citizens or residents have obtained a divorce outside the United States. The problem now arises less frequently since no–fault divorce has become the law in all of the states; however, the desire for a "quickie" divorce may still raise the question. Where residents of foreign countries come to the United States after having married and divorced in their country of residence or some other country, such a divorce is generally entitled to recognition in the United States if it was valid and effective in the country where it was granted and that country was the residence or domicile of both parties. In other cases, recognition in the United States of a divorce obtained in a foreign country will depend on the law of the country and states involved and may also depend on whether the divorce was by mail, default or the appearance of both parties.

Although divorce recognition within the United States is dependent on the concept of domicile, foreign divorces may be recognized where both parties appear in the action, even in the absence of domicile. The question of direct or formal recognition of a foreign divorce obtained by United States residents is often avoided because a court may find that the challenging party is precluded (under the doctrine of estoppel) from denying the existence of the divorce.

2.   Recognition of United States Divorces by Other Countries

Recognition by other countries of divorces and remarriages occurring in the United States and involving aliens or Americans who have married or divorced abroad raises difficult questions. The rules for such recognition vary from country to country. (*See* citations in section VI, Sources of Assistance.)

Although the United States is not a party, the 1970 Hague Convention on the recognition of divorces and separations sets out the broadest possible consensus for recognition, and has become an international model.[6] The Convention reaches a compromise between countries that use nationality as a basis for jurisdiction and those that use domicile. Although the Convention is reciprocal and thus not binding in regard to United States divorces, the

Convention grounds have influenced the rules applied by European courts. The United Kingdom, by legislation, applies the Convention rules generally and has broadened the bases for recognition. There are also Convention rules permitting, but not requiring, non–recognition.

Recognition of a divorce does not necessarily imply recognition of ancillary orders such as support, custody or division of property. The United States has recognized the concept of "divisible divorce," and different rules of jurisdiction govern marital property, support and custody. Jurisdictional rules vary in other countries, some giving the divorce court jurisdiction to decide all issues relating to the marriage, and others controlled in part by conventions that may establish different rules for different issues.

III.   FAMILY SUPPORT

A.   *Relevant Conventions*

Several conventions deal with international enforcement and recognition of support (maintenance) orders. None of these has been ratified to date by the United States.

The United Nations Convention on the Recovery Abroad of Maintenance (New York, 1956)[7] establishes a system for enforcement of the support obligation whether or not the obligation has been established by court order before enforcement has been sought. Currently, 52 countries are parties to this Convention, but the commitment to and service provided for enforcement efforts vary widely from country to country. Some countries will recognize and enforce an existing order in procedures under the Convention either through regular "exequatur" proceedings or pursuant to other treaty–imposed mandate; some merely obtain a voluntary agreement or a new order; and others limit their assistance to helping with the filing and transfer of papers and applications to the legal aid system. The Convention poses a problem for the United States because there is no requirement in the Convention for the provision of legal services in all cases where such services are necessary. At best, the Convention requires that all party countries provide services for applicants under the Convention on the same basis that services are provided for their own residents. In the United States services are provided to all under the federal IV–D program, discussed below in section III.B.

Two conventions dealing with the recognition and enforcement of child support orders have been developed by the Hague Conference on Private International Law: The 1958 Convention on the Recognition and Enforcement of Decisions Relating to Child Maintenance Obligations[8] and the 1973 Convention on the Recognition and Enforcement of Decisions Relating to Maintenance Obligations.[9] Both the 1958 Convention (applying only to child support) and the 1973 Convention (applying to both child and spousal support) accept bases for jurisdiction which conflict with United States constitutional standards of jurisdiction.

B.   *Federal Enforcement Activities*

In 1975, Congress enacted a strong child support program, mandatory for the states, codified in Title IV–D of the Social Security Act (42 U.S.C §§ 551–669), and administered by the Department of Health and Human Services, Office of Child Support Enforcement (OCSE). The program requires the states to establish a single agency to administer the program. State enforcement activities may be carried out by a central state office, by regionally located state offices or by local county offices. The program is mandatory for recipients of Aid to Families with Dependent Children (AFDC), and available to others on request. (Legislation pending in Congress at the writing of this chapter (Fall 1995) proposes to change the AFDC program by providing funds to the states in the form of block grants. The legislation also contains provisions relating to support enforcement but the basic structure of the enforcement system remains the same.) The program is generally free, although a state may charge an application fee and recover costs at state option. Most states charge a minimum application fee which is covered by the state, and do not recover costs for services, considering such recovery not to be cost effective and to be inconsistent with the purposes of the program.

Despite subsequent enactments modifying and strengthening the program, the Congress has not yet addressed the problem of international enforcement of child support, *i.e.*, enforcement when the child is resident in a different country from the parent obligated to pay support.

C.   *State Initiatives*

In the absence of involvement on the federal level, the states have addressed the issue of international enforcement through an expanded use, based on comity, of their individually enacted interstate enforcement acts: the Uniform Reciprocal Enforcement of Support Act (URESA) (first developed in 1950; revised in 1968 (RURESA)[10]; now being replaced by the new Uniform Interstate Family Support Act (UIFSA).[11]) The acts set up what is in effect a two–state lawsuit to establish a court order where no order exists, and a simple registration procedure for registering one state's order for enforcement in another state. Public officials are responsible for establishment and enforcement of the orders without charge to the applicants. These procedures are used for interstate cases in the IV–D system.

Although originally constructed with interstate enforcement as the objective, the acts have been adapted to cover international enforcement as well. The 1968 RURESA (§ 2(m)) defined "state" to include "any foreign jurisdiction in which this or a substantially similar reciprocal law is in effect." The new UIFSA (§ 1(19)) specifies "a foreign jurisdiction that has established procedures for issuance and enforcement of support orders which are substantially similar to the procedures under this act." Using the principle of comity, all of the United States states and territories except Alabama have adopted "parallel unilateral policy declarations" (PUPDs) which recognize the procedures of 13 of the 51 U.N. Convention countries[12] as well as five non-Convention countries.[13] Where the language of the participating country is not English, bilingual forms have been developed, and are used to transmit cases in both directions.

Many of the countries with which PUPDs have been arranged have made their enforcement policy declarations applicable to all of the U.S. jurisdictions that permit enforcement of foreign support obligations under state law. Some countries and the Canadian provinces require an individual state request. Where the foreign declaration encompasses all of the states of the United States, further state action is usually not needed. Therefore, the state IV-D office should be consulted for information on the status of that state's arrangements. If the state does not yet have an arrangement with one of the listed countries, the state may make such an arrangement on request to that foreign country. Any state is also free, of course, under the state's interstate act (URESA or UIFSA), to arrange for enforcement with countries not on the above-cited list. Requests for enforcement must be made through the appropriate state agency, usually the state or local IV-D office, the bilingual forms must be used, and relevant documents must be translated into the language of the country to which the request is sent.

D.   In the Absence of a Convention or Parallel Arrangement

Where neither a convention nor an arrangement based on comity is in effect, the support obligation must be established or enforced through utilization of the country's normal procedures for establishing support or recognizing a foreign support order, associating local counsel as necessary. It is also possible that some assistance may be given by the Ministries of Justice or Foreign Affairs, by the agency handling cases under the U.N. convention or even by a local court (through a letter rogatory). Useful information may be obtained through the country's embassy or consulates in the United States. The U.S. State Department, Bureau of Consular Affairs, tel. (202) 647-3666, fax (202) 647-6201, will also provide information on local counsel, and may have information on laws and procedures.

To establish a foreign support order in the United States, an action to domesticate the judgment in the local state court must be brought under usual civil procedures. An action to obtain a support order where none exists may also be brought under the usual state procedures for establishing a support obligation. There may be problems of proof in the latter case; however, the procedures of the new UIFSA, if the state involved has enacted it, should make the process easier. Legislation now pending in Congress would make enactment of UIFSA mandatory.

E. *Proposed and Potential Federal Action*

The State Department (Office of the Assistant Legal Adviser for Private International Law, L/PIL) and OCSE in the Department of Health and Human Services (HHS) have developed legislation to permit parallel enforcement arrangements on the federal government level. This would result in uniformity of enforcement and procedures throughout the United States. Consideration is also being given to accession to the 1956 United Nations Convention and one or both of the Hague Recognition Conventions. OCSE has recently established an international enforcement liaison officer and is ready to take a more active role in international family support enforcement. Information on the status of federal government involvement may be obtained from either of these offices. (*See* section VI, Sources of Assistance.)

IV. CHILD CUSTODY, VISITATION, AND PARENTAL CHILD ABDUCTION

A. *The Hague Abduction Convention*

The fourteenth session of the Hague Conference in October 1980 completed negotiation of and adopted the Convention on the Civil Aspects of International Child Abduction.[14] The treaty entered into force on December 1, 1983, and for the United States on July 1, 1988.[15] This is one of the Hague Conference's most successful conventions and has (as of June 9, 1995) been ratified by 24 Hague Conference members and acceded to by 18 other countries.

The Convention avoids jurisdiction and recognition questions, and resolves the problem of parental child abductions by requiring the restoration of the *status quo ante*, that is, by requiring the prompt return of a child under 16 to his or her place of habitual residence whether or not a custody order has been issued, thus depriving the abducting parent of any advantage from the wrongful removal of the child. The country to which the child is taken is forbidden from making any decision on the custody dispute. The return remedy under the Convention is in addition to any other means of obtaining the child's return, such as enforcement of an existing order. The Convention contains a provision designed to promote the exercise of visitation rights but has no detailed requirements for carrying out this provision, and its usefulness and effectiveness is still unclear. However, the very existence of the Convention assists in promoting the enjoyment of access rights by ensuring that the child will be returned after visitation has taken place.

United States ratification was subject to two reservations, as permitted by the Convention: (1) The United States would not be bound to assume costs resulting from court proceedings and costs for legal counsel except as covered by legal aid; and (2) requests and other documents submitted to the United States must be accompanied by an English translation.

Implementing legislation was introduced to resolve some potential substantive and procedural problems and provide for uniformity of interpretation. This legislation, known as the International Child Abduction Remedies Act, Public Law No. 100-300, 42 U.S.C. §§ 11601–11610, is in addition to the Convention and serves as interpretive guidance but does not replace the Convention text or its obligations. Among other provisions, it establishes concurrent original jurisdiction in state and federal courts, venue where the child is located, and the burden of proof to establish exceptions to the return obligation, and grants full faith and credit to the disposition of return requests under the Convention.

As required by the Convention, the Act also provides for the designation of a United States Central Authority. By subsequent Executive Order, the president designated the State Department. The Central Authority is located in the Office of Children's Issues in the Bureau of Consular Affairs in the State Department, tel. (202) 647-2688, fax (202) 647-2835. The Central Authority has developed a handbook of information on parental abductions which will be provided on request. The 1993 edition of the handbook is included in the American Bar Association publication noted in the Sources of Assistance. The U.S. Central Authority will assist parents in filing an application with foreign authorities for return of the child.

A major difficulty for the United States in fulfilling its obligations under the Convention is providing representation for foreign applicants. Attorneys willing to provide services in Hague Convention cases should contact the Central Authority (at the telephone and fax numbers provided above) which routinely provides assistance and information in such cases.

B.   Custody Law and Enforcement of Foreign Orders in the United States

All of the states of the United States have enacted the Uniform Child Custody Jurisdiction Act (UCCJA)[16] which establishes the jurisdiction of a state to enter a custody order and requires deference to orders entered by other state courts with jurisdiction under the Act.

The UCCJA is applicable to foreign cases under section 23, which extends its provisions to decrees issued by authorities of other countries if reasonable notice and opportunity to be heard were provided to the affected persons. With the exception of Missouri, New Mexico, Ohio, and South Dakota, section 23 has been adopted by all of the states with some changes in a few.[17]

The UCCJA is not reciprocal, and thus applies whether or not the foreign jurisdiction gives equal respect to orders from the U.S. state involved in the case.[18] The federal Parental Kidnapping Prevention Act[19] does not apply to international cases, and thus states remain free of its provisions in interpreting section 23.

In addition to the section 23 requirement of recognition of foreign orders, the general jurisdictional standards of the Act would operate to require deference by the states of the United States to the jurisdiction of a foreign country when it fit the requirements of the Act. That is, even if some basis for jurisdiction existed under section 3, it should not be invoked. Where the Hague Abduction Convention applies, its terms and requirements control whether or not the UCCJA would apply or require return.

C. *Custody Law and Enforcement of United States Custody Orders Abroad*

The widespread adoption of the Hague Child Abduction Convention has made the question of foreign enforcement of United States custody orders less critical. When the removal of the child is wrongful and the Convention otherwise applies, return is nearly automatic and the issue of custody or custody jurisdiction will eventually be decided in the United States.

Where the Abduction Convention does not apply, the assumption of jurisdiction by a tribunal, the question of recognition or modification of an existing order, and the litigation of the underlying custody dispute will be determined by the law of the country where the child is present. Another Hague Convention, the 1961 Convention on the Powers of Authorities and the Law Applicable to the Protection of Children, establishes jurisdiction over and recognition of custody orders including visitation as well as other measures of protection. It is now being revised by the Hague Conference on Private International Law, and the Convention is, in any event, only applicable to habitual residents of contracting States. The United States is not a party at present.

The Office of Children's Issues in the State Department, through United States embassy and consular officials in the foreign country, can give assistance in locating the child, determining its well-being, give the left-behind parent information on the country's legal system, family laws, and a list of lawyers, monitor judicial or administrative proceedings, provide a point of contact for parents, and assist parents in contacting foreign officials or contact them on the parent's behalf. There is nothing they can do to resolve the dispute even where two U.S. citizens with no ties to the country are involved. The State Department publication previously mentioned contains information on preventive measures that can be taken in certain circumstances (passport restrictions, for example) and the limits on U.S. ability to act in a foreign country.

Except where jurisdiction is limited and recognition is required by a Convention, many foreign jurisdictions will assume jurisdiction to hear a custody case even though there is an existing order and the parties have been or are habitually resident in another country. The nationality of the child or one of the parties or the mere presence of the child are common grounds for exerting jurisdiction. Jurisdiction based on habitual residence and deference to that concept in international cases, even where a Convention does not require it, may also be the rule. Where an order exists, recognition may also be granted in some countries on the basis of *de facto* reciprocity. To argue for the application of this principle, reference to the UCCJA and United States case law will be helpful in establishing that such reciprocity exists. In some countries, the Ministry of Justice determination on this question may be persuasive or even binding on the court considering the case. Consultation with a lawyer in the country involved is recommended. (*See* Chapter 26, *Selecting and Working with Foreign Counsel.*)

V.   INTERCOUNTRY ADOPTION

A.   *The Existing Framework for Intercountry Adoption*

There are more intercountry adoptions to the United States annually than to any other country in the world;[20] an average of about 8000 children a year are admitted to the United States after adoption in a foreign country or release by the country for adoption in the United States. The United States is also a country of origin for intercountry adoptions, although the number of such adoptions is unknown since the United States does not have exit controls, and state laws and procedures govern only those adoptions that take place in the United States.

The National Conference of Commissioners on Uniform State Laws completed work on a new Uniform Adoption act in 1994. Its text may be found in 9 U.L.A. Part I, at 1 (1995 Supp.). Although it has not yet been enacted by any state, its provisions provide useful information on issues and procedures involved in any adoption. It does not deal directly with international adoption because of the concurrent development of an international convention on that subject, discussed in section V.B.

The admission of children to the United States is controlled by two agencies: the Immigration and Naturalization Service in the Department of Justice; and the State Department, which is responsible for the issuance of visas by the United States consulates in foreign countries. Regulations setting out the requirements for the pre–clearance of prospective adoptive parents and the eligibility of children for admission and permanent residence in the United States are set out in 8 C.F.R. Part 204, 59 Fed. Reg. at 38876. Other than the immigration and visa issues, the adoptability of, the adoption by United States residents, and the release of the children of other countries for adoption in the United States are governed entirely by the law of the other country involved.

The country from which a child is sought may not permit direct contact between adoptive parents and birth parents or the child, may impose conditions on such contact, may require adoptions to be arranged only through its own agencies, or may only be willing to deal with one or more particular agencies in the receiving country. It is advisable to exercise extreme care in selecting a foreign lawyer or facilitator, and familiarity with the adoption law and practices of the country of origin is obviously essential.

When the child is adopted in this country by non-U.S. adoptive parents for residence abroad, the law of the state where the adoption is to take place controls. The country to which the child will go will control the child's entry into that country. Where a child is to be removed from the United States for adoption abroad, knowledge of the legal requirements for adoption entry and permanent residence of the country is essential.

The Office of Children's Issues in the State Department (tel. (202) 647-2688), can provide information on the status of adoption law in the foreign countries permitting the intercountry adoption of children, provide general information about U.S. visa requirements, make inquiries regarding the status of a specific adoption case, clarify documentation or other requirements, and ensure that U.S. citizens are not discriminated against by foreign authorities or courts. Other valuable sources of information are the United States adoption agencies offering services in intercountry adoptions and organizations serving the interests of adoption service providers and adoptive (and would-be adoptive) parents.

B.   *The Hague Adoption Convention and Its Effect*

On May 29, 1993, the Hague Conference on Private International Law, with the unanimous approval of the 66 countries participating, both Hague Conference Member Countries and other countries from which children are being adopted, approved another extremely important family law convention – The Convention on Protection of Children and Co-operation in Respect of Intercountry Adoption.[21]

As of September 14, 1995, the Convention had been signed by 23 countries, including the United States. It had been ratified by eight countries, and entered into force on May 1, 1995, after ratification by Mexico, Romania, and Sri Lanka. It entered into force for Cyprus on June 1, 1995, for Poland on October 1, 1995, for Spain on November 1, 1995, and for Ecuador and Peru on January 1, 1996. The State Department is optimistic that United States will ratify this convention in 1996 or 1997.

The importance of this Convention to the intercountry adoption of children throughout the world cannot be overstated. It establishes the primary importance of finding a permanent family for a child, first by adoption in the child's country of origin when that is possible, and then by intercountry adoption provided that the norms and procedures of the Convention are followed and always considering the best interests of the child. By setting minimum standards, forcing re-examination of policies and procedures, and setting up governmental Central Authorities with specified responsibilities, the Convention will have a profound effect on adoptions not just in countries that become a party to the Convention, but also in countries dealing with them. The procedures that countries establish to conform to the Convention's requirements may be extended by many countries to all intercountry adoptions. It is possible that as ratifications proceed, party countries will be willing to arrange adoptions only with other party countries as a means of ensuring that the children involved are protected by the sound practices required by the Convention.

The Convention applies to any child up to the age of eighteen who is habitually resident in one party country and has been, is being or is to be moved to another party country after adoption or for the purpose of adoption by spouses or a person habitually resident in the receiving country. It covers all children in this age group and all intercountry adoptions, whether simple (ties to the birth parents are not completely severed) or full (all previous parental rights are extinguished), involving the two countries. The requirements that must be met by each of the countries are set out in Chapter II (Arts. 4 & 5), and include, for the country of origin, appropriate consents and counselling, determination of adoptability, and considerations of placement and best interest of the child, and for the receiving country, suitability and eligibility of the prospective adoptive parents and a determination that the child will be permitted to enter and permanently reside in the receiving country.

By the provisions of Chapter III, each party country is required to establish a Central Authority, with a few non–delegable functions and other delegable functions, including the procedural requirements of Chapter IV, that may be performed by "accredited" or public bodies. The various procedural steps and the requirements that must be followed are set out in Chapter IV. "Independent" adoptions conforming to the Convention's requirements are permitted at the option of the countries involved, and any country may require that only accredited or public bodies may participate in the adoption process. This flexibility was built into the Convention only through long and difficult negotiations. It is important for the United States because independent providers of adoption services are now permitted to act in most states of the United States, and both agencies and individuals are involved throughout the adoption process through networking. Both accredited bodies and other approved providers must meet Convention standards of integrity, training and experience, and improper financial gain is specifically prohibited. (See Arts. 11, 22(2), 32.)

The Convention does not prohibit prospective adoptive parents from acting for themselves, provided that the Convention requirements for home studies and the submission of an application are met and the country of origin permits it. The Convention does specifically prohibit contact between prospective adoptive parents and birth parents or other person having care of the child until specified conditions are met or under conditions established by the country of origin (Art. 29). Contact with the child and the directors and staff of institutions where the child is being cared for is not prohibited; directors and staff of institutions are bodies and thus are not to be considered a person having care of the child. While setting out a framework of minimum norms and procedures designed to protect the children and the interests of the parents involved, the Convention does not prevent any country from establishing more stringent conditions or requirements.

Chapter V achieves one of the principal objectives of the Convention by requiring that a Convention adoption must be recognized as a matter of law in all party countries, and that recognition may be refused only if it is manifestly contrary to public policy taking into account the best interests of the child. The Chapter also sets out the effect of the adoption: establishment of the new legal parent–child relationship between the child and the adoptive parents; termination of the pre-existing parent–child relationship when the adoption has this effect where made; in the latter case, enjoyment of rights equivalent to those in similar domestic adoptions; and non-prejudice to greater rights.

In the United States, the State Department (with the participation of the Department of Justice (Immigration and Naturalization Service) and the Department of Health and Human Services) is developing implementing legislation. Additional information may be obtained from the State Department – the Assistant Legal Adviser for Private International Law or the Office of Children's Issues.

VI.   SOURCES OF ASSISTANCE

A.   The State Department

In general, the State Department is an excellent source of information on a variety of topics related to family law and children, serves as the Central Authority for the Hague Abduction Convention, and is able at least to provide information on available lawyers in the country involved in the problem.

- Office of Children's Issues
  CA/OCS/CI Room 4800
  United States Department of State
  Washington, D.C. 20520
  Tel.: (202) 647–2688; fax: (202) 647–2835
  Recorded Information: (202) 736–7000
  Consular Affairs Bulletin Board: (202) 647–9225
  (modem number); Internet Gopher Address: DOSFAN.LIB.UIC.EDU
  (Central Authority for the Hague Abduction
  Convention; information on adoption and other issues)

- Assistant Legal Adviser for Private International Law
  Suite 203, South Bldg.
  2430 "E" Street, N.W.
  Washington, D.C. 20037–2800
  Fax: (202) 776–8482
  (Information on conventions)

- United States Department of State
  Office of Passport Policy and Advisory Services
  1111 19th Street, N.W., Suite 260
  Washington, D.C. 20522
  Recorded information: (202) 955-0377
  (Issuance or denial of passports for minors involved in custody disputes)

B.   *Other Agencies and Organizations*

- U.S. Department of Health and Human Services
  Office of Child Support Enforcement (OCSE)
  370 L'Enfant Promenade, S.W.
  Washington, D.C. 20447
  Tel.: (202) 260-5943; fax: (202) 401-5559
  (Information on international child support)

- U.S. Department of Justice
  Immigration and Naturalization Service
  Adjudication and Naturalization Division
  Immigrants Branch
  425 I Street, N.W., Room 7223
  Washington, D.C. 20536
  Tel.: (202) 616-7442; fax: (202) 514-0198
  (Information on requirements for entry and permanent residence of
  children to be adopted and pre-clearance of U.S. prospective adop-
  tive parents)

- National Center for Missing and Exploited Children
  2101 Wilson Boulevard, Suite 550
  Arlington, VA 22201-3052
  Tel.: 1-800-843-5678

- American Bar Association, Family Law Section
  750 North Lake Shore Drive
  Chicago, IL 60611
  Tel.: (312) 988-5603; fax: (312) 988-6281
  (Substantive committees)

- American Bar Association, Section of International Law and Practice
  (General Information)
  740 15th Street, N.W.
  Washington, D.C. 20005
  Tel.: (202) 662-1660; fax: (202) 662-1669

- International Society of Family Law
  Den Hooiberg 17
  4891 NM Rijsbergen
  The Netherlands

- International Academy of Matrimonial Lawyers
  <u>U.S.</u>
  Executive Director
  150 N. Michigan Avenue., Suite 2040
  Chicago, IL 60601
  Tel.: (312) 263–6477

  <u>International</u>
  Executive Director
  13 Claybury
  Bushey Herts, WD2 3ES
  United Kingdom
  Tel.: (44 181) 950 6452

- International Bar Association, General Practice Section, Family Law
  Committee
  2 Harewood Place
  London W1R 9HB England
  Tel.: (44 171) 629–1206; fax: (44 171) 409 0456

- International Children's Institute
  Av. 8 de Octobre 2904
  Montevideo, Uruguay
  Tel.: (598–2) 47 21 50; fax: (598–2) 47 32 42

- Hilton House BBS (Electronic Bulletin System)
  (Information on the Hague Abduction Convention)
  (408) 246–0387 – No fee for access; the file called FILE.DES may be
  downloaded and contains information on the files available from the
  system.

C.   *Organizations Serving Adoption Agencies and Individuals with Regard to Intercountry Adoptions*

- Adoptive Families of America
  3333 Highway 100 North
  Minneapolis, MN 55422
  Tel.: (612) 535–4829; fax: (612) 535–7808

- National Council for Adoption
  1930 17th Street, N.W.
  Washington, D.C. 20009
  Tel.: (202) 328–1200; fax: (202) 332–0935

- North American Council on Adoptable Children
  970 Raymond Avenue, Suite 106
  St. Paul, MN 55114
  Tel.: (612) 644–3036; fax: (612) 644–9848

- Joint Council on International Children's Services
  7 Cheverly Circle
  Cheverly, MD 20785
  Tel.: (301) 322–1906; fax: (301) 322–2425

D.   U.S. Statutes and Regulations

International Child Abduction Remedies Act (Public Law No. 100–300), 42 U.S.C. §§ 11601–11610.

Parental Kidnapping Prevention Act, 28 U.S.C. § 1738A.

Social Security Act, Title IV–D: 42 U.S.C. §§ 551–669.

8 C.F.R. Part 204, 59 Fed. Reg. at 38876.

E.   Uniform Acts

The Uniform Reciprocal Enforcement of Support Act (URESA) 1950, revised 1968 (RURESA), 9B U.L.A. 381 (1987).

The Uniform Child Custody Jurisdiction Act (UCCJA), 9 U.L.A. Part I, at 115 (1988).

The Uniform Adoption Act, 9 U.L.A. Part I, at 1 (1995 Supp.).

The Uniform Interstate Family Support Act (UIFSA), 9 U.L.A. Part I, at 229 (1995 Supp.).

F.   Treaties

Convention on the Recovery Abroad of Maintenance (New York 1956), 268 U.N.T.S. 32 (1957).

Convention on the Recognition and Enforcement of Decisions Relating to Child Maintenance Obligations, 539 U.N.T.S. 29 (1958).

Convention on the Recognition and Enforcement of Decisions Relating to Maintenance Obligations, 1021 U.N.T.S. 209 (1973).

Convention on the Civil Aspects of International Child Abduction, *reprinted in* 19 I.L.M. 1501 (1983), 51 Federal Register 10494 (March 26, 1986).

Convention on Protection of Children and Cooperation in Respect of Intercountry Adoption, *reprinted in* 32 I.L.M. 1134 (May 29, 1993) (English text), 40 Nether. Int'l L. Rev. (1993).

G. Books

AMERICAN LAW INSTITUTE, RESTATEMENT (SECOND) CONFLICT OF LAWS (1971).

JOAN HOLLINGER, ADOPTION LAW AND PRACTICE (1989, Supp. 1994).

INTERNATIONAL CHILD ABDUCTIONS — A GUIDE TO APPLYING THE HAGUE CONVENTION (with forms), American Bar Association (Gloria F. DeHart ed., 2d ed. 1993).

MARTINDALE–HUBBELL INTERNATIONAL LAW DIGEST (1995) (Brief summaries of foreign law, including some family law; texts of selected Conventions to which the United States is a party).

SCOLES & HAY, CONFLICT OF LAWS (1992).

H. Periodicals

American Bar Association, Family Law Section:

Family Law Quarterly:
  Vol. 5, No. 321 (1971)
  Vol. 28, No. 1 (Spring 1994)

Family Advocate:
  Vol. 3, No. 4 (Spring 1981)
  Vol. 9, No. 4 (Spring 1987)
  Vol. 15, No. 4 (Spring 1993)

Journal of Family Law, Univ. of Louisville
  (Annual Family Law Survey)

I.   *Articles*

Monica J. Allen, *Child-State Jurisdiction: A Due Process Invitation to Reconsider Some Basic Family Law Assumptions*, 26 FAM. L.Q. 293 (1992).

Brigitte M. Bodenheimer, *Progress Under the Uniform Child Custody Jurisdiction Act and Remaining Problems: Punitive Decrees, Joint Custody, and Excessive Modifications*, 65 CALIF. L. REV. 978 (1977).

Carol S. Bruch, *The Central Authority's Role Under the Hague Child Abduction Convention: A Friend in Deed*, 28 FAM. L.Q. 35 (Spring 1994).

David F. Cavers, *International Enforcement of Family Support*, 81 COLUM. L. REV. 994 (1981).

Russell M. Coombs, *Progress Under the Parental Kidnapping Prevention Act*, 6 J. AM. ACAD. MATR. LAWYERS 59 (1990).

Gloria F. DeHart, *Conventions, Comity and the Constitution: State and Federal Initiatives in International Support Enforcement*, 28 FAM. L.Q., Vol 1 (1994).

Adair Dyer, *The Tangled International Divorce Web — Abroad*, FAMILY ADVOCATE, Vol. 9, No. 4 (Spring 1987).

Stephen C. Glassman, *The Tangled International Divorce Web — At Home*, FAMILY ADVOCATE, Vol. 9, No. 4 (1987).

James G. Hergen, *How to Practice Law in Europe When You're Not European*, FAMILY ADVOCATE, Vol. 3. No. 4 (1981).

Patricia M. Hoff, *An Overview of the North American Symposium on International Child Abduction*, 28 FAM. L.Q. 1 (1994).

John F. Nichols, *American Courts Look at Foreign Decrees*, FAMILY ADVOCATE, Vol. 9, No. 4 (1987).

Peter H. Pfund, *The Hague Convention on International Child Abduction, The International Child Abductions Remedies Act, and The Need for Availability of Counsel for all Petitioners*, 24 FAM. L.Q. 35 (1990).

Peter H. Pfund, *Intercountry Adoption: The 1993 Hague Convention: Its Purpose, Implementation, and Promise*, 28 FAM. L.Q. 53 (1994).

Linda Silberman, *Hague Convention on International Child Abduction: A Brief Overview and Case Law Analysis*, 28 FAM. L.Q. 9 (1994).

Linda Silberman, *Hague International Child Abduction: A Progress Report*, 57 L. & CONTEMP. PROB. 210 (1994).

ENDNOTES

1 For a discussion of some general problems of law practice internationally, including service of process, taking evidence, and legalization, see James G. Hergen, *How to Practice Law in Europe When You're Not European*, 3 FAMILY ADVOCATE, 24 (Spring 1981).

2 Australia, Luxembourg, Netherlands. Hague Conference Doc.: Actes et documents de la Treizième Session, 4 au 23 octobre 1976, Extract from the Final Act of the Thirteenth Session, Tome III, Marriage, Edités par le Bureau de la Conférence, Imprimérie Nationale, Le Haye (1978), pp. 282–287; *reprinted in* 16 I.L.M. at 18–21 (1977).

3 France, Luxembourg, Netherlands. Hague Conference Doc.: Actes et documents de la Treizième Session, 4 au 23 octobre 1976, Extract from the Final Act of the Thirteenth Session, Tome II, Matrimonial property regimes, Edités par le Bureau de la Conférence, Imprimérie Nationale, Le Haye (1978), pp. 319–326; *reprinted in* 16 I.L.M. at 14–17 (1977).

4 Australia, Cyprus, Czech Republic, Denmark, Egypt, Finland, Italy, Luxembourg, the Netherlands, Norway, Portugal, Slovak Republic, Sweden, Switzerland, United Kingdom, Hague Conference Doc.: Actes et documents de la Onzième Session, 7 au 27 octobre 1968, extract from the Final Act of the Eleventh Session, Tome II, Divorce, Edités par le Bureau de la Conférence, Imprimérie Nationale, Le Haye (1979), pp. 201–208; *reprinted in* 8 I.L.M. at 31 (1969).

5 American Law Institute (1971) §§ 6, 283, 286.

6 A copy of the English text and a translation of the official report of the Hague Conference appears in 5 FAM. L. Q. 321 (1971).

7 268 U.N.T.S. 32 (1957). A list of the parties may be requested from the United Nations: Treaty Section, Office of Legal Affairs, United Nations, New York, New York.

8 539 U.N.T.S. 29 (1958).

9 1021 U.N.T.S. 209 (1973).

10 9B U.L.A. 381 (1987).

11 9 U.L.A. 15 (Supp. 1993).

12 Australia, Austria, Czech Republic, France, Germany, Hungary, Mexico, New Zealand, Norway, Poland, Slovak Republic, Sweden, United Kingdom.

13 Bermuda, Canada (by province), Fiji, Jamaica, Republic of South Africa. Of the additional 20 countries with which the author has discussed the possibility, arrangements may be possible with nine more Convention countries and three additional non-Convention countries.

14 T.I.A.S. 11670, *reprinted in* 19 I.L.M. 1501 (1980).

15 The English text of the Convention and a detailed legal analysis of the Convention are in the State Department notice in the *Federal Register* of March 26, 1986, pages 10494–10516.

16 9 U.L.A. Part I, at 115 (1988).

17 *See* 9 U.L.A. Part I, at 119, Child Custody Jurisdiction, General Statutory Notes; 9 U.L.A. Part I, at 327 (UCCJA § 23) noting variations from official text (1988).

18   It may, however serve to establish *de facto* reciprocity resulting in recognition of United States orders in a foreign country.

19   28 U.S.C § 1738A.

20   The United States does not have the highest per capita rate; at least Canada, France and Australia exceed the United States rate although not the number of adoptions because of their smaller population base.

21   The text of the Convention may be found in Part A of the final Act of the Seventeenth Session of the Hague Conference on Private International Law, May 29, 1993, *reprinted in* 32 I.L.M. 1134 (1993) (English text), 40 NETHER. INT'L L. REV. (1993/2). A copy of the act is also printed as an appendix to Peter H. Pfund, *Intercountry Adoption: the 1993 Hague Convention: Its Purpose, Implementation, and Promise,* 28 FAM. L.Q. 53 (1994).

CHAPTER 26

SELECTING AND WORKING WITH FOREIGN COUNSEL

Elliot R. Lewis*

I. INTRODUCTION

In these times of rapid movement toward a global economy, companies are expanding beyond traditional territorial borders. Economic globalization is the result of significant legislative accomplishments and economic developments, *e.g.*, the North American Free Trade Agreement and the European Union. With these developments comes the necessity for lawyers to be prepared for transactions and dealings worldwide. As indicated in other chapters of this book, the need for local counsel in international practice can arise in a myriad of areas of the law and in diverse contexts.

The intent of this chapter is to suggest ways to identify potential outside foreign counsel and to provide suggestions for retaining and working with the most qualified lawyer. Basics such as selecting outside foreign counsel, working effectively with outside counsel and other advisors, and preparing an engagement letter tailored to the matter at hand will be emphasized. This advice could also be useful for outside counsel in developing business and when working with in-house counsel.

It is important to recognize that each legal matter is unique. You will encounter differences in the legal processes, the applicable laws, the documents and in numerous other elements of each deal or litigation. In addition, you will be faced with numerous administrative (nonlegal) details, *e.g.*, billing, reporting, language barriers, cultural differences, and politics, to name a few. Even the type of legal professional with whom you are dealing may differ.

The advice that follows is intended to help you sidestep potential pitfalls, avoid confusion, and provide you with the necessary tools to select the outside advisor that makes the most sense, given the type of work involved. These suggestions should enhance your relationship with outside counsel and increase the likelihood of success. Take the time at the front end to identify the best choice of outside counsel and to chart out mutual responsibilities; otherwise you will be at a disadvantage from the beginning and may be blamed for subsequent problems.

II.   SELECTING OUTSIDE FOREIGN COUNSEL—WHERE TO LOOK AND FACTORS TO CONSIDER

A.   *Outline Your Matter/Expectations*

Before you interview and select outside foreign counsel and other necessary foreign advisors you may need, take time to sketch out the parameters of your international matter. What exactly are you/your client looking for? Is it researching local laws, drafting, negotiating, meeting with local government officials, handling litigation? Or is it limited to performing due diligence?

Outline your expectations. Review them with the client to confirm that you know your client's full intentions. Your client's short- and long-term objectives must be known as fully as possible, at the outset, in order to select appropriate outside foreign counsel and other advisors.

B.   *Identify the Type of Lawyer You Need*

Most law schools provide little or no training concerning the differences in the structure of the legal profession in different countries. Depending upon the jurisdictions involved, you may be working with more than one type of legal system. To obtain a brief background on the legal system in a particular country, you may wish to consult *The Statesman's Yearbook*, edited by Brian Hunter, 1992-93, 129th Edition. In some systems, the legal profession is organized differently from the U.S. The U.S. lawyer needs to understand the profession's local structure to determine whom to retain to fulfill his needs.

• **Barristers and Solicitors**. The example most often used of how legal systems differ around the world is the English system (applicable in England, Wales, Northern Ireland, and the Republic of Ireland), with its two types of lawyers – barristers and solicitors. In these jurisdictions, there is a distinct difference between a barrister and a solicitor.

Solicitors generally do all of the legal work for clients including negotiating, drafting agreements, forming of companies, drafting wills and trusts and, generally, rendering legal advice. In other words, solicitors perform services which are very similar to those performed by U.S. lawyers with one major qualification: with limited exceptions, solicitors do not argue cases before the courts. Depending upon the jurisdiction, the solicitor may represent the public/client before a limited number of courts.

The role of representing clients before the courts is generally reserved to barristers. The solicitor, however, actually selects and retains the barrister to handle the litigation.

Barristers have a second function, which is to render specialized advice. Frequently, on important issues of law which are significant for clients, a solicitor will instruct a barrister to render a legal opinion. Sometimes the solicitors know what the answer will be in advance; but an opinion from a barrister will serve to reinforce their view and, indeed, cover them in case a problem arises with respect to the advice.

In Canada, the distinction between a barrister and a solicitor is less technical, with the exception of Quebec. Quebec, unlike the other provinces, uses the civil law system; Quebec lawyers are known as "advocates."

In the other provinces of Canada, after being called to the bar (admitted), the lawyer takes the oath of both a barrister and a solicitor. Still, the spirit of the distinction between the two professional designations is present – you consider yourself a barrister if you litigate and a solicitor if your practice is more in the nature of corporate work (although solicitors can appear in the same courts as barristers).

• **Notaries**. Another important example of how legal professionals differ around the globe is the civil-law notary ("*notaire*" in France), ("*Notar*" in Germany) and ("*notaris*" in the Netherlands) (collectively referred to as a "*notary*" or "*notaries*"). *Notaries* trace their profession back to Roman times. They perform a quasi-governmental function, recording and vouching for the legality of a wide variety of private transactions. They are expected to act as honest brokers and to stand behind their determinations of the enforceability of contracts and legality of corporations. The liability that they theoretically assume accounts, at least in part, for the amount of fees charged by *notaries*.

The *notary* in civil-law jurisdictions is a distinct legal profession which does not exist in the United States (except in Louisiana and Puerto Rico). It is *not* the equivalent of the U.S. notary. The types of services a *notary* normally offers include: creating most types of legal entities, *e.g.*, corporations, which require a notarial act; amending articles of incorporation; drafting and executing wills (in the absence of a holographic will); handling land transfers which require the intervention of a *notary*, who prepares the deed and reviews the land register (known as a *cadastre*); authenticating signatures on certain documents, *e.g.*, a power of attorney; and acting for and on behalf of the deceased, which is similar to assisting in a probate procedure in the United States. A civil-law *notary* has much greater responsibility than a notary in the United States.

Fees for a *notary* are generally uniform within a civil-law country and are set forth in a table of fees approved by the respective government. Since only *notaries* are permitted to perform certain required legal functions and the number of *notaries* is limited, some lawyers in these jurisdictions may informally refer to *notaries* having a monopoly (which is really not the case) on handling certain legal tasks. For example, a Belgian lawyer may prepare the articles of incorporation, but would have to seek out a *notary* to register a company. This is not the case in the United States, where any properly trained lawyer could formally create a corporation.

The education and process of becoming a *notary* also vary between the civil-law countries. In some countries, they even vary internally. Generally, *notaries* are fully-trained lawyers, appointed by the government; *e.g.*, in Belgium they are appointed by Royal Decree. In Belgium and France, however, the *notary* is not a member of the bar but could be in other civil-law countries, *e.g.*, in northern Germany.

Germany is an excellent example of how *notaries* may differ within a country. In northern Germany, a member of the bar in good standing, after a certain number of years, may apply to become a *Notar*. If accepted, the individual may remain a member of the bar in addition to being recognized as a *Notar*. In the southwest of Germany, a *Notar* must complete an educational curriculum that is quite different from a lawyer's educational requirements. A *Notar* in this part of Germany is not considered a lawyer. In the southeast of Germany, in contrast, after becoming a lawyer and achieving satisfactory scores on the bar exam, an individual may be appointed a *Notar* without passing another exam. If appointed a *Notar* in the southeast, the *Notar* can no longer remain a member of the bar.

• **Foreign Legal Consultant**. Another type of lawyer you may encounter in the U.S. and abroad is known as the foreign legal consultant ("FLC").

In recent years, a number of law firms have established foreign offices. The expatriates working in those firms may be licensed to practice local law (especially with the elimination in some countries of citizenship requirements for admission to practice), or may not. In some cases they will be licensed as an FLC. The FLC is a lawyer who practices in a foreign jurisdiction and is licensed by that jurisdiction to practice, but not as a local practitioner.

The scope of an FLC's permitted activities depends on local law, but usually does not include advising on purely local-law matters. Virtually all jurisdictions permit FLCs to advise on their home country law, and they usually permit advice on international law as well. There are differences among jurisdictions in the FLC's ability to advise on third-country law. If the FLC is in partnership with local lawyers, the scope-of-practice limitations they personally face may not be a problem. But if the FLC has to go outside his firm for advice on local law, you should consider what value hiring the FLC adds or, conversely, whether the FLC represents another layer of management. Sometimes it is useful, as when the client lacks the language skills to deal directly with the local lawyer; this is really a case-by-case issue.

C.   *Where to Look for Outside Foreign Counsel*

Now that you know what type of lawyer you need, how do you find the right person? Selecting the proper outside foreign counsel to represent you in your international matters can be difficult. Where do you start? Whom do you call? Are there any available directories to consult? Are they neutral sources or self-serving, and are they complete?

There are many sources to tap in creating a list of potential outside foreign counsel choices. The list below represents several sources that the author has found helpful:

*   Word of Mouth – Often the most fruitful. Confirm what legal services the recommended lawyer performed, that the client was pleased, language capabilities and that the lawyer has no troublesome personal/professional quirks;

*   *American Corporate Counsel Association Foreign Counsel Directory* (to order, call (202) 296–4522);

*   *The American Bar Association Guide to Foreign Law Firms* (to order, call (312) 988–5522);

*   Your local primary counsel. Be wary of established business relationships that your local counsel may have, as these may not provide you with the right expertise. Inquire as to the details of the relationship;

*   *Martindale-Hubbell Law Directory* (to order, call (800) 526–4902), which is on-line with LEXIS;

*   *Martindale-Hubbell International Law Directory* (to order, call (800) 526–4902), also on-line with LEXIS;

*   *Campbell's List - A Directory of Selected Lawyers* (published since 1879) (to order, call (407) 644–8298);

*   *Russell Law List – 1993 –* "The Aristocrat of Law Lists" – Legal Correspondents International (to order, call (410) 820–4475);

*   *The American Lawyer - Practice Directories* (to order, call (212) 973–2800);

- *U.S. Customs House Guide* – Official 1995 Version (to order, call (800) 669-3282) (includes an alphabetical and geographical index to law firms specializing in admiralty, customs, international corporate and international trade law);

- *Official Export Guide* – 1995 Version (to order, call (800) 669-3282) (includes law firms specializing in admiralty, customs, international corporate and international trade law);

- *North American Trade Guide®* – 1995–1996 Third Annual Edition (to order, call (800) 669-3282);[1]

- Other lawyers and business professionals, *e.g.*, accountants, in similar positions responsible for international matters;

- Speakers at CLE presentations who have impressed you;

- Authors who have provided you with useful information in the past;

- The U.S. Embassy in the relevant country;

- The relevant country's embassy in your home country – contact the commercial attaché;

- Formal or informal law firm networks; and

- Accumulated business cards – you may have forgotten a contact from an ABA–CLE meeting two years ago.

Consult several sources, and look for recurrent names. If someone's name keeps coming up, especially from word–of–mouth, that's a positive sign.

D. *Factors to Consider When Retaining Outside Foreign Counsel and Other Advisors*

You have now prepared an outline of your expectations and know, to the extent possible, your client's/company's short- and long-term objectives. Next, armed with a list of potential outside foreign counsel, you are ready to embark on the process of interviewing outside counsel, via telephone, fax and whatever other means are possible. Of course, if you have the opportunity to meet the candidate in person, by all means do so. This is especially important if the work will be long–term, expensive or strategically critical to your client.

After making the initial contact with the potential outside foreign lawyer, ask the individual to send a short fax concerning some of the details of your discussion to test the individual's ability to communicate timely in writing. This communique could confirm the lawyer's meeting with your local representatives, billing rates, the team involved, and/or the firm's approach to your matter. If the potential outside foreign lawyer communicates poorly or untimely, these traits could be warning signs of what to expect.

Although the interview and selection process of foreign counsel involves similar skills, criteria and methods used in choosing outside counsel in your home state/country, there are distinctions. Some of the differences include less formality associated with the relationship between you and foreign counsel, language barriers, and perhaps greater difficulty in asking the right questions and evaluating outside counsel's answers.

For the most part, your legal experience and outline of your needs/expectations should serve as guideposts. Above all, do not forget to apply your common sense. To assist you in the decision process, you might consider one or more of the factors listed below:

1.   The Comfort Level

Determine the lawyer's qualifications. How comfortable do you feel that he has the types of experience your transaction will require? For example, if your deal involves multiple parties from multiple countries, do you feel confident that the outside foreign counsel you are interviewing has the requisite expertise?

You might also inquire as to his education and training. For instance, will you benefit from retaining a lawyer with U.S. education (legal or other relevant graduate course work) or U.S. training? Is experience in representing clients from your home country/state important; or stated another way, is knowing the mindset from your jurisdiction important?

Is his office equipped with the technological resources needed for prompt responses and is the equipment and software compatible with your working requirements?

Does the lawyer exhibit any cultural biases? And, remember to ensure at the outset that there are no conflicts of interest (different jurisdictions have different standards).

2.   Existing Representatives in Your Industry

If the firm or contact lawyer represents clients in your industry, this will eliminate much time in explaining how you do business, industry terms and paperwork, etc. On the other hand, existing representations within your industry may be a negative if the firm or lawyer represents your main competitor. In highly specialized areas of practice, it may be difficult to find an experienced practitioner that does not, especially in some countries where the pool of qualified potential counsel is relatively small.

If the lawyer has experience representing clients in your industry, he will be able to flag issues and identify more concerns in much less billable time than a lawyer who has no background in your industry. Another potential benefit from retaining a lawyer with experience is that he may apprise you of other business opportunities.

If the lawyer has little to no previous industry experience, you and your client will lose valuable time explaining the basics. However, depending upon your client's business and philosophy, you might prefer a lawyer who does not represent clients in your industry, which would reduce the risk of a conflict of interest.

Remember, you will be expected to provide your client with the highest degree of sophistication possible, all dependent upon the economic resources at hand, the amount to be invested and the potential risks.

3.   References

If permitted by local law and if prospective local counsel is willing, obtain a list of other clients, the contact person and/or other possible lead attorneys who he has represented.

Depending upon the jurisdiction, it may be appropriate to ask for permission to contact the references. When you do so, be inquisitive. Ask for a general sketch of what was involved in past or present matters. What were the obstacles and significant achievements? Ask about the current status and the future outlook. Evaluate this information and draw your own conclusions.

4.   Substantive Expertise

Evaluate the prospective counsel's expertise by issue area. For instance, can he provide you with the necessary tax guidance? Keep in mind that lawyers in many countries may not be as specialized as those in your home country/state.

Are there tax incentives to help you decide where to locate the business? Will it make a difference if the principal office is located in Holland or Belgium? While you may not have a sufficient grasp of local laws to identify this question as an issue, well-trained local counsel should identify such issues during the initial consultation. Depending on your locale, you might receive tax advice from an accountant, and not an attorney.

Outside counsel, during the initial meeting, can demonstrate his abilities by identifying big picture issues and providing you with a thumbnail sketch of the project or deal to review with the client.

You may also need to determine whether one firm will be able to counsel you on the various areas of law implicated by the matter, *e.g.*, trademark, tax, labor/employment, and environmental, or whether you will need to retain multiple lawyers/firms.

5.   Connections

Does he know any individuals connected to your matter, *e.g.*, the president of the company you intend to acquire, potential investors, key government officials, existing customers, potential customers, and/or the competition? For instance, if your transaction will require the government's consent, *e.g.,* permits, you may be well served with local foreign counsel who has already worked successfully with local government officials. However, this can be a double-edged sword. He may be related to a local official and make an inadvertent disclosure. Also, beware of connections without substance (*i.e.,* the person who is only well-connected), and of the U.S. law risks associated with payments to foreign officials. (*See* Chapter 14, *The Foreign Corrupt Practices Act.*)

6. Language Skills

Can you speak or read the language(s) spoken in the respective location(s) and among the major players in your deal? How fluent are you? Be honest. You could be called upon to interpret a deal-breaking provision. Be confident that either you or the counsel selected possess expert language skills. If not, this could be a disadvantage.

Regardless of the native language, excellent speaking and writing skills will of course be critical. In addition, your outside foreign counsel's fluency in your language, both orally and with the written word, will also play a key role in your success. You may want to avoid the situation where the outside foreign counsel can only speak the language and not be able to communicate effectively in writing.

Requesting a confirming fax after your initial contact with the lawyer will allow you to identify early on whether he has the requisite written language skills.

When negotiating with multiple parties, you may be at the bargaining table listening to several one-on-one discussions in various foreign languages. If your outside foreign counsel is not fluent in all the relevant languages, this may be a disadvantage. You may need to retain another lawyer who has the requisite language skills or hire a translator. A source of foreign translators is the *American Corporate Counsel Association Foreign Counsel Directory*, set forth by language and expertise with various documents (available to members of the Association).

Always try to arrange negotiations in the language in which you are most comfortable speaking unless there are extenuating reasons to do otherwise. Keep accurate meeting minutes. You may prefer to have those present initial the minutes indicating their agreement as to what was discussed. Lastly, take frequent breaks to review what has been discussed to ensure your understanding of the issues and risks involved.

7. Knowledge

What does he know of current developments, *e.g.,* your competition and respective industry trends, that may positively or adversely affect your matter? If the lawyer is lacking in this area, what assurances do you have that he keeps current on changes in local laws and key legal decisions? Also, will you be charged for the lawyer learning the basics of your industry?

8.   Flexibility

What is his degree of willingness to travel, work around your schedule, and the time tables for the deal? Does he have the flexibility and commitment to provide quality service and be mindful of your budget? Will you be charged for travel time? Does he know how to use a computer? Will they use word processing software compatible with your own? Finally, don't make assumptions about work habits or hours (*e.g.*, working weekends) and whether they will call you while they are on holiday.

Do you get the sense that outside counsel will consciously make decisions on whether to expend resources as if he were doing so with his own money? Listen for statements like, "Yes, we could perform that search, but I am not so sure it would be worth your money. There are other ways, which will be less expensive, to provide you with that information to enable you to make this decision."

Also, when interviewing potential outside foreign counsel, do they make it quite clear that it is not critical that they perform all of the work? They should give you the chance to prepare the first draft of documents, perform searches to the extent logistically possible, collect information, and perform other necessary tasks in an effort to hold down costs. Clarify your expectations in this regard up front.

During the course of your transaction, an indication that you are being well served is if you hear this type of response: "We are close to exceeding your budget for the due diligence work. We have four more tasks to perform. I think we should do one and two; perhaps you or one of your staff could perform three. Here's what to do. We can do without number four and this is why."

Cost efficiencies are achieved, not just well intended, when there is periodic discussion of the amount of legal expense compared to the amount invested in the project or the risks associated with the matter.

9.   Worst–Case Scenarios

Before you and your client jump in with both feet, it is critical to assess "worst case scenarios." What does each lawyer tell you can happen if your deal falls apart or you are unsuccessful with the litigation? If two potential outside foreign counsel differ in their opinions as to worst case liabilities, seek out other counsel and call upon whatever other resources are available to draw your own conclusions.

Although the amount of the investment may dictate the type of firm or lawyer you retain, remember, you might "lose the farm" and not just the amount invested. Retain counsel who will adequately protect your client. Although hourly fees are critical, when business opportunities fall apart no one will appreciate that the lawyer you retained was $35 less an hour than any other attorney you interviewed or that the attorney you hired adhered to the budget. Remember, at the end of the day YOU are responsible for the advice given and assistance rendered.

10. Firm Brochure

Review background information on the firm's expertise, the expertise of its members and the firm's office locations by obtaining a firm brochure and any other relevant information. Consult the *Martindale-Hubbell Law Directory* and the *Martindale-Hubbell International Law Directory* to learn more about the individual lawyers, the firm and their expertise and clients. However, many foreign firms don't have brochures; some local ethics rules prohibit them or listings in publications such as *Martindale-Hubbell.*

When dealing in the European Community, a firm with either multiple locations or firm members who have practiced/trained in more than one country may give you an advantage. This could depend upon the number of countries involved in your deal. One factor to consider is whether there is any additional cost, such as travel time and expense, by using lawyers from multiple locations.

11. Fee Factors

There is no right or wrong answer when it comes to the issue of attorney's fees. However, make sure you understand from the beginning on what basis you will be billed if you retain the respective outside foreign counsel. Determine at the outset what types of services and individuals (secretary, assistant, paralegal) for which/whom the firm intends to bill. Also, specify whether you prefer to limit the number (or identity) of lawyers working on the matter. If you do not, you may find you have hired the lawyer's associates when you intended to obtain the services of a particular individual whose skills and experience you are seeking.

Also, you may be in a jurisdiction where the fees are fixed by local law for certain matters. Some countries, for instance, establish a fee scale for litigation. If so, the outside foreign counsel should make you aware of any statutes controlling fee structures at the outset of the relationship.

12. Attorney–Client Confidentiality

Do not presume your communications will be treated as privileged and confidential as they are in your home jurisdiction. Find out the rules and modify your behavior, communications and expectations accordingly. Depending on the nature of your use of foreign counsel, this factor could be highly significant.

Further, in some jurisdictions client listings are kept confidential. Even if they are not, you may prefer to keep your relationship with outside counsel confidential and specifically instruct him not to disclose the relationship.

III.   WORKING EFFECTIVELY WITH FOREIGN COUNSEL

There are a number of tasks and communications which are critical to success when in-house counsel (and/or outside domestic counsel) retains outside foreign counsel and other advisors for representation in international matters. Objectives and expectations should be made clear. Although certainly not exhaustive, the list below should help avoid confusion:

- **Communication.** When interviewing potential outside foreign counsel initially, and throughout the matter, you must properly communicate expectations, budgets, facts, short- and long-term corporate objectives, specific limits on authority, and special concerns, to name a few key factors. Set out preliminary parameters and ask for suggestions. Likewise, foreign counsel should be candid about fulfilling your expectations, adhering to the budget, meeting objectives, etc. Help them to understand the role(s) to be played in the transaction/litigation. They may be unaccustomed to performing certain tasks you take for granted, but nonetheless willing, if your objectives are clarified.

- **Engagement Letter.** After selecting counsel, send a thorough engagement letter, which will serve to bring to light any miscommuni-cations/misunderstandings from the beginning. The engagement letter should cover all foreseeable issues, from expectations, duties and tasks, and fee structure, to reporting responsibility and who has authority to give instructions on the matter. For example, matters such as monthly versus quarterly billing, budgets, etc., should be included in your engagement letter to avoid any confusion. See section IV for a further discussion of the engagement letter.

- **Thank Yous to Those Not Retained.** You should send a thank you letter to the other lawyers/firms/advisors you interviewed, but whom you will not be retaining. Aside from the obvious professional courtesy, you may need them in the future, either on the immediate matter or in another transaction. You never know when your paths will cross. For instance, the firm you select may not be able to provide you a desired service and you may need to retain another law firm to achieve your desired result.

- **Deadlines.** At the outset, establish time frames and calendar reminders to meet deadlines. Remember, the foreign counsel you retain may be a day behind or ahead, depending on locale, and time has a habit of slipping away. Obtain your counsel's home phone number. Also, whether you are discussing deadlines with your outside foreign counsel or referencing deadlines in documents, be specific about whose time zone and date you are talking about when the parties are located in different corners of the world and in different time zones. Also, make clear whether delivery is to be made by voice message, fax, international courier or in person.

- **Billing.** Make sure you have a clear understanding of how, for what, and for whom you will be billed. To whom will outside foreign counsel send the bills? Will they be formatted to meet requirements set forth by your department, accounts payable and/or internal audit?

Also, you may find that the bills are not as detailed as the bills you are used to reviewing from counsel located in your home country/state. Many U.S. companies require detailed billing with a description of how much time was spent for each task on a particular day, total hours spent by each attorney, and/or individual billing rates. If you want this same format from foreign counsel, you will want to provide him with a sample.

Be aware that the terminology used in foreign counsel bills is sometimes misleading. The billing may be phrased to include such language as "telephone attendance," implying that you are being charged for a receptionist taking a message, when in fact, the attorney spent an hour with you on the phone that day, advising you about a multitude of issues.

Lastly, the bill may contain language which is necessary for the firm if there is a dispute. For instance, in some jurisdictions, *e.g.*, New South Wales, it is not uncommon to see the phrase "care, skill and responsibility," on invoices. This language is required by local statutes if the firm intends to receive an amount in excess of the minimum statutory scale of costs/fees.

Will invoices be paid by your client or by you? Foreign lawyers typically assume that when a U.S. lawyer hires a foreign lawyer on behalf of the client, the U.S. lawyer will pay or is the guarantor.

• **Contact.** Allow your key business clients to contact your outside foreign advisor, either via telephone, in person or otherwise. Contact with key business clients allows the outside foreign advisor to get a better flavor for the deal, the dynamics and the parties involved. However, the lawyer should take whatever steps are necessary to keep you in the loop. This is critical. Make sure that your business clients understand this and agree to cooperate.

• **Central Point of Control/Contact.** Depending on the geographics of your transaction, your ability to travel and a host of other factors, it may be essential to make it clear to the outside foreign advisor that he should only receive direction from you, direct his reports to you and not to do so with the client who might be located on site. This precaution will avoid confusion, especially when outside foreign counsel will have significant one-on-one communications with in-house business personnel and your contact with outside foreign counsel is primarily via telephone/fax. You are best suited to provide clear instructions in order to limit the scope of his work to what is truly needed. Conflicting instructions should be avoided.

• **Outside Counsel Manual.** If your company has an outside counsel manual, send a copy to the outside foreign counsel you retain. Ask the attorney whether there are any problems caused by the content of the manual, *e.g.*, provisions that are contrary to local law or practice.

If you do not have a manual, and you often retain outside counsel, you might consider preparing one in the near future. The manual should provide your outside counsel with: additional background information on your company's business; your company's philosophy on retaining outside counsel; to whom outside counsel reports (both oral and written communications); litigation management and strategies; use of attorneys, paralegals and other advisors within the firm being retained; scope of permitted research; whether prior review by in-house counsel of documents/pleadings is required; specifics about working with in-house personnel; and fees and costs. This list is not meant to be all-encompassing, but should serve as a checklist to enhance the relationship between the outside foreign counsel/advisor and your company.

IV.   THE ENGAGEMENT LETTER

The use of an engagement letter in a transnational matter has the same purpose as the one you sent six months ago in your domestic acquisition. The key is to educate outside foreign counsel, set forth the specifics of what is required and avoid confusion about such topics as billing, which no one likes to discuss.

Keep in mind that no two engagement letters need be alike. Each matter is unique. However, you will usually find core topics that will surface. In drafting an engagement letter, you should tailor it to meet your specific needs and recognize that in international matters there will be a number of differences to consider.

- **Local Laws, Practices and Procedures.** One area of concern is the different local laws. In this regard, your questions and concerns should be set forth in the engagement letter. Request outside foreign counsel to identify relevant local laws, practices and whatever differences exist compared to your local laws that he may be able to bring to your attention. Start with the assumption that the laws and practices of the new jurisdiction will be completely different from those of your own country.

- **Deadlines.** Given the geographic distances, time changes may be significant and could have an impact on deadlines. Also, depending upon the type of deadlines, the jurisdiction you are about to enter may have a different view of enforcing deadlines than you do. There may be deadlines of which you are not aware. You might ask outside foreign counsel to identify any and all deadlines and how and to what degree they are enforced.

Overnight mail may become two-day airmail when you are engaged in international matters. This could also have an impact on what type of notice is acceptable, *e.g.*, as set forth in an acquisition agreement, between you and the other party(ies) that is about to unfold.

• **Opinion Letter.** Depending upon the jurisdiction, if you are requesting an opinion letter, the type of product you might receive may differ significantly from what you might receive in your own locale. If you have not already discussed the opinion letter (if one is being sought) on the telephone, spend extra time detailing what type of opinion letter you are seeking.

• **Key Individuals.** Inform outside counsel about key individuals within your organization. Although this would be something you would do in a domestic matter, it becomes more important in an international transaction where the outside foreign counsel may have more "face-to-face" contact with individuals from your company/firm located near counsel. You might never meet the lawyer, but your local client may have significant contact. Do you want to be apprised of all meetings and correspondence? If so, advise outside foreign counsel in the engagement letter as to these details and any others which you deem appropriate when it comes to communicating, either in person, on the telephone, or in writing with local representatives.

• **Communications.** Method of communications is another necessary ingredient in the engagement letter. When doing business in the U.S., the phone and fax are usually considered the most acceptable means. However, depending upon time differences, communication capabilities, and other factors, you might prefer outside foreign counsel to communicate with you via a particular method, *e.g.*, e-mail or the internet.

• **Conflicts of Interest.** Consider whether the standard for conflicts of interest is different from that of your own jurisdiction. The standards may differ significantly. Use the engagement letter to set forth your understanding of local laws and practices in this respect. If you have no knowledge in this area, be sure to inquire. You and/or your client may not find it acceptable that the outside counsel you have just retained may have had a relationship in the past and/or in the present that poses a conflict of interest in your mind, *e.g.*, counsel represents a key competitor. Whether it is a recognized conflict by law or a business preference, define the parameters at the outset to avoid confusion later.

• **Billing.** Billing practices are a basic component of any engagement letter. This topic is worth a few extra lines since these practices seem to have larger variations when venturing abroad. You might request in the engagement letter to have a sample bill faxed to you to ensure that the method and billing format will be acceptable. Billing procedures, especially invoicing software, differ significantly around the world. Ask to see a sample bill at the outset to avoid receiving the initial bill in a format that will be unacceptable to your company's/firm's accounts payable department. Clarify the types of expenses that you will be required to pay, the information that will be set forth in the bill, billing cycles, whether in your own currency or in some other currency, and a myriad of other features. You would be well-served to refer to the types of bills you are used to paying when preparing this section of the engagement letter. Clarify who will receive the bill.

• **Payment.** Specify the currency and exchange rates (when and where applicable). Clarify means of payment (check, wire transfer), and any approval requirements. Clarify who is responsible for payment.

• **The Audience.** Lastly, consider your audience. Who will read and rely on the engagement letter? Remember, the relationship is a two-way street and the geographic distances may make communicating more difficult. The engagement letter should shout clarity and professionalism. Also, many outside foreign counsel appreciate a heightened degree of politeness when it comes to the engagement letter, which flows from the various cultural differences. Before sending the engagement letter, switch places with the outside foreign counsel to ensure it is not peremptory and that you would be pleased to receive it.

V.   CONCLUSION

Whether you are planning a transnational deal or are on the brink of international litigation, your success may hinge on your selection and management of outside foreign counsel. The selection process is a challenge. Be prepared. Refer to these materials and other sources to identify the most appropriate outside foreign counsel. Hasty selection may result in needless headaches and obstacles.

Next, your time will be well spent at the outset if you take steps to ensure the relationship with outside foreign counsel will foster open communication. For instance, a thorough engagement letter will be worth its weight in gold. Attention to routine details should eliminate a layer of confusion and will contribute directly to your success.

Most importantly, of course, you must manage the relationship and execute on the fundamentals as discussed above. Whether you elect a "hands-on" or "hands-off" approach, you are ultimately responsible for the results obtained in utilizing the outside counsel you have chosen. In other words, your success or failure is in your own hands.

Finally, perhaps the most useful piece of advice is do not abandon your common sense at the border.

VI. SOURCES OF ASSISTANCE

A. *Books*

THE STATESMAN'S YEARBOOK (Brian Hunter ed. 1992–1993, 129th ed.).

MARCEL BERLINS & CLARE DYER, THE LAW MACHINE, 1992.

AMERICAN CORPORATE COUNSEL ASSOCIATION, FOREIGN COUNSEL DIRECTORY (to order, call (202) 296–4522).

THE AMERICAN BAR ASSOCIATION, GUIDE TO FOREIGN LAW FIRMS (to order, call (312) 988–5522).

MARTINDALE-HUBBELL LAW DIRECTORY, (800) 526–4902, which is on-line with LEXIS

MARTINDALE-HUBBELL INTERNATIONAL LAW DIRECTORY, (800) 526–4902, which is also on-line with LEXIS.

CAMPBELL'S LIST – A DIRECTORY OF SELECTED LAWYERS (Published since 1879) ((407) 644–8298).

RUSSELL LAW LIST–1993 (Legal Correspondents International (410) 820–4475).

THE AMERICAN LAWYER – PRACTICE DIRECTORIES (various dates) ((212) 973–2800).

U.S. CUSTOMS HOUSE GUIDE – OFFICIAL 1995 VERSION ((800) 669–3282) (includes an alphabetical and geographical index to law firms specializing in admiralty, customs, international corporate and international trade law).

OFFICIAL EXPORT GUIDE – 1995 VERSION ((800) 669–3282) (includes law firms specializing in admiralty, customs, international corporate and international trade law).

NORTH AMERICAN TRADE GUIDE –1995–1996 (3d ed.) ((800) 669–3282).

B. *Periodicals*

International Corporate Law, published monthly by Euromoney, Publications; periodically reviews lawyers and firms in selected countries. Other specialized trade magazines occasionally publish service directories which include lawyers. (*See e.g., U.S./Latin Trade*, January 1995, "International Services Directory for Latin America.")

C.   On-Line Services

As noted earlier, the *Martindale Hubbell* law directories are available on-line through Lexis.

Electronic bulletin boards, such as Counsel Connect, may also be helpful sources of names.

D.   Other

International bar groups are often helpful sources. In addition to the contacts that the general membership may have, the regional committees of these groups, for example, committees in the Comparative Law Division of the ABA Section of International Law and Practice, often include foreign lawyers as well as U.S. lawyers with extensive networks in the region.

ENDNOTES

* This chapter is written from the perspective of an in-house lawyer who was previously with a large law firm. Although many of the ideas, concerns and recommendations flow primarily from an in-house perspective, most apply to the outside lawyer/foreign counsel relationship as well. The author acknowledges the assistance of David L. Teichmann of Sybase in the preparation of this chapter.

1   The *U.S. Customs House Guide, Official Export Guide,* and the *North American Trade Guide* use the same list of lawyers and are published by K-III Corporation.

There are Lots of Things
We Would Like You to Know About
The American Bar Association
and its
Section of International Law and Practice

HERE ARE A FEW OF THEM:

⊕ With a membership of nearly 400,000 lawyers, the American Bar Association (ABA) is the largest private association of legal professionals in the world.

⊕ The ABA's Section of International Law and Practice has approximately 15,000 members, located in the U.S. and throughout the world.

⊕ The Section has three substantive divisions—Business Law, Public International Law, and Comparative Law, and 50 committees and task forces. Find the one that matches your interests and get involved today!

⊕ The ABA works closely with the International Bar Association, the Hispanic National Bar Association, and other bar groups, and hopes to continue to find ways to enhance this cooperation.

⊕ The ABA, and the Section, welcome international members. You do not need to be a U.S. lawyer to join. For further information, call (202) 662-1661.

⊕ The Section of International Law and Practice offers publications that deliver practical, real-world information. Need direction for counseling a client? Consult Counseling Emerging Companies in Going International. Or perhaps Negotiating and Structuring International Commercial Transactions, or any of our other practical publications.

⊕ The Section offers a variety of continuing legal education programs at its Fall, Spring, and Annual meetings and at shorter programs, all featuring top experts in the field.

⊕ There are many opportunities for policy development, designed to provide members with a voice on issues ranging from foreign legal consultants to the future of the United Nations.

more ⇨

⊕ The Section has an ongoing international technical assistance program. Many of our members assist the Cambodia Law and Democracy Project, for example, in providing informational resources to the Government of Cambodia.

⊕ Our Women's Interest Network (WIN) worked to send the ABA's delegation to the U.N.'s Fourth World Conference on Women in Beijing, and will be providing follow–up activities.

⊕ Our Young Lawyers' Forum provides networking opportunities for young lawyers and develops programs and services of interest to young lawyers.

⊕ Each Section member receives, as a membership benefit, complimentary subscriptions to our newsletter, the *International Law News* and to our journal, *The International Lawyer.*

⊕ Our International Legal Exchange (ILEX) delegations travel to destinations of current interest.

⊕ The Section has practical information on the practice of law in an international context, ranging from our *International Practitioners' Workshop Series* to our International Law Practice Management Committee.

⊕ For information on our upcoming meetings and programs, call (202) 662–1660.

TO JOIN THE ABA AND THE SECTION, CALL 1–800–285–2221.

more ⇨

Want More Information on How to Join the ABA Section of International Law and Practice?

FAX THIS FORM TO (202) 662–1669 OR
TELEPHONE (202) 662– 1661

Please send me more information about:

❏ Membership in the ABA
❏ Membership in the Section

❏ Section publications
❏ Upcoming Section Meetings and Programs

❏ The Women's Interest Network
❏ The Young Lawyers' Forum

Other (please specify): _____

Your name (please print):

_____

Your address:

_____

_____

_____

Your telephone number: _____

Your Fax number: _____

Your E–mail address: _____

Fax this form to (202) 662–1669 in the U.S.,
or mail it to Alaire Rieffel, ABA, 740 15th Street, N.W., Washington, DC 20005,
or send us the same information by e–mail, at arieffel@attmail.com.